# PETER CLARKE

# Hope and Glory

BRITAIN 1900–1990

PENGUIN BOOKS

PENGUIN BOOKS

Published by the Penguin Group
Penguin Books Ltd, 27 Wrights Lane, London W8 5TZ, England
Penguin Books USA Inc., 375 Hudson Street, New York, New York 10014, USA
Penguin Books Australia Ltd, Ringwood, Victoria, Australia
Penguin Books Canada Ltd, 10 Alcorn Avenue, Toronto, Ontario, Canada M4V 3B2
Penguin Books (NZ) Ltd, 182–190 Wairau Road, Auckland 10, New Zealand

Penguin Books Ltd, Registered Offices: Harmondsworth, Middlesex, England

First published by Allen Lane The Penguin Press 1996
Published in Penguin Books 1997
1 3 5 7 9 10 8 6 4 2

Printed in England by Clays Ltd, St Ives plc

*For Maria*

# Contents

# Acknowledgements

As ever I am deeply grateful to the Master and Fellows of St John's College, Cambridge, for providing conditions under which it is still possible to combine research with the increasing demands of a full-time academic appointment. Most of the actual writing of this book took place in British Columbia, at what I have come to regard as the Bowen Island Research Centre, and my special debt to its director is recognized in the dedication of this book. The whole manuscript was read in draft by my general editor, David Cannadine, and by Stefan Collini, Ewen Green, John Thompson and Maria Tippett; sections were read by Gillian Sutherland and Simon Szreter. All of them made useful suggestions which have led to the improvement of the final text. I should also like to thank all who helped me at Penguin, led by Peter Carson. But errors may remain; and I must now rely upon solicitous readers and reviewers to alert me to their existence.

Peter Clarke

*Map 1* Great Britain and Northern Ireland

# Prologue

One traditional motive for looking at history, especially national history, has been for inspiration and encouragement. Shakespeare wrote his 'histories', of course, establishing the image of 'this England' as a 'sceptred isle', and Milton introduced a heightened notion of the special relationship between God and 'his Englishmen'. Such phrases, fine coinage when newly minted, passed into the currency of later generations as clichés. Yet 1940 showed that this heroic register still found a resonance. Winston Churchill was able to tap a providential sense that 'the British Empire and its Commonwealth', standing together but standing alone, were capable of saving themselves and thereby the world at an apocalyptic moment. Churchill's gift was to make this 'finest hour' into history while its minutes were actually ticking away. With his aristocratic pedigree and American mother, Churchill was hardly the typical British citizen. Nor, it might be said, was the left-wing writer George Orwell, whose gut reaction in 1940 ranged him, for the moment, firmly behind Churchill's position. Orwell's famous metaphor of his country, as 'a family with the wrong members in control', nonetheless depended on the binding ties of 'its private language and its common memories'.

One difficulty in this nationalist reading of 'our island story' is that it begs the question of what or who constitutes the nation. In 1900 the United Kingdom essentially comprised two large north Atlantic islands. In Great Britain, England took up just over half of the land area, Wales and Scotland the rest. In what Shaw called 'John Bull's Other Island', the predominantly Catholic population, concentrated in the southern counties, had a well-developed sense of their own Irish national identity that disclosed a clear political rift with the mainly Protestant defenders of the Union, concentrated in a number of northern counties. This was already a disunited kingdom, and was to become more so, notably when Ireland established its own independence as a republic, though with a continuing dispute about the border, which continued to define Northern Ireland as part of the Union. The history of the twentieth century has surely shown that partition was no neat and permanent, still less preordained, solution to the Irish question; and that manifestations of national identity in Wales and Scotland – the one more cultural, the other more political – echo more strident and bloody attempts to reassert or reinvent diverse nationalisms worldwide.

British history has generally dealt with nationalism by ignoring it. Churchill and Orwell slipped into a well-established convention of illicitly, implicitly conscripting all Britons into the pageant of English history, with a few tartan-clad spear-carriers and Celtic bystanders, presumed to be muttering the Welsh for 'rhubarb'. It is a mark of changing times that the Penguin History of Britain replaces a series simply called the Pelican History of England. I do not claim in this volume to have given wholly adequate attention to the history of Ireland as a part of the United Kingdom in the first quarter of the century; or to Northern Ireland since then, or to Scotland and Wales throughout the period. But this volume does not, I trust, show itself oblivious of their very existence and it acknowledges that the term Britons is problematic, even if it cannot fully explore the dimensions of 'the British problem'. At any rate, English and British, England and Britain, have ceased to be acceptable synonyms.

History has often been written as a celebration of the present and as a vindication of its particular perspectives, by presenting the past as a story of hard-fought progress towards an ultimately inevitable and satisfactory outcome. A 'Whig' interpretation of British history has taken many forms, all of them, however, grounded in confidence that the present is worthy of celebration. The assumption that we are the privileged legatees of progress makes us confident in awarding marks to our predecessors – depending on how closely *they* succeeded in anticipating and furthering *our* values and achievements. Those who have fallen short by this test have suffered (in E. P. Thompson's famous phase) 'the enormous condescension of posterity'. Nowadays historians are nothing if not alert to the perils of these Whiggish, condescending perspectives (at least in each other's writings). The main reason, however, why British history is no longer in thrall to triumphalist accounts is surely not just because of methodological enlightenment: it is because at the end of the twentieth century British historians lack confidence that there is much to celebrate.

The history of twentieth-century Britain instead threatens to become a history of decline, centred on the question: where did it all go wrong? This vision is understandable but myopic. For it implies a sort of history that is now often regarded as old-fashioned – one in which international rivalry, whether of a military, political or economic kind, is taken as the all-embracing theme. Sellers and Yeatman, in their parody of school textbooks, *1066 and All That*, nicely caught the view that history came to a full stop once Britain ceased to be Top Nation. Nowadays we tend to see it as a semi-colon; after which decline can be remorselessly analysed. A history of Britain between 1900 and 1990 can hardly ignore such perspectives.

In 1900 Britain was arguably the greatest power in the world, though the USA already commanded more resources, which could have been mobilized in a serious conflict, and Germany was preparing to extend its military pre-eminence in Europe into a bid for sea power too. It was the Royal Navy which allowed Britain to capitalize on its natural strategic advantage as an island-based country. Maintenance of naval supremacy, with a string of key bases around the world, was in turn the means by which the British Empire was acquired and maintained. Enormous areas of the world's surface were painted red on the map, from arctic Canada to tropical Africa, from the specialist plantation-crop zones of the West Indies and India to the temperate grasslands of Australia and New Zealand, from the Canadian prairies to the South African gold mines – the produce of the world came to British tables, the riches of the world lined British pockets. For this was no closed protectionist system but a worldwide web based on free markets, with their multilateral transactions delicately regulated through and by the City of London. The Navy, the Empire, and the gold standard, interlocking and mutually supportive, were at once the three symbols and the three pillars of British power and pre-eminence.

It is not surprising that the pillars tottered together as they had once stood together. The First World War shook each of them, though in each case a recovery of sorts was effected, and the 1931 crisis was a shattering moment when their fragility was simultaneously exposed. After the Second World War the Navy was outmatched in an era of air power, the Commonwealth was only the ghost of Empire, and the sterling area was a scaled-down simulacrum for the international gold standard as London had once managed it. Waking up to these new realities proved a painful experience. Yet if no one supposed that Britain was still Top Nation in 1990, whether in economic or political terms, a different kind of historical reckoning remains possible.

What, after all, is history really about? If not about literally everything that happened in the past, it is certainly about a wider range of human experience than used to be recognized. The 'new history' which has come into its own in the last generation has remedied many previous blind spots. Not only has social history received more attention: women and children, families and reproduction, sexual relations and gender differences, leisure and shopping, sport and entertainment, the media and popular culture, have all become serious fields of study. Partly, this represents a shift within social history from the old concerns of labour history, centred on the means of production, to a cultural history more concerned with the forms of consumption. And there is also now a stronger interdisciplinary thrust, breaking down the compartments which used to seal off different sorts of history, as seen, for example, in studies of political economy in twentieth-century Britain, giving a political dimension to economic issues and locating ideas in their full historical context.

Though this volume does not claim to be an example of the new history, it tries to be attentive to it. And this in turn suggests other perspectives on the history of Britain during the twentieth century.

Compared with Britain today, in 1900 most people had shorter lives, and not necessarily happier ones. Diseases like tuberculosis, diphtheria, scarlet fever, influenza and pneumonia were dreaded as killers. Many people, especially mothers with large families, often went hungry. Married women might expect to have up to ten pregnancies, with miscarriages, stillbirths and infant mortality all commonplace. The prospect of more mouths to feed on a labourer's pay of 'round about a pound a week', as the phrase went, could be a nightmare; and multiplying this sum by, say, forty to allow for subsequent inflation hardly transforms the picture. Contraceptive strategies were primitive; even inside marriage, there was much tacit repression of heterosexual activity (while homosexual activity was repressed by being criminalized). Women were excluded from full citizenship rights, reflecting their social and economic subordination; most of them ended up as full-time housewives, coping with back-breaking tasks in the home without electrical appliances, modern detergents or a whole range of later convenience products. Child labour was still common; the overwhelming majority of children in their early teens had finished their education and were working long hours. For many men, the constant fear was of not being able to work, with no state unemployment or sickness benefits to tide them over; and half a century was to pass before adequate medical treatment became available to all.

There is room for more than one perspective on the history of the British people in the twentieth century. What is needed is an account which makes sense of the political and economic changes that transformed Britain, but one which also pauses to piece together other, diverse aspects of the experience of the three entire generations who lived through this era of unexampled change. This story cannot simply be told as one of decline. Though the laurels of international leadership passed to others during the twentieth century, Britain still had its moments of glory, not all of them illusory; and Britons nourished hopes, not all of them misguided, that a condescending posterity should not dismiss but try to understand.

## SOME METRIC EQUIVALENTS OF IMPERIAL UNITS

1 foot = 0.3048 metre (30.48 centimetres)
1 yard (= 3 feet) = 0.9144 metre
1 mile (= 1,760 yards) = 1.609 kilometres
1 square mile (= 640 acres) = 259 hectares
1 hundredweight (cwt) = 50.8 kilograms
1 (long) ton (= 20 hundredweight) = 1.016 tonnes
1 gallon = 4.546 litres

# I

# Hands Off the People's Food
## 1900–1908

## A TRADING NATION

At the beginning of the twentieth century the British people had the testimony of their own eyes as well as that of the Bible for the fact that bread was the staff of life. For many working-class families it was the staple food, bulking large in every meal, sometimes adorned only with a little butter – margarine was now a cheaper substitute – or factory-produced jam. Fresh fruit and vegetables, apart from potatoes, were a rarity in many urban areas. The roast beef of old England was an appealing patriotic sentiment rather than a meal which appeared very often on the tables of the mass of the population.

Yet in 1900 British people were enjoying an average standard of living that was historically unparalleled. Wages had outstripped the rise in prices during the third quarter of the nineteenth century, classically thought of as the great Victorian boom. Admittedly, average wages may have taken longer to improve the nutrition of average families than historians used to suppose; but the gains came through in the end. In the 1880s contemporaries began to talk of a Great Depression, by which they meant primarily a depression of prices and profits. This cast the shadow of looming problems in industry, but for most employed workers at the time money wages generally held steady while the cost of living fell. Real wages thus inched upwards – a process not checked by the steadying of prices in the new century. In agriculture the depression was real, as about one acre in every six went out of arable production. The decline was steepest in wheat-growing. The last year in which over 3 million acres were under wheat was 1882; twenty years later little more than half was left. Agriculture was a victim of falling prices for the foodstuffs that British farmers had traditionally produced, especially corn (wheat, barley, oats and other grains). For the consumers of a corn-based diet, however, this was a bonus. Bread was cheap; wages stretched further. For most people the last quarter of the century brought a sustained rise in the standard of living: it inaugurated not a great depression but a great improvement.

All this was achieved despite a vast increase in population. The population of England and Wales had bounded ahead throughout the nineteenth century. At the first census in 1801 it had approached 9 million and it subsequently grew by well over 1 per cent per annum until it reached 26 million in 1881. Thereafter the rate of growth eased slightly, though it still remained (just) over 1 per cent a year until 1911, at which time the census showed a population of 36 million. The population of Scotland was around one-eighth that of England and Wales; with a similar though slightly less buoyant trajectory of growth, it had reached 4.8 million by 1911. The population of Great Britain had thus virtually quadrupled in the nineteenth century.

In Ireland, by contrast, where the population had touched a peak of 8.3 million in 1845, there was an apocalyptic famine during the late 1840s. By 1901 the Irish population was less than 4.5 million.

It was not decimated by the direct effect of the famine: more important was its indirect effect in reducing fertility and – less important as a cause but more visible in its results – in precipitating a century-long diaspora. Irish emigration was largely to Great Britain in the first instance; it was often seasonal or at any rate temporary. But there was a tidal wave of more than a million permanent emigrants, primarily to the USA, in the decade following the famine. In the 1880s Irish immigrants into the USA still numbered over 60,000 a year, though this figure had dwindled to less than half another thirty years later. Well beyond the first generation of immigrants, the Irish community in the USA remained linked to its native land by family bonds and ethnic loyalty, both of which generated flows of dollars. Remittances from Irish-American relatives played a vital role in the Irish domestic economy. Political contributions, moreover, from the time of the new departure in Nationalist politics under Parnell, sustained the agitation for Irish Home Rule. This was one reminder that the politics of the United Kingdom in the early twentieth century were crucially influenced by sentimental ties with kith and kin overseas. It was a phenomenon with not only an Irish dimension but also wider imperial implications.

In Great Britain there were four mouths to feed at the beginning of the twentieth century for every one mouth a hundred years previously. How was it to be done? This question lay at the heart of nineteenth-century political economy. The terrible example of Ireland showed how high the stakes were. An island rich in agricultural resources had failed to sustain a population which bred at a rate greater than that at which the indigenous food supply could be increased. The economist Malthus had notoriously warned of a widening chasm between an arithmetic rate of increase in food production and a geometric rate of increase in human reproduction; and Ireland, it seemed, had fallen into the Malthusian trap in the 1840s. Why should the rest of the United Kingdom, where the geometry of population growth was set at an equally steep angle, not suffer the same fate?

Politics and economics together spelt out the answer. The repeal of the Corn Laws, undertaken at the time of the Irish famine in 1846, opened the British market to imports of wheat at prices which the mass of consumers could afford (though this hardly addressed the immediate crisis in Ireland). British wheat production, still buoyed up by strong home demand, was not to suffer until thirty years later when steam transportation brought a revolution in freight prices.[1] The long-term effect of the repeal of the Corn Laws was that imports first surged and then soared. The year 1846 was the last in which wheat imports were less than 10 million hundredweight (cwt); in 1875 this figure reached 50 million cwt; by 1910 it was over 100 million cwt. British wheat production was now enough to feed only one in four of the British people. This tenfold increase in imports of the basic ingredient of the British diet marked the triumph of Free Trade. But it was only half the story.

It was British steam technology, on both land and sea, which made the North American prairies into the real competitor for British farms. Not only was it British capitalism which helped to build American railroads – exports of railway materials exceeded a million tons a year in the late 1880s – but British shipping enterprises also played a key role. Though it was not until 1903 that the number of ships under sail registered in the United Kingdom was overtaken by the number of steamships – just over ten thousand of each – in tonnage the advantage had been with steam for twenty years. By 1895 steamships of over 10

---

1. In 1877 British wheat still fetched 56s 9d (£2.84) a quarter, much the same as in the last years of the Corn Laws. But during the next fifteen years shipping freight rates were cut by 40 per cent, and they were to fall further over the following decade. In 1894 the price of wheat dipped under 23s (£1.15), and 30 shillings (£1.50) remained a high price until the First World War.

million gross tons were registered; and by 1914 this figure had almost doubled. About half of the world's merchant marine was flying the British flag.

The whole point of abolishing tariffs was to maximize production through an international division of labour and thus maximize the exchange of goods produced by the most efficient methods at the cheapest prices. Free Trade worked by expanding the volume of world trade between countries which, through nature or nurture, possessed specialized resources or skills. The volume of British foreign trade, both imports and exports, was over six times higher by 1910 than it had been in the mid-nineteenth century (or three times as much per head). The breakdown of imports by category in the early twentieth century was fairly constant. Food, drink and tobacco accounted for not far short of half the bill; raw materials for up to one-third; and manufactured imports for the remaining quarter. On the other side of the account, manufactured goods provided two-thirds of Britain's export earnings.

Here was the living demonstration of the highly developed division of labour which the theory of Free Trade implied. In accordance with the axioms of classical economics, Britain had ceased to grow food on a large scale and instead concentrated on adding value to manufactures, which were traded for cheap food grown under more advantageous conditions overseas. In fact Britain's trade was even more highly specialized, since three major items dominated the export account. It is hardly surprising that one of these comprised all goods – pre-eminently railways again – made from iron and steel, which made up over 10 per cent of domestic exports. So did coal; there were a million coal miners in the United Kingdom by 1910. The export industry *par excellence*, however, was cotton textiles, which alone made up a quarter of the value of all domestic exports before the First World War.

Not only was the export trade largely dependent on one industry; that industry was uniquely concentrated in one English county, Lancashire, and was in turn disproportionately dependent on one overseas market, India. Here is the industrial counterpart to the overwhelming import penetration of foreign food in the British market, established under an international division of labour during the late nineteenth century. Exports of cotton piece goods, which stood at 1,000 million yards at the time of the repeal of the Corn Laws, had doubled within ten years – and doubled again by 1880. Exports continued to climb, passing 5,000 million yards by 1890, exceeding 6,000 million by 1905, and in the unique boom year of 1913 touching 7,000 million. Since the total domestic market for all cotton goods used in the United Kingdom was only 1 million yards, seven out of every eight Lancashire mills were plainly dependent on the export market.

The textile industry's reliance on the unimpeded flows of a vast foreign trade can be measured in another way. In the boom years raw materials for textiles, chiefly raw cotton, were over 20 per cent of all British imports, costing around £130–£150 million in 1907 and 1913. Exports of textiles in those years earned £180–£200 million. The difference between the two figures is a crude measure of the value added in Lancashire – an understatement in view of the fact that the people of Britain were also clothed in the process of converting the raw cotton into manufactured cotton goods. This rough-and-ready calculation suggests that the profit of the cotton trade for Britain was generated by this difference between two much larger numbers and that it was of the order of at least £50 million a year.[2]

The romance of the rise of the cotton trade was part of a Manchester mythology which underpinned an almost providential sense that Britain would retain its position as the workshop of the world. There is room, however, for a less complacent view of what was going on, which suggests its precarious footing. For in the late nineteenth century Lancashire had increasingly concentrated on producing cheap cotton goods, of the coarser counts (fineness of yarn), for mass consumption in India. The richer and more sophisticated market for fine counts had already come under competition from producers in other industrial countries, especially in Europe. In this sense it was bad news that Lancashire was driven to specialize in the coarser counts, where less value was added to the commodity in the course of production and

2. Part of this went in profits to the capitalists of Lancashire, but most of it was paid out in weekly wages to the millworkers. In 1907 there were just over 200,000 full-time male workers and 350,000 full-time women workers in the cotton industry. If the men were paid an average of £2 a week – rather less than a mule-spinner could earn but more than most weavers got – and the women around a pound a week, this gives a round total of £750,000 a week or £40 million a year. At such rates of pay, it is easy to see how the cotton trade directly supported its workforce of more than half a million workers – probably a couple of million family members in all. This makes no allowance for the indirect impact on the regional economy of Lancashire, where the population was approaching 5 million on the eve of the First World War.

the margin of profit was narrower. This made the cotton trade acutely sensitive to any increase in prices.

Despite the rise of other industrial countries, the United Kingdom continued to dominate world trade. Unlike Germany and the USA with their largely self-sufficient agricultural output and their protected domestic markets for industrial goods, the United Kingdom was dependent on importing food and exporting manufactures. Its share of world exports of manufactures, which had been over 40 per cent for much of the late nineteenth century, had fallen to around 30 per cent in the Edwardian period. This was still an impressively high proportion of an ever-increasing global total. Moreover, London was the centre of the web of international finance through which world trade was conducted. Gold was the medium in which international settlements were ultimately made; but before the First World War the pound sterling was, as the phrase went, as good as gold.

The gold standard meant that the Bank of England guaranteed to exchange the currency for a prescribed weight of gold. This fixed the value of sterling against other currencies which were also on the gold standard. In the forty years before 1914 the pound was invariably worth just over 25 French francs, just over 20 German marks, and – a parity which was to become an icon – 4.86 US dollars. In practice it was sterling which dominated international exchange parities. Prices of imports and exports were set in sterling; settlement was made through British banks; insurance and other financial services were provided through a network based on the City of London. These services, of course, no less than exports of commodities, were being sold to foreigners – they were Britain's invisible exports. Indeed, these earnings were a crucial item in the United Kingdom's balance of payments with the rest of the world.

The fact is that Britain habitually ran a deficit on visible trade. Imports exceeded exports in value by well over £100 million in most years around the turn of the century. The gap then narrowed somewhat, so that in 1913 (which was exceptionally favourable for exports) the deficit stood at £82 million. A deficit it remained – and nobody turned a hair at the time.

With the aid of subsequent statistics, the reason is not hard for us to see, though it is 'invisible'. The earnings of the City alone were sufficient to fill the payments gap in the years immediately before the First World War. Even in buoyant years, like 1900–1902, when net earnings from services covered under half the visible deficit, other invisible income, derived from property abroad, still produced a small surplus on the overall current balance. It was this rising income from Britain's overseas investments which cushioned the balance of payments in the lean years. In the fat years, since there was no claim on it to finance imports, it provided a source of further capital for export. Britain thus possessed capital overseas which not only produced a rentier income but provided a self-financing accumulation of progressively greater wealth. This was the 'Land of Hope and Glory' which, according to A. C. Benson's Edwardian panegyric, God had made mighty – mighty rich, anyway – and was implored to make mightier yet.

Likewise, when an older patriotic song demanded that Britannia rule the waves, it was affirming a hard-headed business proposition. British shipping companies dominated many international routes, both for passenger and freight traffic. This, too, was a source of invisible export earnings, making exports even more profitable and offsetting the costs of imports to the balance of payments, since freight charges in sterling accrued on both inward and outward voyages. The strategic task of the merchant navy was to transport the bulk of the nation's food from overseas. The task of protecting it rested on the Royal Navy – the ultimate form of flexible response in safeguarding a worldwide maritime network of trade routes. By the parsimonious standards of Victorian public expenditure, defence did not come cheap. Like the Army, the Navy soaked up almost a fifth of the budget in the late 1890s. But, as some contemporaries argued, seen as an insurance payment of £20 million a year on an external trade forty times bigger, this premium of 2.5 per cent might not seem unreasonable. In the twentieth century, however, the premium was to rise.

## IMPERIALISM

Though Victorian radicals had liked to talk of Free Trade as God's diplomacy, knitting together a pacific world through the nexus of commercial interest, the reality was sterner. Historians have identified an imperialism of Free Trade which relied, not on annexation, but on an informal empire of economic advantage. Informal imperialism was based on a calculus of minimum effort on Britain's part – a sufficient exertion of power to secure an open market in which contracts would be enforceable. These were the conditions under which competitive capitalist enterprise could flourish. Once these conditions had been established, it was up to individual British businessmen to take advantage of them, as they had done to such good effect throughout the nineteenth century. All that was demanded was a fair field and no favour, for a sporting contest in which, having made up the rules and having been in training longer than anyone else, Britain started as favourite.

Other competitors, however, were becoming reluctant to see the best man win. Increasingly protectionist in their domestic markets, France and Germany in particular threatened to establish protectionist empires of their own, in which British entrepreneurs would naturally be at a disadvantage. British participation in the late-nineteenth-century scramble for Africa was in this sense a defensive move, appropriating new colonies in a largely pre-emptive way, designed to protect them from protectionism and to enforce the strategic priority of safeguarding Britain's older empire, east of Suez.

There is no need to suppose that British imperialism was in any way reluctant. The fact that the British Empire grew, on average, by 100,000 square miles a year throughout the nineteenth century speaks for itself. But the new gains in territory, especially the African colonies acquired in the last twenty years of the century, were no great economic prize. Compared with the rich markets of western Europe and North America, the African trade was, and was to remain, of minor importance to the metropolitan economy. It was, of course, of major importance to the British companies involved in that trade, and naturally they formed pressure groups designed to promote their own interests by enlisting the aid of the British Government and fostering public opinion. But in general such methods did not yield very conspicuous results.

The noticeable exception was South Africa. The Boer War of 1899–1902 was the last of Britain's imperialist adventures and the greatest, at least in aspiration. Its rationale was threefold, appealing in different ways to three different constituencies. The strategic concern was the most traditional. This saw the Cape of Good Hope as the guardian of the ocean route to India, regarded the protection of the existing British colonies at the Cape and Natal as essential, and viewed the pretensions of the settlers of Dutch origin, now established inland in the two Boer republics, as an intolerable threat to British paramountcy. Though the thinking here might seem rather paranoid, it was well within the canon of British imperial statecraft to which the prime minister, Lord Salisbury, had subscribed throughout his long tenure of the Foreign Office. What troubled Salisbury about the war, over which he presided with aristocratic disdain, was the infusion of two new ingredients into the imperialist rationale: plutocracy and democracy.

Money always talks, but during the Boer War its tones were particularly raucous. The fact was that when an earlier generation of Boers, a pastoral people attached to a peculiar sort of fundamentalist Christianity, had gone on a trek into the wilderness of the veldt, to get away from the British, they inadvertently ended up sitting on the world's richest goldfield. As the scale of the discoveries became apparent in the 1890s, just when the need for more gold to lubricate world trade was driving its value through the roof, British business enterprise was stimulated to do for the Boers what they seemed incapable of doing for themselves: to mulct the mines of the Rand. It was just the sort of overseas investment opportunity that the London market relished, as British companies fuelled with British money scrambled for the prizes, while arriviste South African millionaires jostled their way into London drawing rooms. All that stood in the way of the realization of this golden imperial project was the froward obscurantism of the so-called independent republic of the Transvaal (and its ally the Orange Free State). Little wonder that the City of London showed a thirsty impatience or that radical critics talked disparagingly of stockjobbing imperialism.

But imperialism had to be sold to the democracy. It was not axiomatic that it would be popular. Statesmen like Salisbury shuddered at the recollection of Gladstone's Midlothian campaigns, culminating in the Liberal triumph of 1880 on a tide of anti-imperial rhetoric. Disraeli (ennobled as Earl of Beaconsfield) showed a fascination with the notion of a British Raj – he had had Victoria made Empress of India – that had failed to grip the popular imagination. Gladstone had promised an 'extrication from Beaconsfieldism', even though in practice his own Government stumbled into an occupation of Egypt. What politicized imperialism and redirected its thrust was Joseph Chamberlain's period in office as Colonial Secretary from 1895 to 1903.

A former Radical, who had broken with Gladstone over Irish Home Rule, Chamberlain was now in Salisbury's Unionist cabinet, serving cheek by jowl with Conservative ministers. One implication was that many of his old schemes for domestic reforms would have to be shelved or at least repackaged in imperial measures. It was an implication he was ready to accept since in any case he was now consumed with a passion for the British Empire that the Conservative Party more readily shared.

Chamberlain's main concern, however, was not Disraeli's Empire, centred on the British Raj in India. In this he was quite different from a Tory imperialist like Lord Curzon, who ascended a dizzying pinnacle of power and fame as Viceroy of India from 1899 to 1905. It was not just that it was Curzon's job to talk up India: he manifested a lifelong commitment to maintaining the British Raj. 'As long as we rule India we are the greatest power in the world,' he maintained. 'If we lose it we shall drop straight away to a third rate power.' Curzon's imperious temperament turned duty to pleasure, as he organized the magnificence of the Coronation durbar in 1903, which ritualistically asserted the supremacy of the King-Emperor, splendidly represented by the person of his viceroy. Yet underneath the pomp there were hard-headed businesslike reasons for prizing India as the imperial jewel. In land area and population alike, it dwarfed other British territories, at a stroke putting the Empire into a world league alongside Russia and the USA. In trade, it was India which balanced the books for Britain, with steady profits from cotton exports compensating for chronic deficits in other markets. Above all, in military and fiscal resources, it was the self-financing Indian Army which provided the bulk of the the land forces at Britain's disposal, called upon regularly to do the dirty work at the behest of its unheeding imperial masters, just as Rudyard Kipling often mordantly observed.

Chamberlain, by contrast, reserved his imperial enthusiasm for a Greater Britain of white settlement. Canada had long been self-governing as a Dominion and the colonies in Australia and New Zealand were to be formally granted similar status in 1907. Chamberlain was all in favour of self-government, seeing the Dominions as adjuncts in the mobilization of Britain's maritime Empire, in turn implying a stronger naval commitment as compared with the Indianists' concentration on military preparations against putative Russian designs. If a link could be maintained between the mother country and its sturdy offspring overseas, then British emigration could be seen as a strategic redeployment of imperial manpower: relieving pressure on resources at home while peopling new territory under the Union Jack. In this way the intractable inferiority of Great Britain to the rising power and population of Germany and the USA might perhaps be countered. Chamberlain began brooding on some way to 'call in the new world, the Colonies, to redress the balance of the old'.

In the 1880s, net emigration from Great Britain had run at an annual rate of about 100,000. According to British statistics, more than half went to the USA; according to US statistics, even more. By the late 1890s net emigration from Great Britain had dwindled to a trickle of perhaps 20,000 a year, at a time when Irish emigration, from a far smaller population, was still virtually double that figure. Emigration to Canada was overstated in the early figures – much of it was indirect immigration into the USA – and it is doubtful if it ever exceeded 10,000 in any year in the 1890s. The figures for Australasia were now even lower, following a heady burst in the mid-1880s; while those for South Africa, which peaked at 12,000 in 1895, had actually turned negative at the outbreak of war in 1899. It is readily apparent that the lure of successive gold rushes explains many fluctuations in the figures, with a boom-and-bust cycle which led some hopeful globe-trotters from one El Dorado to the next.

Opportunities for settlement, in rich new lands under the dear old flag, were surely one benefit of Empire which the working-class electorate could be brought to appreciate. All that was necessary was to bang the drum. The last decade of Chamberlain's political career was to be governed by a mission to create a popular imperialism. South Africa dropped into this picture. Here was a gilt-edged opportunity for the British race to go forth and multiply their wealth. Chamberlain talked of making South Africa into a white man's country – an argument with a strong democratic appeal, as the Unionist victory in the general election of 1900 seemed to affirm.

There was to be a brief flurry of British emigration to South Africa at the end of the war, totalling over 50,000 in 1902–3. But the openings for white labour were not all they had been cracked up to be. Under Milner, the British High Commissioner, a policy of using indentured Chinese labour in the gold mines was seen as the quickest way of getting the economy moving. It provoked an outcry in Britain from Liberals who denounced 'Chinese Slavery' – a fine humanitarian cause in a philanthropic tradition that stretched back to earlier campaigns for emancipation of the less-favoured races. Chinese labour had a stronger economic resonance for British labour, since it was seen as an attempt to undercut trade-union rates and conditions. No one had fought to make South Africa a yellow man's country, and there was an ugly racist undertow to the ostensibly high-minded exploitation of the issue by Chamberlain's opponents. One way or another, South Africa failed to realize the dizzy dream that had been conjured up.

The true, workaday opportunities lay elsewhere in the Empire – in the antipodes and, above all, in Canada. What the colonial immigrant could realistically expect was a hard but wholesome life in an under-developed country where food, land and work were all more plentiful than in Britain. Emigration picked up dramatically in the Edwardian period. Well over 1 million emigrants left the United Kingdom in the seven years 1903–9 and another million in the next four years. These figures fully matched the peak years of the early 1880s; but meanwhile two historic changes had taken place. In the 1880s, more than half the total, year by year, had come from Ireland; after 1910 nearly 90 per cent of the emigrants were from Great Britain. Their destination too had changed. The USA still drew the bulk of the Irish but the English, Welsh and Scottish emigrants now opted for the Empire.

British immigration into Australia and New Zealand boomed in a decade, from a combined total of 15,000 for the three years 1901–3 to a total of over 200,000 for the three years 1911–13. The figures for the USA contain discrepancies which probably conceal some British immi-gration via Canada; but even so, it is striking that Canada was the destination of more than a million British citizens in the early twentieth century, half of them during the four years 1910–13.

The reasons for this spurt in imperial migration are not straight-forward, though economic motivations, both push and pull, bulked large. The Empire was certainly better promoted. Propaganda aimed at potential migrants was purposefully stepped up at this time by the Canadian Government. 'Only farmers need apply' was its slogan; but the great exodus from British farms had already taken place, and the new generation of British emigrants were mainly urban workers. Some of these British settlers became farmers, *faute de mieux*, as the prairies were opened up. Thirty per cent of all immigrants to Canada in 1901–11 were headed for the western provinces of Saskatchewan and Alberta, whose population quadrupled in a decade, by 1911 containing a rela-tively higher British-born proportion than Ontario (though in absolute terms the weight of numbers remained in the east). With the closing western frontier now pushing American farmers north, the drain of population from Canada to the USA was at last reversed.

Though it would be naive to attribute too much to imperialist fervour in pushing British immigrants out to the Empire, sentimental ties clearly played a part in pulling some of them back – all too soon. A million and a half troops from the Dominions were to serve in the First World War. It would be interesting to know how many of them were recent migrants who, having made one fateful voyage to the ends of the Empire, made a subsequently fatal one back to the old country. Given the relatively narrow margin of victory, the contribution of Greater Britain was to prove crucial.

Here was a complex process of equilibration between land and population, capital and labour, all on a global scale. Frontiers were not yet restricted by deterrent quotas on white immigrants and in Britain no embargoes or tariffs inhibited economic forces. As a result, the imperial granary was set up in business in a big way, with fine prospects and higher hopes. British imports of Canadian wheat, which first passed ten million cwt in 1903, were to touch thirty million in 1914. It was indicative of a shift in the focus of Imperial interest – from the Raj in India a generation previously to the goldfields of South Africa at the turn of the century and then to the wheatfields of Canada and the new pastures of Australia and New Zealand.

## JOE'S WARS

Chamberlain's diplomacy in South Africa gave imperialism an explicitly democratic twist; the Boer War was the continuation of this diplomacy by other means. It all turned on an appeal to the ballot box. The Government's *casus belli* was not, of course, stated in naked economic terms. 'We seek no goldfields,' Salisbury had intoned. Instead, it was the grievances of the Uitlanders, the British migrants into Johannesburg, which dominated the headlines; and foremost among these was the fact that the Transvaal enforced a long qualifying period of residence before allowing them to vote. How undemocratic! To be sure, the arguments used on the hustings betrayed many inconsistencies, not all of them on the Unionist side. Those Liberals, steeped in the Gladstonian tradition, whose hearts went out to the Boers as a small people rightly struggling to be free, were often as blind as their Unionist opponents to the claim that South Africa might properly be considered a black man's country.

They called it a 'khaki' election in 1900. It is undeniable that 'Joe's War' eclipsed other issues. Polling took place at a time when the war appeared to be on the point of a victorious conclusion, and the jingo- ism of Chamberlain's electioneering was unabashed. He sent one tele- gram to a supporter saying: 'Every seat lost to the Government is a seat gained to the Boers.' Its controversial impact was not muted by the substitution of 'sold' for 'gained' somewhere along the line. Perhaps it is not surprising that the outcome was a solid Unionist majority of over a hundred seats at Westminster. To contemporaries this seemed the more striking because they expected the pendulum to swing against the party in power, as it had at every election since household suffrage had been introduced. Salisbury was the first prime minister in more than thirty years to survive a general election with his majority intact, and the old man was curiously troubled at what this portended.

Maybe Salisbury was right to suspect there was something artificial about this victory, snatched on a single issue at an opportune moment. Though the average vote for opposed Unionist candidates was only 4 per cent more than for Liberals, this is a misleading figure. For this was truly the last nineteenth-century general election, in that over one-third of all MPs were returned without a contest; and the fact that no fewer than 163 Unionist MPs were returned unopposed (compared with only 22 unopposed Liberals) shows that the Unionist triumph was a fore- gone conclusion. The results, it soon appeared, represented a pre- mature triumphalism, since the Boers staged a long guerrilla action which mocked the imperial pretensions of the noisy jingoes. This was a point not lost upon that keen but introspective imperialist Rudyard Kipling, who blamed the insular British themselves:

It was our fault, and our very great fault, and *not* the judgment of Heaven.
We made an Army in our image, on an island nine by seven.

For Chamberlain the protracted nature of the messy war in South Africa had held one great consolation. It showed that the colonies were loyal. Soldiers from Australia and New Zealand, and volunteers from Canada, were sent to fight on the veldt alongside British troops – and often fought rather more effectively. Was Kipling right to think that 'We have had no end of a lesson: it will do us no end of good'? His hero, Chamberlain, brooded on the moral to be drawn. This demonstration of the limits of British power suggested a need to work on a bigger canvas than nine by seven – a need to cement the wonderful loyalty which the Empire had displayed with the concrete reinforcement of institutionalized self-interest. It is no coincidence that it was while Chamberlain was away from Britain for several months in the winter of 1902–3, on a post-war tour of the British colonies and annexed republics in South Africa, that his big idea came to fruition: a scheme for imperial preference based on tariffs.

The ex-Radical Chamberlain still remained a radical (with a small r) in one fundamental respect: he believed in the agitation of mass opinion behind great popular causes as the means of achieving his political objectives. He was not a great orator but he made himself into a forceful platform speaker, projecting a strong image to the people. With his well-known props – a monocle in his right eye and an orchid in his buttonhole – he was a cartoonist's dream. As caricatured by the most talented of them, F. Carruthers Gould, whose cartoons were widely printed in the Liberal press, 'Joe' was inimitable. His fiscal policy might be satirized but he was not diminished in the process – quite the reverse. Chamberlain put his faith in 'a raging, tearing propaganda' to get his message across. He had used such methods all his life and was now too old to change (he turned sixty-seven in 1903). This was a break in style with traditional Conservatism, which had relied on the forces of social conservatism – land, property and established institutions, notably the Church of England – to recruit deferential support for an aristocratic governing class. Chamberlain had little time for any of this. Socially, he was a self-made businessman from Birmingham who had made his name denouncing the landed interest as parasitic; and his religious affiliation (if no longer his faith) was Unitarian and Dissenting.

Though prepared to work with the Conservatives, Chamberlain was not of them. Their leader, Robert Arthur Gascoigne Cecil, third Marquis of Salisbury, was a figure from another world. Chamberlain was happier hobnobbing with the colonial prime ministers at the imperial conference held at the time of King Edward's coronation in 1902. Ironically, it was during the conference that Chamberlain suffered a cab accident which temporarily immobilized him; and while he was out of action, Salisbury, the great survivor of the Victorian era, quietly took his leave. The succession was kept in the family: Arthur Balfour, whose mother was a Cecil, took over from his uncle as head of a government which seemed to be so packed with his relatives that wits called it the Hotel Cecil. Educated at Eton and Trinity College, Cambridge, Balfour had been bred for office; though more than ten years younger than

Chamberlain, his ministerial experience was longer, stretching back into the 1870s. He was a cold fish whose languid elegance belied his intellectual acuity and his political ruthlessness.

With Salisbury, perhaps curiously, Chamberlain enjoyed relations of mutual respect: with Balfour of muted respect. Their uneasy cooperation got off to a bad start. Two episodes ruffled Chamberlain's *amour propre*. First, his status as the custodian of Liberal Unionist support for the Government was challenged by the Education Bill, introduced in Salisbury's last days, which Balfour insisted on pushing through. Its administrative rationale was sound enough. In place of the school boards, which were elected locally in an ad hoc way, the 1902 Education Act made county councils responsible for elementary education in England and Wales. Moreover, they would henceforth constitute the local authority for all the schools in their areas: not only elementary schools, educating children up to the age of fourteen, but also new secondary schools for pupils continuing their education beyond the elementary level. For the first time a ladder of opportunity, albeit a narrow one, could help the publicly educated child to gain academic qualifications which compared with those of the fee-paying schools, of which the most famous were the 'public schools', patronized by the upper and professional classes.

Moreover, all elementary schools with approved educational standards were now eligible for support from the 'rates', levied as a local property tax. Here was the political sting. For schools under religious control thus qualified for assistance. It meant 'Rome on the rates' in those districts, notably large cities with Irish communities, where Catholic schools had been set up. More important at the time, the Church of England's many thousands of elementary schools also had to be assisted by their local county councils. To most Liberals this was an anathema. Many of them had a principled objection to subsidizing any kind of religious activities and (as Chamberlain had done in the 1870s) campaigned for secular public education.

It was the Nonconformists – Methodists, Baptists and Congregationalists especially – who objected most violently to the 1902 Act; some went to the length of passive resistance by withholding rate payments. Historically, Dissent challenged the notion of conformity within a confessional state. This corpse had been interred; but its latter-day ghost, manifested in the lingering privileges of the Church of England, still needed exorcism. Since 1870 Nonconformists had tolerated the continuing provision of state grants for building (not running) Church schools while favouring board schools (run at public expense), in which no specifically denominational instruction was given. This smouldering issue was disturbed by the Balfour Education Act, rekindling the historic animosities of church and chapel which had energized Victorian party politics.

To this Chamberlain could hardly remain indifferent, however agnostic his own beliefs. The only way that his breed of Liberal Unionist had been able to cooperate with the Tories since 1886, and join them in government since 1895, was by avoiding mention of such sensitive matters and, whenever they were raised, quickly changing the subject to Ireland and Empire. Chamberlain knew that, up and down the country, the agitation against the Education Act was reminding some of his old supporters, still loyal chapel-goers, of their suppressed Liberal affinities. The Colonial Secretary did not break ranks in public, but his position was well understood, and his decision to spend the winter of 1902–3 in the sunshine of South Africa spared him the necessity to say more.

On Chamberlain's return, he received a second affront from the Balfour Government. The Budget of April 1903 abolished the corn duty recently imposed on all imported grain; this had been at the nominal level of only five shillings (0.25p) per ton, so any protection it gave to home production could only be marginal. Why, then, meddle now? Clearly because Chamberlain was already toying with the idea of introducing some preference for colonial wheat over foreign wheat in the British market, in line with the pleas recently put in his ear at the imperial conference. If the minimal corn duty were to be waived – but only for colonial imports – it would be a gesture towards imperial preference at no appreciable cost to the British consumer. This was the opening which the Chancellor of the Exchequer, Charles Ritchie, now closed by scrapping the tax altogether. Chamberlain was angry at the decision itself, resentful at the lack of support from his colleagues.

If Ritchie and Balfour really imagined that Chamberlain would be so easily thwarted, they little knew their man. In May 1903, at a packed meeting in the town hall of his beloved Birmingham, Chamberlain launched his campaign for tariff reform. In one sense his proposals were nothing remarkable. He had given many previous hints about the desirability of preferential tariffs to bind the Empire together. The trouble was that the only preference worth anything to Canada had to be on grain; the food imports from Australia and New Zealand, mainly frozen meat and dairy produce, faced less competition. A new tariff on foreign corn was therefore inescapably the main plank in Chamberlain's platform.

He did not apologize; that was not his way. The Unionists were already in low water before Chamberlain ever made the Birmingham speech. When reproached later, he flatly denied that tariff reform was the immediate cause, still less the real origin, of the Government's troubles, which he blamed on the Education Bill. Chamberlain was playing for higher stakes than his critics, inside or outside his own party. He proposed nothing less than a crusade to avert British decline through an exercise of will. To his eager young supporters, like Leo Amery, the moment was like that when Luther nailed his theses to the church door at Wittenberg, and it was to effect a sea change in the politics of Edwardian Britain.

To some extent the fiscal debate was a clash of interest groups. The oldest protectionist interest, of course, was agriculture (hence the Corn Laws until 1846), but here imperial preference was not protectionist enough; it had little to offer British farmers who had already been swamped by imports of Canadian wheat, which would presumably continue to flood the market. By contrast, the mercantile and financial interest tended to be cosmopolitan. Dealers and traders, shippers and insurers, discounters and bankers: these, if anyone, were the men with a vested interest in Free Trade. Along with the gold standard, it established the framework of an international free market in goods, in labour and in capital, with the City of London ready and able to siphon its percentage from each of these lucrative flows.

Chamberlain offered a businessman's policy to producers – like those in the metal trades within a thirty-mile radius of Birmingham – who felt threatened by foreign competition in the domestic market. Conversely, within a thirty-mile radius of Manchester, the cotton trade had little to gain and much to lose from proposals which were bound to push up British costs of production. Here was the problem for the export industries. If cost increases, caused by compensating workers for higher food bills, were passed on in export prices, markets would be lost overseas; this was the major headache for the bosses. Alternatively, if labour costs were held steady despite a rise in the cost of living at home, this would mean lower real wages, which was the immediate worry for wage-earners.

It was an economic argument with strong moral overtones. Tariff Reformers soon discovered that the Free Trade orthodoxy of the previous half century was deeply entrenched. It was part of a 'fiscal constitution' which had been established in mid-Victorian Britain, notably through Gladstone's great budgets of 1853 and the early 1860s. Abolition of import duties, satisfying the Radical demand for the 'free breakfast table', was made possible by relying on income tax for revenue, making the wealthier classes bear the burden of direct taxation. The Gladstonian doctrine of Treasury parsimony, however, deliberately limited the size of that burden. The role of the state, by general consent, was minimized: the working class freed from undue interference, the middle class spared from undue expense. The ideological triumph of Gladstonianism was to make these conceptions popular by making them seem fair.

The virtue of Free Trade was that it offered insider privileges to no one: no favoured class, no special interest. Hence the moral opprobrium which Chamberlain aroused when he seemed to be opening the door to a competitive scramble for sectional advantage at the expense of the community at large. The fact that he had long been held responsible for the Americanization of British politics, through his development of the 'machine' or 'caucus' of party activists, added colour to the charge that, via tariffs, he was about to usher in the sort of political corruption notorious in the late-nineteenth-century USA.

Chamberlain realized full well that he would have an uphill struggle in making Tariff Reform popular. Having introduced the fiscal issue, his instincts were to follow through hard by making a virtue out of the necessity to tax food. For taxes, in the nature of things, raise revenue; new taxes raise new revenue; with new revenue, new government expenditure becomes possible. Social reform and Tariff Reform might be yoked together, offering the working-class electorate welfare gains to compensate for any marginal economic loss.

This kind of logic was spelt out in a typically provocative way by the Fabian Socialist Bernard Shaw, who argued that both imperialism and social reform embraced a much stronger role for the state than the laissez-faire orthodoxy of the nineteenth century allowed; thus, on the basis of a common opposition to Gladstonianism, state socialists ought to have no quarrel with imperialism and protectionism. Chamberlain, for his part, had for some time toyed with the idea of introducing a state-assisted scheme of old-age pensions, but had delivered nothing. Taunted in the House of Commons by a Liberal backbencher (David Lloyd George), Chamberlain now threw out the hint that pensions might become affordable with the revenue generated by his proposed tariffs.

Somehow, during the summer of 1903, Chamberlain let this grand design slip between his fingers. Instead, locked into the tactical infighting of the Balfour cabinet, he became sidetracked. The prime minister, wearily worldwise, evinced little enthusiasm for imperial preference (or for anything else). He once said that the difference between himself and Chamberlain was the difference between Youth and Age – but with Balfour, twelve years the junior, adding the twist: 'I am Age.' Balfour's sceptical and subtle mind saw that it was no use defending the old doctrine of Free Trade, or 'Insular Free Trade' as he liked to call it. Scepticism took him as far as supporting tariffs, in principle, for the purpose of retaliation against other country's tariffs. Subtlety then led him to claim that, if this strategy succeeded in reducing tariffs all round, it would make retaliationists freer traders than the doctrinaire Free Traders.

Such arguments left Chamberlain wholly unpersuaded; they were frivolous distractions which he ignored. He did, however, seek to conciliate the Free Traders in the cabinet, notably the Duke of Devonshire, the nominal leader of the Liberal Unionists. Devonshire and Chamberlain had been thrown together in common opposition to Home Rule. They had usually been at odds when, twenty years previously, they had served in Gladstone's cabinet; Balfour's was now riven by the incompatibility between the old Whig's antique fiscal conservatism and Chamberlain's impatient economic radicalism. Devonshire and his followers took their stand against taxing food. Chamberlain sought to conciliate them by claiming that his scheme need not raise food taxes for the average family.

The fact was that tea and sugar – plantation crops with no domestic competition – were already subject to revenue duties which could not be regarded as protectionist and were therefore permissible under Free Trade doctrine. This enabled Chamberlain to make a clever move – too clever by half. By promising to offset the extra cost of his prospective wheat duty by an abolition of the tea and sugar duties, he balanced a hypothetical working-class household budget, down to the last farthing – but at the price of depriving the Exchequer of the windfall that would be required to finance old-age pensions. Having promised to produce social reform like a rabbit out of his fiscal hat, Chamberlain was then left with an empty hat. The trick did not even succeed in impressing the duke, who remained as hostile as ever to Tariff Reform.

The split in the Government came to a head in the autumn of 1903. Chamberlain resigned as Colonial Secretary in order to be free to crusade for his policy in the country. Balfour took the opportunity of getting rid of Ritchie and other doctrinaire Free Traders, but inadvertently lost Devonshire too in the manoeuvre. Young Austen Chamberlain was installed as Chancellor of the Exchequer to appease his father and the Tariff Reformers.

The sort of factionalism which had for years debilitated the Liberals now infested the Unionist Party instead. The fervent Chamberlainites wanted the 'whole hog' of imperial preference, food taxes and all. The Free Fooders were a disintegrating remnant; some crossed the floor and joined the Liberals, like the young Winston Churchill, MP for the cotton town of Oldham; others looked, increasingly vainly, for a lead from the Duke of Devonshire. Meanwhile the Balfourites colonized the middle ground, some leaning towards Tariff Reform, some towards Free Trade, most of them simply good Conservatives who were ready to accept any formula which would keep the party together. Most of Balfour's own erudite points went over the heads of his supporters. Repeatedly challenged by the Opposition in the House of Commons, he was reduced to preserving a show of party unity by a series of desperate tactical ploys, on one occasion leading his supporters out of the chamber rather than face a vote on the Free Trade issue.

Chamberlain took his case to the country. A Tariff Reform League was set up to mount a ceaseless propaganda against Free Trade. It was well funded and well organized, bringing a new professionalism into campaigning methods, ready to exploit the new technology of the gramophone and motion pictures to get its message across. The star attraction remained Chamberlain himself, setting out the case against Free Trade in a series of cogent speeches. When told by an expert adviser that some of the statistics he cited were inaccurate, he simply replied: 'I have used them before.' He took the war to the enemy, unafraid to address vast meetings in Free Trade Lancashire. He pointed to the erosion of Britain's manufacturing base, with one industry after another going into decline. 'Cotton will go,' he warned. He dismissed the idea that the commerce of a great nation could depend on 'jam and pickles' or the manufacture of 'dollseyes'. A long-running debate had thus been inaugurated over the importance of the manufacturing base in the British economy. Though now living off a rentier income himself, Chamberlain remained the spokesman for industrial producers, despising what historians have termed the 'gentlemanly capitalism' of the City of London, with its commitment to the logic of a cosmopolitan free market.

## THE ROAD TO 1906

The Home Rule crisis of 1886 had split the Liberal Party and depleted its support in the country. For twenty years the Unionists were to be the largest group in Parliament, with only the minority Liberal Government of 1892–5, dependent on Irish Nationalist support, to punctuate their period of office. The Boer War merely added to the Liberals' difficulties, with their new leader, Sir Henry Campbell-Bannerman, uneasily straddling divisions between 'pro-Boer' and 'Liberal Imperialist' groupings. Both of these labels were terms of art. 'Pro-Boer' started life as a jingoist taunt to the Government's critics – who defiantly adopted the appellation – and there was hardly more literal accuracy in 'Liberal Imperialist'. The fact remained that the Liberals were in a bad way. On his retirement Salisbury could reflect on how unexpectedly well the Conservative Party had weathered the advent of democracy. It had been his achievement to use Home Rule for his lifelong political purpose: to rally the possessing classes into a formidable party of resistance.

The class basis of the Government's support, however, raised an awkward question – what about the workers? A party of organized labour was not a new idea. In a sense it had been expected since urban workers were enfranchised (with the introduction of household suffrage in the parliamentary boroughs of Great Britain) under the Second Reform Act in 1867. But all that had materialized was an informal arrangement with local Liberal organizations to run a number of trade-union candidates. These were the so-called Lib-Labs, initially representatives of the craft unions for the most part. It was one achievement of Gladstonian populism to make this possible without, of course, turning the Liberal Party into the instrument of organized labour, still less of socialism, in the process. The Trades Union Congress (TUC) used lobbying methods, with considerable success, on matters of labour legislation. By 1900 there were over 1,300 trade unions with a total of

2 million members. Sixty per cent of them belonged to a hundred big unions with an income of £2 million a year.

The Third Reform Act of 1884–5, by extending household suffrage to county divisions, opened the door to another platoon of Lib-Lab MPs: the miners. On most coalfields, where a Nonconformist political culture (usually Methodist) was strong, the Liberal organization became virtually an adjunct of the lodges (union branches) of the Miners' Federation. Under household suffrage there was thus no difficulty about achieving labour representation, provided two conditions were satisfied: that one trade union could call the shots in a given constituency and that virtually all its members were of the same party-political persuasion (in practice, Liberal). The first condition, however, was satisfied only by the miners and the cotton operatives; the second by the miners alone – and not even them on the Lancashire coalfield. The reason was the presence of enough Conservative working men in Lancashire to thwart the extension of the Lib-Lab system, which plainly had no future as a general method of labour representation.

Yet, as the twentieth century dawned, direct representation in parliament was exactly what the trade unions decided that they needed. This was now seen as the only way of protecting their own interests when they found their legal status threatened by a series of adverse judgements in the courts. Since 1893 there had existed a body called the Independent Labour Party, with a name apparently proclaiming the same aspiration. This was an invitation by socialists, of whom Keir Hardie was the best known, for trade unionists to join their party. This grand design failed and electorally the ILP was a flop.

The Labour Representation Committee, set up in 1900, tackled the problem the other way round – through an invitation from the TUC for socialist organizations to join its own party. As well as the ILP, with branches concentrated in Yorkshire and Lancashire, the Fabian Society joined – a small think-tank of metropolitan collectivists, seizing disproportionate attention through the irrepressible talent of Bernard Shaw in publicizing the formidable researches of Sidney and Beatrice Webb. As in all European countries, there was a Marxist organization, albeit a small one: the Social Democratic Federation. Secularist in outlook, prominent in godless London, it was distinguished from the provincial, Nonconformist political culture of the ILP as much by style as by doctrine. The SDF pulled out of the LRC almost immediately, correctly perceiving that this was no socialist party.

The LRC brought together a number of affiliated trade unions, whose number was opportunely boosted by further court decisions, notably in the Taff Vale cases of 1901–2. The cumulative effect of these judgements was to undermine the legitimacy of peaceful picketing and to make unions liable for the payment of damages to employers who suffered loss through trade disputes. A generation of trade unionists had grown up believing that Gladstone and Disraeli between them had given industrial action the cover of law. Now they discovered the Taff Vale catch: if they lost a strike, they lost, and if they won, and were successfully sued, they still lost.

Following the establishment of the LRC, relations between the Liberal Party and Labour were put on a new footing. The key step was an agreement between the Liberal chief whip, Herbert Gladstone, whose father had first brought organized labour under the Liberal umbrella, and Ramsay MacDonald, an able socialist publicist who had recently been appointed as secretary of the LRC. The Gladstone–MacDonald pact earmarked up to forty constituencies in England and Wales for Labour candidates. Gladstone could give no absolute guarantee that Liberal candidates would withdraw in favour of Labour any more than MacDonald could be sure of preventing Labour or socialist candidates sprouting up elsewhere. Nor was the pact made public. For all that, it laid out the ground rules for electoral politics until the First World War: a new template for cooperation between Liberals and Labour which, with the obsolescence of the Lib-Lab model, contemporaries called a Progressive Alliance.

What really made the Progressive entente effective was the substantial ideological affinity between Liberals and Labour. For years the Liberal leadership had made approving but ineffective noises about encouraging working-class candidates. Now they were offered a job lot of around forty Labour representatives – mainly comprising solid and sensible trade-union officials, recognized and funded by a proper national organization under the control of the TUC, all of them determined to get a fair settlement of labour legislation, but otherwise, almost to a man, imbued with a strongly Liberal outlook. The Fabian logic of social imperialism did not sway Labour politicians who might sometimes call themselves socialists but who were steeped in the Gladstonian tradition. Hostile to Joe's War, they were to prove immune to Joe's blandishments. If reassurance were needed on this point, it was immediately forthcoming through the virtual unanimity with which

Labour rallied to the defence of the greatest of all Liberal causes, Free Trade.

The need to defend Free Trade stuck the old Liberal coalition back together again for the first time in twenty years. Leading Liberals rehearsed their lines, blowing the dust off the hymn sheets of their old-time religion, confident that if it was good enough for Cobden it was good enough for them. Campbell-Bannerman was a fat and comfortable rentier, with a fondness for foreign spas, or for French novels when he was not actually on the Continent. Though his hock-and-seltzer lifestyle made it clear that he had no quarrel with the cosmopolitan ethos of Free Trade, he was content to leave the hard slog of speech-making to others.

The real leadership in the Free Trade campaign came from H. H. Asquith, marking him out as the heir apparent to 'C-B'. Born in Yorkshire, known by his first name (Herbert) in his youth, Asquith was a self-made barrister with a well-oiled mind which had been put into meticulous working order, thanks to a scholarship in classics, at Balliol College, Oxford. As Home Secretary he had been the youngest, brightest member of Gladstone's last cabinet, and had got married, with the Grand Old Man as chief guest, to a highly articulate heiress, Margot Tennant (his first wife having died leaving a young family). With his second wife, his second name (Henry) was thought more fitting, and Margot's egregious influence was to be apparent in more than the stylish parties she gave.

Asquith followed Chamberlain around the country, marshalling the brief for Free Trade with relentless pertinacity and imperturbable aplomb. During the Boer War he and his colleagues, R. B. Haldane and Sir Edward Grey, had been known as Liberal Imperialists and had lived in the shadow of the former prime minister, Lord Rosebery. Now the perspective shifted. Rosebery moved out of the Liberal orbit altogether; Asquith emerged as his own man; and he successfully mended his fences within the party by championing Free Trade. In fact, Liberal Imperialism had never amounted to much more than a readiness to look further than the Gladstonian agenda in domestic policy as much as in foreign policy. Asquith's instincts were centrist, just as Campbell-Bannerman's were; it was only late in the war that the pro-Boers made a hero out of 'C-B' when he denounced the Government for using 'methods of barbarism'. Now, magically, rancour and mutual suspicion were dispelled under the wand of Free Trade. After hearing Asquith,

Campbell-Bannerman mused: 'How can these fellows ever have gone wrong?'

Chamberlain's ability to 'make the weather', as Churchill later put it, was never seen to more dramatic – or more perverse – effect than in 1903–6. The sun went in for the Unionists; they got doused in a number of spectacular by-election defeats, and then found themselves swept away in the deluge of the general election. Partly it was a matter of bad timing. In the four years after Chamberlain started preaching doom and gloom, British exports increased by 50 per cent. Unemployment, which had peaked at 6 per cent in 1904, then fell sharply. Chamberlain's slogan, 'Tariff Reform means work for all', with its implied protectionist appeal, had little to bite on – as yet. Instead, the simple, populist, time-worn Free-Trade slogans carried the day – 'Hands off the people's food' or 'Your food will cost you more'. On countless Liberal platforms the Big Loaf, which Free Trade brought to the humble poor in their cottage homes, was contrasted with the Small Loaf, which was all that rapacious Tariff Reformers would allow. Liberal scaremongers had loaves baked, to show credulous audiences the contrast between a fat, fecund Free-Trade loaf, fit for the British table, and a puny, parsimonious protectionist loaf, such as foreigners had to tolerate. The real poser about reciprocal imperial preference – whether the protectionist colonies would admit British goods freely rather than further increasing their own tariffs on non-imperial imports – was barely debated.

Balfour's final tactical ploy came in December 1905, when he resigned rather than dissolve parliament. Thus a Liberal Government had to be formed before rather than after a general election, which Balfour hoped would create trouble and expose fissures. In fact it had the opposite effect. Asquith, Grey and Haldane had a plan up their sleeves ('the Relugas compact') for kicking Campbell-Bannerman upstairs into the Lords, for the good of his health, leaving them to run the new Government. They had not envisaged conducting this political assassination under the limelight of an impending election; nor reckoned with Campbell-Bannerman's determination to accept the King's commission to form his own administration; nor appreciated that, since Asquith was offered the Treasury, Grey the Foreign Office, and Haldane the War Office, they would virtually be running the Government anyway. Cabinet-making, in short, cemented the unity of the Liberal Party and Campbell-Bannerman was at last free to set January 1906 as the date of the long-heralded appeal to the people on the issue of Free Trade.

There were, of course, other issues. The Unionists claimed, as they had at every election for the last twenty years, that the Union was in danger. But even the Duke of Devonshire could not be terrified this time, conceding that Campbell-Bannerman's 'step-by-step' policy for Ireland excluded another Home Rule bill in the next parliament. There is little doubt that many Unionist Free Traders felt able to vote Liberal. Some of them did so as Nonconformists, still incensed over the Education Act. This was an issue which stirred the historic Liberal constituency, recharging activists with righteous indignation.

Chinese labour had a similar effect in touching tender consciences, but its real impact was its coded message to the new Progressive constituency. In urban and industrial seats, where trade unionism was strong, Chinese labour served as an object lesson on how the Unionist Government regarded labour in general. This larger symbolic meaning escaped most Unionist candidates, who bitterly regarded the prominence of the issue as nothing but Liberal humbug. It is true that it filled a vacuum since, so far as specific measures of social reform were concerned, the Liberal programme offered virtually nothing to the working-class electorate.

Before the First World War polling was spread over a couple of weeks, with the big cities and boroughs generally voting first, and then the county divisions. This gave the results added drama in 1906, for the first day was dominated by the stunning Progressive gains in Lancashire, where the Unionists had been predominant for a generation. Balfour himself lost his seat in Manchester. This was not just cotton speaking up for Free Trade. The Liberal landslide was across the whole of Great Britain, even in the English shire counties and cathedral towns. Moreover, 30 Labour members were returned. Both the Labour MPs from Scotland defeated Liberal opponents; but in England and Wales all but a couple of Labour's successes came through Progressive cooperation in the constituencies, which maximized both Liberal and Labour representation.

In Great Britain the average fall in the Unionist share of the poll was over 10 per cent. In England only 4 Unionist MPs were returned unopposed, compared with 15 Liberals – a big difference from 1900. Indeed it was the Irish Nationalists, with 74 of their 83 MPs returned without a contest, who now accounted for the bulk of unopposed returns. The new parliament neatly reversed the balance of the old, in that 402 Liberals replaced 400 Unionists as the largest party. Only the

Irish representation was substantially unaffected: 82 Nationalists in the South, 15 Unionists in the North (plus 3 Liberals and 1 independent). In addition, 1 Irish Nationalist was returned for the Liverpool Scotland division, as at every election until 1929. In 1900 there had been 402 Unionists in the House, now they were cut to 157 – only 130 from the 560 constituencies in Great Britain. In 1900 there had been 184 Liberal MPs; in 1906 there were 400. This understates the strength of the new Government's position since the Labour Party (to use the name it henceforth adopted) supplied an extra thirty reliable votes, and the Irish Nationalists were hardly likely to support the Unionists.

The real division on the opposition benches was not between Liberal Unionists and Conservatives (they were to merge formally in 1912): it was between Chamberlainites and the rest. Though Tariff Reform had gone down to defeat, it had strengthened its hold on the Unionist Party, which Chamberlain now looked poised to capture. Certainly the divisions within the party had done it little good, and those candidates who had distanced themselves from Imperial Preference still found themselves tarred as protectionists. But Chamberlain himself had little time to exploit his opportunity. In the summer of 1906 he had a stroke. The family hushed up the seriousness of his condition for as long as they could; Balfour was reduced to poring over newspaper photographs through a magnifying glass to form his own prognosis. The invalid Chamberlain lived on till 1914 in his Birmingham villa, fitfully intervening by telegram in the course of subsequent political developments which he had set in train but which he could no longer dominate, direct and determine.

## THE ROAD TO BIARRITZ

A majority Liberal Government was a novelty. Queen Victoria had not had to put up with one during the last fifteen years of her reign. King Edward VII was less politically prejudiced than his mother, who had been charmed by Disraeli into becoming a fierce anti-Gladstonian. The King got on well enough with Campbell-Bannerman when the two indolent and overfed old men were taking the cure at Marienbad. The political influence of 'Edward the Peacemaker' was much overrated at the time, though *l'oncle de l'Europe* naturally wanted to keep on good terms with his relations, Tsar Nicholas as much as Kaiser Wilhelm – it was all in the family. He approved of the Entente Cordiale with France which the Unionist government had sealed in 1904. But then, who did not?

The Entente was one of several diplomatic steps which Britain took to remedy an international position that suddenly looked vulnerably lonely. Chamberlain might speak of the British enjoying 'a splendid isolation, surrounded and supported by our kinsfolk', but the Boer War brought home the reality that, fully extended in their imperial role, the British needed to avoid conflict with the other great powers. The Marquis of Lansdowne, Salisbury's successor as Foreign Secretary from 1900 until the fall of the Unionist Government, had a basically Whig instinct for adroit accommodation as the price and means of survival amidst unwelcome change. He could see that Germany was no longer content, as in Bismarck's day, to respect British naval and imperial hegemony; a new navy was under construction and the Kaiser, dissatisfied with Germany's meagre place in the sun in tropical Africa, kept turning hungry eyes on promising territories, from China to the Sahara. Ideally, Lansdowne would have liked a treaty with Germany, to cut the roots of potential conflict; but since Germany's price was a pledge of British support against the Franco-Russian alliance, Lansdowne was forced to think again.

The fact was that Britain still had no interest in entering the system of alliances between the European powers. Instead it proved easier to settle outstanding difficulties in the western hemisphere, basically by accepting that the Royal Navy could no longer compete with the US fleet (especially once the Panama Canal was constructed). Likewise, in 1902, Lansdowne limited Britain's naval commitments in the Far East by concluding a treaty with Japan, the first Asian country to flex its muscles as an industrial and military power. No serious British interest was compromised by thus ruling out war with either the USA or Japan – though if war should break out between Japan and Russia (as soon happened in 1904), it would now pit the ally of Great Britain against the ally of France, threatening to import hostilities back to Europe. This was just what Britain – and France too – wished to avoid; so the effect was to spur the two countries into concluding their Entente. It was a determined effort to restore harmonious relations, chiefly by clearing up outstanding colonial rivalries; it was hardly an alliance, still less an alliance against Germany. A similar settlement with Russia proved possible (under the Liberal Foreign Secretary, Grey) in 1907, once a Japanese victory had ended the war in the Far East. All told, in a process of give and take, these two Whigs – one now a Unionist, one still a Liberal – seemed to have achieved through negotiation the sort of peace in Europe which well suited a satisfied power like Great Britain – much the same objective which Lansdowne was to seek, under far less promising conditions, in 1916–17.

The Edwardian era was short but had a distinctive tone which the King set (or lowered, as some whispered). The Victorian age was soon identified in retrospect as heavy with respectability and decorum: un-amusing and notoriously unamused. The old Queen's death seemed to release a psychic burden. Edward was no rebel but nor was he wholly respectable. He had mistresses; he eased the opprobrious rigour of the court and made it less exclusive. He greedily hobnobbed with pluto-crats of dubious social origin, accepting their hospitality with lax acquiescence. Under his patronage, the Upper Ten Thousand set new standards of conspicuous consumption by the wealthy. On the grouse moors, aided by armies of beaters, shooting parties measured the day's bag in thousands: carnage on a scale that anticipated the trenches. Vast meals were served, course by course, for guests to pick over, washed down by the finest wines. Champagne became a fetish; in some circles it was consumed at every meal (a lifelong habit in Winston Churchill's case).

There had never been so many millionaires. They generally made their money in finance rather than industry; even if they had lived in the North they tended to die in the South, buying their way (or their chil-dren's way) into landed society. This was an old pattern of elite mobil-ity in Britain, with the aristocracy renewing and refreshing itself with new money in each generation. The old money, however, had never felt so much threatened as in the Edwardian period. Socially it felt affronted by plutocratic vulgarity. Economically, thirty years of agricultural decline had taken their toll; it brought lower land values, reduced rents and declining incomes for landlords who had always thought of them-selves as rich (and lived accordingly). Politically, the landed interest suddenly found that the Hotel Cecil had gone out of business and that 'the best club in London' (the House of Commons) had been occupied by a horde of Radicals.

The House of Lords was indeed 'another place', as parliamentary language put it. There the political balance had not shifted since, in 1893, the Lords had rejected the second Home Rule bill by a 10-to-1 majority. The fact that, despite Gladstone's fulminations, the Lords had got away with it shows two things. First, of course, the reality of their constitutional role as a hereditary second chamber, despite all the talk in the late nineteenth century about the triumph of representative government. Twenty years during which Unionists had outnumbered Liberals in both Houses of Parliament had masked but not removed the potential for conflict beteeen them. The other point about the Home Rule fiasco was its Irishness. There was no majority for Home Rule in Great Britain; the bill had been put through the Commons by Irish Nationalist votes. While this was perfectly proper in procedural terms, it also meant that an appeal to the electorate against the Lords' action would be doomed by the unpopularity of the substantive proposal. In short, the issue was not constitutional but political.

No one recognized this point more clearly than Balfour. Returned to Westminster in a hastily contrived by-election in 1906, he found himself confronted by the biggest Commons majority since the Great Reform Act. When he attempted one of his characteristically feline debating ploys, Campbell-Bannerman simply brushed it aside, to thunderous cheers, with the comment, 'Enough of this foolery.' Disraeli's dictum, that a majority is the best repartee, was thus brutally confirmed. But Balfour realized that he too commanded a repartee that made him the most powerful Leader of the Opposition of modern times. The Unionist peers were led by the Marquis of Lansdowne. He and Balfour adopted a very simple principle: that the inbuilt Conservative majority in the Lords should be used in the interests of the Conservative Party. Thus bills that were popular, however misguided their provisions were thought by the Tory peers, would be let through. Bills which simply appealed to partisan Liberals, by contrast, though they might be part of the platform on which the party had won the 1906 election, were fair game for obstructive action.

The Lords did not impede the Trade Disputes Act of 1906. Here was the response to the Taff Vale difficulty, fulfilling the Government's debt of honour to the Labour Party. After some fumbling by the Government's law officers, trying to define a sound but not invidious legal status for trade unions, it became apparent that so many Liberal MPs felt themselves already committed that a simple capitulation to the TUC's own solution was the easiest recourse. The bill reverted to the anomalous provision, originally enacted in the 1870s, which protected trade unions by giving them a unique legal immunity from being sued over trade disputes. This legal settlement was a mark of an arms-length approach to British labour legislation that was to survive for most of the century. Politically it showed the power of organized labour.

The Government's other debts to its supporters were less easily redeemed. The temperance interest had, as usual, been vocal in the Liberal campaign, just as the brewers and publicans had on the Tory side. The Unionist Government's Licensing Act (1904) was felt to be too lenient to the vested interest of 'the trade' and had little effect in extinguishing liquor licences, which were staggeringly profuse in many urban areas. The Liberals duly passed their own bill in 1908; the Lords rejected it. Liberal propaganda pointed to the significant number of Tory peers with interests in brewing. It is true that the 'beerage' comprised the largest section of British industrialists to become ennobled, partly because brewing was the longest-established large-scale British industry. It is also true that 'the trade' was a significant financial contributor to Conservative funds. But licences were in fact being reduced, prohibition no longer had serious support (outside north Wales), and the Liberals were certainly not going to fight an election on the drink issue, which was rapidly becoming passé.

A similar fate awaited the Government's attempts to modify Balfour's Education Act. Its tenderness towards the Church of England had rankled with many Liberals, but the idea of returning to the school boards was a non-starter, and the Government simply wanted a decent compromise which would leave honour satisfied all round. This Balfour was determined to deny them. The first effort in 1906 (the Birrell bill) was conceived to propitiate the Nonconformists, while offering a loophole for Catholic schools. The House of Lords employed stealthy tactics, to maim rather than kill it. The hobbled bill, trapped in the Lords' procedural snare, was put out of its misery by the Government. The second try in 1908 (the McKenna bill) laboriously modified the Liberal proposals so as to protect Nonconformists, on one flank, and secure the assent of the non-partisan element on the bench of bishops of the Church of England, most of whom sat in the House of Lords. The Conservative Party did not want to upset the bishops, just upset the bill; this they eventually succeeded in doing, since at the grassroots it really pleased neither Church nor chapel.

Within a couple of years of its greatest triumph, the Liberal Party had dissipated much of the heady enthusiasm which had carried it to victory. The fact was that the Government was in no position to fight back against the tactics employed against it, because it lacked a strategy that promised popular appeal. It was living in the past, fiddling around with measures on schools and pubs that no longer seemed relevant to most of those who had voted Liberal in 1906. The negative nature of that victory was belatedly revealed by the fact that its major election cry (Free Trade) implied no agenda for action.

One thing was plain. It was no use looking to Campbell-Bannerman for a lead. He was much loved in the Liberal Party, for reasons that are now elusive; and not much hated by the Tories, for reasons that remain much more understandable – he gave them no reason either to hate or fear him. The fatal illness of his wife, who had crucially stiffened his resolve to occupy 10 Downing Street, blighted his time there; he suffered more than one heart attack; and by April 1908, when he submitted his resignation, he was a dying man. The constitutional niceties were observed – just. The King was abroad, taking the cure, and could not be bothered to come home, so it was Asquith who had to travel to kiss the hand of his monarch, in a French hotel. Where more appropriate for Edward the Peacemaker to appoint his last prime minister than Biarritz?

# 2

# Wait and See
## 1908–16

## WELFARE

Virtually anyone living in Great Britain had a much better chance of seeing their next birthday in 1980 than if they had lived in 1900. Up to the age of forty-five, the death rate for males in 1900 was six times higher than in 1980. Among females it was ten times higher – not because women had been more vulnerable than men in 1900 but because their pre-existing advantage over men was to open out in the course of the century. Death was, of course, related to age; in this sense old age came ten or twenty years sooner in those days.[1] Only after the age of sixty-five did a woman in 1980 have less than a 99 per cent chance of surviving the next year, whereas in 1900 a woman had the same expectation from as early as her forty-fifth birthday.

The most dramatic changes in life expectancy, as is usual, were those affecting the very young rather than the very old. In England and Wales in 1980 there were 12 deaths per thousand babies under the age of twelve months, whereas in 1900 there had been 163 – the sort of level which we now associate with the Third World. Thus in a family of six children – still not uncommon among manual labourers – it was probable that one baby would die. Other children might easily fail to survive to adulthood. Young people from five to thirty-five years old faced a chance of death which was only approached well into middle age later in the century. Little wonder that Edwardian as well as Victorian novels contained harrowing deathbed scenes in which men and women, boys and girls, were snatched away from sorrowing relatives – an incidence of mortality among the young which reached its gruesome climax with the First World War.

The English *Book of Common Prayer* was speaking literally when it

1. The death rate for men aged 55–64 in 1980 was less than that for men aged 45–54 in 1900 – a ten-year remission of mortality. For women aged 55–64 the death rate in 1980 was virtually like that for women aged 35–44 in 1900 – a twenty-year remission.

proclaimed that in the midst of life we are in death. Death was a fact of life with which Victorians had coped in various ways. For some it was a transcending religious experience, especially if a shared faith in salvation united the whole family around the deathbed. It may seem natural that Christianity, with its promise of an afterlife, should have brought comfort to many families prematurely ripped apart by the ravages of mortality; though it is equally understandable that Joseph Chamberlain, after being twice widowed, lost his Christian faith, as did David Lloyd George, unreconciled to the loss of his favourite daughter. For believers and unbelievers alike, the rituals of mourning, which could be very elaborate, were a practical way of coming to terms with bereavement. In a small way euphemisms softened the blow; it was said that the deceased 'passed on' or was 'called away' or even, as on the tombstone of General William Booth, the founder of the Salvation Army, who died in 1912, 'called to higher service'.

The people of Britain in 1900 were not only shorter-lived but shorter than us. The two facts are, of course, connected since height is a clear long-term indicator of standards of nutrition, which in turn influence life expectancy. At the end of the nineteenth century the average height of adult Englishmen was around 5 ft 7 in (1.7 m) and Scotsmen were probably an inch taller. It was exceptional for a man to grow to six feet, so much so that to be a 'six-footer' became a mark of distinction which persisted in the language long after the physical achievement of growing to 1.8 m had ceased to be remarkable. From about 1870 each cohort of children grew taller – and more quickly. Until the 1930s the rate of change was not striking, at perhaps an inch a century; but in the next half century the rate quadrupled until British heights reached their genetic plateau in the 1970s. Adult males now averaged 1.76 m, with the English slightly taller than the Scots. The gains were greatest for teenage boys since the tempo of growth was to speed up in the twentieth century, especially for working-class children. Differences in height and weight were related to social class in obvious ways. The boys at Eton and other public schools, drawn from the well-fed classes, were already as tall as nowadays by the end of the nineteenth century. Undergraduates at Oxford and Cambridge were likewise more obviously distinguished from working-class youths by brawn than by brain in 1900. The stature of Lancashire cotton operatives, by contrast, was stunted by a combination of child labour and a diet which later generations would regard as meagre.

Poverty was hardly a new problem. In the early nineteenth century people spoke of 'the condition of England'; by the end of the century of 'the Social Question'. Horrifying overcrowding in the slums of London had been the shock issue of the 1880s; the epic investigations of Charles Booth and his team of helpers were steadily being published throughout the 1890s, in a series of fat volumes. In later generations such a project would have been conducted by academically qualified sociologists, with funding from research councils or foundations: not paid for by a Liverpool shipowner, who initially wanted to show that socialist propaganda was alarmist, and who invented his methodology as he went along. Booth literally mapped out the impressions formed by his team of investigators, street by street. What distinguished See-bohm Rowntree's book *Poverty: a Study of Town Life* (1901) was that he got inside the problem, house by house.

Rowntree was another well-heeled amateur, a member of a well-known Quaker family of cocoa and chocolate manufacturers in York. Again his work bears his own peculiar stamp, with procedures which a later code would regard as gross intrusion into the privacy of the working-class households which he investigated. He used his connections to find out, from the family firm or other employers, what income each household in York received. Then he drew on current research in nutrition to establish how much food was necessary for subsistence, and found out how much it currently cost. Putting the two sets of information together was Rowntree's coup. At a stroke he could tell how many households had an income simply inadequate to provide for subsistence ('primary poverty') and how many, though possessed of such an income, were reduced to the same condition by unwise spend-ing ('secondary poverty').

In the long run, this concept of the 'poverty line' promised an elegant solution to the problem of primary poverty, through ensuring a sub-sistence income to every household. In the short run, Rowntree's book had a considerable impact on a public inured to the idea that the hor-rors of the rookeries were a problem unique to London. On the contrary: in a respectable, provincial city like York, blessed with philan-thropic Quaker employers, 10 per cent of the population was in acute need and up to 30 per cent in some degree of poverty. Whether the Rowntrees were to blame, or their workers, or the capitalist system, or Free Trade, was a matter on which Tories, temperance activists, social-ists and Tariff Reformers naturally held different opinions, which they sought to support by bandying selective findings from Rowntree on their different platforms in subsequent years.

Rowntree himself, as might be expected with his Quaker background, was an earnest Liberal. His family subsidized a weekly paper, the *Nation*, recently founded as the Liberal rival to the long-established *Spectator* (which was currently the mouthpiece of the Unionist Free Trade views of its editor, John St Loe Strachey). The Cadbury family, also Quakers, likewise subsidized the *Daily News*, giving the Liberals the support of the 'cocoa press' in the popular as well as the highbrow market. Seebohm Rowntree was thoroughly at home with the *Nation* and the band of talented contributors recruited by its editor, H. W. Massingham: notably the economist J. A. Hobson and the social philosopher L. T. Hobhouse. 'The two Hobs', as their friend the social historian Barbara Hammond called them, were the leading intellectual spokesmen for a New Liberalism of social reform which was now to come into its own.

Both Hobson and Hobhouse had been influenced by the Fabian Society, which was where young collectivists learnt their trade in the 1890s. They were indebted to Sidney and Beatrice Webb for lessons in painstaking social inquiry; and were almost as impressed with Shaw's brilliance as he was himself. Graham Wallas was the other leading Fabian: a student of political behaviour whose book *Human Nature in Politics* (1908) was to suggest that social psychology had a generally unacknowledged importance in shaping the democratic process. It was Wallas with whom Hobson and Hobhouse developed a deeper affinity; conversely Wallas was to break with the Fabianism of the Webbs and, above all, Shaw in 1904 (over Free Trade) and identify with the New Liberalism.

It was essentially the logic of Chamberlainite-cum-Shavian imperialism, supporting the big state at home and abroad, which precipitated the rupture between Fabianism and New Liberalism. Hobson's famous book, *Imperialism* (1902), identified imperialism as an economic and political force which was the enemy of social reform, not its ideological ally against Gladstonianism. Imperialism was the means by which parasitic plutocratic interests distracted the attention of the people in pursuit of adventures – notably in South Africa, of course – which were profitable for the vested interests concerned but bad business for the nation as a whole. Only redistribute wealth at home, Hobson urged, and the purchasing power of the mass of the people would provide all the markets that a prosperous economy needed.

'Under-consumption' is the way this tradition of economic thinking is generally known, and at the time it was regarded as heretical by orthodox academic economists. But though Hobson was broadly under-consumptionist in his economic views, not all New Liberals were. The neoclassical analysis developed by Alfred Marshall, the doyen of professional economists in Britain, countenanced everything that the Liberal Party came to adopt under Asquith and Lloyd George. Not only had Marshall, professor of political economy at Cambridge, rallied academic economists against Tariff Reform: his successor, A. C. Pigou, established the term 'welfare economics' in arguing out principles of distributive justice which justified interventionist reforms. New Liberalism was not necessarily under-consumptionist in economics, any more than it was necessarily Idealist in philosophy.[1] What united New Liberals was a more directly political sentiment.

The way Hobhouse put it was to say that the task of Liberalism in the nineteenth century had been the achievement of political democracy; in the twentieth century it would be social democracy. There were senses of 'socialism', therefore, which were acceptable to Liberals; and certainly labour, representing a special case of the maldistribution of wealth in the community, ought to be part of the Liberal coalition. In arguing that liberalism and social democracy were compatible, the notion that liberalism was essentially a doctrine of the free play of the market was discarded. Maybe Liberals had historically been identified with laissez-faire, in fighting the battles of their own day against an aristocratic state; but that was no reason for modern Liberals to fear the democratic state or pit themselves against its benign collectivist potential. When the New Liberals put a new foot forward, this was it. Equally, it was held illiberal to pursue otherwise desirable collectivist ends by statist, bureaucratic or undemocratic means – the New Liberals' liberal foot. Little wonder that they kept shifting the weight of their arguments from one to the other.

What the New Liberals required from a Liberal Government was a double agenda. Most of them had opposed the Boer War; they wanted

---

1. The posthumous influence of the Hegelian philosopher T. H. Green, dead for a quarter of a century by 1906, has been too freely invoked in understanding the outlook of the Edwardian Liberal Party. Plainly not all New Liberals were philosophers, still less neo-Hegelians; and Green's politics of moral regeneration did not envisage anything like a welfare state.

an extrication from Chamberlainism. All of this made them partisans of Campbell-Bannerman, for they believed that liberalism was safe in his hands; they remained to be convinced that Asquith had lived down his Liberal Imperialist past. So much for the traditional idiom of Radicalism. But there was also an emerging political language which talked of 'the left' and of 'welfare'. Of the new side of the New Liberals' agenda there was little sign on the statute book before 1908. Whatever the Government's other deficiencies, they were as nothing to its almost total failure to address the issue of social reform. As H. G. Wells was to put it in his *The New Machiavelli* (1911), it seemed tremendously clear what the Liberals were against – 'The trouble was to find out what on earth they were *for*!'

## A POPULAR CULTURE

In 1906 Shaw turned fifty and Wells forty; they were the dominant figures in the literary life of the Edwardian period. Their near contemporary Kipling already seemed the voice of an earlier era, that of the triumphant imperialism – which, it should be remembered, he had himself presciently chastised for its hubris since before the Boer War. His poem 'Recessional' (1897) marked Victoria's diamond jubilee; and in the twentieth century his mood was indeed recessional, almost as if he had retired early, like one of his own Anglo-Indian subalterns, to tend his garden in Sussex. His established international fame was confirmed by the award of the Nobel Prize for Literature in 1907, whereas Shaw had to wait until 1925. Kipling at forty was a great Victorian whale washed up on the beach.

By contrast, Shaw and Wells made their names by teaching and preaching self-consciously post-Victorian attitudes. Keynes, another twenty years younger, later called them the 'grand old schoolmasters' of his generation: Shaw the divinity master and Wells, with his scientific bent, the 'stinks' master.

Shaw's secularist morality invoked Darwin, Nietzsche, Samuel Butler and, above all, Ibsen, whose quintessence he aspired to transfer to the English stage. This ambition proved initially difficult to realize, and not just for artistic reasons. It long remained the law that the Lord Chamberlain had to grant a licence for all public performances on the stage, and Shaw's agenda fell foul of this restriction. Indeed *Mrs Warren's*

*Profession* (1893), which suggested that there were more immoral earnings in the world than those that came from prostitution, had to wait thirty years for the Lord Chamberlain's ban to be lifted, and many of Shaw's plays were originally put on by the Stage Society in nominally private performances. In other provocative plays, like *Widowers' Houses* (1892), which showed the squalid foundations on which a nice little investment in property might be built, Shaw succeeded in dramatizing the arguments even when he failed to make the characters much more than vehicles for his dialectical set-pieces. His *Plays, Pleasant and Unpleasant* (1898) offered texts, complete with full prefaces and stage directions, which could be read like novels – and without hindrance from any Lord Chamberlain.

By turning bourgeois morality inside out Shaw the socialist may have sought to expose the rottenness of capitalism. But the cold-eyed Fabian style, abjuring sentiment, meant that his offence was conducted most offensively against conventional Liberalism, with its propensity to strike moral attitudes. In *Major Barbara* (1905) every stripe of do-gooder is satirized: not only the internally inconsistent upper-crust Radical professions of Lady Britomart, and the ineffectual academic agonizings of Adolphus, but the well-meaning palliatives of the Salvation Army's social work in the slums, carried on by Major Barbara herself. The real hero, by contrast, is the international arms dealer Undershaft, revealed not as the 'merchant of death' of Radical demonology but as the wholesale provider of a living wage to workers otherwise condemned to the ultimate sin: poverty. Little wonder that Shaw's audiences squirmed in their seats, mocked for the same tender consciences which had brought them to attend these dramas of social concern.

Shaw, moreover, had a trick up his sleeve which ensured that they would come back for more: his genius not just with language but with ideas, seen in a dazzling gift for paradox which laced these plays with sardonic wit. Shocked, affronted, chastised – often unpersuaded – his audiences might be: but not bored. His ambivalent stance as an Irish exile, by extenuating the froth of words and the outrageous opinions, helped his accreditation as licensed jester. As 'GBS' he was as much a public figure as politicians like 'C-B' or 'LG', with fully as many newspaper profiles and biographies in his own (long) lifetime. The distinctive forked beard, the spare figure and the twinkling eye were easily recognizable. 'GBS' was a walking, talking caricature of the sandal-wearing Fabian lifestyle: the pure wool Jaeger knickerbocker-suit which he designed for himself as hygienic clothing; the vegetarianism which he upheld, not through soppiness over animals but through disgust over devouring dead bodies; the teetotalism which was not a moralistic reproach to the drinking classes but an almost Martian incomprehension about the alcohol habit.

Wells was more easily placed in the English social structure. Sprung from a lower-middle-class background of precarious gentility, he was shut out of the still exclusive ancient universities as surely as the eponymous hero of Thomas Hardy's *Jude the Obscure* (1895). Unlike Jude, Wells happily pursued his studies at the Normal School of Science, South Kensington, which had established a leading role in the training of science teachers. Wells celebrated the rise of a professional and managerial ethos, the triumph of an expertise that would later be called technocratic, seen most dramatically in the promise of science to unlock new potential in society. The fact that Britain lagged behind Germany and the USA in the priority given to scientific education was generally acknowledged in the early twentieth century. True, science now had a secure foothold in the universities, as illustrated by the sharp increase in the number of candidates for the Natural Sciences Tripos at Cambridge, albeit from a low base, or the burgeoning number of BSc degrees given by London and the newer civic universities. The perceived failure – which the foundation of Imperial College in 1908 was intended to remedy – was in coordinating academic specialization with the needs of industry (with new chemical technologies as an object lesson in German superiority). 'There is a gap in our public mentality at the present time,' Wells was to tell the British Science Guild in 1917, meaning that in Britain the ordinary man and the scientific specialist were hardly on speaking terms. He saw a mission in filling if not closing that gap.

Wells's novels partook of his own complex persona. There are his early best-sellers in science fiction, opening a window from the known to the unknown in an almost surreal way, as in *The Time Machine* (1895) or *The Invisible Man* (1897). There is, in *Love and Mr Lewisham* (1900) and *The History of Mr Polly* (1910), a fine evocation of the thwarted aspirations of the unknown England of the shabby suburbs.

Wells developed too a genre which closely – sometimes mimetically – reflected the life of their successful Edwardian author. Typically, a striking young woman falls for a man twice her age; and scandal threatens to engulf them. She is a 'new woman', set on having her own career; he encourages her advanced views on social and political issues, with his own blend of idealism, experience and iconoclasm, which is plainly rather attractive to women – and evidently not unsympathetic to the author as an idealized self-portrait. The power of these novels to shock was fuelled by autobiographical references which inflamed some of Wells's critics. *Ann Veronica* (1909), which reduced St Loe Strachey to apoplexy in the *Spectator*, had a reception which can only be explained in this way. *The New Machiavelli* (1911) contained a portrait of the Webbs – as Oscar and Altiora Bailey, with a passion for bureaucratic reform which would have replaced trees with green-painted sunshades – a portrait which was as unmistakable as it was unfriendly. Wells's tactlessness, however, was pure artistic gain and helped him to make *The New Machiavelli* the equal of any political novel in the English language, animating the story with a real sense of the important issues at stake, rather than just using Westminster as a backdrop.

Writing made 'GBS' and 'HG' rich as well as famous. The Dickensian legacy of a large reading public for works of acknowledged literary quality was not exhausted. There were, of course, best-selling authors whose work is little read today. Silas Hocking had his public for novels imbued with high-minded religiosity; 'Marie Corelli' (Mary Mackay) had a distinctly lighter touch in her romantic fiction; and Elinor Glyn trespassed on the boundaries of public taste, especially with her erotically charged *Three Weeks* (1907).

'Thrillers' or 'shockers', plainly intended as entertainment, came from diverse hands. In *The Riddle of the Sands* (1903), Erskine Childers exploited the spy theme, allied with a passion for messing about in boats – all quintessentially English but for the fact that Childers himself later became an Irish Nationalist; a member of the Irish Republican Army, he was to be shot after a court martial in 1922. It was in the early part of the First World War that the Unionist politician, historian and publisher John Buchan found his vocation with books like *The Thirty-Nine Steps* (1915) and *Greenmantle* (1916), fantasies of espionage and political intrigue, pushing hard at the borders of plausibility. In 1920, on retiring from the Royal Engineers, Lt-Col. Cyril McNeile was to assume his own mantle as 'Sapper' and introduce Bull-Dog Drummond, an upper-class vigilante with a taste for violence that was both proto-fascist and photogenic, as a string of films testified. These were books without high literary pretensions. But they were joined on the best-seller lists of the first quarter of the century by an impressive number of novels which have survived the subsequent vicissitudes of critical taste.

Arnold Bennett was the spiritual successor of Trollope in his unabashed thirst for success and his utilitarian accounts of his annual production of words. Like Trollope, Bennett found that his reputation was to suffer as a result, especially when he became the prime butt of Virginia Woolf's increasingly influential disdain in the twenties. Maybe by then he was past his best; but the years which saw the publication of *Anna of the Five Towns* (1902), *The Old Wives' Tale* (1908) and *Clayhanger* (1910) were hardly barren of artistic achievement, despite their lucrative results. John Galsworthy was to endure similar condescension from coterie critics who dismissed his 'Forsyte Saga' and scorned his Order of Merit in 1929 and his Nobel Prize in 1932; yet the trilogy, *The Man of Property* (1906), *In Chancery* (1920) and *To Let* (1921), has continued to give later generations an insight into the social norms of Edwardian England. The comedies of manners by E. M. Forster were more finely drawn and had to wait for recognition – not only *Maurice* (posthumously published, 1971), with a homosexual theme that consigned its manuscript to a drawer for fifty years, but even *Howards End* (1910), with its culture-clash between the aesthetic values of the Schlegels and the 'telegrams and anger' of the worldly Wilcoxes. There was too a distinguished literary old guard: not only the immigrants Joseph Conrad (from Poland) and Henry James (from the USA) but, above all in popular acclaim, Thomas Hardy, who received the Order of Merit in 1910.

The really popular art form at the turn of the century was music hall. Originally based in pubs, it offered 'turns' of all kinds; comedy and popular songs trod an emotional tightrope, with a cynical undertow of sharp social comment. When Albert Chevalier offered the apparently sentimental tribute to forty years of married life together, 'My Old Dutch' (rhyming slang: Dutch House/spouse), the turn was performed against a backdrop which showed the workhouse, to which aged paupers were consigned. The otherwise bland refrain – 'We've been together now for forty years/An' it don't seem a day too much' – was bitterly undercut by the implications of the separate entrances on each side for Men and Women.

Music hall had a beery camaraderie, with plenty of audience participation from a plebeian crowd of men and women alike, while the new palaces of variety reached upmarket to an audience of clerks and rakish toffs, slumming while they eyed the chorus girls. At the time of the Boer War the music hall was looked on as a source of jingoism; but it was essentially the amplifier of the visceral response of the crowd to targets of approbation or derision, either noisily given. Topical references were quickly taken up; catchphrases were propagated across the country via a hidden network of which the nerve centre was Crewe Junction on a Sunday afternoon, when itinerant artistes changed trains en route to the next week's engagement. This was the hard school in which Charlie Chaplin came up, before one day abandoning Crewe for California, where he captured some of his old acts on celluloid. George Robey, 'the prime minister of mirth', continued to tread the boards with a technique which, as Lloyd George realized, showed the affinities of the stage and the platform. Music hall finally became respectable when one of its greatest stars, the stage Scotsman Harry Lauder, was knighted in 1919.

In the late nineteenth century religion and recreation had often gone together. In much of provincial Britain they still did, with a wide range of social activities based on church and chapel: girls' friendly societies or lads' clubs, choirs or amateur dramatic groups. Choral works had long been the forte of English music; north-country town halls resounded to performances of oratorios like Handel's *Messiah*, another reflection of the religiosity with which popular culture was still impregnated. Among secular works, Gilbert and Sullivan's Savoy operas formed a mainstay of the amateur repertoire. All of this was in an active tradition of participation and self-help, common to the artisan ethic as much as to that of middle-class self-improvement. Lt-Gen. Robert Baden-Powell started the Scout movement in 1909 and it flourished, not because of its mildly imperialist proselytism, but because it was a passport to accessible outdoor adventures, where smoke-tainted food and damp canvas provided a fine escape from mean streets.

Sports clubs in urban areas were often started under religious auspices, with subsequently famous soccer teams springing from origins which would have surprised their mid-twentieth-century fans. Most clubs, of course, remained amateur in every sense of the word, with players who would turn out for St Swithin's on a Saturday even if they did not often turn up for worship on a Sunday. Such transfers of attention and allegiance, from the religious life of the churches to the secular activities they sponsored, may have had the effect of diluting denominational rivalries. The rise of professional football in the big cities, however, could foster and fan divisions between teams affiliated with the (indigenous) Protestant and (Irish) Catholic communities: in Glasgow it was Rangers versus Celtic; on Merseyside, Everton versus Liverpool.

Association Football (soccer) had become the people's game by the end of the nineteenth century, especially in industrial Scotland and Lancashire, where the professional League clubs offered a chance of vicarious participation to workers who finished at noon on a Saturday, in time for the big match. Professional footballers were working-class heroes in a double sense. Treated as gods by their fans, they were treated as proletarians by their employers, and kept till 1961 in a form of wage slavery through flat-rate contracts which denied them the financial fruits of their talent. Their star status was affirmed by their depiction on 'cigarette cards', distributed in each packet by rival brands. The rise of football was also fuelled by its association with working-class gambling, hardly less than horse-racing, though more legally once the weekly football pools had become established. A surrogate for a British national lottery, filling in a pools coupon on the kitchen table offered a relatively respectable way of having a flutter, whereas the furtive presence of bookmakers' runners on street corners testified to the fact that working-class gambling long remained (ineffectually) criminalized.

In 1911 virtually every English town with a population of over 50,000 had a Football League club. The big teams represented the big money, with the composition of the League charting the economic history of the country. The northern conurbations were represented among the twelve founder members of the League in 1888: Birmingham by Aston Villa, Merseyside by Everton – both of them teams which were still to be in the Premier League over a century later. It was still true five years later, with two divisions instituted, that none of the twenty-eight League clubs was south of Birmingham; though professional football was now creeping south. The Woolwich Arsenal, in south-east London, with waning prosperity after the Boer War, abruptly lost its connection with its eponymous football team, which moved to its present Highbury ground in Islington; but Arsenal remained 'the Gunners' just as their north-London rivals, Tottenham Hotspur, were 'the Spurs'. Likewise the name Sheffield Wednesday commemorated the midweek fixtures on early closing day, which gave shopworkers the afternoon off. These big-city clubs lived on even when they had moved on from their origins. But at the beginning of the twentieth century it was still possible for the small northern cotton town of Glossop, boasting the largest spinning mill in the world, to enjoy its hour of glory in the First Division. Towards the end of the century it was the more prosperous south which was prominent in the upper reaches of the Football League, with clubs like Wimbledon, Southampton, Ipswich, and Norwich in the Premier League, and with Luton, Swindon, Oxford, Peterborough, Brighton, Cambridge and Bournemouth appearing in the First or Second Divisions.

In Wales rugby football acquired a mass working-class following that it lacked in England or Scotland, where its status as the amateur code was designed to keep it socially exclusive. Indeed the issue of amateur status had prompted the formation of the Rugby League, as a professional code, mainly on the coalfields of Lancashire and Yorkshire. Rugby Union, by contrast, was played in most public schools and 'Old Boys' teams, or 'Former Pupils' in Scotland, were one of its mainstays. In south Wales, however, 'football' meant the Rugby Union code, amateur status and all, with heroic teams of pitmen from the valleys carrying the national honour. No fewer than six times between 1900 and 1912, Wales won the 'triple crown' by conquering England, Ireland and Scotland in the international championship; and the achievement of the Welsh XV in beating the All Blacks, hitherto undefeated on their 1905 tour from New Zealand, was to become legendary.

Unlike either code of football, cricket was played and followed by all social classes in England (and parts of south Wales too, but only by small Anglo-Scots and Anglo-Irish contingents). At its highest level of proficiency, accredited as 'first-class cricket' since the county championship began in 1873, it had always been a spectator sport in which the upper classes had insisted on participating, like horse racing. The governing body of the sport remained until 1969 the Marylebone Cricket Club (MCC) – nominally private, socially exclusive – established for more than a century at the present Lord's cricket ground in north London. Cricket solved the problem of professionalism by making a distinction in first-class cricket between Gentlemen, who were amateurs, and Players, employed by the county clubs. In a microcosm of the English class system, they took the field each day as members of the same team, though through separate gates at Lord's, and were distinguished by the fact that Gentlemen alone had initials before their surnames on the scorecard. Lord Hawke (the seventh baron) was captain of the Yorkshire XI from 1883 to 1910, leading his side to the county championship eight times. He also took MCC teams abroad, in proselytizing missions which may have had little lasting impact on the sporting culture of the USA, Canada, or South America. But Australia, with its tiny population, very soon proved more than able to take on the old country in Test matches, with the winner of each series awarded the purely notional trophy of 'the Ashes' (of English cricket). Hawke had the satisfaction of seeing other countries which he had toured, like India, the West Indies and South Africa, acquire international Test status – in the end a more lasting legacy for Commonwealth unity than anything Chamberlain achieved.

In England the status of cricket as the national game was culturally secure. Village teams, playing on village greens, preferably with the shadows of ancient trees lengthening across the wicket, with the blacksmith as fast bowler, and the squire's son as a stylish batsman, were mythologized in prose and verse. Literary figures like J. M. Barrie, the author of *Peter Pan*, doted on the game and were joined in their dotage by many indulgent readers who found here a potent metaphor for all that was best in English life. To call something 'not cricket' was to make a moral judgement.

For some people, the joke goes, sport is not a matter of life and death: it is more serious than that. When it is referred to as a religion, the comment may be suggestive as well as ironic. The ability of sport to capture the popular imagination, to infuse a sense of common commitment in the outcome of an epic contest, to provide a strong narrative line – even when busy people can only eavesdrop on the story on the back page of a newspaper or snatch at the latest Test score – this is not just a trivial matter. In twentieth-century Britain organized mass sport may have filled some of the psychic space which was being vacated by organized mass Christianity.

## FISCAL CRISIS

Asquith stepped effortlessly into the premiership in 1908 and looked the part immediately. His strength lay in an executive capacity to transact business, with a mastery of exposition on paper which recalled Gladstone, and an adroitness in managing personalities which enabled him to nudge discussion towards consensus. He would bide his time in apparent indolence until he spotted a favourable turn, on which he would seize incisively. The dictum which became notorious – 'Wait and see' – was originally uttered during the Irish crisis, with a hint of menace as much as procrastination behind it. His intellectual dominance over his cabinet meant that, until the War came, he exacted respect from even the most forceful and self-confident of his lieutenants – indisputably, David Lloyd George and Winston Churchill. By immediately promoting them to key positions, Asquith injected his cabinet with a dynamism which Campbell-Bannerman's had lacked. Grey as Foreign Secretary and Haldane as Secretary of State for War remained closer to the prime minister, and together they determined defence and foreign policy; but the initiatives now came in domestic politics.

Asquith chose Lloyd George as his Chancellor of the Exchequer, knowing full well that this did not mean a quiet life. Like himself, Lloyd George was a self-made lawyer; but a Welsh country attorney, as he liked to call himself, rather than an Oxbridge-educated barrister. His background in Welsh-speaking, Nonconformist Caernarvonshire gave Lloyd George's Radicalism a fiery, populist flavour, especially when directed against English landlords; but this 'cottage-bred man' had been pampered in the finest cottage in the village of Llanystumdwy and was a tribune voicing historic wrongs, not a victim of personal deprivation. His was a small people rightly struggling to be free of English oppression – hardly less than the Boers, whose cause he had naturally championed. Through the pro-Boer network he had broadened his political base, forming long-lasting bonds with New Liberals, like C. P. Scott, the magisterial editor of the *Manchester Guardian*, the leading anti-war paper. Scott, the high-minded patron of Progressive politics, reconciling Liberals with Labour, was to make a life's work out of 'saving Lloyd George's soul'.

Lloyd George stood out as the minister with green fingers, able to make the garden bloom through an intuitive flair, in ways that he hardly understood, let alone foresaw. Above his bed was the motto: 'There is a path which no fowl knoweth and the eye of the vulture hath not seen' (Job 28: 7). An apprenticeship as President of the Board of Trade confirmed his ministerial calibre, showing that he was not just a Radical platform orator. More than anyone else, he was responsible for giving the New Liberalism a real purchase in Edwardian politics; yet he had no more read his Rowntree or his Hobhouse in 1908 than he had actually read the Reports of the Royal Commission on the Poor Law in 1909, when he airily began citing them in his speeches. Talking to Rowntree or Hobhouse, or to others who had read them, gave Lloyd George more in half an hour than anything he got from book learning; and though his manifest deficiencies in mastering the contents of his ministerial red boxes were as exasperating to colleagues as his blatant negligence as a correspondent, his methods had the unanswerable virtue of success, sometimes under conditions which needed drastic remedies.

Under Asquith some significant steps had already been taken at the Treasury, probing the frontier of traditional Free Trade finance. The 1907 Budget granted remissions of income tax on earned incomes, thus throwing the burden more on to investment incomes. This was frustrating for Tariff Reformers; it countered their strategy of relying more on indirect taxation by instead moving towards a progressive scale of direct taxation. Asquith's trump card, moreover, was old-age pensions.

The Victorian poor law held out the prospect of the workhouse as a deterrent influence on its clients, thus providing an incentive to self-reliance and independence. The principle was that, under ordinary conditions, the worker had the means of avoiding pauperism in old age by the exercise of foresight, industry and thrift. So by foreseeing that old age comes to all, by industriously earning a living, and by thriftily setting enough aside for the future, the individual could reap the rewards of the individualist virtues. This was a scheme of things which many Liberals found appealing; they were by no means minded to throw it over, capriciously, in favour of a doctrine of collectivist provision. It was the manifest practical breakdown of existing arrangements which put the case for pensions on its feet. As life expectancy increased, more people lived to an age which they had never foreseen reaching, became unable to support themselves through their own industry, and were liable to exhaust whatever thrifty provision they had made. Moreover, the idea that all working-class incomes allowed a surplus for adequate endowment of old age was itself unrealistic. Furthermore, the friendly societies, through which many respectable artisans had accumulated pension rights, were now caught between the actuarial assumptions about life expectancy which had set their contributions levels and their ever-increasing liabilities to aged beneficiaries who, according to the yellowing life tables, ought to have been dead years ago.

The economic provisions of the 1908 Old Age Pensions Act were meagre by later standards. A pension of five shillings a week – only a quarter of even a labourer's wage – was to be paid, and only after the age of seventy. A means test tapered payments to recipients of an income of more than ten shillings a week; and married couples were paid at a lower joint rate, thus further limiting the cost to the Treasury. Also anyone on poor relief was initially ineligible for a pension. This was an unsatisfactory stipulation, since paupers were the one group of old people manifestly in greatest need, but a wish to discriminate between the deserving and undeserving poor died hard. Even with such restrictions, since the scheme was non-contributory, the estimated burden was £6 million a year (an underestimate by 50 per cent as it turned out). The political impact was enormous: the more so since Chamberlain had for years been half-promising pensions. The Liberals smugly claimed that they had not promised them, just implemented them – and had done so without abandoning Free Trade.

Lloyd George inherited old-age pensions, not least as a commitment which he had to finance. The estimates of cost turned out to be under-estimates; and the Government's backbenchers insisted on removing the pauper disqualification, which enhanced both the consistency and the expense of the scheme. Not only that: further measures of social legislation were now in the pipeline, with a Royal Commission on the Poor Law about to report. Worse still, especially for a Government elected on the old Liberal cry of Peace, Retrenchment and Reform, were the naval estimates.

Here were the twin causes of the Edwardian fiscal crisis. Visions of a Liberal Government financing social reform from the money it would save on defence spending were blasted out of the water with the advent of the Dreadnought: a state-of-the-art battleship rightly renowned for its mighty firepower, its mighty armour and, not least, its mighty expense. The first ship of this class had been launched in 1906, giving the Royal Navy a clear technological edge over Germany – temporarily. For, once the Germans decided to compete, as they did in 1908, with a programme of lookalikes, only Dreadnoughts counted in the great game for mastery of the North Sea. Germany might thus leapfrog into the lead over a whole generation of outclassed British ships of an older vintage. Or so the alarmist propaganda of the Navy League, amplified through the Tory press, readily suggested, in a campaign to step up the construction of Dreadnoughts. 'We want eight,' was the cry; six was the Admiralty bid; four the sticking point of the 'economists' in the cabinet, led by Lloyd George and Churchill. After protracted disputes in 1909, the cabinet agreed to a compromise brokered by Asquith: four Dreadnoughts immediately, four more later, if found to be necessary, as they duly were.

Grey's foreign policy was not hostile towards Germany, and more than one attempt was made to defuse the naval rivalry. But since Great Britain was in an essentially defensive position, it was inexorably pitted against constant challenges from the rising power of the Wilhelmine Reich, its thrusting nationalist ambitions fuelled by its dynamic economy. In 1900 Germany produced 13 per cent of world manufacturing output compared with nearly 19 per cent in Britain; but by 1913 Germany was breasting 15 per cent while Britain's share had fallen below 14 per cent. Though both economies manufactured over twice as much as that of France, the combined size of all three was now only slightly greater than that of the new giant, the USA, fast approaching one-third of world manufacturing output. Such statistics spell out, with the sophistication of hindsight, a relative decline of power which was perhaps inevitable, but which excited apprehension among Britons who had been brought up to think differently. Periodic anti-German panics did not drive the Liberal Government into a full alliance with France, let alone with Tsarist Russia, and overtures continued to be made to Germany until 1912. But the 1909 crisis was significant because Germany was seen as challenging the position of the Royal Navy, the guardian of the sea routes on which depended both the security of the Empire and the political economy of Free Trade.

So it was that the Liberal Government became committed to financing a naval race with Germany at the same moment as the bills were coming in for its new programme of social reform. Existing taxes could not meet such calls, as Tariff Reformers kept reiterating, whereas their own proposal to 'broaden the basis of taxation' stood ready. Lloyd George's answer was forthcoming in the distinctly unsuccessful speech – he hardly seemed to understand some of his own proposals – with which he introduced the 1909 Budget.

The People's Budget, as he called it, found the bulk of the new revenue it needed by a sharp rise in direct taxation, especially by increasing the progressive impact of income tax on higher incomes, notably through a supplementary 'supertax' on the very rich. Measures to hit back at the drink trade were brought in by the back door, and the ground was prepared for taxes on land by initiating a valuation of all real property in the United Kingdom. All this made for a large and unwieldy Finance bill, arguably 'tacking' social legislation which the Liberals were unable to get through the House of Lords on to the budget, which was conventionally Commons business alone. The guts of the budget were pure New Liberalism: redistributing income from rich to poor via progressive taxation and social reform in a way that would have profoundly shocked Gladstone. But Lloyd George's political cunning was to attach Old Liberal sentiment to its fate, by taxing the drink trade, by making faces at the landed interest, and by parading the vestal purity of Free Trade. Liberal finance, moreover, though it hit those who were seriously rich, was not unfriendly to a taxpayer in the professional class on an earned income of up to £1,000 a year.

Since 1906 by-elections had run against the Government, in a way that we now discount as 'mid-term blues', but which led contemporaries (and some subsequent historians) to more sweeping judgements about political trends. A short recession meant that unemployment in 1908–9 was at double the level of 1906–7, which gave Tariff Reform just the opening it needed; and a series of Unionist by-election victories helped dispel the taint of the electoral verdict in 1906. Partly as a result of the recession, more emphasis was now put on protection of domestic industries through a general tariff on manufactured goods, rather than on Imperial Preference. These two planks in the platform, plus the old Balfourite favourite of retaliatory tariffs, were joined by a fourth plank – revenue – which was to become the clinching argument in finally converting the party to Tariff Reform. Faced with the People's Budget, the Unionists needed to point to an alternative source of revenue. The Budget could hardly be challenged on the expenditure side, since more Dreadnoughts had been a Unionist demand in the first place, and a repudiation of pensions spelt electoral suicide. Tariff Reform, in this domesticated form, thus became the Conservative answer to 'Lloyd George finance'.

The Budget's role in reviving the electoral fortunes of the Liberal Party seems unmistakable. It became the spine of a vertebrate policy of social reform, going beyond pensions into what Churchill called 'the untrodden field in politics'. By this he meant unemployment; and as the new President of the Board of Trade, he had the field to himself. In so far as the problem was frictional unemployment, during the interval while a match was made between unfilled vacancies and the workers seeking them, he had an answer in 'labour exchanges', which were introduced in 1908. The idea had been worked out by one of

Churchill's advisers, William Beveridge, then beginning an influential career in social administration. This was hardly socialism: it was a means of making the free market in labour work more efficiently by means of a little interventionist lubrication. It provided, too, the passport to a further exercise in intervention which was now coming to fruition: unemployment insurance.

'Unemployment' spoke a language hardly more than twenty years old. The traditional term was 'able-bodied pauper', the client of the Poor Law, which was the administrative responsibility of the Local Government Board, which might be supposed, therefore, the seat of operations in a Government set on social reform. Not so under John Burns, the flamboyant Lib-Lab MP for Battersea, President of the Local Government Board since 1905. This striking appointment was 'the most popular thing you have yet done', Burns had confidently assured Campbell-Bannerman. Burns retained an emblematic membership of the class from which he had made his well-advertised rise – and showed all its social conservatism, not least in the artisan's contempt for the undeserving poor.

If this was one reason why the Poor Law remained unreformed, another was that its potential reformers could not agree on their proposed reforms. The Royal Commission, which had been at work since 1905, found itself polarized between the two remarkable women who sat on it. Helen Bosanquet represented the individualist ethic of the Charity Organization Society, reinforced with the Hegelian social philosophy of her husband, Bernard Bosanquet; and she made the running in a majority report which wanted to retain the Poor Law as the authority dealing with destitution but to devolve many of its functions on to specialized agencies. With much of this the minority report in fact agreed; but Beatrice Webb had been determined to write it as a coherent statement of a case to break up the Poor Law. The unemployed would be required to register at labour exchanges, permitted to take out unemployment insurance, and guaranteed a minimum support from the state, on one crucial condition: that they submit to measures to reform and retrain them.

Faced with a choice between two reports, the Government chose neither. Instead of the Webbs' package of voluntary unemployment insurance and conditional relief, Churchill opted for a scheme of compulsory insurance (in specified industries) but essentially unconditional entitlement to unemployment benefits. Registration at labour exchanges established a test of willingness to work and was thus the passport to benefits. This was to become Part Two of a vast National Insurance Act, passed in 1911, initially covering 2½ million workers in trades subject to cyclical unemployment. Part One was Lloyd George's responsibility, covering sickness – though, appreciating that death insurance was always sold under the name life insurance, he adopted the term Health Insurance. 'The Lloyd George' (as it became known colloquially to its participants) covered all employed workers, about 12 million, but was less innovative than 'the Winston Churchill' (as, inequitably, it did not become known). Churchill's scheme for unemployment-insurance benefit did not have German precedents upon which to build.

National Insurance protected the breadwinner by insuring him (almost always the male) against pauperization through unemployment or sickness. Medical help was subsidiary: basically it aimed to get the man back to work again, by giving him access to panels of approved doctors registered under the Act. The fact that the scheme was financed by weekly contributions from the insured worker and the employer, as well as a state subsidy, limited the Exchequer liability. If this was the financial rationale for choosing this approach, the political reasoning was equally revealing. First, it showed Lloyd George's populist touch. He knew the revulsion with which people regarded the workhouse; he would have nothing to do with the machinery of the Poor Law in administering National Insurance, any more than in paying pensions, which came across the post-office counter. In this way the Liberals dealt with the Poor Law by ignoring it, coping with its traditional concerns through other means. Second, the point which the Webbs failed to grasp was that the unconditionality of insurance benefits, to which workers felt they had earned the right, was the means of winning assent for state intervention. Liberal collectivism thus made an appeal to Labour, bypassing socialist objections, which surely explains why the British welfare state was built on the foundation of National Insurance.

Without the People's Budget, the Liberals' welfare reforms would have had neither resources nor political clout. Social reform became big politics when it was meshed with partisan concerns in 1909–10, when the New Liberalism provided a language for addressing the predicament in which the Liberal Government found itself. The rejection of the Budget by the House of Lords in November 1909 led to a constitutional crisis, only settled, after two general elections, by the passing of the

Parliament Act in 1911. This has sometimes obscured the fact that it was fundamentally a political conflict, resolved not by constitutional arguments but because the Liberals hit upon a winning political strategy.

The Unionist majority in the House of Lords blocked the Budget because they thought they could get away with it – and they almost did. The appearance of a number of 'backwoodsmen' to inflate the ordinary Tory majority – the Budget was lost by 375 to 75 – was a picturesque touch of the kind which fed Lloyd George's rhetoric. He talked of being governed by 'five hundred men, chosen accidentally from among the unemployed'. But he had been nearer the mark when he had claimed that the House of Lords was not the watchdog of the constitution but 'Mr Balfour's poodle'. The Unionist leader knew that if the Budget could meet the Government's revenue needs, the case for Tariff Reform would be much weakened; and the Lords carefully claimed that they were acting only so as to refer the matter to the people. No one doubted their legal right to vote against the Bill; likewise no one was surprised by Asquith's response in calling a general election for January 1910.

This argument between a Liberal majority in the Commons and a Conservative majority in the Lords had been in rehearsal for at least twenty years. What gave it a cutting edge in 1910 was the electoral appeal of the underlying social and economic issues at stake. Social reform depended upon the People's Budget; Tariff Reform relied upon defeating it. This was the core of the argument, especially in industrial and working-class seats. Lloyd George had already made his biggest splash in 1909, with his barnstorming taunts against the peers at Limehouse in east London becoming a synonym for demagogy (and upsetting the King into the bargain). Churchill spearheaded the campaign for the Budget, with a Lancashire campaign reminiscent of Gladstone's in Midlothian, in which he impressed his view of the 'fundamental issues' – 'They are great class and they are great economic and social issues.' This was strong stuff from a duke's grandson.

The progressive case was essentially the same whether it was made on Liberal or Labour platforms; and though there were more three-cornered contests than in 1906, the forty Labour MPs elected were overwhelmingly those with Liberal backing. The increase in numbers over 1906 was due to the belated affiliation of the Miners' Federation of Great Britain to the Labour Party in 1908, changing the label under which a dozen 'Lib-Labs' sat, in some cases without their acknowledging the difference. One incident, however, showed that the Lib-Labs were not going to fade away quietly. In 1909 a Liberal activist called Osborne obtained an injunction preventing his union, the Railway Servants, from using union dues to support Labour. The Osborne judgement was to cause a temporary financial crisis for Labour, which naturally pressed for remedial measures. The Government readily implemented a measure for the payment of £400 per annum to MPs in 1911. More reluctantly, it eventually brought in the Trade Union Act (1913), which directly dealt with the Osborne judgement by stipulating that any union could establish a political fund, which in practice was used simply to support Labour.

In the General Election of January 1910 the Unionist poll was 5 per cent higher than in 1906 in England, though only 2 per cent higher in Wales and Scotland. The Government's majority at Westminster was cut as the Unionists gained more than a hundred seats, mainly in the south of England. In the north, however, as in Scotland, the progressive gains of 1906 were generally retained, not only in the historic Nonconformist areas of Yorkshire and the north-east but in Lancashire too; and much the same was true in the working-class districts of London, where the Liberals were now in their strongest position for a generation. The new House of Commons contained 275 Liberals and 273 Unionists, and the usual eighty-odd Irish Nationalists, who in theory could have voted the Government out. Leaving aside all 103 MPs from Ireland, the real electoral division in Great Britain was between 315 Progressives and 252 Unionists, giving the Government a majority of at least sixty. Since in Ireland the Nationalists likewise had a majority of sixty over the Ulster Unionists, this had the effect of doubling the Government's working majority. The second general election of 1910, held in December, though it brought offsetting changes here and there, barely disturbed this parliamentary arithmetic. If few expected the new parliament to be as short as that elected in January 1910, no one predicted it would last eight years.

## IRELAND

England and Wales together have roughly twice the land area of either Ireland or Scotland. In area, Great Britain is thus three times as big as

Ireland. But the demographic shifts of the nineteenth century brought an increasing imbalance within the British Isles, which contributed to the instability of the Union with Ireland. The catastrophic Irish famine of the mid-1840s had precipitated changes which virtually halved its population by the time the island was partitioned after the First World War. Meanwhile the burgeoning population of Great Britain, which had been little more than twice that of Ireland in 1841, was nearly ten times as big by 1911. Under the Act of Union between Great Britain and Ireland, the Irish representation in the Westminster parliament was fixed at 103 seats – say 15 per cent of the House of Commons. In the early nineteenth century this meant that, relative to population, Ireland was under-represented by half. But by 1910, Ireland was over-represented by half.

Unionists claimed that the tail was now wagging the dog: that the Liberal Government was in thrall to the Irish Nationalist Party. Its leader, John Redmond, was called the 'Dollar Dictator', because of the subventions which the Nationalists received from their expatriate supporters in the USA. This was melodramatic stuff, fit for the hustings. The Unionists, however, had a serious point about representation and they used it to justify their obstruction of Liberal measures of electoral reform in Great Britain. Their further contention, that it was improper for a Liberal Government to enjoy the parliamentary support of the Irish MPs, was less tenable – especially on the Unionist argument that the United Kingdom was one and indivisible. What was the principle of the Union if not that Ireland was to be represented at Westminster by MPs with full voting rights? Moreover, not all Irish MPs were Home Rulers: and the bulldog of British Toryism was soon to be wagged by its own Ulster Unionist tail.

Home Rule had been a non-issue in 1906. Many Liberals secretly hoped that it it might remain in limbo and not return, like Gladstone's ghost, to spoil their long-awaited electoral feast. But the compromise Irish Council bill of 1908 was a fiasco; like other measures proposed by the Campbell-Bannerman Government, it disconcerted its friends while failing to appease its enemies. It was an illusion, therefore, to suppose that anything short of Home Rule would suffice. To be sure, successive land-purchase schemes had already given a glimpse of twentieth-century Ireland as a nation of peasants, by creating a generation of well-fed petty proprietors whose complacency their fellow-countryman Shaw mercilessly satirized in *John Bull's Other Island* (1904). The Irish

Nationalist Party no longer displayed the raw political hunger for red meat which had gnawed at Parnell, now safely dead these twenty years. He was posthumously revered and commemorated with a hollow piety which James Joyce surely captured in his perfectly achieved short story, 'Ivy Day in the Committee Room', published in his collection *Dubliners* (1914).

The post-Parnellite Nationalist Party faced a problem not dissimilar from that of its mainland ally, the post-Gladstonian Liberal Party. There was talk at the time of a 'crisis of liberalism', as the Liberal Party, with its historic bourgeois image and Nonconformist identity, faced up to the problems of economic and social change in the twentieth century, with a potential challenge from a working-class party if its nerve should fail. The New Liberalism, as developed in practical politics under Asquith and Lloyd George, went a long way to confound such fears and to give evidence of the 'illimitable character of Liberalism, based on the infinitude of the possibilities of human life'; so J. A. Hobson argued in a book on this theme. A later historian, George Dangerfield, was to go further and write of 'the strange death of Liberal England', a phrase which retains a hold almost like that of scripture: mythopeically enshrined in the minds of even those readers who doubt that the story is actually true. But perhaps Redmond's party faced its own crisis of liberalism that portended the strange death of Nationalist Ireland, outflanked by a new wave of cultural politics which looked for salvation to Sinn Fein ('ourselves alone') rather than the British parliament.

The third Home Rule bill was conceived as a thoroughly parliamentary proceeding from first to last. It was intended to repay the Liberal Party's historic debt to Ireland, now that there was no excuse for default. Home Rule had handicapped the Liberals in the 1910 elections, especially in December 1910 in the west of England, where losses of some seats held in January offset the modest gains the Progressives registered in industrial England. Almost all Liberal and Labour candidates had given pledges for Home Rule, usually in the small print at the bottom of their election addresses. It was the Unionists who, as usual, claimed that Home Rule was the headline issue; and they did so with more verisimilitude on this occasion because of developments in the political situation during 1910.

The January 1910 election sealed the fate of the Budget but not that of the House of Lords. Asquith had not obtained from the King an undertaking to use the royal prerogative, which would be necessary to enforce the supremacy of the House of Commons by threatening to create enough new peers to outvote the old ones. Otherwise the Lords could simply reject proposals for constitutional change, like any other bills which they disliked. This revelation of Asquith's nakedness shook the confidence of his supporters; but he was able to retrieve the position nicely. First King Edward died in May 1910; and, amid the fulsome obsequies, efforts were made to negotiate an agreed constitutional settlement among all parties.

Home Rule was the stumbling block. The Government would not countenance any arrangement that precluded Home Rule, the Unionists any that facilitated it. Behind the scenes Lloyd George went further, seeking to leapfrog over the constitutional obstacle by making an overtly political deal, via a national government which would roll up social reform, Tariff Reform and Home Rule into one constructive package of measures. Again Home Rule was Balfour's sticking point. Indeed the lengths to which he would go to defend the Union were seen in the December elections. With days to go before the first polls, he appalled loyal Chamberlainites by giving a pledge that a Unionist Government would be prepared to submit Tariff Reform to a referendum before implementing it, thus further emphasizing the Home Rule issue.

Asquith meanwhile had put irresistible pressure on the new King, George V, to back a Liberal Government by creating as many peers as were necessary to override the House of Lords. The Government's election victory in December 1910 therefore determined the political outcome; the legislative steps followed inexorably. Asquith now had the right cards in his hand and took his tricks with the finesse of a man who enjoyed his bridge. The Parliament Bill of 1911 made noises about reforming the composition of the House of Lords but in fact just removed its veto on legislation. In future, finance bills would need approval by the Commons alone, and any other bill rejected by the Lords would nonetheless become law once it had been passed by the Commons in three (normally annual) sessions.

Passing the Parliament Bill itself, of course, needed a Lords majority, which the Government did not possess, and most Tory peers professed their determination to die in the last ditch. But the 'ditchers' were cheated of their martyrdom. The bishops, under the leadership of the Archbishop of Canterbury, Randall Davidson, were enlisted in the bill's support – an early sign that in the twentieth century the Church of

England was no longer simply 'The Tory Party at prayer'. Crucially, enough Tory peers broke ranks ('hedgers') to avert the prospect of a mass creation of Liberal peers. That this was a serious possibility is shown by the survival in the Liberal chief whip's papers of a list of several hundred names – such as Bertrand Russell, Robert Baden-Powell, Thomas Hardy, Gilbert Murray, J. M. Barrie – which would actually have increased the calibre of any second chamber.

The third Home Rule bill, introduced in 1912, could be expected to complete the procedure required under the Parliament Act by 1914. Unlike Gladstone's original Home Rule bill, which had excluded the Irish from the Westminster Parliament (to Unionist outcry), and the second Home Rule bill, which had included them (to renewed Unionist outcry), the new bill offered the compromise that the Irish representation would be reduced at Westminster, just as the Unionists kept demanding.[1] They were no better pleased, however. The proposal was essentially one for devolution, giving an Irish parliament significant domestic authority but reserving some powers to the Westminster parliament. Defence was one, fiscal policy another – a thorny issue since, left to themselves, most Irish Nationalists would have opted for protection. What most distinguished the Third Home Rule from its two predecessors was the real prospect that it would become law and be imposed on Ulster.

The nine counties in the north of Ireland that comprised the historic province of Ulster contained most of the Protestant population. Since there was also a strong Catholic presence, the province's parliamentary representation was pretty equally divided between Nationalists and Unionists. For, despite a distinguished line of Nationalist Protestants – Parnell, for example – the conflict was basically between communities defined by religious labels. The notion that Home Rule meant Rome rule was an agreeable joke in the southern provinces of Ireland; for the Protestant Orangemen of Ulster it was a nightmare. Their hostility to Home Rule, in any of its previous incarnations, had never been in doubt; it was back in 1886 that Lord Randolph Churchill had talked of playing 'the Orange card' against Gladstone. The British Unionists

---

1. The 1893 Home Rule bill would have reduced the number of Irish MPs at Westminster to 80; but this was still full representation as measured by current population. By 1912 Ireland was entitled to 64 MPs on a strict population basis; the Home Rule bill would have reduced this to a total of 42 (including Ulster, of course).

were as determined as ever to support Ulster in 1912, if possible to scupper Home Rule altogether. But this time, from an early stage, there was a fallback position: an implicit concession of Home Rule for southern Ireland so long as Ulster was excluded.

If this meant sacrificing the Unionists' traditional supporters among the Anglo-Irish landowners, like Lansdowne, their own leader in the Lords, at least the patricians could be bought off, as many had been already, through land purchase. But the plebeian Protestants of Belfast had nowhere to run, and no money to run with. Little wonder that more than 400,000 of them, harking back to the seventeenth century as usual, were to sign a 'solemn covenant' declaring that they would not submit to a Dublin parliament. Others had gone further: no fewer than 80,000 Orange Volunteers were drilling by April 1912 – and who should turn up to take the salute but the new leader of the British Unionist Party.

Andrew Bonar Law was an unexpected choice to succeed Balfour, who had resigned at the end of 1911, having exhausted the tolerance of the Tariff Reformers by losing three elections in a row. Their preferred candidate was Chamberlain – Austen since they could no longer have Joe. But another candidate, a much more traditional Tory who could play the squire, was found in Walter Long; and to avoid further conflict they both did the decent thing and withdrew in favour of Law. He was a leading Tariff Reformer, a businessman from Glasgow who had been born in Canada; but at least he was a Conservative, through and through, who made no pretence of magnanimity. Once invited to agree that Gladstone was a very great man, Law simply said: 'He was a very great humbug.' This was all in a different tenor from Balfour – Asquith sarcastically called it 'the new style' – which was, of course, the whole point of changing the leadership. What the Chamberlainites misjudged was that Law's single-minded fervour for Tariff Reform would be out-matched by his single-minded fervour against Home Rule.

Law's presence in Belfast was one visible sign; and in the course of 1912 he publicly declared, both in the House and outside, that 'there are things stronger than Parliamentary majorities'. By committing the Unionist Party to supporting armed resistance to Home Rule, Law was not only making Ulster the sticking point: he was raising the spectre of civil war. Here was another constitutional crisis following at the heels of the last. Perhaps it is wrong to be surprised that the Conservative Party, the traditional upholder of law and order, should have taken this course. After all, until the passing of the Parliament Act, Tories had never needed to challenge the verdict of the ballot box in this way; they had been able to thwart their opponents through the House of Lords. Historians who complacently celebrate the smooth transition from aristocratic to democratic government in Britain perhaps overlook the Ulster crisis as the moment of truth for a politically emasculated governing class, resisting the implications of representative government.

One democratic resolution of this conflict, of course, would have been a referendum. There was a case for appealing to the people on a fundamental issue, especially one of a constitutional character. This proposal attracted Unionists who were confident that the majority which the Liberals had jobbed together between British Progressives, on the basis of economic and social issues, concealed the fact that Home Rule was as unpopular as ever. But the expedient of a referendum was not to be tried for another sixty years.

Since Home Rule remained inextricably mixed up with other party issues, therefore, it was a question of priorities on both sides. The Government sadly came to appreciate how much of the momentum of its emerging new policies was lost after 1911, when its obsolescent old policies – not only Irish Home Rule but, in minor key, Welsh Disestablishment – instead hogged the business. This was why Lloyd George launched his land campaign in 1913, with a think-tank headed by Seebohm Rowntree to dream up new ideas, such as state intervention in housing and a minimum wage, to reinforce old Radical cries. 'God gave the land to the people,' was the chorus of the Lloyd George land song, which would have been the Liberal theme in the general election envisaged for 1915. On the Unionist side, conversely, the change of ground, from social reform to Ulster, was a welcome boost, as the mid-term by-elections seemed to confirm; but the worry was that Tariff Reform would still blight the party's appeal in a general election.

Whether he was clearing the decks for a civil war or just a general election, therefore, Law's priorities became clear in the course of 1912. He knew that the pledge which Balfour had given in December 1910, to submit food taxes to a referendum, would kill Imperial Preference; and at the end of 1912 he initially endorsed Lansdowne's announcement that the pledge had now lapsed. Law also knew, however, how strongly feelings ran in Lancashire; his experience in contesting a Manchester seat at the previous election had brought him to clutch at the pledge in the first place; and when the local magnate Lord Derby could no longer keep the Lancashire Tories in check, Law realized that the moment had come for a volte-face. Food taxes were written out of the programme; Imperial Preference was thereby ditched and only industrial protection retained. By the time Joseph Chamberlain died in 1914 Tariff Reform had become a ghost policy.

The Unionists now put all their chips on Ulster. The Home Rule bill was duly passed by the Commons in 1912 and 1913. There was, at this late stage, serious discussion of schemes to exempt Ulster, or at least those counties of Ulster which had a Protestant majority, at least temporarily if not permanently. The clear Protestant majority in Belfast and four of the northern counties did not, however, live in well-defined segregated areas, susceptible of neat partition, as subsequent history has fully demonstrated. It is not obvious, at the end of the twentieth century, that partition was ever a real solution; certainly it commanded insufficient support in 1914. As Law had foretold, there was a difference between passing a Home Rule Act and implementing it. The position of the Army was delicate, the more so since many officers had Irish connections. The so-called mutiny by a number of army officers at the Curragh in May 1914 showed the uncertainty of the Government's grip at this juncture. A messy situation faced a messy outcome, one way or another.

What happened, of course, was that European War eclipsed any threat of civil war in the summer of 1914. The Government got its Home Rule Act on to the statute book at last; but with the provision that it would only come into operation a year after the conclusion of peace. Redmond was not happy with this, but he supported it because he supported the United Kingdom war effort; and really he had little alternative. The pugnacious instincts of the Ulster Volunteers were likewise now diverted to the western front. Once again, England's danger was Ireland's opportunity – this time an opportunity to be forgotten. Indeed it was only with the Easter Rising that Irish affairs burst back on to the front pages of British newspapers.

At Easter 1916 the headline news was that the Dublin Post Office had been seized by Sinn Feiners, in a largely symbolic move. Any threat of insurrection was quickly dispelled since the general feeling in Dublin, when not apathetic, was against Sinn Fein. What transformed the situation was the Government's crass response. True, efforts were made to negotiate a compromise, with Lloyd George's emollient skills coaxing Nationalists and Ulster Unionists to the brink of an agreement to implement Home Rule for twenty-six counties, excluding six in Ulster.

But all of this was to break down. Above all, in the eyes of most ordinary Nationalists, the execution of the ringleaders of the Rising turned them into martyrs, and Redmond's denunciation of it as a German plot turned him into a stooge. The scenario in which Asquith and Redmond would lead their nations to reconciliation through an Irish Home Rule Act was brought to a bloody end.


## THE POLITICS OF WAR

There are potent literary evocations, ranging from Siegfried Sassoon's *Memoirs of a Fox-Hunting Man* (1928) to L. P. Hartley's *The Go-Between* (1953), of a blissful Edwardian garden party, a golden age of peace and prosperity, suddenly brought to an end in August 1914. For a small elite, whose double privilege it was to enjoy unfettered amenities before Armageddon and to provide the junior officer corps for the impending slaughter, it is surely understandable that subsequent reminiscence was to carry a heavy freight of nostalgia. Their experience, however, was not the whole story.

For most people in Britain life was hard in 1914. The burst in emigration was one testimony. To be sure, social reforms now alleviated some of the terrors of old age, sickness and unemployment – an incremental gain in welfare at a cost of 10 per cent of a Budget that touched £200 million in 1914. The purchasing power of wages, which had been rising as prices fell in the late nineteenth century, faltered in its advance once prices started to rise in the mid-1890s. Nobody supposes that average real wages fell; the older statistics show that they were exactly the same in 1914 as in 1895, and recalculations suggest that there may even have been some improvement. This tallies with other indications that nutrition and physical welfare were now steadily improving for the population in general.

The cost of living, however, rose by 20 per cent in twenty years, sometimes outstripping the annual rise in money wages (notably in 1905–7) with unsettling effects on wage bargaining. Indeed the sharp cost-of-living increases from 1910 to 1913 brought a rash of strikes on a scale not seen since the 1890s. In 1912 40 million days were lost through strikes, notably a national coal dispute which was eventually settled through Government intervention – a sign of the times. But this 'labour unrest', unlike the Ulster crisis, had subsided by 1914.

The pre-war years, while hardly seeing 'the strange death of Liberal England', were not trouble-free. It was the direction from which trouble came in the summer of 1914 that was unexpected. In H. G. Wells's *Mr Britling Sees It Through* (1916), its hero stood representative of all those who were 'mightily concerned about the conflict in Ireland, and almost deliberately negligent of the possibility of a war with Germany'. Sarajevo suddenly became a city to find on the map, with the assassination there of the Austrian Archduke Franz Ferdinand igniting a powder trail across Europe that, by 1 August, faced Asquith's cabinet with an unpalatable decision: whether to support France (and Russia) against the Central Powers (the Habsburg and German Empires).

Alliances had pulled the continental powers into conflict; Britain was not committed. True, there was an Entente with France, and military talks had taken place between the two general staffs; there was also an understanding between the fleets. These were only contingency plans. If they were not implemented, however, France would be vulnerable, creating an obligation of honour which weighed heavy on Grey as Foreign Secretary. Grey worked hard for peace in the last days but he had become bound to France more closely than he cared to admit; though those members of the cabinet who later accused him of misleading them – the Lord Chancellor, Loreburn, spoke of a Liberal Imperialist plot – must have been wilfully myopic not to see the implications of facts which they all knew.

The fact is that the drift of opinion in the cabinet was quite inadequately conveyed by the conventional divisions between 'Liberal Imperialists', in support of a strong foreign policy, and 'Radicals' against it. Lloyd George, though he continued trying to trim the naval estimates, had shown in the 1911 Agadir crisis – the Kaiser had sent a gunboat to Morocco – that he was quite ready to face up to German pretensions. It was Lloyd George's Mansion House speech, agreed with Grey, which publicly declared the position of His Majesty's Government. Churchill was no longer the 'economist' of 1908; he was now a free-spending First Lord of the Admiralty, determined that the mighty British fleet should retain its historic supremacy. The old pro-Boers whom Lloyd George consulted in August 1914 – C. P. Scott hopped on the train from Manchester – were unable to count on their man any more for the peace party. In the end only two cabinet ministers resigned when Britain declared war on Germany: the old Lib-Lab John Burns and the aged biographer of Gladstone, John Morley. Whatever other factors disposed towards British intervention, what brought almost all Liberals round to supporting the war was the German invasion of Belgium.

Serbia was belatedly seized upon as a small nation rightly struggling to be free – Lloyd George was to make a speech about how much the world owed to 'the little 5-foot-5 nations' – but it was Belgium which immediately fitted this familar paradigm. The point was that a war on behalf of Belgium was not seen as an assertion of realpolitik in the national interest, which Conservatives would have supported anyway, but a struggle of right and wrong in the Gladstonian tradition. Radicals, whose readiness to resist public obloquy their pro-Boer stand had testified, and who had long stood accused of being anti-British, were persuaded that this time it was, for once, their own country that was in the right. It was to be a Liberal professor of Greek at Oxford, Gilbert Murray, who wrote the classic defence of Grey's foreign policy in 1915. It may have made an anti-war protestor like Bertrand Russell angry, and left the sceptical Shaw unmoved, but it tapped a rich vein of Liberal self-righteousness, which, stage by stage, helped to invest war-making and peace-making with high moral objectives. It is not at all odd, therefore, that the most impassioned call for patriotic sacrifice came from Lloyd George in his first public utterance of the war at the Queen's Hall in London in September 1914.

The Labour movement, too, despite much pre-war rhetoric about the international solidarity of the working class, generally supported the Government's decision to go to the aid of Belgium. This is not surprising since the Gladstonian tradition was part of the progressive ideology that encompassed Liberals and Labour, so that they split over the war on much the same lines. Ramsay MacDonald, who, very much the progressive in outlook, had debated whether to accept a cabinet post only a few months previously, now resigned as Labour leader in the Commons and was to work with Liberal critics of Grey's foreign policy in setting up the Union of Democratic Control, aimed at securing peace in future through international cooperation. The trade unionist Arthur Henderson took over from MacDonald, becoming uniquely powerful in shaping his party's destiny during the war years. Labour support for the war was obviously more readily forthcoming under a Liberal than a Conservative Government.

The prime minister kept so far as possible to the methods that had served him well in peacetime. His only immediate concession was to find a new Secretary of State for War – he had held the post himself since the fiasco at the Curragh – in the august person of Lord Kitchener. This was the stern visage, all brass hat and mustachios, which was to stare out from the recruiting posters: pointing the finger at potential volunteers. Since the cabinet was clearly an unsuitable body to determine strategy, this meant that Kitchener's control of the war effort went virtually unchallenged. A War Council was set up, which took over the secretariat that had served the Committee of Imperial Defence, as established by Balfour back in 1902; indeed not only did the War Council inherit Colonel Maurice Hankey from the CID as its secretary, it also took on Balfour as a member – the only Unionist directly enlisted in the war effort.

The slogan, 'Business As Usual', was coined by Churchill, but exemplified by Asquith. Asquith's conception of the war was traditional. For a couple of centuries Britain's role in continental wars had been to leave most of the fighting to the mass armies of her allies while acting as paymaster; the preservation of her economic and financial resources was thus crucial. This was a highly rational model, which, through two World Wars, greatly profited the USA as 'the arsenal of democracy'. But how far was such a strategy any longer available to the United Kingdom?

Unusually, Kitchener predicted the likelihood of a war that could last for years, with a need for millions of men. His 'new armies' were thrust into the breach, since the sector of the western front assigned to Britain, though perhaps commensurate with the relative French and British populations, was clearly beyond the capacity of the puny British Expeditionary Force of trained soldiers, even when reinforced by the Territorial Army of part-time reservists that Haldane had created. Volunteers came flooding in, at a rate which took the authorities aback. The problem was training and supplying them, not finding them. They were reinforced too by troops from the Empire. Australia and New Zealand sent troops altogether out of proportion to their population; Canada came in to the war despite internal divisions in Quebec; and so, more remarkably, did the Boer-led Government of South Africa, where General Smuts emerged as a key figure.

The appalling losses on the western front – they were still higher on the eastern front – soon provided a chilling rebuff to many of the easy assumptions of August 1914. The prospect of a quick breakthrough on either side was poor.

In this context the War Council came up with a plan to switch the attack to another theatre and to bring the Royal Navy into play. The defensive role of the Navy was to protect British shipping routes and in this it was generally successful, at least against surface attack. The only full-scale naval engagement was to be the inconclusive encounter at Jutland in May 1916; and the Kaiser's claims of a famous victory by his High Seas Fleet were belied by the fact that it never again put to sea. But if the British were able to secure their essential defensive objective, the Royal Navy found more difficulty in securing an offensive advantage. This is where the ill-fated plan for naval action to take the Dardanelles, at the mouth of the Black Sea, went badly wrong, committing Imperial forces to a futile battle at Gallipoli. British and Australian troops bore the brunt of the carnage. Churchill's dream of finding an alternative strategy thus became ensnared by compromise, muddle and indecision, which was hardly his sole responsibility – but more his than that of the men who perished at Gallipoli. Politically Churchill was saddled with it, and he lost the Admiralty in May 1915.

It was not the Admiralty crisis alone which prompted the reconstruction of the Government; allegations in the press that the British Army in France faced a shell shortage forced Asquith's hand. As in previous crises, he showed that he was still the master and that Lloyd George was still his principal adjutant. Together they disposed of the offices in a new administration, including the Unionists. This was hardly an equal coalition; Law was only given the Colonial Office and Liberals continued to hold all the top jobs, including the Treasury, which went to Reginald McKenna. Lloyd George's move to the new Ministry of Munitions was the big change. He threw himself into the task of improvising a better supply structure by doing deals with the armaments industry and vastly extending state intervention through munitions factories under his own control. He became the apostle of state intervention, finding allies where he could.

The new Minister of Munitions went so far as to say: 'We are fighting Germany, Austria and drink; and, as far as I can see, the greatest of these deadly foes is drink.' The real drink problem at the time was not beer but spirits. The peak year had been 1900, when 25 million gallons of proof spirits were consumed in England and Wales (well over a gallon for each adult) and over 8 million gallons in Scotland (well over three gallons per head). Despite a slightly rising population, these totals had dropped by 1913 to under 17 million and under 6 million gallons respectively. It was the War that gave a temporary boost, as war workers spilled their earnings. Lloyd George's temperance supporters, thwarted by the Lords before the War, saw their chance in 1915. Not only was beer watered in strength but the hours of licensed premises were regulated. In London, for example, pubs were henceforth open only from 12 noon to 2.30 p.m. and from 6.30 to 9.30 p.m. The immediate objective was achieved; in Great Britain consumption of spirits in 1918 was only 40 per cent of its pre-war level, and little more than a quarter of the levels of 1900. The effects, moreover, were long-term. Despite a temporary post-war boost, these levels of consumption were to remain normal until the 1960s; and the distinctive British licensing hours, with compulsory afternoon closing, were set for the next seventy years.

The coalition had been formed partly to blunt press criticism of the Government. In getting rid of Haldane, the architect of an efficient army, in face of grotesque allegations that he was pro-German, Asquith sacrificed not only an old friend but also an old friendship. The press attacks continued regardless, but on a more selective basis. Lloyd George was the one Liberal who was exempt: a mark of the fact that his position was now much more sympathetic to Unionists who generally favoured belligerent measures. It was in the summer of 1915 that the prime minister lost Lloyd George's confidence. 'Wait and see was an excellent precept for peace,' he now said privately. 'But in war it is leading us straight to destruction.'

The great divisive issue was conscription. Many Unionists had favoured it anyway, as a means of state-building which marched alongside a policy of national economy and tariffs. The needs of the new armies converted many more, who wondered aloud why the flower of British manhood should perish while men at home failed to do their patriotic duty. In fact there was no absolute shortage of volunteer recruits. The real case for conscription was a matter of logistics – to implement manpower priorities which would prevent essential civilian workers from joining up and keep them on the job in factories and mines. This was not, however, the emotional level on which the issue was approached in the winter of 1915–16. Instead Asquith exhausted every tactic of dissimulation to appease Tory demands while simultaneously appeasing Liberal consciences. He encouraged Lord Derby, 'the King of Lancashire', to come up with a scheme that ostensibly preserved the voluntary principle, by getting men to attest their willingness to serve, while assuring the married men that none who attested would be taken until the single men had gone, and then telling single men who had not attested that they were 'deemed' to have attested. The Derby scheme was laughable or despicable, according to taste. Conscription was finally introduced in Great Britain (not Ireland) at the beginning of 1916. It was Asquith's final essay in consensus.

In 1914 the parties had called an electoral truce; they agreed to give an unopposed return to the party in possession at by-elections. But politics did not stop just because some peacetime quarrels were shelved. Labour issues, for example, were as crucial as ever, once a war of production gave a wholly new leverage to the trade unions.

The key issue was whether the unions would permit the 'dilution' of their position by allowing less skilled workers to do some of the jobs without the traditional union ticket. These working practices, called 'protective' by the unions and 'restrictive' by the employers, maintained a 'closed shop' under union control. This was the problem which Lloyd George addressed in the Treasury Agreements, early in 1915, securing concessions from the trade unions on 'dilution' but strictly on the understanding that the restrictive practices would be restored at the end of the war. This was a considerable victory for the trade unions, whose leaders patriotically responded to the nation's needs – but on their own terms.

In all these ways the conduct of the war became the stuff of politics. It was on this protean issue, not on pre-existing rivalries or ideological divergence, that the working alliance between Asquith and Lloyd George came unstuck. By the end of 1916 Lloyd George was ready to make a bid for control of the war effort – not initially for the premiership, but stating terms for the establishment of a small war committee, excluding Asquith, which would have made a mockery of his position. The crisis of December 1916 found Asquith less steady on his feet – allegations about his drinking now dogged 'Old Squiffy' – and one sign of the toll of a long premiership was that he overestimated his own following. When he backtracked on a compromise with Lloyd George, Asquith found himself displaced. Their partnership had been the axis of the Government for the past eight years and the mainspring of Liberal success; their vendetta over the next six years was to push the Liberal Party to the edge of the grave.

# 3

# The Man Who Won the War
## 1916–22

We often speak of the *First* World War to distinguish it from the Second. Yet it was as early as 1920, in a book by Colonel Charles à Court Repington, *The Times* war correspondent, that this term was first given currency. Repington was stressing the unprecedented *worldwide* dimensions of a war that spread to Africa, where the German colonies were taken; to the Middle East, where the Ottoman Empire was the enemy; and to Asia, where Japan had been Britain's ally since 1902. Yet not only the origin but the main theatre of the war lay in Europe. It was here that most of the troops from the Dominions of Canada, Australia and New Zealand fought, initially as part of the British Expeditionary Force (BEF), leaving the Indian Army to play a crucial role in the Middle East.

The western front, running from the Belgian coast, between Ostend and Dunkirk, winding across Flanders and France to the Swiss border, was settled by the end of 1914 and was to change little until 1918. So stable was the line that London stationers found it worth while to stock maps showing it. The trenches symbolized this war: a stage in the development of military technology in which defence had temporarily triumphed over offence, stacking the odds against attack. To gain even a few hundred metres of ground produced casualties on a scale never before seen in Europe (though the American Civil War had given a glimpse of the future).

The term contemporaries generally used was the Great War. From an early point the recruiting propaganda projected the stance into the future, asking women: 'When the War is over and someone asks your husband or your son what he did in the great War, is he to hang his head because you would not let him go?' A classic poster shows a pensive father dandling his embarrassingly interlocutive offspring: 'Daddy, what did *you* do in the Great War?' This projection into the future was one indication of a self-consciously momentous, heroic posture. It was an appeal to an idea of a Great War imagined, not a reflection of the immediate experience of the trenches.

One obvious contrast is between the early and late war poetry. Rupert Brooke was not unknown before the war, as one of the new generation of 'Georgian' poets. If it was one irony that the name of the new King, a wonderful philistine, should bless this aesthetic endeavour, it was not the last in Brooke's charmed, doomed life. A Cambridge undergraduate of striking good looks, he had made women swoon (as well as Lytton Strachey). No nationalistic Tory in his politics – he and his Cambridge friends, like Hugh Dalton, were Fabians – Brooke found that the elevated diction of Georgian poetry was matched by the romantic patriotism which seized him in 1914.

> Now God be thanked who has matched us with His Hour,
> And caught our youth, and wakened us from sleeping.

His was a soldier's death foretold in his war sonnets:

> If I should die, think only this of me:
> That there's some corner of a foreign field
> That is for ever England.

What he could not have known was that this corner was to be on a Greek island, not Flanders; the cause of death a mosquito bite, not a German bayonet or bullet. But in the spring of 1915 his England needed a war hero. His friend Edward Marsh was private secretary to Winston Churchill, and Margot Asquith had more than once made Brooke welcome at 10 Downing Street. The publication of the war sonnets posthumously transformed him into a national figure who spoke for the idealism – and idealization – of the early part of the war.

Laurence Binyon's much-quoted poem 'For the Fallen' remains memorable:

> They shall grow not old, as we that are left grow old:
> Age shall not weary them, nor the years condemn.

Remarkably, this was written only seven weeks after hostilities began. It is plain that Brooke was not the first but he became the most famous of the war poets, an early casualty who did not write at first hand of the western front. Though it is a mistake to suppose that the heroic register was lost, even in some poems composed right up to the Armistice, the sordid reality of life in trenches increasingly pervades the poetry – as in Wilfred Owen's '. . . truth untold, / The pity of war, the pity war distilled'.

There was to be an extraordinarily rich harvest of war poetry from soldiers who stuck it out in the new armies during the years to come. Some of it was published at the time, like Siegfried Sassoon's anti-war barrage, *Counterattack* (1918). Other poems, notably a full edition of Owen's arguably homo-erotic oeuvre, had to wait half a century to appease the sensibilities of bereaved relatives. Together with Edmund Blunden and Robert Graves, these are the voices that cry out from the trenches in 1917–18; and the three survivors (Owen was killed a week before the Armistice) went on to recapture their experience in prose. In particular, with *Good-Bye to All That* (1929) Graves caught the crest of that mighty wave of anti-war literature which reared up at the end of the 1920s.

The privileged background of Sassoon, the fox-hunting man, is sufficently signalled in his work; Graves had been subjected to a hearty public-school education at Charterhouse, bullied because his middle name was von Ranke; Blunden was a scholarship boy who got to Oxford; Owen, from a fairly similar lower middle-class background, missed university. One way or another, they were all officers and gentlemen. Though the ideal temporary officer was straight from the Officers' Training Corps of a recognized public school, a class analysis does not indicate the essential dichotomy which the western front imprinted on the war poets as on other subalterns serving in the line. Though they spoke as officers, they spoke for the men who were with them there – and spoke against almost everyone who escaped their unique, shared, incommunicable experience.

In peacetime the total size of the armed forces was about 400,000. By 1915 the figure had reached 2½ million; by 1916, with conscription, 3½ million; and in 1917–18 it stabilized at between 4 and 4½ million. At the peak this was one in three of the entire male labour force. It was one in two of the men of normal military age (eighteen to forty-one years old) subject to conscription from 1916. It was a higher proportion still of the young single men in Great Britain (conscription was never implemented in Ireland) who were the real target successively of the moral opprobrium of the recruiting posters, of Lord Derby, and finally of conscription. (In the final British assaults in 1918 half the infantry were under nineteen.) Not all of these 4½ million were soldiers, and not all soldiers served in Flanders or France; conversely, more British soldiers served in the Army, with periods at the front, than are shown in a snapshot at any one moment. Whichever way it is added up, the western front was, for a large proportion of men born in the last decade or so of the nineteenth century, the experience of a lifetime, sometimes the ultimate experience.

The casualties were horrific. It is the sheer cumulative impact of the losses, week by week and month by month, which is staggering. Perhaps the most remarkable record of the toll of war on this highly exposed generation is that by a woman, Vera Brittain, whose *Testament of Youth* (1933) was to be rediscovered, undiminished in its impact, through television in the 1970s. When she interrupted her studies at Somerville College, Oxford, engaged to an undergraduate now serving in France, and became a military nurse (VAD) in 1915, she was pitched into a sickening, wearying nightmare round of clearing up in the wake of an unending trail of carnage. It was all a long way from her comfortable, constricted upbringing in the spa town of Buxton. Her own brother and her own fiancé gave up everything when they contributed their invisibly minuscule fractions to the total of British deaths, which reached three-quarters of a million.

Between the wars there was much talk of a 'lost generation' of young men. Demographically this is not easy to find, partly because the war had the effect of turning the torrent of emigration into a small net inward flow; in four years 1 million Britons would have been lost anyway (though of both sexes). The 1921 census was admittedly the first time that the inter-censal increase for England and Wales dropped below 1 per cent a year; but this was to be the trend of the twentieth century. There was still an increase in population during the war, albeit twice as large for women as for men. Statistically, over half a million men were missing after the war, widening the surplus of women in the population of Great Britain from 1.3 million to 1.9 million. In 1921 there were 110 women to every 100 men in England and Wales; but in 1911 there had already been 107. In Scotland the change was even less: 108 in 1921, up from 106 in 1911. The idea that, as a result of the war, there was an absolute shortage of men is better borne out by folklore than statistics. In considering the impact on marital prospects what matters most, to be sure, is the balance between younger people. In Great Britain in 1911, there had been 11 per cent more women in their twenties than men; and this surplus increased to 19 per cent by 1921.

This would have been noticeable. Yet the difference it made to the proportion of women getting married in each age group is not very marked, since marriage rates were subject to long-term shifts of a more complex kind than simply a slight temporary shortage of eligible young men.

It is not the demographic but the human impact of the losses which burned so deep. Bereavement was a more common experience anyway in the early twentieth century, but that does not rationalize away the poignancy of parents burying sons, or of wives and lovers losing young men in their prime. Women at home bore this special burden, dreading the arrival of a telegraph boy on his bicycle – in working-class streets telegrams were only received from the War Office, with their invariable bad news. 'Futility' is the title of Owen's classic poem: 'Was it for this the clay grew tall?' The 'comrades' of 'the fallen', in the elevated diction which became conventional, felt a special pang. The 'lost generation' was an emotional and psychological reality which made a life-long impact on its surviving members. Politicians from this generation who achieved fame later – first Oswald Mosley and later Anthony Eden, Clement Attlee, Hugh Dalton and Harold Macmillan – took with them an abiding sense of admired contemporaries lost, especially in two battles, the Somme and Passchendaele.

The British sector of the front was muddy. Whether the mud of Flanders around Ypres ('Wipers') was worse than the mud of the Somme valley around Albert ('Bert') was a hotly disputed, finally un-resolved question. 'In Flanders field the poppies blow / Between the crosses, row on row,' wrote the Canadian John McRae, in what became the most popular poem of the war, published posthumously in *Punch* in December 1915. The 'Roses of Picardy', celebrated in the popular song, likewise symbolized the Somme valley. Such songs, memorably performed beneath a rattling scoreboard showing the running total of war dead, in Joan Littlewood's *Oh What a Lovely War* (1963), have gone down to posterity. The banal lyric of 'It's a Long Way to Tipperary', or the false cheer of 'So, pack up your troubles in your old kit-bag, / And smile, smile, smile,' are evocatively redeemed by the context. The mere words, from cloying sentiment to cynical ribaldry, stand in ironic juxtaposition to the grim fate of the troops who sang them. Who knows with what mixture of emotions they sang: 'The bells of hell go ting-a-ling a-ling / For you but not for me'?

Back at headquarters, it was decided to launch a major offensive on the Somme, where the French and British lines joined, in the summer of 1916. The new British commander-in-chief, Sir Douglas Haig, planned a frontal assault, piercing the German wire, letting his massed cavalry through, and thus bringing the war to a victorious conclusion. It was unfortunate – for the British troops at any rate – that the bloody and protracted defence of Verdun scaled down the French participation. Kitchener's new armies filled the breach. The 'pals' battalions', Lord Derby's brainchild, had joined together and now served together, formed through the networks of local communities. The great conurbations of Liverpool, Manchester and, above all, Tyneside, were home to recently recruited battalions, the deficiencies in their training matched by the inadequacy in their equipment.

On the first day of the Somme, 1 July 1916, the casualties of the British forces were 60,000 – half the total size of the British Expeditionary Force which had been shipped to France two years previously. Of these, 21,000 were killed, most within an hour. These were the heaviest losses any army ever sustained in a single day.

Once Verdun had sapped the French army, the responsibility for any further offensive would have to fall on the British sector of the front. With Lloyd George as prime minister, committed to the policy of fighting on to 'a knockout', previous limitations of the British commitment were cast aside. Haig was now given more or less what he demanded. This was the logic of Passchendaele in the summer of 1917. Again the bombardment was immense: its intention to cut the German wire, its effect to make the terrain, which was already difficult, pretty well impassable. And the mud, the mud . . .

British soldiers met death by water when they escaped German fire. The British army was literally bogged down in Flanders at just the time when the Russian collapse meant that the Germans were now able to give the western front their full attention. In hindsight, Haig's failure to appreciate the possibilities of the tank, which the British had developed, as a means of superseding trench warfare, seems blinkered. There is no need to suppose that there was some easy way for the Allies to win this war to take a dim view of the strategy pursued by the British general staff.

So it seemed in the sodden trenches. Staff officers, identified by their scarlet tabs, received the routine contempt of those who served in the front line, officers and men alike, who had to endure conditions far removed from those enjoyed by 'chateau generals'. Sassoon said it all:

> If I were fierce, and bald, and short of breath,
> I'd live with scarlet majors at the Base,
> And speed glum heroes up the line to death.

The politicians, too, were cocooned, though it would be a vulgar error to suppose that they had no personal stake in averting bloodshed: the leader of each political party at Westminster (Asquith, Law, Henderson, Redmond) lost a son in the war; Law lost two. Rudyard Kipling, no kind of conscientious objector to a war in which he lost his son, spoke mordantly for his generation in the gnomic epitaph:

> If any question why we died,
> Tell them, because our fathers lied.

The face of war, however, was now far different from the heroic stereotypes which had been evoked at the outset and were still being purveyed to an anxious public at home, seemingly many thousand rather than a few hundred miles away. Back for medical treatment in 1916, Graves found Britain a strange land: 'The civilians talked a foreign language; and it was newspaper language.' Yet when he heard Lloyd George – 'The power of his rhetoric amazed me' – he admitted that he 'had to fight hard against abandoning myself with the rest of his audience'.

The visual image of this war was created by the impact of first-hand impressions upon a distinctively twentieth-century aesthetic sensibility. The work of the post-impressionists had already been brought to London in 1910. British painters like Percy Wyndham Lewis began experimenting in a new, Vorticist style, forsaking the fidelity of representational conventions for a stark creation of violent images – an adumbration of the western front before war was ever declared. Their magazine was called *Blast*. Institutionally what gave the war artists their chance was the inception of a government-sponsored scheme for commissioning them to work at the front.

The young Canadian millionaire Max Aitken, as avid a Tariff Reformer as his friend Bonar Law, found that the war presented him with a unique opportunity to hustle his way into the top echelon of British political life. One of Lloyd George's first acts as prime minister was to give Aitken a peerage, as Lord Beaverbrook. No great connoisseur himself, Beaverbrook relied on artistic advice from experts; but the dynamic behind commemorating the war in this way came from him. The

Canadian War Memorials Fund became the model for a similar British scheme (and it was to be replicated under Kenneth Clark, the art historian, in the Second World War). In fact, since Beaverbrook used British as well as Canadian artists from the outset, these were overlapping projects, both in personnel and achievement.

War artists no less than war poets found the stereotypes, whether of military valour or English pastoral, challenged and subverted by the evidence of their own eyes. It was soon apparent that, as one artist put it, 'the old heroics, the death and glory stuff were obsolete'. What replaced portraits of high-ranking generals or canvases of colourful cavalry charges were images of the land. Nothing came to epitomize the war like the pock-marked terrain strewn with bleached bones and all the refuse of modern warfare. Perhaps the most successful artist in capturing this was Paul Nash. In *Void* (1917) Nash abandoned his earlier lyrical style and thrust the viewer into a landscape of shell-blasted trees, broken shafts of Very lights, and the incongruous rise and fall of broken earth.

In *A Battery Shell* (1918) Wyndham Lewis kept his distance, putting his mechanical soldiers into a no man's land which he recognized as consonant with the austerity of his own 'abstract vision'. C. R. W. Nevinson, too, easily bridged the transition from peacetime to wartime painting. His *Marching Men* (1916) are not just uniformed but uniform, expressing the brutalizing violence of their emotional response. William Roberts's *The First German Gas Attack at Ypres* (1918) is a rare attempt to portray combat. A former gunner in the Royal Field Artillery, Roberts seized on an incident during the battle when the Canadians push through the African colonial troops to take their place in the line. A less imaginative artist might have shown the Canadians gallantly moving forward. But Roberts chose to depict the moment of truth when every soldier makes his choice between self-preservation and duty. Some are moving forward; one seems to be joining the gassed troops in their retreat. The work of the official war artists, which was only fully displayed after the Armistice, thus helped to create a new perception of war. It achieved an aesthetic success, opening a window to a modernist style of painting – though the window was subsequently closed again, even by some painters like Nevinson who had been more experimental in wartime.

If the project failed as a war memorial, it was because the popular instinct for commemoration was channelled into totally different forms, which people could invest with their own meanings. On the second anniversary of the Armistice, 11 November 1920, the King unveiled the Cenotaph war memorial in Whitehall, in a simple but moving ceremony, culminating in the playing of the last post. These arrangements were improvised under the direction of Lord Curzon, the former Viceroy of India, drawing on his experience in organizing the Coronation durbar of 1903. The Cenotaph was designed by Sir Edwin Lutyens, the architect of New Delhi. But whereas both Curzon and Lutyens opted for grandeur in promoting the Raj, the idiom of Remembrance was that of stark simplicity. This set the tone for an annual commemoration of Armistice Day, with the widespread observance of a two-minute silence proving eloquent enough for the survivors and the bereaved. The symbolism of the poppy, chosen by the British Legion, likewise provided a spare but sufficient evocation of the western front.


## LLOYD GEORGE AND THE WAR

Lloyd George became prime minister in December 1916 because he was widely thought to offer the best chance of bringing this seemingly interminable war to a victorious conclusion. This gathered him support from the Conservative leaders, with the exception of Lansdowne who was now toying with the possibility of a negotiated peace. The Liberal members of the cabinet, almost to a man, followed Asquith out of office; Grey left the Foreign Office after eleven years. It was, however, possible for Dr Christopher Addison, a junior minister of firmly progressive views, to rally sufficient support on the Liberal backbenches to make the new Government a genuine coalition. Addison took over his chief's former post as Minister of Munitions for six months until he was succeeded by Churchill, the only former member of the pre-war Liberal cabinet to join a Government that was undeniably Conservative in balance. Lloyd George did, however, secure the support of the Labour Party under Arthur Henderson, who joined the new war cabinet.

Here was Lloyd George's first innovation. The structure of government was rebuilt around the necessities of waging war. It was one of the weaknesses of Asquith's administration that his cabinet was neither ready, willing nor able to exercise effective control over the direction of the war effort. Not only was a cabinet of twenty-odd unwieldy when it came to taking quick decisions: it had no record of its decisions other

than a letter after each meeting from the prime minister to the King. All
this was changed when the secretariat which Hankey had first established at the Committee of Imperial Defence, and transferred to the
War Council, was now brought in to serve a war cabinet of only five
members.

The leaders of the Labour and Conservative Parties had to be there;
but Lloyd George sidestepped the party hierarchy in picking as the
other members the two pro-consuls, Curzon and Milner, the former
High Commissioner in South Africa. Law, as Chancellor of the Exchequer, was the only member of the war cabinet with departmental
responsibilities. This was a compact group of strong ministers, meeting
every other day, articulating its decisions, through official cabinet minutes, to the departments in Whitehall responsible for carrying them
out. Lloyd George, the bad correspondent, thus got out of the historic
prime ministerial chore of writing to the King. He also made sure that
the prime minister was better serviced. He looked for indispensable
support, emotional and political alike, to Frances Stevenson, his mistress since 1912; she occupied a key role as his personal secretary. New
office accommodation was constructed at the back of 10 Downing
Street to house a 'garden suburb' of personal aides. Philip Kerr was one
who was recruited from the staff which had served Milner in South
Africa; and the irony of members of this 'kindergarten' ending up as
lieutenants of the former pro-Boer did not go unnoticed.

Another administrative reform was to parallel the Ministry of Munitions – the first time the French-sounding term 'ministry' had been used
– with other new Ministries, responsible for Labour, Shipping and
Food. There was some extension of Government control here, especially in the introduction of food rationing, but also a better public-
relations exercise for measures that had been in train under Asquith.
Lloyd George made new appointments from outside party politics,
bringing in businessmen, sometimes in ways that suggest the development of a rather cosy corporate ethos. The Minister of Shipping was a
shipowner. Likewise the Minister of Labour was a trade unionist.

Everywhere Lloyd George brought a conspicuous new vigour to the
conduct of the war. His courage and vitality were less in doubt than his
strategy. It was all very well to run the British war machine flat out –
maybe that was the only way to feed the insatiable appetite of the
western front. But was that really what Lloyd George wanted? He had
never been a resolute 'Westerner', even though he had (correctly) been

sceptical about Gallipoli, and his mind always sought ways of avoiding the frontal attack by finding a way round. The Chief of the Imperial General Staff, Sir William Robertson, was a man of few words. He would not or could not argue out the available options with Lloyd George, who reciprocated with instinctive distrust of him and Haig.

Lloyd George plotted against Robertson and Haig, as he had been accused of plotting against Asquith, whose supporters were accordingly inclined to side with the soldiers. Robertson and Haig had the War Secretary, Lord Derby, in their pocket, and Haig had a private line to the King, which he exploited to protect his position. This sort of politico-military trench warfare reduced Lloyd George to the expedient of backing the French rather than his own general staff; but since the French generals, notably Nivelle, proved no better able to achieve a breakthrough, Lloyd George eventually acquiesced in the British plans for another assault in Flanders – what became Passchendaele. It was Passchendaele which highlighted Lloyd George's dilemma: how to squeeze all possible resources out of the British war machine without letting Haig squander blood and treasure in the mud.

The immediate crisis in 1917 was at sea. The British naval blockade of the Central Powers was highly effective, possibly the most effective means by which the ultimate outcome of the war was determined. The submarine, however, enabled Germany to strike back at Allied merchant shipping, and the steady losses in 1916 already threatened Britain's capacity to last out for more than a matter of months. In February 1917 Germany raised the stakes, in a desperate gamble, by adopting the policy of unrestricted submarine warfare. The attitude of the USA was crucial. Following his re-election as President in November 1916, Woodrow Wilson had sought to bring the war to an early end, calling for a 'peace without victory'. Back in 1915, however, the sinking of the Cunard liner *Lusitania*, which had been carrying American citizens (as well as war materials), had led the US Government to take a firm stand against such provocation. When the U-boat policy duly led to the sinking of American ships, Wilson declared war on Germany in April 1917.

The ultimate gains to Britain were immense since, apart from military supplies and troops, which were inevitably slow to arrive, the impending crisis in war finance was averted as the USA took over as the Allies' lender of last resort. But the immediate losses – of merchant shipping – might meanwhile have been fatal. The German calculation depended on their ability to sink 40 per cent of Allied shipping capacity, and to reduce wheat imports proportionately, within six months. In fact their target for ships sunk was almost met. In 1917 over 6 million tons, 30 per cent of the British merchant fleet, were sunk. But the grain still got through. Though the American wheat harvest was short in 1917, nearly three-quarters of the Canadian crop was exported. Stocks in Britain actually rose, and only in March 1917 did sinkings reduce supplies of wheat by more than 10 per cent – far short of German expectations. Improvisation and the enforcement of new priorities by Government saved the day. This is a story which shows Lloyd George at his incomparable best, at least as told in his *War Memoirs*, striding into the Admiralty and imposing the convoy system upon the barnacled admirals. Maybe he was pushing at an already open door when he got there, but the importance he gave to convoys was well justified since it succeeded in staunching, though not stopping, the haemorrhage of losses by the autumn of 1917.

The case for a negotiated peace, however, was cogent, the more so if the USA's combatant status gave it more muscle in imposing terms acceptable to the Allies. This was a policy which went begging in the political muddle of 1917. In opposition, as he now clearly was, Asquith gave little leadership. It was left to Lansdowne to make a public statement in November 1917 of a plea he had privately made twelve months previously for an exploration of peace terms.

Labour was now sympathetic, the more so since Henderson's resignation from the war cabinet in August 1917. No one could have been a more loyal supporter of a war for democracy, which was what everyone now claimed it was. But when Henderson visited Russia, where revolution had deposed the Tsar in February, he judged that it could only be kept in the war if the social-democratic forces among the Allies stirred themselves more conspicuously. Henderson therefore favoured sending Labour delegates to a conference in Stockholm at which German Social Democrats would be represented. After being kept, as he put it, 'on the doormat' while his colleagues in the war cabinet discussed the propriety of his conduct, he eventually resigned, amid sharp personal exchanges with Lloyd George. Though replaced in the war cabinet by another Labour minister (G. N. Barnes), Henderson remained, more than ever, the leader of the Labour Party. 'Labour and Lansdowne', an improbable combination if there ever was one, filled a political vacuum at the end of 1917 since Asquith offered no coherent alternative to the Lloyd George coalition.

In March 1918 the German armies, reinvigorated under Ludendorff's leadership, now that the eastern front had been closed down, broke through on the western front. The British position on the Somme, maintained for so long at such cost, crumbled in days, and the collapse was as much in morale as anything else. Lloyd George's nerve did not crack. He strode into the War Office, as he had into the Admiralty the previous year; he ordered troops on leave back to France, he demanded the commitment of American forces. The desperation of the position was indicated by Haig's order of the day on 12 April: 'With our backs to the wall and believing in the justice of our cause each one of us must fight to the end.' This received wide publicity at home, if no great respect among the troops. The overtones were of Captain Scott's fatal expedition to the South Pole six years earlier.

In the aftermath, Asquith made his one faltering bid as a real leader of the Opposition. Robertson had been deposed before the German offensive; his aggrieved deputy, Sir Frederick Maurice, who was also dismissed, now decided to create a public fuss. Stung by Lloyd George's denials that he had starved Haig of troops, Maurice challenged the figures given by the prime minister. There is little doubt that Maurice was correct and that Lloyd George destroyed the relevant evidence. But when Asquith demanded a debate, the issue was politicized in the starkest way as a vote of confidence in Lloyd George. While over 70 Liberal MPs supported the Government, nearly 100 voted with Asquith; the remaining 85 or so did not vote. Lloyd George survived with massive Conservative support.

The vote in the Maurice debate revealed the polarization of the Liberal Party which had taken place over the previous eighteen months. When it came to a general election later that year, virtually every Liberal MP who had voted against the Government was denied the coalition 'coupon' of approval and most of them lost their seats. The Asquithian legend is that this shows the retributive vengeance which Lloyd George wreaked upon his old colleagues. In fact what it shows is that, once Lloyd George had opted to fight in coalition with the Conservatives, he was able to secure a high degree of protection for a limited number of his own supporters; and naturally, in rationing his patronage, the Maurice debate was one indication of past loyalty and future allegiance. Coalition Liberals were among the recipients of the formal endorsement by himself and Law but it was not this 'coupon' – so called from the rationing analogy – which saved them: it was the absence of Conservative opposition.

The break-up of the Liberal Party was the main consequence of the Maurice debate. Lloyd George's position as war leader was confirmed; his commitment to continuing the struggle, through thick and thin, was underlined. The switchback course which the war took in its final stages dramatized his leadership and gripped public attention as never before. Well into the summer of 1918 the Allies were on the defensive: in June the Germans stood on the Marne, within 100 kilometres Paris. This needs to be remembered in order to appreciate the intense surge of relief at the turn of the tide in August. After the collapse of one ally, Russia, in 1917, it had been a close race as to which belligerent power would be next; in fact it was to be Austria–Hungary, then Germany – leaving France exhausted, and Britain stunned with an unanticipated plenitude of success when an armistice was negotiated for 11 a.m. on 11 November 1918.

Little wonder that Lloyd George was hailed as 'the man who won the war'. Little wonder that he decided to cash in his political chips as soon as possible. On 14 November he called a general election. Polling took place a month later. The coalition which Lloyd George had put together for war purposes two years previously now addressed the problems of peace. Feeling against Germany was naturally running hot; demands for reparations were common; so was the demand to bring the Kaiser to trial. But there was also a coalitionist programme of domestic reform, for which Addison, as Minister of Reconstruction during the previous sixteen months, had a particular responsibility. The coalition platform thus addressed the future as well as the past in its professed aspiration for 'a fit land for heroes to live in'. The verdict of the electorate was much like that of the House of Commons in the Maurice debate: to endorse Lloyd George, with all his faults, for want of a better alternative.

## WOMEN AND LABOUR

In a double sense one could say that women and organized labour won the war. Their contributions to the war effort were difficult to ignore, either socially or economically. Their gains from the war, especially politically, were equally conspicuous – the 1918 Reform Act went almost all the way to full adult suffrage and the Labour Party quickly emerged as the official Opposition. These were all highly significant developments, though the relation between them is not altogether straightforward.

Most married women filled traditional roles as wives and mothers, conventionally described in the census as 'unoccupied', though hardly lacking unpaid occupation in the household. The statistics about women's employment and earnings, of course, conceal as much as they reveal. In an age when such activities as home-baking and home-brewing had been commonplace, but naturally performed without recompense, a busy housewife who took a job might instead start buying her family's bread and beer – thus boosting the economic indicators for earnings and consumer expenditure out of all proportion to any real change in the amount of work or consumption which took place.

Married women often found their lives dominated by childbearing and child-rearing. At the beginning of the twentieth century the wife of a manual labourer could expect to have half a dozen pregnancies, producing four or five live births. Children took their toll; women were far more likely to die in childbirth than later in the century. The great killer, however, especially for young women, was tuberculosis, a disease linked, in ways that are still less than fully clear, with poor living conditions and poor diet. Access to medical attention was difficult and Health Insurance only provided a panel doctor for a worker paying contributions. In practice this meant the male head of the household; wives and children were not covered, despite the fact that their medical needs were usually greater. The small but significant exceptions were a maternity grant and the provision of sanatorium care for the treatment of tuberculosis.

There was a crude economic rationality to the hierarchy of the male-dominated household. In the early twentieth century, many British families bought meat once a week and it was often fed primarily to the man of the house, as the breadwinner. Women and children last was the watchword in apportioning the working-class diet. Girls growing up in working-class households were systematically undernourished (one reason for their proneness to tuberculosis) and when they became mothers they would often stint themselves in later life.

Deprivation was thus engendered in the family as well as institutionalized in the wider society. Even in parts of the country where weekly wages were 'tipped up' on the kitchen table, to be counted up by the housewife as family treasurer, a man was generally allowed his pocket money, if only as his beer money. More beer was drunk per head before the war than in the middle of the century, and mainly by men. The matey environment of the British pub was male-centred. Drink was the prime example of luxurious expenditure by the working class, as moralistic Liberals had never failed to point out. For many family men beer was a luxury which they enjoyed when they could, and forewent when money was tight. Precisely because it was not a fixed commitment, as mortgage payments would have been, it could act as an inbuilt stabilizer of the working-class budget. But over-indulgence by the breadwinner, especially in spirits, could easily put the rest of the family on to short rations. The sight of underfed children waiting at the pub door for the emergence of their errant father was not just temperance propaganda but expressed a grim struggle of domestic priorities. The wartime and post-war fall in the consumption of alcohol marked a victory for the family home over the public house.

The household, then, was polarized around two gender-based roles: that of the breadwinner, the head of the household, who was in paid employment; and that of the housewife, who was not.

There was a political dimension to this separation of spheres. Since 1867 in the towns, and since 1884–5 elsewhere, the parliamentary franchise had been founded on household suffrage. There were other ways of qualifying for a vote, through the ownership of real property, which gave rise to about half a million plural votes in 1915, the last year in which a register was compiled. But the other 6¼ million names stood there as householders. Why so few out of an adult population of 20 million? Because only the male head of the household qualified for the parliamentary vote. Thus women were excluded, even if they happened to be householders in their own right; and so were other adult men, notably sons living in the parental home. The net result was that only two-thirds of adult men were registered to vote before the war.

Though this was not what we would nowadays regard as democratic, contemporaries innocently commended the British system as 'democracy', especially when fighting wars on its behalf. This claim was not absurd. The fact is that, whatever its other flaws, the male franchise did not produce a strong bias against the working class, for the obvious reason that sons of wealthier parents were excluded as much as other, poorer sons. On a conventional definition of the working class as manual workers, they comprised 80 per cent of the population. By this definition, in 1915, 70 per cent of the electorate was working class. In urban and industrial areas the working class already dominated the electorate, even though half of them might not be on the register. And household suffrage had plainly not prevented Labour from establishing itself at Westminster.

The premises of household suffrage, however, were under increasing challenge in Edwardian Britain. The Liberal Government had tried to abolish plural voting in 1906 – one of the bills thrown out by the Lords. What really made the suffrage a hot issue, however, was the agitation by women – not just the 'suffragettes', who grabbed the headlines with their militant tactics, but the much greater number of 'suffragists', organized in the National Union of Women's Suffrage Societies under Mrs Millicent Garrett Fawcett. By and large progressives were sympathetic (though Asquith was not) while Conservatives were hostile (though Balfour was not). What prevented a settlement was the way the women's claim intermeshed with other aspects of electoral reform. Conservative suffragists were more likely to support a simple removal of the sex disqualification; progressives were suspicious of this minimalist approach since they assumed that it would add female property-owners to a franchise already biased enough through the plural vote.

Two private members' bills in 1910 and 1911 failed to find a compromise along minimalist lines, and in 1912 the Government brought in its own Electoral Reform bill. This broadened the issue by proposing universal suffrage for men – and women too, if the Commons should so decide on a free vote. What happened, quite unexpectedly, was that the Speaker ruled the woman suffrage amendment out of order, which caused the collapse of the whole measure. Suffragettes responded by accusing Asquith of treachery; though why he should have wanted to sabotage such an exquisitely Asquithian manoeuvre, designed to get the Government off the hook, is difficult to say. To be sure, his slowness to perceive the merits of the women's case was partly to blame for his difficulties; but, better late than never, in 1914 he signalled that woman suffrage would become Government policy in its next attempt at electoral reform.

This impasse was overtaken by the outbreak of war. The suffragette campaign, organized by the Women's Social and Political Union, was called off. By the end of 1914 Mrs Emmeline Pankhurst, its leader, and her favourite daughter, Christabel, had made the transition from militants to super-patriots. (Sylvia Pankhurst, by contrast, with her Labour commitment, was a critic of the war.) Since the militant campaign (employing arson) had been increasingly counter-productive in generating support for its avowed objective, while the Government response (employing forcible feeding) had also aroused distaste, both sides were ready for a truce – in order to wage war. When the issue was reopened, it was in a wartime context much more favourable to women, subduing all but the most bigoted opponents.

The pressing new problem of manpower shortage had one manifest answer: woman-power. The munitions factories were the most obvious way in which young single women were mobilized for war production. There were already 200,000 women employed in the metal and chemical trades in July 1914; by the Armistice there were nearly a million. A quarter of them were directly employed by the Ministry of Munitions; no fewer than 11,000 women worked at the national cordite factory at Gretna, on the Scottish border. With the increasing demands of the Army, moreover, women took over jobs in traditionally male occupations. They were highly visible on the tramways and railways, generally acting as ticket collectors or conductresses.

The most emotive example of women responding to the call was in care for the wounded. The Voluntary Aid Detachments (VADs), of which Vera Brittain wrote, were in origin an extension of the Territorial Army; they contained over 40,000 women in 1914, over 80,000 in 1920, often serving under conditions as unpleasant as those of any troops. Dr Flora Murray and Dr Louisa Garrett Anderson formed their Women's Hospital Corps in 1915; it became a lever for fuller professional recognition of women doctors, of whom there were three times as many by 1921 as ten years earlier. The Women's Army Auxiliary Corps (WAAC) was officially established by the Army Council in 1917, with four sections (Cookery, Mechanical, Clerical and Miscellaneous), serving under a woman director; by the time of the Armistice it had a strength of 40,000, 20 per cent serving abroad.

These numbers, however, are tiny when set against the mass of women in paid work. In July 1914 there were 1.65 million women in domestic service, traditionally the greatest source of employment, but the least loved because of its confining nature. When girls could find an alternative, by and large they did. By 1918, despite four years of unparalleled sacrifice by the employing classes, saturating the pages of *Punch* with tearful jokes about the servant crisis, there were still 1.25 million domestic servants. In the United Kingdom as a whole women's employment seems to have increased by nearly 1½ million during the war. The most significant change came in commercial and clerical posts; the number of women office workers practically doubled. The 'lady typewriter' had arrived – and was to stay. The 1921 census for Great Britain disclosed over 1 million women engaged either in commerce or in typing or clerical tasks, rising to 1.35 million by 1931.

The total size of the female workforce in 1921, however, showed virtually no net change since 1911. Despite the wartime bulge, it was still around 5.7 million, compared with 13.7 million men. It is apparent that much wartime employment was a transient phenomenon, especially in fields where the intrusion of women had been most shocking and had attracted most publicity. Photographs of women driving trams, buses or ambulances became well known, not because of their typicality but because of their novelty. In 1921 as in 1911 there were only 3,000 women employed on the railways, less than 1 per cent of the total. During the war the workforce was diluted with women, only to be purposefully undiluted afterwards, just as the Treasury Agreements had specified. The process was reinforced by the post-war slump, which likewise helped solve the servant problem. The 1921 census showed 1.85 million women in 'personal service'; this was a more elastic definition than just domestic servants and represented a fall from the figure of 2.13 million recorded in 1911. By 1931, however, it was back at 2.13 million, exactly the same as twenty years previously, in Archduke Franz Ferdinand's prime. Despite all the fuss, the war had not created vast new opportunities for women, just photo-opportunities.

Wartime manpower shortage also explains a lot about the changed position of organized labour. At the beginning of the war the immediate worry was about workers who lost their jobs through dislocation of trade. Relief funds were set up. Equally, there was an economic explanation for the flood of military enlistment just as there had been for emigration. For many men in marginal employment, the Army meant a guaranteed wage and a better diet. Soon, however, the logic of mobilization turned the material advantage in favour of civilian workers at home. The simple fact is that the war economy meant a continuous boom, with high Government spending and inflationary pressure, soaking up surplus labour in a way that seems more obvious to us than it did to contemporaries.

Before the war began, unemployment was already well under half its peak level of 1908–9, running at around 3 per cent of the labour force.

From 1915 to 1918 1 per cent unemployment was a high figure.[1] The tight labour market, especially for skilled workers like engineers, had the effect of bidding up wages. The rate for the job rose most in occupations where the war increased demand for goods or services in short supply at home: food and coal, new buildings and transport. By July 1918, wage rates for agricultural workers, coal miners, bricklayers' labourers, dock labourers and railwaymen had all increased by 90 per cent in four years.

The increase for cotton operatives, by contrast, was less than 60 per cent, reflecting the wartime decline of the export trade. Even if the markets were still there, shipping space was at a premium – even more so for imports, which included war materials for the Allies. Allowing for price changes, imports had dropped to 70 per cent of their 1913 volume by 1918; exports had dropped to below 40 per cent. In this Free Trader's nightmare, import substitution was encouraged by market forces and Government intervention alike.

In 1918 British wheat production was back at a level not seen for a generation and imports were likewise the lowest since the 1880s. But increased demand for home-grown food, as well as giving Hodge a decent wage, inevitably meant price rises to the consumer, as did the increased freight costs caused by the shipping emergency. The cost of food in the average working-class diet was double its pre-war level by 1917 and still rising. The overall cost of living likewise doubled in four years. Since the general rise in wage rates was slightly less than this, the real improvement of the standard of living went to those workers who were able to put in more overtime in meeting war production targets.

There were also important differences within particular trades, between skilled men, whose pay rates stood still in real terms, and their labourers, who often did better out of the war. In engineering, for example, where the rate for a fitter was 75 per cent above the pre-war level in 1918, a labourer had meanwhile more than doubled his wage rate. Here was ample cause for resentment among workers with deeply entrenched notions about differentials. The war had the effect of eroding the traditional status of the skilled workers, organized in craft unions to maintain the rigour of the apprenticeship system. The labour

---

1. Even as measured by the new National Insurance scheme, which tended to exaggerate the overall level. This was because National Insurance had deliberately been introduced first in occupations which were particularly at risk from cyclical unemployment.

disputes on 'Red Clydeside' which erupted in 1916 owed as much to such considerations as to ideology.

Labour shortage put trade unions in a strong bargaining position. Their membership had been rising before 1914; from 2.5 million in 1910 it had bounded up to 4 million in three years before slackening off. It was the later years of the war, however, which saw a sustained growth, to 5.5 million in 1917, 6.5 million in 1918, and a brief peak of around 8 million in 1919–20. Most of them were men, though the fact that there were 1¼ million women trade unionists by the end of the war was significant. Previously women had accounted for only one out of ten trade unionists, with few outside the cotton industry; in 1918 this proportion was more like two out of ten. Affiliation to the TUC and to the Labour Party ran behind these totals; but the fact that Labour's natural constituency had doubled in size, not to mention confidence, was a fact of unmistakable political significance. It was a fact not overlooked by President Wilson, who took British Labour very seriously in 1917–18.

It was at this opportune moment that the intractable suffrage issue was at last settled – on terms highly favourable to Labour and women alike. Indeed, a big measure which could satisfy everyone was the only way of cutting through the difficulties; and it was the war which made a big measure possible. An all-party conference under the Speaker of the House of Commons helped to formulate proposals which were knocked into shape in 1917, when the flame of idealism about reconstruction was burning at its brightest. What made the claim for universal male suffrage irresistible was the record of the new armies. Conservatives who had their doubts about democracy if it meant enfranchising the proletariat had no such qualms about our soldier lads. In 1918 there were 5.3 million men in the trade unions; 4.4 million in the armed forces. All men over twenty-one got the vote, and all soldiers regardless of age.

This increased the male electorate to over 12 million. Had the suffrage been given on the same terms to women, there would, of course, have been more of them. This was too much for the Commons to swallow. But there was still plenty of room for a large measure of woman suffrage without the (rather unreal) risk of 'swamping' the male electorate. The solution adopted was to give parliamentary votes to women over the age of thirty – on the condition that they were local-government electors or the wives of local-government electors. As householders, some women had for years qualified for the local-government franchise, since an outright gender bar had not been in force, and they were now joined by the wives of other householders.

Under the Reform Act of 1918, then, women got the parliamentary vote in a ghostly perpetuation of household suffrage. One implication is that the women who were excluded after 1918 were much like the men who had been excluded before 1918. They were young and single, for the most part still living with their parents. In short, they were the very sort of women who had so conspicuously shown that 'women can do it'. The Minister of Munitions, Edwin Montagu, had rhetorically asked the Commons: 'Where is the man who now would deny to women the civil rights which she has earned by her hard work?' As it turned out, the logic here was as faulty as the syntax, and household suffrage was now buttressed by housewife suffrage.


## LLOYD GEORGE AND THE PEACE

Arguably, the strength and prestige of Lloyd George's position at the end of 1918 were unrivalled in British history. In the general election his coalition swept the board. In the new House it had the support of well over 500 MPs – an exact figure is difficult to give since not all of them had received the 'coupon'. No fewer than 380 of the Coalitionists were Conservatives, which meant that they alone held a majority of the seats in the Commons. At the time many of them were full of gratitude to Lloyd George; conversely he was held responsible by the Asquithians for delivering the Liberals' former majority into the hands of the enemy. The reality of the position was that a substantial swing to the Conservatives was in the offing anyway; by fighting in coalition with them Lloyd George ensured that a block of his Liberal supporters were saved; but in the process he became the prisoner of the Conservative Party.

Lloyd George's obvious strategy was to institutionalize his position by merging the two wings of the coalition into a new centre party, of which he would be the undisputed leader. When he made moves in this direction at the beginning of 1920, he cleared the high hurdle of securing Conservative endorsement for the idea; but he stumbled on an unforeseen obstacle – the stubborn Liberal loyalties of his own supporters. Though a number of Liberal businessmen, like Sir Alfred Mond, head of the chemicals conglomerate Brunner Mond (later part of ICI), were to find the Coalition a bridge to an ultimate destination in the Conservative Party, the Lloyd George Liberal Party (now with its own organization) retained authentic Liberal credentials. Called 'Coaly Liberals' by the Asquithians, they were not as black as they were painted, and it was their input which gave social reform a prominent place in the Coalition manifesto. In particular, state responsibility for housing – the unfinished agenda of Lloyd George's land campaign – underpinned the promise of 'homes for heroes'.

One reason why the split in the Liberal Party was so damaging was that it was so equal. Both factions claimed legitimacy; each had a powerful leader, trailing the authority of the premiership; neither was a mere rump, destined to disappear quickly. The division was sharper at Westminster than in the country, where ordinary members often pined for a 'prefixless' Liberal candidate to heal and unify them. This reflected the fact that the sort of split which had always been on the cards – between the left and right wings of the party – was not the one that occurred from 1916. Lloyd George, the former Radical, was now working with the Tories; Asquith, the erstwhile Liberal Imperialist, was now the champion of left-wing progressives who remained close to Labour on many issues. The election results in 1918, distorted by the coalitionist pact, exaggerated the disparity between the two factions. Just as the strength of the Lloyd George Liberals was flattered by their 130 seats, so the Asquithians were under-represented with their thirty or so. Still, it was a miserable showing; Asquith lost the East Fife constituency which had returned him since 1886 and was temporarily out of the House.

Labour did better, though not as well as had been expected in 1917. It was now fighting as a fully fledged independent party, no longer a pressure group within a progressive alliance. Henderson had used his time well since the 'doormat' incident, building a Labour organization throughout the country, albeit on trade-union foundations. A new constitution had been adopted in 1918, with its famous Clause IV committing the party to 'the common ownership of the means of production', which gave it a distinctive stance. There was now a Labour view on more immediate aspects of policy, even on foreign policy, where ex-Liberals recruited through the Union of Democratic Control were influential. It became possible for individual members to join the Labour Party directly, rather than through affiliated organizations like the ILP or, above all, the trade unions, though the block vote of the big unions continued to control the party. All this was gain. The disappointment was that, with manhood suffrage, and with nearly 400 candidates in Great Britain, Labour did not poll much over 20 per cent. With about sixty seats, this was a significant but not dramatic improvement on the forty it had won in 1910.

Ireland went its own way in 1918. In the north, of course, the usual twenty or so Ulster Unionists were returned to Westminster. But in the south, the old Nationalist Party was reduced to a handful of six, and 72 Sinn Feiners (including the first woman) were elected. The victorious Sinn Fein candidates refused to go to Westminster and instead met in Dublin as an Irish parliament, the Dáil. It proclaimed independence in January 1919 with an appeal to the peace conference, now assembling in Paris, on the Wilsonian formula of national 'self-determination'.

Here was Lloyd George's first problem. He had inherited it from a long line of British statesmen, some of whom had tried to make it better, all of whom had made it worse. Lloyd George had had several tries at fixing up a deal over Home Rule: after the Easter Rising in 1916 by offering to combine Home Rule with partition, in March 1918 by simultaneously offering Home Rule to please the Nationalists and conscription to satisfy the Unionists. The package deals which he tried to bundle together (hastily, in his spare moments from winning the war) fell apart before they were wrapped up. Home Rule was now a dead letter and the plan for Irish conscription had been a fatal blow for old-fashioned Nationalists.

The Coalition Government, with its Unionist majority, could hardly be expected to adopt a conciliatory line, faced with a challenge to its authority from the Dublin Dáil, with its pretensions to establishing its own system of administration. Throughout 1919 and 1920 the situation went from bad to worse, with the Irish Republican Army (IRA) now engaged in a guerrilla struggle, to which the British response was the recruitment of an equally deadly paramilitary force, the 'Black and Tans'. What really alienated liberal opinion in Britain from Lloyd George was the policy of reprisals which his Government now sanctioned. He tried, as ever, to find a carrot as well as a stick. This was the Government of Ireland Act of 1920, which established separate devolved parliaments for the north and south, with reduced representation at Westminster. This suited the Protestants of Ulster, and was to define relations with Northern Ireland for the next half century.

It was not, of course, enough to satisfy the Dáil. A further deterioration in the Irish situation prompted a final initiative on the British side. The King was wheeled into action; his appeal for peace, delivered in Belfast, brought a truce in July 1921; negotiations began in earnest for an Irish treaty. This brought out the best and the worst in Lloyd George, as he bargained with the irreconcilable factions, telling each as much as he judged it prudent for its partisans to hear, and finally threatening the Irish delegation with renewed war unless they signed. For Ireland it was a shotgun divorce, severing six of the counties of Ulster from the twenty-six in the south, which became the Irish Free State. This was a constitutional hybrid, maintaining the fiction that Ireland enjoyed a peculiar sort of Dominion status, while ceding the substance of autonomy (as shown by the subsequent proclamation of sovereignty in 1937). It was a solution which was only accepted in the south at the expense of a bitterly divisive civil war in 1922–3, but it marked the moment at which the history of Ireland formally parted company with that of the now disunited United Kingdom.

Lloyd George had thus persuaded the Unionists to end the Union. He liked to think of his Government as one in which the Liberal yeast had worked a powerful effect upon its doughy Conservatism. Yet whatever he touched, his Liberal critics impugned his Liberal credentials. This was as clear over the peace settlement as over Ireland. When Lloyd George went to Paris in January 1919 it was as one of the Big Four who called the shots. If he was not so big as Wilson, exercising the new hegemony of the USA, he was at least bigger than the French premier, Clemenceau, and a lot bigger than Orlando of Italy. This was personal diplomacy at the summit in a style which suited Lloyd George so nicely that he took to attending a whole string of post-war conferences in the watering places of Europe. He lost touch with the House of Commons in the process, and subordinated his Foreign Secretary, Curzon, into a role which Sir Edward Grey would never have contemplated but which later Foreign Secretaries were to find customary.

All Lloyd George's instincts were for a just post-war settlement rather than vindictive retribution, especially if justice consorted with British interests. One problem was war debts. Britain had run up vast debts to the USA on behalf of its Allies, who were now clearly unable to pay. The British, who were owed about as much as they in turn owed the Americans, suggested that these debts were surely on a par with reparations, to be scaled down correspondingly, or waived altogether as between allies in a common cause. Not so, according to the USA.

In practice Lloyd George's aspiration for a just peace became a quest for a deal that would stick. Moreover, he was not altogether a free agent. He found himself bound in three ways. Clearly, he was bound to his own coalitionist supporters. In the most famous account of the conference, Keynes's *Economic Consequences of the Peace* (1919), there is a description (which we now know came from Stanley Baldwin) of the new House of Commons as 'hard-faced men who look as if they had done very well out of the war'. Keynes suggested that here was the influence which made for an unjust peace, exacting disproportionate reparations from Germany. His message was to be relayed not only by his friends in the Asquithian Liberal Party but by Labour and a wide swathe of liberal opinion.

What it omitted to say, however, was that Lloyd George was bound also by his own utterances, in a style which Liberals had themselves fostered. 'Hang the Kaiser' is the election cry that has been remembered; but behind it was a demand to put him on trial, couched in the same idiom of law and morality which had justified the war effort all along. This came to nothing in Paris. However, the argument over reparations, also justified on the basis of Germany's war guilt, proved vexatious.

At this point Lloyd George found himself bound by the ties of Empire. The fact was that the Empire had played an indispensable part in the war effort, mobilizing 3 million men (half of them in the Indian Army). For the Dominions, this served the function of a war of independence, assuming a central part in the mythology of national self-assertion. For Australians the formative experience was Gallipoli, for Canadians it was Vimy Ridge: heroic, bloody battles in which the chief gains, perhaps, were of national self-respect and pride, tinged with a rueful sense that their troops had been left to pull Britain's chestnuts out of the fire. One makeshift expedient, recognizing the Dominions' contribution, had been the constitution of an Imperial War Cabinet: a forum in which Smuts of South Africa assumed a notable role. Whereas in 1914 the King had simply declared war on behalf of the colonies, in 1919 – at Canada's insistence and despite US reluctance – there was separate representation at the peace conference for Canada, South Africa, Australia, New Zealand and India, albeit within the British delegation. This was an important step in itself, and had the effect of giving an imperial twist to the issue of reparations.

The British on the whole wanted to keep down the total demanded in reparations, realizing that the Germans' ability to pay was limited by their productive resources (in line with the advice which Keynes had given before his resignation as the Treasury's representative). This implied limiting Germany's liability to the direct damage suffered by the belligerents (excluding Russia). Since this had been inflicted overwhelmingly along the western front, it implied that France would receive the lion's share of reparations, and Australia, for example, virtually nothing. To the prime minister of Australia, the populist Labour leader Billy Hughes, this was intolerable. Egged on by Hughes, therefore, Lloyd George demanded that indirect costs be assessed, inflating the total bill to a wildly unrealistic figure, but enhancing the share due to the British Empire.

Keynes may have been right to insist that the reparations in the Versailles Treaty were uncollectable except on the unrealistic assumption of a self-denying German economic miracle; but Lloyd George secured the best deal available at the time and reckoned on the terms being revised later – as in fact happened. Other provisions of the peace treaties were similarly flawed in using the high rhetoric of liberal internationalism and self-determination, its prose polished up by Wilson from an old draft by Gladstone, to justify compromises brokered between the cynicism of Clemenceau and the opportunism of Lloyd George. This was the fate of the League of Nations, intended as the linchpin of Wilson's new world order. Though hobbled by the failure to secure US participation, the League promised conciliation of international disputes, sanctions instead of war, collective security instead of great armaments. It was seized upon by liberal opinion in Britain as the embodiment of hopes which had not emerged unscathed through the transition from war to peace. Lloyd George became a convenient whipping boy for disappointments of which he was not the sole author.

Lloyd George found that his diplomatic finesse was, as often before, needed on the industrial front as much as in international affairs. Demobilization was not easy. Faced with the problem of reintegrating 4 million men into the civilian workforce, the Government proposed to give priority to those with jobs awaiting them, often those whose enlistment was most recent. Economically rational, this was emotionally insupportable for troops who had sweated it out in the trenches. The British Army had been virtually alone in avoiding large-scale mutiny; but now it threatened. Churchill, with his own eight months of experience on the western front in 1916, stepped in as the new War Secretary

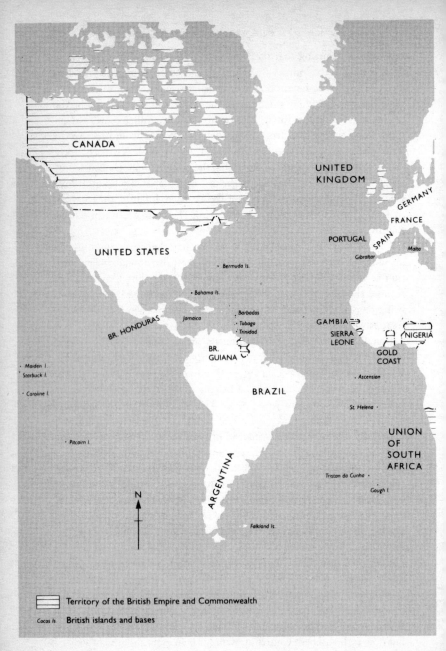

**Map 2** The British Empire in 1920

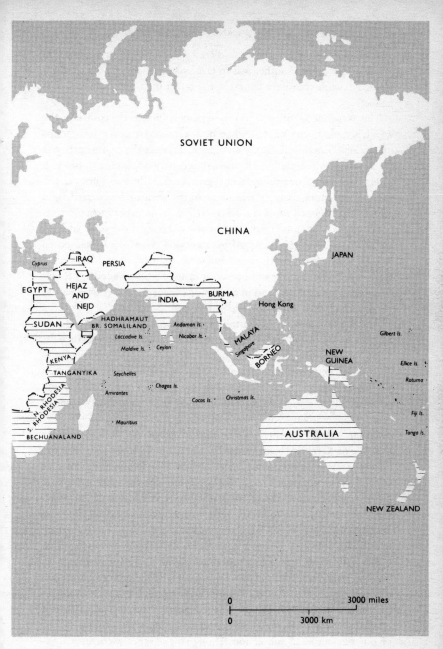

(After T. O. Lloyd, *The British Empire, 1558–1983*, Oxford, 1984)

and ordered that long-serving soldiers be demobilized first. This was one ad hoc remedy. Another was to give ex-servicemen an 'out-of-work donation' while they were unemployed, rather than designate heroes as paupers.

This was a decision with serious repercussions. In the course of the war, Unemployment Insurance had been extended to cover new groups of workers, notably those in munitions. In 1920 the major step was taken of including almost all manual occupations, except those with little incidence of unemployment (agriculture, railways, domestic service). Thus more than 11 million workers were to be covered by a scheme that seemed to have worked well since its experimental beginnings in 1911. So sound were its finances, during these years of high employment, that the actuarial assumptions on which it was based were now relaxed – just at the moment when the boom suddenly came to an end. In 1921 nearly 17 per cent of insured workers suddenly found themselves unemployed and in danger of exhausting the entitlement to benefit which their contributions had earned.

Again, the Government flinched from simply letting the Poor Law take the strain, faced with unemployment on a scale not seen since the 1880s. Instead it improvised arrangements for workers to go on drawing an 'uncovenanted' benefit, notionally covered by future rather than past contributions. In acknowledging that mass unemployment could not be met by mass reliance on the Poor Law, the Coalition Government thus inadvertently invented 'the dole'.

Perhaps it is not surprising that Lloyd George trod warily, with the example of Kerensky before him. The spectre of Bolshevism in Britain, however, was mainly just that: a phantasm. The Communist Party of Great Britain, set up in 1920, was tiny; and the fact that it took its orders from Moscow was not so much sinister as inhibiting. The representatives of 'Red Clydeside', briefly arrested in 1919, when a red flag flew over Glasgow City Chambers, included men like James Maxton, who could put on a passable impression of Robespierre as a parliamentary turn, and the young Emanuel Shinwell, who was to end his days as a centenarian peer. Guild Socialism, with the young Oxford don G. D. H. Cole as its prophet, inspired a short-lived interest in syndicalism, with cries like 'The Mines for the Miners'. And the security forces naturally had a professional interest in providing spine-chilling reports on other examples of subversion. Though the significance of such activities was largely in inflating the red menace, for theatrical effect and political advantage, Lloyd George took a serious view of industrial disputes.

The pre-war 'labour unrest' was put in the shade by the record under the coalition. Every year was another 1912:

>1919 35 million days lost in industrial disputes
>1920 27 million
>1921 86 million
>1922 20 million

The underlying reason was the instability of prices. Until the end of the war wages had chased prices quite closely, so that both stood at roughly double their 1914 level. By 1920 the cost of living had increased by another 25 per cent; wages responded more unevenly. It was natural that the trade unions, now 8-million strong, should engage in a scramble for competitive advantage, if only to relieve their members' apprehensions about falling behind.

The so-called Triple Alliance of miners, railwaymen and transport workers huffed and puffed to some effect in 1919. Their grievances had a directly political aspect since during the war the Government had assumed a large degree of control over the mines and the railways, two industries poised on the cusp of decline and increasingly dependent on state subsidy. The Miners Federation had strong political leverage through the Labour Party – half the Labour MPs were from the coal-fields – and its insistent demand was for nationalization. The Government set up a commission to report on the matter, and the casting vote of its chairman, Mr Justice Sankey, came down in favour of public ownership. When Lloyd George reneged on his half-promises of action – a specie in which he often traded – the miners were incensed. They were bought off temporarily by wage increases. Then, with the state having shed its direct responsibility for the mines in 1920, the miners looked again to the Triple Alliance for support when they went over the top in April 1921.

It was like the Somme, where not a few of them had fought. J. H. Thomas of the Railway Servants was a corpulent Labour MP with no stomach for this kind of frontal assault; the rising star of the trade-union movement, Ernest Bevin, likewise had no ambition to play Haig in the Transport and General Workers' Union. The miners were left stranded on the barbed wire, bitter and bloody but unbowed.

Disputes about pay were complicated by another factor. The end of the war saw one of the greatest changes of the twentieth century in the pattern of work. For forty years before the war the average working week had been 56 hours; after the war it stabilized at 48 hours. This made the 'eight-hour day' a normal expectation; and demands for a 40-hour week soon looked ahead to a normal five-day week. The implications for unit costs of labour in industry were to be less happy.

Until 1920 the Government might as well have been running a war economy. Its own expenditure remained at levels unprecedented in peacetime. Lloyd George's 1914 Budget had been thought shocking for edging towards a total of £200 million; but in 1917 the Budget exceeded £2,000 million. Public spending in the first post-war Budget in 1919 was hardly less than that of 1918, at over £2,500 million. Admittedly, inflation distorts these comparisons, since the relevant price level had doubled by 1917 and was to touch three times its pre-war level in 1920. When the inflationary bubble was pricked in 1920, the Government was forced to declare its priorities. Interest rates were put up; spending was cut back; social reform became a dispensable luxury which the country could no longer afford.

The prime victim was the housing programme, which was at the centre of the ambitious plans for reconstruction which Christopher Addison had hatched in the idealistic mood of 1917–18. He had become Minister of Health in 1919, with responsibility for state promotion of a programme of housebuilding. This operated at one remove, through the local authorities, to whom Exchequer grants were made available as a subsidy. In the overheated conditions of 1920–21 this made the houses a very expensive investment, though around 170,000 council houses were under construction by the time the subsidy was withdrawn. Addison was left to carry the can. He left the Government in 1921, alienated from the man whom he had helped become prime minister five years previously.

Though other coalition Liberal ministers, like the historian H. A. L. Fisher at the Board of Education, fought their corner, the Government's priorities were now clear. Faced with a populist 'Anti-Waste' campaign, which notched up a couple of by-election victories in June 1921, Lloyd George decided to throw it a sop by appointing a committee of businessmen to report on possible economies. It sat under the chairmanship of Sir Eric Geddes, a former coalition minister, and worked closely with the Treasury in deciding on its targets. Lloyd George's own instincts were to seek an alternative to deflation, perhaps through interventionist measures to stimulate employment; but Treasury orthodoxy prevailed and, having fashioned the 'Geddes Axe', the Government had to use it. The committee's recommendations became the basis of a new round of cuts in 1922, although they were somewhat scaled down after representations from the Navy and the teachers, both of whom escaped the full rigour of the exercise. Increasingly, however, the Government was discovering its centre of gravity in the Conservative majority which had always been its mainstay.

If the Government was Conservative in drift, why not Conservative too in name and personnel? This was a question which had surfaced in the minds of many of its backbenchers by 1922. At the top, the Government was united in mutual admiration of its own brilliance. The Lord Chancellor, Lord Birkenhead, had as F. E. Smith been a hard-hitting Tory polemicist; now he was a hard-drinking comrade of Winston Churchill, unable to imagine what had ever divided them politically. The Coalition reeked of cronyism; hence the catch: 'Lloyd George knows my father, / Father knows Lloyd George.'

This is why the honours scandal was so serious for Lloyd George. An aura of sharp practice had hung around him since the pre-war Marconi affair, in which he and other ministers had been accused of abusing their position for financial gain (and their cause had been pleaded in the courts by none other than F. E. Smith). Yet every Government, the Liberals under Gladstone as much as the Tories under Salisbury, had been guilty of what so shocked all decent people when it was revealed in 1922: that the Honours List included men who had made major contributions to party funds. One part of the trouble was that the Coalition had become crude, with a tariff showing the price of a peerage, a baronetcy or a knighthood. Another part of the trouble arose from Lloyd George pocketing the proceeds when, so the Tory whips felt, they should have been shared. The Lloyd George Fund was to finance him, and dog him, for twenty years.

Only a Government already in trouble would have been so damaged by a side issue that seemed to symbolize its flaws. A Coalition which relied for defence upon Birkenhead's arrogant homilies seemed to have degenerated into a coterie motivated by mutual admiration rather than any other principle. An inner ring of ministers perpetuated the methods of the war cabinet; the full cabinet of twenty rarely met. Law had withdrawn from the Government on health grounds in 1921, to be succeeded as Conservative leader by Austen Chamberlain. But the new leader, a true Coalitionist, did not have the same hold over the party and was unable to restrain it when it became restive, as it did in October 1922.

When Chamberlain called a party meeting at the Carlton Club, it provided an opportunity for revolt not reconciliation. News of a by-election at Newport, showing that an independent Conservative had beaten the Coalition candidate, was on the ticker-tapes as the meeting assembled. For the first time, Stanley Baldwin, appointed President of the Board of Trade in the previous year, caught the ear of his party with an almost conversational intervention. He acknowledged that Lloyd George was, as Birkenhead claimed, 'a dynamic force', only to throw the words back in the faces of the Coalitionists: 'A dynamic force is a very terrible thing; it may crush you, but it is not necessarily right.' Above all, Law had turned up, and now spoke up, restored in more ways than one. His advice to fight the next election as an independent party was accepted by a two-to-one majority. Lloyd George resigned the same afternoon.

# 4

## Safety First
### 1922–9

### COMMUNICATIONS

The British railway network was created in Victoria's reign. In 1837 there had been only 500 miles of track; by 1901 the network was virtually the same in extent as it was to be in 1960. It actually reached its maximum between the world wars, with lines totalling just over 20,000 miles. Throughout the first half of the twentieth century more than 300,000 men were employed on the railways. The railway companies were vast enterprises, the pioneers of big business in Britain, with a share capital of over £1,250 million at 1913 prices.

The position of these companies was recognized as containing an element of monopoly and, though the nineteenth century is thought of as the heyday of laissez-faire, they had therefore been subject to a good deal of parliamentary regulation, stipulating the provision of early-morning 'workmen's trains', for example. Some Liberals (Churchill was one) wanted to push the case for protecting the public interest one step further through nationalization of the railways. It looked as though this might happen during the First World War since the railway companies were put under state control, though administered through their existing managers, in a way typical of Lloyd George's leanings towards corporate solutions. It seemed portentous that his Government set up a Ministry of Transport at the end of the war – what was the need if not to run nationalized railways? But instead the cry of 'decontrol' carried the day and the old corporate arrangements were rejigged (until after the next war).

With decontrol in 1921 came an amalgamation into four great companies: Southern; London, Midland, & Scottish (LMS); London and North Eastern Railway (LNER); and Great Western Railway (GWR). With their distinctive liveries and regional attachments, they inspired an almost patriotic loyalty, especially in retrospect when infused with nostalgia for the great days of steam, on which British industrial pre-eminence had been built. The spectacle of the *Mallard*, in LNER colours, establishing the world record speed of 126 m.p.h. for a steam train was one which many found inspiring in 1938; not only small boys whose hobby was 'train-spotting' but countless grown-ups lined the track for a fleeting glimpse of the mighty locomotive as it sped on the east-coast line between London and Edinburgh. With the electrification of the commuter lines on the Southern Railway well under way, however, this celebration of British mechanical prowess was already tinged with elegy.

Great Britain was knitted together by its railway network. No two stations were more than a whole day's journey apart. Rich and poor used the train; luxurious dining and sleeping carriages, First Class and Third Class compartments (no Second Class since the nineteenth century), offered a service for all pockets. By 1901 there were well over 1,000 million passenger journeys a year; by 1913 1,500 million; in 1920 a peak of over 2,000 million. This represents a train journey every ten days for each man, woman and infant in Great Britain. Obviously that is not how the network was used. In the inter-war period about a third of the journeys were by holders of season tickets, mainly commuters, who can be presumed to have travelled twice each working day. But excluding the season-ticket holders still gives an average of one journey every twelve days.

Most of the railways' revenue came from freight. Since it could only be transported between railheads, this implied a vast system of secondary distribution on short-haul journeys to the ultimate destination. This is where the horse and the iron horse formed their characteristic Victorian partnership. There were 3.5 million horses in Great Britain at the peak in 1902. The coming of the railway had boosted the number of horses used in urban Britain; conversely, the coming of the internal combustion engine was to signal their common eclipse, sooner or later. The demand for vast numbers of horses on the western front is often overlooked; when transport ships were sunk in the English Channel, the sea was full of hay. Nonetheless, the number of horse-drawn vehicles, over a million in 1902, had slumped to 50,000 by the end of the 1920s. Immediately before the First World War more than 500 million tons of freight was being carried annually by rail. The peak post-war figure was only two-thirds of this level and in the early 1930s it dropped to half. Part of this decline was due to the slump; but the failure to bounce back above 300 million tons a year during the recovery of the mid-1930s shows the potent competition now offered by motor vehicles, which could deliver goods from door to door in a single journey.

The railways, however, were still unrivalled in two specialized kinds of freight which facilitated communication through the written word. They carried nearly all the mail, enabling the Post Office to provide a cheap service of extraordinary efficiency throughout the country. This achievement was to be rhapsodized by the GPO film unit's documentary *Night Mail* (1936), which, with its commentary by W. H. Auden – 'This is the Night Mail crossing the Border, / Bringing the cheque and the postal order' – has become a classic. During the war, post had generally reached troops in the trenches within two days. The total number of letters, postcards and packets posted in the United Kingdom was over 5,000 million in 1920 – about four items a week for each adult; and mail traffic was to rise in every decade until the 1970s. Mail trains, moreover, were paralleled by newspaper trains, running overnight, which made it possible to achieve national distribution of London daily newspapers throughout most of England and Wales.

It was this distribution network which enabled British national newspapers to gain a circulation unparalleled anywhere in the world. Scotland was protected not only by distance but also by cultural nationalism. At the top of the market, the *Scotsman*, printed in Edinburgh, continued to hold its own throughout the century. Scottish editions of most national newspapers were printed in Glasgow, facilitating distribution on Clydeside, where most of the customers lived. The *Daily Record*, for example, was a lightly transmogrified version of the *Daily Mirror*. One way or another, mass-circulation newspapers were London newspapers.

In the second half of the nineteenth century, with the development of wire services like the Associated Press, the provincial press had been a great force. Newspapers like the *Manchester Guardian*, the *Yorkshire Post* and the *Western Daily Post*, often under the control of editor-proprietors, relied primarily upon a bourgeois readership with a strong sense of regional identity. Merchants and brokers on the Manchester cotton exchange, for example, relied on the *Manchester Guardian* for its commercial pages, not for the left-wing Liberal politics which C. P. Scott propagated. It was to be unique in achieving a national circulation by the middle of the century, just like a London paper; it followed this logic by renaming itself the *Guardian* in 1959 and by effectively relocating to London in 1970. But the mass-circulation papers printed in London steadily seized the market. Already under pressure in the Edwardian period, the forty provincial morning papers which survived the First World War faced competition of a wholly new intensity. By 1937 only twenty-five remained.

It was Alfred Harmsworth's *Daily Mail* in 1896 which first showed the possibilities of a national daily paper, selling at a halfpenny, and relying on advertising revenue to offset the low cover price. This was frankly aimed at the lower middle class, especially the growing numbers (of both sexes) in clerical jobs. Harmsworth had made his money in the 1890s with weekly papers geared to the interests of women; he insisted that the *Daily Mail* develop a women's page as well as a sports page. With the *Daily Mirror* in 1903 Harmsworth even tried the experiment of a paper written by as well as for women. When it failed to prosper, it was relaunched in the following year in a new format, only half the size of the conventional broadsheet. Harmsworth called this 'tabloid journalism'; it specialized in news photographs, using improved technology to produce halftone pictures with new speed and quality. Here too Harmsworth was revolutionary, though he cribbed many of his other ideas from the USA.

The striking innovation of the rival *Daily Express*, founded in 1900 with R. D. Blumenfeld as editor, was to put news on the front page, at a time when other papers consecrated it to grey columns of classified advertisements. Popular papers henceforth used 'streamers' which broke across more than one column, or splashed the main news in a 'banner' right across the page, with multi-deck headlines to lead the readers' interest into a story. Harmsworth resisted this in the *Daily Mail*, and he showed a similar disdain for the prominence of advertisements, blenching at the course of the revolution which he had begun. Display advertising spread across several columns, using bold founts and pictures to get the message across. The London department store, Selfridge's, was a pioneer in taking full-page advertisements, illustrated with line drawings.

The war not only made news and sold newspapers: it taught quality newspapers about news values. The main news page of *The Times* in Edwardian days was a relentless compilation of the 'latest intelligence' from around the world, with no headlines spreading beyond the column, and little indication in them of the substance of the stories, let alone sub-heads to lead a busy reader through the thicket of closely packed print. It was during the war that clear priority was signalled for the urgent news, which was sometimes put on to the front page (instead of customary columns of personal advertisements). By the 1930s *The Times* was ready for a facelift from the print designer Stanley Morison, who created the Times Roman fount, which has become a classic. Headlines for the first time broke across more than one column, though it took another thirty years before the paper became the last of the dailies to put news on the front page.

To British newspapermen of the first quarter of the twentieth century, this was a golden age, when giants stalked Fleet Street and Governments hung on every word which dropped from the press – or so it seemed when they wrote their (copious) memoirs. In the Edwardian period famous editors like J. A. Spender of the Liberal *Westminster Gazette* and J. L. Garvin of the Conservative *Observer* could build great reputations on the strength of the leading article alone, relying upon indulgent proprietors to support their endeavour to shape the fate of the nation. The new press lords, however, were unashamedly interested in giving the public what it wanted.

Alfred Harmsworth acquired a peerage in 1905, as Lord Northcliffe, and completed his journey to respectability by acquiring *The Times* in 1908. The first of the press lords, Northcliffe was emulated by others, not least in the sonorous titles they chose: Lord Rothermere for Alfred's brother Harold Harmsworth, who kept the *Daily Mail* in the family; Lord Beaverbrook for Max Aitken, who had bought the *Daily Express* in 1916; Lord Southwood for J. B. Elias of the Odhams Press, which went into partnership with the TUC in 1930 to resuscitate the *Daily Herald*; Lord Camrose for William Berry, the proprietor of the *Daily Telegraph* from 1928, while for his brother Gomer, with whom he had earlier built up the *Sunday Times*, there was a peerage in due course as Lord Kemsley. Lloyd George's friend, George Riddell of the *News of the World*, however, stuck with plain Lord Riddell.

The fall of Asquith was rather indiscriminately attributed to the power of the press; and Northcliffe was certainly an imperious figure who was determined to make his influence felt. (His growing megalomania indeed was pathological, and he died in 1922.) It is true that Lloyd George cultivated the press in a manner that was only later to become commonplace among ministers. The fact that his was a Coalition Government, lacking a declared party basis, also helped inflate the reputation of the press as a proxy for public opinion. Beaverbrook thrived in the Coalition milieu; Max loved to pick up the champagne bills when he kept open house for LG and FE and Winston, in an era when parties seemed to have replaced party as the glue of politics. Just as Northcliffe's *Daily Mail* had pioneered a popular daily press, so Beaverbrook's *Daily Express* set the pace in the race to mass circulation in the inter-war period.

At the end of the First World War, national dailies were selling 3 million copies; by the beginning of the Second, their sales were over 10 million. The *Daily Express* was the first to sell over 2 million a day in the mid-1930s; the *Daily Mail* was selling 1½ million; the TUC's revamped *Daily Herald* more than 1 million; and the *News Chronicle* (a recent amalgamation of the two surviving Liberal popular dailies) somewhat less. Their circulation wars in the early 1930s, with as many as 50,000 canvassers offering rival editions of encyclopedias and sets of classic novels as free gifts, had helped drive up these figures, albeit at a heavy cost. By 1934, 95 morning and 130 Sunday papers were sold for every 100 families in Britain.

The role of newspapers was both buttressed and challenged by the rise of the newer media. The film industry, with its star system, created a whole new realm of human-interest stories; newspaper publicity helped to promote films and a good way of selling newspapers was to write about Hollywood, which provided 95 per cent of the films shown in Britain in the 1920s. The cultural threat of Americanization had always aroused fears among traditional elites in Britain; when it meant rampant commercialization it also aroused the suspicions of the anti-capitalist left. Here was the making of a consensus which helped ensure that radio broadcasting would be developed under public auspices rather than left to the free market.

The British Broadcasting Corporation (BBC) was the result. It built upon the Post Office's responsibility for regulating radio transmission, and, after a transitional period, was finally established in 1927 as a public corporation, under a board of governors appointed by the Government, vested with a monopoly of public radio broadcasting. By charging an annual licence fee for radio receivers, the service was freed from dependence on advertising. Indeed, the strict BBC code of the early years forbade any mention of brand names on the air. This was an arrangement which suited the press lords well since commercial radio would have threatened their advertising revenue. Broadcasting boomed from the start. The number of licences grew from 125,000 in 1923 to nearly 2 million by 1926, 3 million by 1930.

The precarious semi-autonomous status of the BBC was converted into an ethic of independent public service by its strenuous Director-General, John Reith, still in his thirties. High-minded, puritanical, domineering, Reith dedicated his life to the improvement of public taste through a carefully regulated regime of programmes, with just enough concessions to variety, entertainment and popular music to stave off mutiny by the listening public. The careful elocution of the BBC announcers was all part of Reith's master plan for 'improvement': helping to establish one variant of an upper-middle-class London accent as 'standard English'. Only on the regional networks were other accents regarded as acceptable.

The regime which Reith initially imposed was based on giving the public what he thought was good for them. In belated over-compensation for his own failure to secure a place at one of the ancient universities, he packed the BBC with Oxbridge graduates. Donnish talks enlightened the listening public on topics which ought to have interested them. Music meant live relays of symphony concerts, hogging the prime-time slots, evening after evening, with dance bands only allowed on the air after the normal programmes had finished. There were long-lasting triumphs along the way. Sir Henry Wood's Promenade Concerts were saved by the intervention of the BBC in 1927; and the subsidized Proms became a feature of summer broadcasting for the rest of the century. Broadcast drama needed to innovate since relays from West End theatres did not work. This prompted the BBC to develop studio performances in adaptations of plays suitable for the microphone.

The BBC thus began by catering to minority tastes, but it was overtaken by its own success. From 3 million licence-holders in 1930, the number doubled by 1934 and trebled by 1939 – not far short of saturation coverage. The 'cat's whiskers' of the early days, with headphones running off a crystal set, offered a hobby in the tradition of fiercely individualist artisan tinkering; but the valve radio sets on sale by the 1930s, with their tasteful Art Deco modelling, claimed pride of place in the family sitting room for a shared experience. To have missed a popular programme became a minor social disability, excluding the non-listener from a range of common references.

In Reith's later years there was a more flexible adjustment of the programme schedules and the BBC even began to use listener research to find out more about its audiences. Listeners were thus permitted to tap their feet to famous dance bands like those of Henry Hall and Jack Payne. The launch of *Band Waggon* in 1938, starring Arthur Askey and Richard Murdoch, signalled the emergence of a new breed of radio comedians who were not just stand-up comics but began to develop a real situation comedy. Special events were covered by outside broadcasts. Cricket commentaries were particularly successful, with the slow unfolding of the game, hour by hour and day by day, lending itself to verbal transmission. Millions who never saw the great Australian batsman Donald Bradman nonetheless listened to him destroying England's bowlers. Radio coverage of test matches developed into a minor art form, so much so that it was able to withstand the later competition from television. From 1931 the University Boat Race between Oxford and Cambridge improbably acquired a large vicarious following through live coverage from the BBC launch by John Snagge (educated at Winchester and Pembroke College, Oxford), one of the best-known announcers on the National Programme.

The frankly posh tones of the newsreaders, who were required to wear dinner jackets in the early days, may have helped buy credence for the BBC's authoritative pretensions. Its claims to impartiality and objectivity were seldom challenged. There was no overt political bias, just a reflection of the fact that the BBC aspired to become part of the Establishment. Its duty to represent the Government's position was impressed upon it behind the scenes at times of perceived crisis, notably the General Strike, which it weathered with some characteristic trimming by Reith. During election campaigns the parties were allowed air time which they initially misused by treating the microphone like a public meeting. Baldwin was the first to project a fireside manner successfully; radio was a medium for which his curiously intimate talents in communication were well suited. The Baldwinian ascendancy and the Reithian ascendancy coincided nicely. Reith's balancing act was successful in cultivating an ethos of public broadcasting which survived him – he was eased out in 1938 – and in preparing the way for the BBC's apotheosis as a national institution during the Second World War.

## RIGHT, LEFT, RIGHT

The fall of the Lloyd George Coalition in October 1922 stemmed from a conscious decision by most of the Conservative Party, eagerly endorsed by Asquithian Liberals and Labour, to restore the party system. This was indeed accomplished, but not directly. Not only did it take until 1924: what was restored was a new party system – much more favourable to the Conservatives than the old, with Labour as the natural party of opposition. During the next seventy years the Conservatives were only to be out of power for eighteen.

Three general elections were held in quick succession. In 1922 the Conservatives won a majority, only to lose it again in 1923. The first Labour Government took office in 1924, for a few months only, until a further general election gave the Conservatives a secure majority. For the Liberal Party, these were like successive punches to the head of an ageing heavyweight: a right jab which caught it off balance, a deceptive left which set it up for more punishment, and a devastating right swing which put it out for the count.

| General Election | | Conservative | Labour | Liberal |
| --- | --- | --- | --- | --- |
| 1922 | Votes (m.) | 5.5 (39%) | 4.2 (30%) | 4.1 (28%) |
| | MPs | 344 | 142 | 115 |
| 1923 | Votes (m.) | 5.5 (38%) | 4.4 (31%) | 4.3 (30%) |
| | MPs | 258 | 191 | 158 |
| 1924 | Votes (m.) | 7.9 (48%) | 5.5 (33%) | 2.9 (18%) |
| | MPs | 419 | 151 | 40 |

The influence of the electoral system itself on these results is worth noting. The Conservative triumph of 1922 and the Conservative setback of 1923 were each achieved on virtually the same share of the poll. It was the distribution of the vote between their opponents that made the difference. On one flank, in 1923 the Liberals succeeded in winning half of the agricultural seats, in a style reminiscent of their strong performance in by-elections in the days of the pre-war Land Campaign – a message which Lloyd George took to heart in bringing forward new land proposals in 1925.[1] On the other flank, Labour was steadily consolidating its position as the party of urban and industrial Britain, with a string of victories in working-class constituencies, not only in the coalfields as hitherto, but in most of the big conurbations. This was

1. There were 86 constituencies in which more than 20 per cent of the male workforce was engaged in agriculture. The Liberals won 43 of them in 1923 but the Conservatives won 74 in 1924.

class politics, but with some curious twists. In the two British cities most divided on ethnic and religious lines, this sort of cultural politics worked for Labour in Glasgow, allowing it to gather Catholic votes, but against it in Protestant Liverpool; so a phalanx of Clydesiders, but not Merseysiders, appeared as Labour MPs.

In general the fact that Labour's support was skewed on class lines was a clear advantage under the first-past-the-post system. Concentration of its support gave Labour more seats than the Liberals on the same share of the national vote. It was not that the Liberals were a third party nationally, subject to a squeeze on their support through fears of wasted votes: this was a secondary handicap that they faced chiefly from 1924. The fact was that they were the wrong sort of minority party, with support spread fairly evenly throughout Great Britain, and across social classes. This had been an advantage before the war; but became a fatal handicap when their national vote fell below a critical threshold. The crude logic was that they were able to finish second to Labour in working-class constituencies, second to the Conservatives in middle-class constituencies.

Under the three-party system of the 1920s a party that could nudge 40 per cent was a potential winner, a party stuck on 30 per cent was an also-ran. Yet in many electoral systems, of course, a party with 30 per cent of the votes is formidably represented. Here the Liberals had only themselves to blame for fumbling their opportunities to reform the voting system during the twelve years in which they had held a majority in the Commons, culminating in a Reform Act in 1918 which, almost at the last minute, abandoned the measure of proportional representation which was initially part of the package.

The Conservative backbenchers relished their display of power in repudiating the Coalition in 1922; thereafter they were to institutionalize their regular meetings under the name 'the 1922 Committee'.[1] After the Carlton Club decision to fight the next election on independent lines, Lloyd George obviously had to go, but many Conservatives regretted this. Not only did Austen Chamberlain resign as party leader, allowing Bonar Law to pick up the reins which he had so recently laid down: the first-class brains of the Coalition cabinet — the fading

1. Its original composition in 1923, however, was restricted to the new MPs elected in 1922 — exactly the group who had not been present at the Carlton Club meeting. It was only in 1925 that membership was extended to all Conservative backbenchers.

laureate Birkenhead, the evergreen Balfour – spurned the new Government. Marquess Curzon of Kedleston, though enormously grand, stayed on – the last of an unbroken line of aristocrats since Canning had left the Foreign Office in 1827.[1] Law formed his cabinet as best he could. He initially tried to get the Liberal McKenna to go back to the Treasury, which he had occupied under Asquith, in place of Sir Robert Horne, another Coalitionist. Only when this ploy failed was the inexperienced Baldwin promoted instead. This changing of the guard made it plain that partisan and personal allegiances were in flux.

The Conservative Party could hardly repudiate the entire record of a Coalition Government of which it had been the mainstay. Much was therefore left unsaid during the election campaign in November 1922. The Conservatives lost 40 – but only 40 – of the seats which they had won in the Coupon Election. This showed that they had a future with or without Lloyd George. Without was the preference of many, notably Baldwin, who accordingly took comfort from the result. By contrast, Austen Chamberlain, who had loyally stuck to Lloyd George through thick and thin, found that he had yet again played the game and had again lost.

To refer simply to a 'Liberal' performance in the 1922 general election can be misleading. The 'National Liberals' under Lloyd George had no interest in alienating Coalitionist goodwill; and many of them enjoyed at least tacit Conservative support. Lloyd George and Asquith each had between fifty and sixty followers in the new parliament. This was a come-down for Lloyd George, still licking his wounds, but a welcome boost for Asquith, if only in comparison with his previous weakness; though in many constituencies 'prefixless' Liberals were what the activists really wanted.

The real gains were Labour's. Given that a number of its victories in the Coupon Election had been by grace of the Coalition, Labour's true strength was increased by up to 100 seats, putting it well clear of the Liberals, howsoever enumerated.

---

1. Throughout a century, it had been unusual for the Foreign Secretary to be less than an earl: the notable exceptions being Russell (the son of a duke), Palmerston (an Irish viscount) and Grey (a baronet and a collateral of Earl Grey of the Reform Act). Since 1924 only the 3rd Viscount Halifax (Foreign Secretary, 1938–40), the 14th Earl of Home (1960–63 and 1970–74), and the 6th Baron Carrington (1979–82) have had such a pedigree.

Labour had made a big advance since 1918. It was not due simply to the votes of trade unionists; with the onset of recession, their 5.6 million members could not have comprised more than 27 per cent of the electorate. Nor was it simply a product of the new parliamentary franchise. Labour's increasingly broad appeal had come through in the 1919 local election results, fought on a register effectively based on household suffrage. The fact is that the Labour breakthrough was not sociologically determined but a product of the politics of the period. Its ability to channel the support of anti-Coalitionist forces in the country had been signalled in the Spen Valley by-election in 1920, when, fighting on traditional Liberal and Nonconformist territory, Labour had triumphed over both older parties. If Labour was now the people's party, it was also becoming a toffs' party – at least in its parliamentary leadership. The election as Labour MPs of educated professional men like Clement Attlee and Hugh Dalton showed the shape of the future.

For the present, a purely Conservative Government was a novelty – the first since 1905 (or even earlier, depending on how the Liberal Unionists are regarded). A proper peacetime cabinet of sixteen ministers was restored, though retaining the secretariat through which Hankey had serviced the war cabinet since 1917; the cabinet secretary henceforth occupied a key post in the power structure of Whitehall. The Government got off to an inauspicious start when Baldwin did a deal in Washington over the war loan – to pay the USA, on easy terms, irrespective of whether the UK was able to collect its own war debts – and, on docking at Southampton, leaked it to the press without squaring the cabinet first. He was lucky that most of them backed him – though not the prime minister, who first vented his feelings through an anonymous letter to *The Times*, attacking his cabinet's proposed settlement, then caved in under the weight of City advice. This was an odd way of doing business; but Law hardly had time to make an impression as prime minister. Forced to retire from the Coalition on doctor's orders in 1921, he had been given a clean bill of health in 1922, only to discover in May 1923 that he had terminal cancer. When he was buried in Westminster Abbey later that year Asquith remarked that the Unknown Prime Minister was being buried alongside the Unknown Soldier.

An unexpected vacancy thus opened in the leadership. Law had insisted on being elected as party leader before accepting the King's commission as prime minister; but the constitutional propriety of doing things the other way around was now reasserted. Nor was this a mere formality, as it had been when Asquith succeeded Campbell-Bannerman. Since Chamberlain was out of the Government at the time, the choice was between Curzon, a long-serving cabinet minister, and Baldwin, with only a few months' experience as Chancellor of the Exchequer. George V was thus faced with a decision of real weight. Since Law offered no advice, Balfour's was sought. The old man, who harboured a feline malice for Curzon ('dear George'), left his sickbed to go and see the King. Balfour's case was that a peer was not acceptable as prime minister – a constitutional doctrine which might have surprised his uncle Robert but which certainly meant that 'dear George' was not chosen.

Stanley Baldwin was to be the pivotal figure in the government of Britain for the next decade and a half. Though his tenure was sometimes shaky, even as late as 1930, in the end he established an extraordinary grip on power. Under him the Conservative Party managed the transition to a fully democratic electorate, which it had so long feared, and weathered an economic slump which brought down regimes throughout Europe. Yet few predicted the rise of a Tory backbencher who had succeeded his father in the Worcestershire seat of Bewdley back in 1908: a wealthy ironmaster whose works were administered on old-fashioned paternalist lines, with time for a chat with men whom Mr Stanley had always known by their first names – a style which he effortlessly transferred to the Tea Room of the Commons, where he could be found, even as prime minister, hobnobbing with Labour's old guard of trade-union MPs, over their pipes. All of this was good politics, especially when Baldwin projected heartfelt Christian verities and the sentiments of an English patriotism rooted self-consciously in the soil – all depicted with an art that sometimes reminded his hearers that Rudyard Kipling was a cousin.

Baldwin's accession closed the door on Coalitionist projects. He wanted nothing to do with Lloyd George and was ready, if need be, to give Labour a chance in government. Nor was he hasty in mending his fences with the old Coalitionists. The new shape of the Conservative leadership was indicated by his choice at the Treasury, which went to the Minister of Health, Neville Chamberlain. Son of Joseph, half-brother of Austen, by whom he had hitherto been overshadowed, Neville was more faithfully a chip off the old block, both in his steely wish to succeed and in his retention of close ties with the economic and civic life of Birmingham. Only two years younger than Baldwin and even newer to the Westminster elite – Chamberlain was nearly fifty when he became an MP in 1918 – he exemplified the business ethic of the post-war Conservative Party. He too despised Lloyd George and the fleshpots of his Coalition; but he was naturally ready to welcome home the prodigal half-brother, should that prove possible.

As a Midlands industrialist, Baldwin had long been a Tariff Reformer, with an eye to domestic protection rather than any imperial vision; but he was no ideologue. He knew the electoral dangers of an issue that had happily lain dormant in Conservative politics for ten years. During the war it was the Liberal Chancellor McKenna who imposed duties on certain luxury goods, justified on the grounds that this rationed shipping space by price (rather than protecting domestic producers). But this was a fine line to draw, as was that between 'protection' and the measures of 'safeguarding' which the Lloyd George Coalition had introduced. After Versailles, to be sure, there was no large-scale resort to the sort of post-war economic warfare which many Free Traders had feared. The fiscal issue dropped out of prominence, assisted by Law's pledge in 1922 that no change would be made in the next parliament. Why, then, did Baldwin revive the cry for protection?

Since the Government was precipitated into a general election which it lost, whereas it could have soldiered on for years, Baldwin met accusations of tactical ineptitude at the time. But since the chain of events led, within a year, to an impressive consolidation of the Conservative position, Baldwin has also been credited with a master strategy of great subtlety. He himself offered conflicting accounts. Though he proved adept at turning events to advantage, it is not clear that he foresaw the consequences of his declaration to the Conservative Party conference in October 1923 that Law's pledge should lapse at the end of the parliament. His case was squarely based on unemployment, which he proposed to fight by protecting the home market. There is no need to doubt that he believed this; he knew it would go down well with his party; he knew too that Austen Chamberlain could hardly fail to rally to the cry of Tariff Reform, which headed off any new challenge from Lloyd George. Whether Baldwin also appreciated how soon an election would have to be called, once the genie was out of the bottle, is more doubtful; but he went ahead anyway.

The general election of 1923 was the nearest thing to a restoration of the pre-war party system, turning on the axis of Free Trade, with Lib-

erals and Labour defending it from Conservative attack. The reunifica-
tion of the Conservative Party around Tariff Reform was as nothing to
the spectacle of the Liberal Party reuniting around Free Trade. Lloyd
George and Asquith appeared on the same platform, their respective
womenfolk hissing at each other beneath their breath. The fact is that,
despite everything that had happened, the two men got on fairly well,
left to themselves (though they seldom were by their stridently partisan
followers). The Liberals racked their brains to remember the arguments
that had served them well in 1906 and trotted them out again. The
Liberal poll in 1922 had been an amalgam, still partaking of Coalitionist support in many places; the improvement in 1923 was thus substantial, showing surprising resilience in a party that could survive seven
lean, mean years.

The rebuff to the Conservatives' plea for protection was clearer in
the parliamentary than in the electoral arithmetic. The Government
had lost its majority, and Labour had appreciably more seats than the
Liberals. Since Baldwin chose to meet the new House, rather than
resign at once, there was time for reflection, which the Liberals would
have been wise to put to better use. Asquith was not worried about a
Labour Government as such; but he naively supposed that it could be
sustained, to mutual advantage, by the ad hoc cooperation between the
progressive parties which had worked when he had himself been prime
minister. The Liberals therefore voted down the Baldwin Government.
In allowing Labour to take office, without prior agreement on the terms
on which Liberal support would be forthcoming, Asquith displayed a
goodwill which he fondly hoped would be reciprocated.

The first Labour Government marks an epoch. On his return to the
Commons in 1922, Ramsay MacDonald had narrowly been elected
leader instead of J. R. Clynes, a Lancashire trade unionist who had
been a stopgap, given the dearth of talent at Westminster since the
Coupon Election. MacDonald's opposition to the war had done him
little permanent harm, given growing post-war disillusion, while it reinforced his left-wing credentials within the party. Ideologically, he
remained a progressive in the mould of his old friend J. A. Hobson
(now a Labour supporter), arguing that Labour represented this outlook more faithfully than the Liberal Party. Tactically, therefore, Mac-
Donald was bent on replacing the Liberal Party.

The Government he formed in 1924 was a crucial step in achieving
this objective. His defeated opponent Clynes was easily accommodated

as Lord Privy Seal; Arthur Henderson became Home Secretary and J. H. Thomas Colonial Secretary. The Chancellor of the Exchequer was Philip Snowden, an intellectual equal of the prime minister and a colleague of thirty years' standing in the ILP, where his fiercely moralistic utterances, though giving him an awesome reputation as a socialist, signalled a Gladstonian pedigree which made him welcome at the Treasury. These were Labour's Big Five. Since MacDonald had more jobs than that to dispense, he had to root around for some of his other appointments, of which the most distinguished was the ex-Liberal Haldane as Lord Chancellor.

There was little in the policy of the Government with which Liberals disagreed. Snowden's Budget was impeccable, so pure in its fiscal orthodoxy that it even abolished the McKenna duties. In the House Labour relied on Liberal support, not only in supplying votes but also some necessary legislative proficiency. For example, John Wheatley, the Clydesider who became Minister of Health, was responsible for one of the Government's few effective measures, the Housing Act of 1924. Following the collapse of the Coalition's building programme, Neville Chamberlain had put through a Housing Act in 1923 which opened the field to private enterprise; what Wheatley did was to provide a state subsidy for the construction of council houses too. Though he received considerable help from the Liberals in passing the Act, this was not acknowledged.

The point was to demonstrate that Labour could form a proper Government. This MacDonald achieved. He served as Foreign Secretary as well as prime minister, playing both roles with aplomb, striking a handsome figure, seemingly at ease in even the grandest social circles – a point increasingly made against him. With every week that passed the idea of a Labour Government seemed less shocking, the notion of calling back Asquith more outlandish. The fact that Labour was gaining the kudos, while taking Liberal support for granted, naturally did little to improve relations between the parties. This was the real reason for the Government's fall. The occasion was a vote of confidence in October on its handling of the prosecution of a Communist agitator – a trivial matter in itself had a concordat between Liberals and Labour been in force. As it was, the Liberals voted the Labour Government down, just as they had voted the Conservative Government down ten months previously.

Here was the flaw in the Liberals' position. Having fought on the left in 1923, they were now fighting on the right in 1924. The election campaign showed that the fiscal issue had been consigned to oblivion – Baldwin in effect revived the pledge of inaction – and instead the issue was 'socialism'. Little enough of this had been seen in action, but the very existence of a Labour Government was enough to fuel the Conservatives' propaganda machine. MacDonald had spent a good deal of time trying to normalize relations with the Soviet Union, which was an opening for widespread allegations that the country was at the mercy of a Bolshevik conspiracy, aided and abetted by MacDonald. For those who needed evidence, Conservative central office excelled itself by producing an ostensibly compromising letter over the signature of the president of the Communist International, Zinoviev; and the Foreign Office managed to release the text while MacDonald himself was campaigning.

It is now known that the Zinoviev letter was a forgery; but it served its purpose in the election campaign; and it entered Labour Party legend as an example of Tory dirty tricks. In itself, however, its impact was probably marginal. The Labour poll, after all, went up by more than a million, or 3 per cent of votes cast on a higher turnout, giving Labour more seats than they had held in 1922, and establishing their clear role as the Opposition. What made the 1924 general election so decisive was what happened to the Liberal Party. This was a disaster worse than 1918. With a drop in their national poll to well under 20 per cent, the Liberals ended their career as a major party. Their 40 seats in parliament banished them to the 'Celtic fringe', holding constituencies in north Wales and the highlands of Scotland but almost wiped off the map in urban England.

Baldwin was now the master. The Conservatives benefited from the increase in turnout with almost 2½ million extra votes. At nearly 8 million, they were in a different league to the other parties and within sight of an absolute majority of the votes cast. With over 400 MPs they were back to the golden days of Lord Salisbury. One attraction of the post-war Coalition had been as a great rally of moderate opinion against the threat of Labour; now the Conservatives had shown that they could achieve this on their own. The former Coalitionists were thus at Baldwin's beck and call. His former leader, Austen Chamberlain, who had been in the cabinet before Baldwin was even in the House, served under him, as Foreign Secretary. Birkenhead was sent to the India Office. The aged Balfour prepared to return – the fossilized missing link with the party of Disraeli.

The most striking of the new appointments, however, was the Chancellor of the Exchequer. Amazingly, Neville Chamberlain did not want to go back to 'that horrid Treasury', preferring the Ministry of Health. So Baldwin turned to Winston Churchill, who was not even a paid-up Conservative at the time. Churchill had been deeply unhappy since the break-up of the Coalition, and was plainly no longer a Liberal except in the undiminished fervour of his attachment to Free Trade. He anticipated the new shape of politics by standing on anti-socialist lines at a by-election in 1924, before finding a berth at Epping as a 'Constitutionalist'. The demise of the fiscal issue as the dividing line in politics was a precondition of Churchill's return, after twenty years, to the Conservative Party; equally Baldwin could not have given a clearer signal of the new turn in Conservative strategy than by choosing Churchill.

## ECONOMIC CONSEQUENCES

By 1924 it was clear that the British economy was less robust than it had been ten years previously. An obvious reason was the war. The most direct and frightening way of counting its cost was the total figure for the national debt, which in 1914 stood at £620 million – a burden far less in real terms than a far smaller population with far fewer resources had shouldered at the end of the Napoleonic wars. By 1920 the total public debt was nearly £8,000 million. Inflation helped make this manageable – prices in 1920 temporarily reached a level about two and a half times higher than before the war. Even so, the debt charges were a heavy load on the Budget in the 1920s: in round terms £300 million out of a total annual expenditure of £800 million. The standard rate of income tax, which the People's Budget had so daringly raised from 1s (5 per cent) to 1s 2d (6 per cent), reached 6s (30 per cent) in 1919–22 and stood at 5s (25 per cent) at the beginning of 1924.[1] On each £100 pounds of unearned or investment income, £25 went in tax, of which £10 simply serviced the national debt.

---

1. These rates of tax were less onerous than similar rates today since earned incomes were charged at a lower rate. There was also a graduation of the tax rates on lower incomes; so in 1919 standard rate, charged on incomes over £250 a year, was only paid by 1.25 million out of a total of 3.5 million taxpayers.

These were chiefly matters for financial adjustments between different groups of British citizens. After all, some of the public debt could have been paid off with accumulated private capital at the end of the war. Baldwin, whose ironworks had profited from war contracts, made a donation of £120,000 to the Treasury for this purpose – a fine but lonely gesture. A number of Liberal and Labour economists proposed a capital levy, partly appealing to social justice and partly to simple logic in breaking out of a crazy spiral. It was a spiral because many of the people who would have had to pay such a levy on their accumulated assets had not only benefited from debt-financed wartime expenditure but now held those assets in the form of war debt and were being taxed on the interest – in order to meet the Government's debt charges. The money went round and round, though not, of course, to the equal advantage of everyone.

There was also, within the total, over £1,000 million of external debt, owed chiefly to the USA. This had to be financed by the UK across the foreign exchanges, in just the same way as reparations had to be financed by Germany. One way of meeting the costs of the war to the nation was out of its capital; British foreign investments had accordingly been run down during the war. Income from property abroad was one measure of this. In the 1920s this was still worth 5 per cent of GDP – as compared with 1 per cent sixty years later – but this was appreciably less than in the immediate pre-war years.

Britain's magnificent foreign investments had thus served as a war chest; but the bottom line was that the UK had more need to pay its way in the post-war world through current earnings and current output. After the inflationary peak of 1920, commodity prices stabilized at about 175 per cent of their 1914 level. Invisible earnings, however, had not kept up with this increase; in the early 1920s they did not produce any more than pre-war in money terms. In real terms, therefore, the two items – rentier income from abroad and invisible exports – which had handsomely made up the pre-war deficit in visible trade were much diminished in value when measured at constant prices. This was not so, however, on the debit side of the foreign trade account. Measured at 1913 prices, the volume of imports was much the same as pre-war in the 1920s, whereas in real terms exports never again reached the 1913 level. What with the shortfall in property income and invisible exports, this meant that the balance of payments was now continually under strain.

The British export performance continued to rely on the old staples. In the exceptionally good year of 1920 coal still made up 9 per cent of domestic exports, only 1 per cent down on 1913. Cotton outdid itself by providing 30 per cent of all exports, an even higher share than in 1913; and the misplaced euphoria of this moment fuelled an investment boom in new mills, some of which never subsequently came into production. Coal was already slipping, relatively as well as absolutely, down by 1925 to 7 per cent of an export total which was itself below par. Cotton's misery, exacerbated by the post-war over-expansion, was more prolonged: down to 25 per cent of all exports by 1925, well below 20 per cent by 1929, with worse to come.

The regional impact was devastating. In the export coalfields of north-east England and south Wales, and increasingly in Lancashire, communities found themselves with no future. When George Orwell published *The Road to Wigan Pier* (1937) he was writing about a town on the Lancashire coalfield where young men had traditionally gone down the pit and young women into the mill – a double catastrophe when both went bust. Markets for coal in eastern Europe, for textiles in Asia, were inexorably slipping to competitors with lower costs than Britain in producing these fairly unsophisticated goods. What is really remarkable, of course, is not that this eventually happened but that it took so long.

British export prices were crucially affected by three other prices: that of labour in the form of wages; that of the currency, as shown by the parity of sterling; and that of money, measured by interest rates. These prices were out of kilter in the 1920s, setting costs of production in Britain at levels which were no longer competitive, with resulting unemployment. If all these prices had been perfectly flexible, Britain might have adjusted to new trading conditions with some temporary dislocation but with no permanent loss. The signals of the market, indeed, provoked some diversion of resources to the new skills which were to flourish in the middle of the century – science-based industries like electrical goods and chemical processes, often geared to the demands of more affluent consumers, at home or abroad. A sign of the times was amalgamation which, in 1926, turned Brunner Mond into Imperial Chemicals Industries (ICI). This was what Americans had termed a trust, what we would now call a multinational, and it was paralleled by the soap company, Lever Brothers, combining with Dutch partners in 1929 to form Unilever. British industry does not therefore present an unrelieved picture of stagnation; but the widespread un-employment of the period surely points to a significant failure in market responses, faced with the challenge of change.

The biggest change was in labour costs. In 1924 the cost of living was 75 per cent higher than in 1914 but wages were nearly double. This meant that the standard of living for employed workers was at least 10 per cent higher than pre-war. Moreover, this understates the real gain since the normal working week had meanwhile been reduced by ten hours, or one-sixth. For employers, of course, it was a real problem to pay appreciably more for fifty hours' work than they used to pay for sixty. Ideally productivity gains would fill the gap, but this was a tall order given the suddenness of the change. Producers for the domestic market might be able to pass on some of the increase in higher prices, but this course was hardly open in trades where prices were set by international competition. It is not surprising that export industries where labour constituted a high proportion of total costs should have run into recurrent trouble on the linked issues of pay and hours. Hence the great coal disputes of the period.

A second change affected the currency. At the outbreak of war the gold standard had been suspended. No longer was the parity of sterling fixed at $4.86; it traded at $4.76 for most of the war. The British Government maintained a commitment in principle to return to gold and kept hoping that the sterling and dollar rates would converge sufficiently to make this easy. In 1920 the average rate had been as low as $3.66; but it edged toward four dollars in 1921 and from 1922 to 1924 was around $4.40. This was a full 10 per cent short of the historic pre-war parity – or a mere 10 per cent, as some people preferred to put it. The option of returning to gold at this lower parity was not seriously considered. Since the object of the exercise was to restore confidence, to get back to the happy days of 1914, it was thought essential that the pound should, as the phrase went, 'look the dollar in the face'.

Interest rates were the third crucial price. The Bank of England had historically set its discount rate at the level necessary to keep the gold reserves in equilibrium. Released from the obligation to sell gold at a fixed price, it had the alternative option of letting the exchange rate take the strain of a run on the currency. Such a course was inflationary, which is why City opinion was against it. Bank rate had gone as high as 7 per cent in 1920–21 to check the inflationary boom. This was one reason why the exchange rate subsequently strengthened, and this in turn permitted bank-rate to be lowered. By July 1923, the rate had stood for twelve months at 3 per cent before being raised by one point. Now interest rates of 3 or 4 per cent may not seem high, but the context of deflation should be remembered. Not only were prices falling: unemployment remained at least double its pre-war level. Industry was crying out for cheap money to lower its costs and make investment profitable again. The question was, did restoration of the gold standard require a prolonged dose of dear money?

This was the dilemma which Churchill faced on becoming Chancellor at the end of 1924. The weight of expert advice in favour of gold was formidable. The Controller of Finance at the Treasury, Sir Otto Niemeyer, marshalled the case for the Chancellor with steely logic. An advisory committee under the successive chairmanship of Sir Austen Chamberlain, twice previously Chancellor himself, and Lord Bradbury, a highly respected public servant and former head of the Treasury, came down in favour of an early return to gold. For Bradbury the economic arguments about whether sterling was overvalued against the dollar were secondary to the quasi-constitutional case for removing monetary policy from political influence. The great merit of the gold standard, he liked to say, was that it was 'knave-proof'.

The 'authorities' – the Treasury and the Bank of England – stood firmly together. The Governor of the Bank, Montagu Norman, was an enigmatic, neurotic figure who, hardly less than God, moved in mysterious ways. He modestly affirmed that the Gold Standard was 'the best "Governor" that can be devised for a world that is still human, rather than divine'. Such comments indicate a suspicion about the bad effects of political meddling that is partly timeless, as ongoing arguments about the role of a central bank sufficiently demonstrate; but this feeling was exacerbated in the mid-1920s by widespread revulsion against Lloyd George's legerdemain and by fears of socialism. Government failure was more feared than market failure in opinion-forming circles. At the time when the decision had to be made, there were few voices against gold. As Labour's Treasury spokesman, Snowden could be counted in favour, and the position of the sceptical McKenna, the once and nearly Chancellor, now chairman of the Midland Bank, was not in the end clear-cut. In a double sense Churchill wanted to be persuaded of the case for gold: that is, he rigorously interrogated his experts rather than simply rubber-stamping their opinion, but his mindset was also one which prized the self-adjusting mechanism of traditional sound finance. In announcing the return to gold in his Budget speech in 1925 Churchill identified only one prominent critic.

This was J. M. Keynes, who was to capitalize on the fame he had acquired through his critique of Versailles by calling his case against the gold standard *The Economic Consequences of Mr Churchill* (1925). The crux of his argument was that, since sterling was overvalued, British costs would have to be brought down through a mechanism which Churchill, misled by the authorities, did not properly understand. It could only be done by using bank-rate to squeeze profits, intensifying unemployment as the means by which these fundamental adjustments would take place. Thus the argument was essentially about market flexibility. Churchill, consistent with his long-standing faith in Free Trade, was still assuming that the economic system would adjust to the parity of $4.86 which he now imposed, and that the gold standard simply shackled Britain to the realities of international competitiveness. Keynes suggested that too much had changed since 1914, meaning that unemployment would not be a transitory side-effect of adjustment but a chronic symptom of disequilibrium.

There is no need to castigate the gold standard as the root cause of all Britain's economic difficulties in the late 1920s; but it did nothing to bring recovery at a time when the USA, for example, was enjoying a boom, while recovery in Britain remained as elusive as ever. Bank-rate, which had gone up to 5 per cent to launch the new parity, briefly dipped to 4 per cent on the strength of City sentiment but was back at 5 per cent by the end of 1925, and it stayed within half a point of this figure throughout the rest of the decade. The evidence of whether sterling was really overvalued is here; had it not been overvalued dear money would not have been needed, year in, year out.

Moreover, the deflationary effect of the policy can clearly be seen. Between 1924 and 1929, wholesale commodity prices fell by 17 per cent. In the same period the cost of living fell by more than 6 per cent. Money wages, however, hardly declined at all. One implication was benign: real wages, for those in work, rose from 11 per cent above their 1914 level in 1924 to 18 per cent above it five years later. The other implication spelt bad news for British industry and those who depended on it for jobs. The pressure of unemployment had not brought down wages to the extent required by the gold standard, and British costs accordingly remained uncompetitive. Modern estimates show that unemployment persisted in the range of 7 to 8 per cent. Since the level was higher in the insured occupations, the official figures, as published at the time, therefore showed unemployment at around 10 per cent.

With good cause, therefore, unemployment became a central issue in the politics of the period. Baldwin had offered to tackle it through tariffs in 1923. This approach was ruled out on electoral grounds in his new Government, except for the reinstatement of the McKenna duties, to which Churchill did not object. Otherwise his policy was constrained by the principles of sound finance, as traditionally conceived: Free Trade, the gold standard and balanced budgets. Given these assumptions, costs of production measured in sterling should have fallen to internationally competitive levels, so as to make sense of the ambitious parity of the pound at $4.86. But they did not. The Treasury privately complained that British workers were choosing unemployment instead; that trade unions insisted on maintaining existing levels of money wages, thus increasing real wages for those in work – at the expense of a million unemployed. The role of National Insurance in giving the unemployed a third option between work and starvation was also relevant. The principles of sound finance may have been as elegant as ever; it was their relevance to the real world that was now in question.

## BALDWIN IN POWER

Baldwin set the tone of the new Government. His was a new Conservatism, seeking to establish a moderate consensus in clear opposition to Labour but abjuring the strident rhetoric of the class war. His most famous utterance of these sentiments came in a speech in 1925, when the Commons was debating a private member's bill to abolish the trade unions' political levy, thus cutting the Labour Party's financial lifeline. Baldwin killed the bill in a wholly characteristic way, catching the ear of the House with a low-keyed emotional appeal, concluding: 'Give peace in our time, O Lord.' There is abundant testimony to the effects which he could achieve when on form, though print can hardly recapture the resonance of such addresses. Some were collected in the best-selling volume *On England* (1926), where he rhapsodized over 'the sight of a plough team coming over the brow of a hill, the sight that has been seen in England since England was a land, and may be seen in

England long after the Empire has perished and every works in England has ceased to function, for centuries the one eternal sight of England'.

Eternal? Baldwin was right to think that the Empire might perish, though he hardly foresaw that it would go out of business within forty years – barely surviving plough teams, and with a Conservative Government presiding over the obsequies. On paper at least, the Empire was at its fullest extent in the 1920s. Several of the former German colonies had been annexed under the peace treaties, with the League of Nations used to camouflage a division of the spoils between the victors. In west Africa, Britain and France partitioned Togoland and the Cameroons, but did so with an international mandate from the League to act as trustees. In east Africa, Britain got Tanganyika (and had even turned covetous eyes on Abyssinia for a moment) while German South West Africa was mandated to South Africa – which had conquered and occupied it during the war.

In the peace settlement possession inevitably made its own strong case: one which aided Britain in establishing a mandate over much of the Middle East. Here the Ottoman Empire's intervention in the war on the German side had been successfully countered, mainly by the traditional British resource of deploying the Indian Army. True, Britain had long occupied Egypt; but by the Armistice large tracts of territory, from Jerusalem and Damascus to Baghdad, had been conquered under General Allenby's command. The trouble was that, in the process, the British had given contradictory promises: to their French allies, promising them Syria; to their Arab allies, promising them much the same; and finally (the Balfour Declaration of ·1917) to the newly influential Zionist interest, promising a Jewish national home. In Paris, Lloyd George had wriggled out of these diverse commitments as best he could, coming out of the negotiations with new British mandates over Palestine and Iraq. The war aim of self-determination, which had seemed to spell the end of imperialism, had plainly not stopped the post-war expansion of the British Empire, which now covered one-quarter of the world.

But it covered it thinly. British control had always meant empire on the cheap, relying on bluff to shore up its prestige and power. The new strategy was to assimilate the new territories by invoking the new technology of air power, subduing tribesmen in the most cost-effective way yet devised. It was the making of the Royal Air Force. Meanwhile, on the ground, British officials were haplessly caught in simmering conflicts which threatened increasingly during the inter-war years to come to the boil (and often did so after the Second World War). Thus as High Commissioner for Palestine, the Liberal ex-minister Sir Herbert Samuel, the embodiment of disinterested rationality, sought to mediate between immigrant Jews and aggrieved Arab nationalists, leaning over backwards (as a Jew himself) to reconcile the irreconcilable. In India, too, the Montagu–Chelmsford reforms, implemented in 1919, sought to propitiate a rising tide of nationalism through an extension of representative government, while squaring the circle of imperial control.

As for the Dominions, their de facto independence was to be recognized in the fuller definition of Dominion status formulated in 1926, accepted by the imperial conference of 1930, and enacted as the Statute of Westminster in 1931. The crown was thereby acknowledged as the symbol of the free association of 'the British Commonwealth of Nations'. Thus the question of whether the Great War had reinvigorated the Empire, or pushed it into decline, could henceforth be ducked by pointing to the phoenix-like evolution of the Commonwealth. It was a concept which owed much to the Round Table group – often recruited from members of Milner's 'kindergarten' in South Africa, like Philip Kerr (Lord Lothian) and Lionel Curtis, author of *The Problem of the Commonwealth* (1916). In their formulation, the Commonwealth was a laudable example of international cooperation, claiming strong affinities with the League of Nations, and drawing support from the same ecumenical swathe of liberal opinion to which Baldwin now pitched his appeal.

Britain's real concerns remained focused on the Empire, where it had its hands full, perhaps its stomach too. This had been shown by Britain's readiness, at the Washington conference in 1921–2, to accept not only naval parity with the USA but the American condition that the Anglo-Japanese alliance must be abandoned. Resources for another naval race were simply unforthcoming, as Churchill made clear while he was Chancellor; indeed it was he who institutionalized the 'ten-year rule', meaning that defence planning should assume no major wars within that horizon. Britain's European role was therefore relatively attenuated. It saw itself as honest broker, sustaining the League of Nations, rather than as France's ally, exacting vengeance on Germany. As Foreign Secretary, Austen Chamberlain was given a lot of latitude and achieved a gratifying personal success at Locarno in 1925. This was essentially a completion of the work begun by Lloyd George to welcome back Germany as a full partner – 'no victor, no vanquished' – and secure German assent to the post-war settlement, notably mutual recognition of frontiers.

Detailed policy-making, abroad or at home, was simply not Baldwin's forte, any more than it had been Disraeli's. Moreover, his public image was not always the face seen by his colleagues, who were sometimes exasperated at his inconsistencies and his apparent lack of strategic grasp. In domestic policy, the Government depended overwhelmingly on Churchill and Neville Chamberlain.

Neville Chamberlain had learnt to love the Ministry of Health in 1923 and returned in 1924 for a five-year stint, with his plans already prepared. He had a string of measures ready, some of them on technical lines, drawing on an expertise in local government which was unrivalled in his party. Lloyd George's gibe, that Chamberlain had been a good lord mayor of Birmingham in a lean year, had some truth in it; but it also betrayed the disparaging attitude of the Westminster talking-shop for a minister whose executive grasp was seen to best advantage in Whitehall. Chamberlain was determined that a Conservative Government should show itself as fit as any Liberal or Labour Government to legislate on social questions.

Chamberlain took up pensions where Asquith and Lloyd George had left off. The withdrawal of older men from the labour force was to become one of the major social and economic changes of the twentieth century. Whereas in 1881 three out of four men aged over sixty-five were still at work, a century later nine out of ten had retired. It is tempting to see the Widows' and Old Age Pensions Act of 1925 as the hinge of this change. This was an extension of the National Insurance scheme, providing for contributory pensions to insured workers or their widows, with sixty-five instead of seventy henceforth established as the pensionable age. The 1931 census, for the first time, recorded a majority of men aged over sixty-five as retired. Yet the level of pension was hardly enough to provide an incentive for retirement, although it may have cushioned it; and it was not until after the Second World War that retirement was made a condition for drawing the old-age pension. Chamberlain's Act, significant as it was in recognizing the need for pensions, was following rather than setting a trend towards retirement at sixty-five.

What appealed to Chamberlain here was the administrative consolidation and the self-financing nature of the scheme in the long term.

What seized the imagination of his colleague Churchill was the development of Tory Democracy, as preached by his father, so as to attach the self-interest of millions of contributors to the well-being of the capitalist system. The aid of the Treasury was needed to finance the transition until the point in the future when contributions would balance outgoings, since benefits became payable immediately. Through such interdepartmental negotiations Churchill and Chamberlain, though not personally close, reached a good working relationship. This was seen to best effect in the quid pro quo eventually embodied in the Derating and Local Government Acts of 1928 and 1929.

Chamberlain wanted nothing less than a comprehensive reform of all local government, subsuming the old Poor Law structure within the ambit of omnicompetent local councils. It was a complement to the Education Act of 1902, which had abolished the ad hoc school boards; now the functions of the ad hoc Poor Law Guardians were likewise to be given to specialist committees of existing local councils. The Act thus fulfilled the ambition to break up the Poor Law, as declared by the Webbs in their minority report twenty years previously. Local councils were to provide specialist services for childcare and for health. Old people's homes were to replace the Poor Law's provision for aged paupers – though since the same buildings often continued in use, old people for a generation were to continue speaking of going (or not going) 'into the workhouse'.

The residual responsibility of the Poor Law – for the able-bodied destitute or unemployed – was given to new Public Assistance Committees, which local authorities were required to set up. This had the political attraction for Chamberlain of removing the hard-core unemployed, who had exhausted all benefits under the National Insurance scheme, from the ministrations of those Poor Law Guardians, in Labour-controlled areas, who had insisted on paying relatively high levels of relief. This practice, called Poplarism from the east London borough where it was prevalent, had not only bankrupted the Poor Law Unions in some of the unemployment blackspots but offered informal competition to the dole among claimants who often calculated which paid best. Chamberlain was now able to stamp out Poplarism as part of his grand design to clean up local government.

The design became even grander once Churchill got into the act. The fact that local government had long been financially dependent on central government gave the Chancellor his entrée. The old system was to give grants-in-aid from the Treasury for certain functions undertaken by local councils – so that the affluent areas which spent most got most, while the indigent, which needed most, got least. In place of this, Chamberlain's rational mind devised a plan for Treasury block grants, related to assessed needs, area by area. Churchill would not agree to such a simple adjustment of public funding. Since he had to find the money, it was his plan which took over.

Its origin lay in Churchill's frustration in face of persistent unemployment, which sound finance permitted him to tackle neither through tariffs nor through cheap money nor through devaluation nor through Budget deficits. He relied therefore on fiscal incentives on the supply side, to try to stimulate enterprise. Income tax, which had been reduced in Snowden's 1924 Budget from 5s (25 per cent) to 4s 6d (22.5 per cent), was further reduced by Churchill in 1926 to 4s (20 per cent), at which level it remained until 1930. His distinctive scheme, however, was to relieve industry of local taxation. Industry was exempted from local rates ('derated') by a full 100 per cent and railways by 50 per cent.

The shortfall in revenue for local government was made up from central government – by redesigning the block-grant arrangements which Chamberlain had first suggested as a far bigger fiscal merry-go-round. Moreover, those who lost on the roundabouts would win on the swings – that was guaranteed by Churchill's further provision that no local authority would suffer a net loss. The richer authorities, usually in Conservative areas, would not suffer in order to subsidize the depressed authorities, usually Labour. The political finesse of these arrangements can be gauged from the contrast with the comparable revolution in local-government finance, sixty years later: the ill-fated poll-tax experiment.

Initiated by Chamberlain, supported by Churchill, most of the Government's social programme worked out according to plan. But Baldwin's aspiration for 'peace in our time' was mocked by events. Although the Conservatives were determined to disentangle the state from responsibility for the coal industry, there proved to be no easy way of achieving this. The return to gold exacerbated the export difficulties in 1925 and prompted the mine-owners to cut wages. With the miners' union, under its intransigent leader A. J. Cook, now threatening a strike, the Government agreed to pay a subsidy while a Royal Commission reported. This task was put in the hands of Sir Herbert Samuel, fresh from Jerusalem. The Samuel Report, published in March 1926, endorsed rationalization of the pits into larger combines to secure a long-term future for the industry, but in the short term advised that there was no alternative to some reduction in wages. The passionate response of the miners' leader – 'not a penny off the pay, not a minute on the day' – showed that he was not on Samuel's plane, hardly on his planet.

The Government was let off the hook. Restive backbenchers who thought Baldwin soft had been worried that he might settle. The bad tactics of the miners' union, the bad grace of the mine-owners, the bad conscience of the TUC – perhaps the bad faith of the cabinet – now conspired to produce the long-heralded General Strike. It was actually selective rather than general. On 3 May 1926 the TUC brought out 1½ million key workers, mainly in energy and communications industries, in support of the miners. It is not clear what they hoped to achieve or how. A General Strike had often been regarded as a doomsday scenario, in which Government would be humbled by the might of organized labour. But the TUC leaders, like its general secretary Walter Citrine and Ernest Bevin of the Transport and General Workers' Union (TGWU), had no ambition or illusion of revolution; they were responding, like many of their members, to a sentiment of loyalty, a feeling that they could not decently let the miners down. The Government, by contrast, had a simple strategy forced upon it – to resist.

Churchill's combative instincts made him a prominent figure during the General Strike. Instead of sitting in 11 Downing Street, poring over the fine print of the next financial statement, he enjoyed a dizzy ten days as a newspaper editor, able to hold the front page whenever he dreamt up another bloodcurdling headline about the threat to constitutional government. His *British Gazette* had a virtual monopoly and exploited it without scruple to put the Government's point of view. Its distribution far outran that of the TUC's *British Worker*. The real competition was from the BBC, which Churchill wanted to take over too. Instead Reith stalled, Baldwin prevaricated; the worst that happened was that the Archbishop of Canterbury was kept off the air for fear that he might talk unseasonably about peace in our time. For many undergraduates the Strike was fun – the chance of a lifetime to drive a tram or, more rarely, act as an outrider for the march of the proletariat. The famous myth of the General Strike is that strikers and policemen played football – which they did, but only on the odd occasion, never repeated, rather like the Christmas truce in the trenches in 1914. In industrial areas where the issues were most pointed this was a real conflict while it lasted.

It only lasted for nine days. The TUC, desperate to call off an exercise that they could not win, seized on a compromise formula put forward by Samuel. The miners were thus again left to fight on, and did so with grim resolution, facing inevitable defeat. Once the Government had won, unexpected fissures appeared within the cabinet. It was now Churchill who spoke up for magnanimity, reaching out to offer an honourable retreat to a beaten foe; it was Baldwin who sat out the miners' strike until they were starved back, on the owners' terms, after a siege of six months. All told, 1926 was the worst year for industrial disputes in British history. More days were lost than in 1912, 1921 and 1979 put together. But it was the miners' strike, not the General Strike, which accounted for 90 per cent of the total.

The General Strike had an impact on each of the political parties. The Tories thenceforth had their tails up, and in 1927 Baldwin let his backbenchers have the sort of bill which he had vetoed in 1925, stipulating that trade unionists must 'contract in' if they wished to pay the political levy, not, as previously, simply 'contract out' if they were opposed. The Labour Movement, conversely, opted firmly for moderation. Bevin became the dominant figure in the TUC, and the parliamentary party sought to assert its independence. For the Liberals, too, the General Strike was a turning point, as the occasion of a transfer of the leadership from Asquith to Lloyd George.

Asquith had hung on as leader, despite his own defeat at Paisley in the 1924 General Election, partly because his supporters still could not bear the thought of Lloyd George, who now led the Liberal MPs in the Commons. The Earl of Oxford and Asquith (as he became) was by this stage a remote figure, into his mid-seventies. When his henchman Sir John Simon endorsed the Government line that the strike was unconstitutional, Lloyd George had had enough and broke ranks; moreover he carried with him even left Liberals, like Keynes, with personal loyalties to Asquith. So Lord Oxford finally bowed out; he died in 1928. The factional animosities in the party went deep and were never to be fully healed. Asquithian loyalists, increasingly looking to Simon for a lead, were to set up their own Liberal Council as a party within a party. The Lloyd George political fund, instead of being a boon to the hard-pressed finances, became a bone of contention between the new leader and the old guard of Asquithians, like Viscount (Herbert) Gladstone, back in charge of the party machine, twenty years on from his days of glory as Chief Whip. For all that, as one Asquithian had the grace to admit, 'when Lloyd George came back to the party, ideas came back to the party'.

Lloyd George succeeded in making the most of the Liberals' remaining assets. Labour might have the trade unions and the Tories might have the money, but the Liberals were confident that they still had the brains. The Liberal summer schools, which Lloyd George patronized, were one way to enlist the intellectuals; the Liberal Industrial Inquiry which he set up was another. Its report in 1928, known as the Liberal Yellow Book, was full of ideas – perhaps rather too full – about the current state of the British economy and about what could be done to revitalize it through Government coordination and support. Some of these suggestions were hammered into a manifesto, under the direction of Seebohm Rowntree, which was published in March 1929 with the title *We Can Conquer Unemployment*. It was built around Lloyd George's pledge to bring down unemployment to its pre-war level through a two-year programme of loan-financed public investment. The intellectual inspiration came from Keynes; the political leadership from Lloyd George.

Lloyd George's achievement, starting under a multiple handicap, was to seize the political initiative and put the Liberal policy agenda at the centre of the electoral battle. To be sure, there were also Labour proposals on unemployment, with which the young Oswald Mosley was prominently involved; but socialists proved better at castigating the evils of the capitalist system than explaining how to remedy them. Likewise, there were Conservative backbenchers like Harold Macmillan, the MP for the blighted industrial town of Stockton-on-Tees, who wanted action on unemployment. Furthermore, within the cabinet the case was covertly made for a development programme which might pre-empt Lloyd George, even though it meant abandoning the policy of sound finance to which Churchill was committed. His own advice to the cabinet was that a Conservative Government should not make a U-turn of this kind at the last moment. Rather than compete with Lloyd George, therefore, Churchill used his Budget speech in April 1929 to declare the established 'Treasury view': that it was impossible to achieve any net reduction in unemployment through state borrowing and state expenditure.

By this point a general election was in the offing. The Conservative

Government's record, especially on unemployment, was clearly to be the main issue. Baldwin opted for the slogan 'Safety First', which had been used in road-safety propaganda, and hoped to project his reassuring image in preference to his opponents' wild experiments, as he had done so successfully in 1924. Since then a Liberal revival had clearly occurred, though its scale remained in doubt. Two by-elections on successive days in March 1929 brought Liberal gains from the Conservatives, suggesting the favourable impact of the unemployment proposals. But though they remained at the centre of the campaign until polling day at the end of May, there is evidence of some faltering in the Liberal momentum, and of an even bigger last-minute swing back to the Conservatives from Labour.

The general election of 1929 was the first to be fought on a fully democratic franchise. Ever since 1918 the inequality between the male and female suffrage had been contentious. Fears about broadening the electorate had largely died down after an increase approaching 200 per cent had failed to produce any dramatic change. The Conservative Home Secretary, Sir William Joynson Hicks, rather inconsequentially committed the Government to legislation on equal suffrage, and, since it was unrealistic to disfranchise younger men by setting the age qualification at twenty-five, this meant bringing in the single and younger women hitherto excluded at a uniform age of twenty-one.

There is no reason to suppose that this 'flapper vote' hurt the Conservatives; rather, the pressure was on Labour to modify its male-orientated appeal. The electorate increased by over 30 per cent to nearly 29 million. Labour and Conservatives both polled over 8 million; the Conservatives got 300,000 more votes but Labour got more seats – 287 to 260. The Liberals polled over 5 million votes; their share of the poll, at 24 per cent, was nearly 6 per cent up on 1924, but plainly it was not high enough to break out of the third-party squeeze. It yielded only 59 MPs. Labour stood only 21 seats short of an absolute majority. 'Safety First' had been rejected; Baldwin resigned at once; a Labour Government took office, with the problem of unemployment to be addressed, if not conquered.

# 5

## Economic Blizzard
### 1929–37

### BRICKS AND MORTAR

A good investment was often said by the British to be 'as safe as houses'. House ownership had become socially widespread by the end of the nineteenth century, with working-class landlords as well as tenants. But the national figure for owner-occupiers was not very high before the First World War, only about 10 per cent of all dwellings. In an era when prices were fairly steady in the long term, it was not rational to acquire a house simply as a hedge against inflation. People of all social classes were content to rent their houses. Even the aristocracy, with their vast landed estates, might rent town houses for the season. Professional families did not see owning their own homes as a necessary part of keeping up appearances. Working-class families, especially in big cities, got used to 'flitting' between rented accommodation, whether to seek work, or slightly more adequate space, or cheaper rents. Conversely, home ownership was spread patchily over the country. Miners, like agricultural workers, characteristically lived in tied cottages made available by their employers; but textile workers in Lancashire and the West Riding of Yorkshire often bought their houses. If a two-up, two-down terrace house in Oldham might go for as little as £150, that represented a year's wages for a top-rate cotton spinner.

Mortgages had originally been developed by cash-strapped members of the landed interest as a means of raising funds on the security of the real property which they already owned. By the end of the Victorian era this device had been inverted, both financially and socially, so that funds could be advanced to prospective house-purchasers, who then paid off mortgages on the homes which they occupied. Instead of allowing improvident aristocrats to turn fixed capital into ready money, mortgages thus became the means by which thrifty artisans turned their own rent payments into capital. Some Victorian building societies were like cooperatives or friendly societies, run by their own members, bent on self-help through pooling their resources; and disbanding once they all had their own homes. What 'permanent' building societies did was to institutionalize this function, taking on new generations of members, not only as borrowers but as savers, earning a modest but steady return ultimately secured by a good portfolio of residential property, with interest paid net of income tax through mutually advantageous arrangements with the Inland Revenue.

One way or another, the British put a lot of money into bricks and mortar. Around the turn of the century, buildings and works accounted for upwards of half of all the new capital created annually. Though this proportion declined slightly in the Edwardian period, after the war it again stood at over half, and within this total it becomes possible to distinguish dwellings. In the 1920s houses represented about one-quarter of the country's annual fixed-capital formation, and by the mid-1930s over one-third. This tells us what people were prepared to invest; what did they get for their money? Housebuilding enjoyed a great boom around the turn of the century – 1 million new houses in seven years – though falling back to little more than 50,000 a year just before the war, which brought a savage cutback in construction. By the late 1920s, however, a rate of 200,000 a year was normal.

The big changes came after the First World War, when the aspiration for home ownership increasingly became a middle-class norm. More than one in three of the new houses built between the wars and, by 1939, well over a quarter of all dwellings, of whatever age, were owner-occupied: a figure that did not change substantially over the next twenty years. Building societies adjusted to the pressure of demand by becoming more user-friendly, extending the normal term of a mortgage to twenty years and making it easier for customers to put down small deposits on suitable properties – usually newly built houses which satisfied current building regulations. Suburban housing developments were now targeted firmly at mass owner-occupation rather than renting. Those who could afford to buy were thus encouraged to move out of older properties in town centres, which inevitably tended to move downmarket and were increasingly seen as the visible sign of the housing problem, to be solved by slum clearance. For half a century, until the tide of conservation turned, some fine urban domestic architecture from earlier centuries was at risk from philanthropic demolitionists.

Housing became a hot political issue after the First World War, which intensified the housing shortage by enforcing cuts on the supply-side while the pent-up demand for decent accommodation soared. The Lloyd George coalition was remembered for its promise of 'homes fit for heroes' – bitterly remembered, as it turned out. The sensitivity of housebuilding to changes in interest rates was accentuated by the post-war growth of owner-occupation. The rise in bank rate to 7 per cent in 1920–21 spelt the doom of the post-war housing programme; and the dear money of the 1920s continued to inhibit building. Nonetheless the state was now in the housing business. The Conservatives preferred to offer subsidies to private enterprise, trusting that the benefits would trickle down to the needy once the market was stimulated; about 400,000 houses were built in the 1920s under legislation which Neville Chamberlain introduced. Labour directed subsidy towards municipal provision for rent to the working class, and in ten years the Wheatley Housing Act of 1924 produced over half a million 'council houses', often on large green-field estates on the outskirts of towns. By 1939 10 per cent of households were council tenants. The total capital expenditure of local authorities, which had generally been between £20 and £30 million a year before the war, now usually exceeded £100 million. The main difference was housing, which accounted for more than one-third of this total (more than half in Scotland).

For county councils, the other major item in the capital budget was roads. Local-authority investment in highways and bridges had been around £2 million a year before the war; in the late 1920s it was nudging £10 million. The reason is obvious. In 1913 the number of private cars for the first time exceeded 100,000; in 1922 it exceeded 300,000 and in 1930 1 million, with more than another million licences held for motorcycles and goods vehicles. Motor-vehicle duties produced £7 million a year for the Exchequer in 1921, five times as much by 1939. Notionally these revenues went into the Road Fund (established by Lloyd George in 1909) at least until Churchill raided it to balance his budget in 1927; but the county councils, who were actually responsible for roads, had no claim to the money beyond what they could negotiate in Treasury grants.

The impact of the internal combustion engine was felt in many ways. The slogan 'Safety First' was used in campaigns to cut the rising toll of road accidents, and establishing liability gave new prominence to the law of tort. Increasing numbers of drivers were convicted of motoring offences – nearly half a million a year by 1938, 60 per cent of all convictions. In an era when criminal statistics had fallen to a historic low, this was a major social change. Previously the police had spent much of their time in petty harassment of the working classes on the streets for moral lapses – sex, drink and gambling – which generally went unpunished when money bought privacy and discretion. With their new motor cars, the middle classes for the first time found themselves systematically on the wrong side of the law.

In 1920 the new Ministry of Transport started classifying roads and numbering the main routes, like spokes in a wheel with London as the hub. The Great North Road to Edinburgh became the A1, the Old Kent Road to Dover the A2, and so on. This looked fine on the new maps produced for motorists. The trouble was that many of these 'first-class' roads were second-rate. They straggled through villages which resented the intrusion of motor traffic; ancient bridges and town centres inevitably created bottlenecks. G. K. Chesterton might celebrate the fancy that 'the rolling English drunkard made the rolling English road' but it left something to be desired when seen as part of the infrastructure of a modern industrial nation.

The German response, under Hitler, was the creation of the autobahn network; in the USA the public works of the New Deal were to be distinguished by the engineering of great modern bridges. Such plans proved too grandiose for the British. The politicians who urged them, notably Lloyd George for the Liberals and Oswald Mosley for Labour, were themselves rather suspect for their Napoleonic ambitions, which irked solid citizens who had no desire to be dictated to. Likewise civil servants tended to dismiss the supporting arguments from Keynes as too clever by half.

What Keynes was saying in 1929-30 was not actually so different from other economists, though he said it louder and more insistently. The point was that the economy was out of balance (disequilibrium), as shown by the fact that 1 million workers were unemployed. The reason for this must have been that British costs were uncompetitive; and, failing other means of getting them down, that meant that wages were too high. Virtually all economists would have agreed with this analysis; where they disagreed was over the remedy. A few said that wage cuts were therefore the only solution. Most, however, agreed with Keynes in saying that reductions in labour costs would indeed be a solution if they were readily forthcoming, but that in the real world wages had failed to adjust fully to the parity of sterling imposed by the gold standard, and therefore other expedients had to be found.

Everyone could see that wages were 'sticky' – they would not adjust. But sterling was also sticky – it could not adjust. So the British economy was trapped between these two unadjustable prices. Since something had to give, unemployment rose. This is what Keynes told the Macmillan Committee on Finance and Industry, which the Labour Government set up in 1929, and essentially it is what he wrote in his book *Treatise on Money* (1930). He looked for a remedy which accepted the gold standard as a political fait accompli, which accepted the current wage level as an economic fact of life, and instead sought to stimulate the domestic economy so as to create employment. Keynes's own preference was public investment, which was something the Government could control. This would have several objectives, of which the most immediate was to give jobs through public-works projects. But the broader aim was to mobilize savings which currently were not finding their way into real productive investment ('bricks and mortar') and thus kick-start the economy by making up for this shortfall.[1] Furthermore, he urged, whether or not the other objectives were fully achieved, such schemes would leave Britain with a modernized infrastructure in the form of roads and bridges.

Historians at one time supposed that a Keynesian programme of this kind was bound to do the trick and portrayed its opponents in a poor light; but nowadays the poor light is more often reserved for Keynes, who has been accused of facile over-optimism. To be sure, able civil servants, like Sir Richard Hopkins of the Treasury, approached the problem not by simply reiterating the dogmatic 'Treasury view' of 1929 but with a hard-won administrative experience from which Keynes had something to learn (as he came to see). It is true, moreover, that even a public-works programme on the scale he advocated would have had a limited impact on unemployment. But in 1929, it should be remembered, with 1 million out of work, the aspiration was also limited. Maybe this total could not have been cut by 600,000, as Lloyd George pledged; but the Labour Government's own programme, which was half as big, seems to have got halfway there, according to modern

---

1. Exactly how Keynes defined saving and investment at this time, so that he could claim that they were not necessarily equal, was a topic for much dispute among economists. The salient point is that by investment, as he told the Macmillan Committee, he meant 'bricks and mortar'; and I use the term in this sense, to cover all investment in new plant or infrastructure.

estimates. In the two years to the summer of 1931 public-works schemes costing more than £100 million were brought into operation. The real tragedy was that the scale of the unemployment problem had by then escalated owing to the world slump.

Failing a British New Deal, road-building proceeded by traditional methods, though on an increased scale. A national responsibility for 'trunk roads' was assumed in 1936, a step towards the idea of an integrated transport network. At the bottom of the slump, moreover, local authorities were investing nearly twice as much in highways and bridges as in the 1920s. Furthermore, their budget for housebuilding was also maintained. To some extent, then, the construction industry could look to public investment to tide it through lean times. But its real salvation, in the absence of major public works, came through private, market-led demand for bricks and mortar.

Housebuilding did not drop below 200,000 even in the worst year (1930) and it averaged 360,000 a year in the years 1934–8. Naturally the new houses were built in places where people wanted to live and where they could afford to pay for them. The high-wage regions of Greater London and Greater Birmingham saw a disproportionate growth – or rather saw an adaptation of these conurbations to the new economic and demographic pattern of the mid twentieth century, leaving the old industrial North behind. Though 'ribbon development' along the main roads out of towns was to provide an object lesson in the need for planning to prevent erosion of the countryside, suburban development was not wholly unplanned. There was a major investment in the infrastructure of Greater London. The Metropolitan Railway came up with the concept of 'Metroland', promoting suburban development in London's north-west suburbs. And the purposeful extension of the Underground rail network left its mark, not least through the influence of its commercial manger, Frank Pick, who came to exercise enormous patronage in sponsoring clean, spare modern design in everything from posters to new stations for London Transport (including its well-known circular logo).

It was this new England of sprawling suburbia – in contradistinction to the two old Englands of declining industrial North and historic rural South – which the novelist J. B. Priestley spied, with mixed feelings, in his *English Journey* (1933). At its best, it showed a new consciousness of the importance of modern design in urban and commercial settings. The burgeoning 'picture palaces' of the period did not generally evoke the rococo extravagance of traditional theatre-building, all gilt and red plush; instead massive modern structures, loosely derivative from ancient Egyptian models, were brought to a hundred high-street Luxors or Odeons, all showing the same film. The functional elegance of the international style, derived from the Bauhaus, also left a distinctive mark, even if it was only the use of steel-framed windows, with the gimmick of turning them around corners. It was the Americanization of the chromium-plated suburbs, spawned around London, which struck George Orwell, leaving him not only cold but nostalgically musing about green fields in his novel *Coming Up for Air* (1938). The Hoover factory on the A40 out of west London shows what he meant: it fitly represents the industrial archaeology of the period (1932–8), set amid residential development which was home alike to some of its affluent workers and to the customers for the consumer durables, from electric irons to vacuum cleaners, which it supplied.

New housing estates, especially council houses, were often built to a uniform plan, exploiting economies of scale both in design and in mass production. While well-known architects scrambled for prestige commissions, it was David Adam, on the staff of the building firm Laings, who designed more actual houses than any of the big names. 'Stock-broker's Tudor' became a term of art at the top of the market for a rustic idiom which was derived from the garden suburbs of the early part of the century. But it was susceptible of infinite and ingenious adaptation, to suit every pocket. The suburbs of the 1930s offered solid family homes with gardens and usually space for garages. The semi-detached house symbolized the bargain that was being struck between genteel aspirations and cost-effective accommodation. There was more good basic design in such houses than Osbert Lancaster's telling satires on 'bypass variegated' might suggest; in the late twentieth century it was thirty-year-old tower blocks not sixty-year-old semis which were unloved by those who had to live in them. For many workers in employment the dream of home ownership came true, because of a combination of developments. Smaller families were a factor; so were higher real incomes; but what tipped the balance was the reduced cost of a mortgage in the 1930s, which was transformed into an era of cheap money. This only happened after Britain had been forced off the gold standard.

## CRISIS

The fate of the second Labour Government was bound up, to a degree unprecedented in British history, with the performance of the economy. In 1929, when Labour came in, high unemployment was already the key issue. At that time, it could be blamed on the capitalist system; but since the Government had neither a plan for socialist transformation nor a parliamentary majority, such talk served largely as an alibi for inaction. Or it could be blamed on Free Trade; this many Conservatives did privately, though publicly they were temporarily inhibited by having to defend Churchill's (Free Trade) record at the Treasury. Or it could be blamed on the return to the gold standard; but reversing the painful decision of 1925 was not advocated even by its arch-critic Keynes, who instead set about devising expedients for managing the consequences. Or, finally, unemployment could be blamed on the economy's senescent rigidities; but the problems of wage stickiness, and of structural unemployment in old industries that were now past it, were easier to identify than to remedy.

One way or another, the weakness of the UK's competitive position stood out. After all, world trade was buoyant; the USA was forging ahead. The Wall Street crash in the autumn of 1929, however, suddenly ended the American boom and a cumulative contraction in world trade took hold in 1930. MacDonald called it an 'economic blizzard'.

It meant that economic depression was no longer a peculiar British problem but part of a world problem, bringing cyclical unemployment on top of pre-existing structural unemployment. This made it more difficult to find a solution along orthodox lines, by improving competitiveness, since even if British exports somehow managed to cut costs, their foreign markets were now impoverished. Previously it had been domestic supply which was inelastic, unable to stretch to meet the prices which overseas customers were prepared to pay. Now international demand became inelastic, unlikely to expand much whatever price reduction was made. The assumptions of Free Trade, underpinned by the self-adjusting mechanisms of the gold standard, suddenly looked vulnerable. Before the war, the necessary adjustments had generally been easy for Britain; since 1925 they had proved hard to make; by 1930 they were beginning to look impossible.

But though an orthodox policy now looked fallible, the economic blizzard simultaneously made it more difficult to tackle unemployment with an unorthodox policy – or at least one which ignored the international dimension. Bad times naturally depressed tax revenues while increasing government commitments through the dole. Worries about the budget deficit, and even about the pound sterling itself, highlighted the importance of confidence. The City's reflexes were all for belt-tightening – usually other people's belts – not for a further increase in public expenditure. In hard times, where was the money to be found? Saying that it would all be financed by loans only made matters worse; and, whatever the rationality of these fears, such a lack of confidence could prejudice the Government's credit if it were to seek a sum like £200 million for road-building. A run on the pound was seen as the horror of horrors. Moreover, public works might have measured up to the challenge of unemployment in 1929, when its level stood at around around 7 per cent; but in 1931 and 1932 it averaged over 15 per cent.

These statistics indicate a major recession, with unemployment rising in all parts of the country, not just in the old industrial black spots. But the problem looked even more frightening to contemporaries because the 'headline' figures for unemployment, now regularly published in the newspapers, covered only insured workers, who were in occupations particularly susceptible to cyclical fluctuation. The public had got used to unemployment figures of 10 per cent in the late 1920s: a bit more each winter, a bit less each summer. In 1930 the monthly average exceeded 16 per cent, rising to over 20 per cent for the next three years running. These figures inevitably generated concern – not only about the plight of the unemployed but about the cost of maintaining them.

'Work or maintenance' was Labour's slogan, going back to the Right-to-Work bills of the early part of the century. In practice the emphasis fell on the second, reflecting the fact that Labour's constituency in industrial Britain was immediately at risk, whether or not government proved able to master the underlying economic forces. The assumptions which the 1920 Insurance Act made about average unemployment had long since been invalidated, yet the continued payment of the 'dole', which successive Governments extended piecemeal to groups of unemployed workers who had exhausted their entitlement to benefit, showed the political popularity of the insurance principle – or rather the popular revulsion against falling back on the Poor Law. In an effort to shore up the system in 1927, the Conservatives had accepted the proposals of an all-party inquiry (the Blanesburgh Report) aimed at

putting the payment of benefit on a sound financial basis by introducing more realistic actuarial assumptions. Meanwhile, purely as a
transitional measure, until prosperity returned, the dole would again be
extended. In hindsight, this stored up double trouble, since the unanticipated failure of the upturn, followed by an intensified downturn,
mocked the notion that the scheme could now balance its books; while
'transitional' benefit further institutionalized the dole.

This was the bad situation which the Labour Government inherited.
It acted quickly – to make things worse, at any rate for the National
Insurance fund. The borrowing limits on the scheme, under pressure
from the numbers of long-term unemployed on the dole, were progressively relaxed, as were the conditions under which it could be claimed.
No longer did the onus of proof rest on claimants to establish that they
were 'genuinely seeking work' (as well as being registered at the labour
exchange). These changes undoubtedly had some effect in pushing up
the unemployment statistics, which showed increases from 1.5 million in
January 1930 to over 2 million by July and 2.5 million by the end of the
year. To infer that they also pushed up unemployment, by removing an
incentive to find work, is another matter. It is equally plausible to infer
that authentic claimants, who had previously been cheated of relief by
arbitrary tests, now got their due. There is no reason to suppose that
large numbers of people started living off the state as a preferred way
of life, though there is evidence that clients maximized the support they
could obtain from the competing agencies of National Insurance and
new public assistance committees (which had taken over responsibility
for the residual unemployed when the Poor Law was wound up in 1929).
The truth is that, whatever the administrative flaws in the system, or the
marginal disincentives it created, the shocking increase in the number
of men who were on the dole was driven by the slump itself.[1]

The workshop of the world, built on Free Trade, had fallen on hard
times. In this context, it was little wonder that protectionist ideas

---

1. For women the picture is not so clear. The number of insured men continued to rise
every year during the slump from just under 9 million in 1930 to 9.5 million in 1935; but
the number of insured women, which peaked at 3.58 million in 1931, declined slightly
to 3.53 million by 1935. Women were thus a quarter of the insured workforce and
accounted for 25 per cent of those registered unemployed in 1930. But by 1932 only 12
per cent of the registered unemployed were women. This was mainly an effect of
the Anomalies Act, passed in the dying weeks of the Labour Government in 1931,
in tightening the conditions under which married women could claim benefit. Thus

resurfaced. Lord Beaverbrook seized his chance to relaunch Imperial Preference. Since talk of Tariff Reform had always upset the electors, the great newspaperman now started talking of Empire Free Trade instead. The *Daily Express* was joined by Lord Rothermere's *Daily Mail* in this initiative, masquerading for a time as the United Empire Party, but really the hobby horse of two press barons. Baldwin saw that there was a protectionist wind blowing in the Conservative Party, and was increasingly free to trim his sails once his restive colleague Churchill had virtually jumped ship. So Baldwin made concessions on policy, talking of safeguarding industry and putting food taxes to a referendum, but stood his ground in asserting his own leadership. Indeed he turned the tables on Beaverbrook and Rothermere by making their presumptuous demands the issue in rallying his party's support. The by-election at St George's Westminster in March 1931, when a dissident Conservative candidate was put up, allowed Baldwin to administer the *coup de grâce*. Borrowing a phrase from his cousin Kipling, he denounced the press lords for aiming at 'power without responsibility – the prerogative of the harlot throughout the ages'.

Shakily supported by the Liberals, the Government remained firm at least in its commitment to Free Trade. Philip Snowden, as Chancellor of the Exchequer, was as firm in the faith as his predecessor Churchill – firmer as it turned out. Snowden gave the axioms of financial rectitude the stiffening of an inflexible Nonconformist conscience; he was determined to vindicate Labour's reputation for financial responsibility; his worry was what to do about the gaping budget deficit created by the dole. J. H. Thomas, as Lord Privy Seal, presided with initial bravado over a ministerial committee charged with tackling unemployment. Its fitful activities had the effect on its junior member, Mosley, of demonstrating that the old men and the old methods would get nothing done.

The veteran socialist George Lansbury had free-spending instincts, as his involvement in Poplarism had showed; as Commissioner of Works, he and the Scottish Secretary, Thomas Johnston, sided with Mosley against Thomas, in the committee. The argument came to a head during 1930. Mosley was a dashing figure whose impatience to tackle unemployment induced him to advocate a revolution in the

---

women who would have been willing to work were being pushed off the register. The official figures, which overstate men's unemployment, to this extent *understate* women's unemployment.

structure of government. When a plan for a new bypass around a town was formulated it had to endure a cautious Treasury appraisal of its cost-effectiveness and an endless series of negotations with the several local authorities who would be responsible for surveying the route, acquiring the land and building the road itself. Mosley wanted to create his own bypass – around the Whitehall traffic jam. He produced a memorandum for the cabinet, proposing a dirigiste economic strategy which rode roughshod over the austere traditions upheld by the British Treasury. The Mosley memorandum proposed cutting the workforce by raising the school-leaving age and reducing the retirement age; then using easier credit to stimulate the economy behind a tariff wall, with special arrangements for imperial trade.

Mosley's response to its rejection was his resignation from the Government in May 1930 and his subsequent campaign to rally sufficient support in the Labour Party to impose his views. At the party conference in October he came close to winning the vote, but already the support he received for his proposals was being compromised by suspicion of his domineering personality. A manifesto he published in December 1930 drew minority Labour support (as well as some covert sympathy from others like Keynes and Harold Macmillan) but the New Party which he went on to launch was seen by his respectable supporters as a false step – and Mosley's subsequent lurch into fascism as a reprehensible one. With a brilliant parliamentary career in ruins, he took to the streets (some said the gutter).

Whereas, ever since Lloyd George's pledge to conquer unemployment in March 1929, the argument had been mainly about public works, after Mosley's resignation the argument was mainly about tariffs. As prime minister, Ramsay MacDonald had created the Economic Advisory Council to offer expert advice; and its committee of economists, with Keynes as chairman, produced a report in the autumn of 1930 which endorsed a series of expedients, of which tariffs proved much more controversial than public works. Such policies were tainted by the support of Mosley and Beaverbrook. Though MacDonald himself brooded on the alternatives, he knew that any change of course would involve the loss of his Chancellor, a pillar of Free Trade. Still, the march of protectionist ideas in 1930–31 made more headway than in the whole of the previous quarter-century. It was the unlikely sources from which they now gained support that was significant. This was not just the familiar song from the industrialist lobby but a swelling chorus from the City of London, academic economists, trade unionists, even partisan Liberals who had now lost faith in the old cries of Free Trade.

The Government stumbled on. It paid some of its debts to its supporters, for example the Coal Mines Act of 1930 which traded shorter hours to please the miners against cartelization to help the owners. The Agricultural Marketing Act of 1931 could also be seen as loosely corporatist; it was the work of Christopher Addison, ex-supporter of Lloyd George and ex-scapegoat, and it set up marketing boards with price-fixing powers. Herbert Morrison, Labour's party boss in London, made his mark as Minister of Transport by bringing in proposals for setting up London Transport as a public corporation to take over the capital's bus, tram and tube operations. The fact that the measure was actually enacted by the successor National Government in 1933 suggests its lack of pronounced ideological content but is equally a tribute to its administrative rationale.

What the Government lacked was a strategy. Spurning that offered by Mosley, it then started talking to Lloyd George, who was likewise never stumped for ideas. At best this offered the promise of support from the Liberals for an agreed programme. The talk now was of tackling unemployment, not conquering it. The real trouble was that by the autumn of 1930 Lloyd George was unable to deliver solid support even if policy agreement proved possible. Sir John Simon, a survivor of Asquith's cabinet, had never been happy with either the leadership of Lloyd George or an accommodation with Labour; now he rejected both, making it clear that he and his group of Liberal MPs could not be counted on. What Lloyd George got from the Government was the introduction of an Electoral Reform bill, providing for the alternative vote, which would have helped shore up the Liberals' parliamentary representation to some extent. This was a suffecent inducement to keep most Liberal MPs in line for most of the time until the summer of 1931, when the bill was eviscerated by the House of Lords.

In February 1931, however, there were parliamentary ructions, with more serious implications in train. Faced with Conservative attacks on its wasteful expenditure – the dole again – the Government accepted a Liberal amendment setting up a committee to report on economies. It was the Geddes Axe all over again. Snowden, exasperated by his own backbenchers, hoped that this would protect his back; in fact it opened his flank. For the committee, under Sir George May of the Prudential Assurance Company, took a stern auditor's view of its responsibilities.

It opened the government's books, briskly insisting that they should balance, just like any responsible firm. One liability which ought to be met out of income, most of the auditors agreed, was the annual provision for the sinking fund, which paid off the national debt. Modern statistics show that revenue still covered government expenditure, as it had in every year since 1921. But this is with hindsight, and without allowing for a sinking-fund transfer, which modern conventions would treat as a residual balancing item, not a binding commitment. Even by the standards of the time, especially by classing all expenditure on unemployment relief as a charge on income, the bottom-line figure the May Committee came up with was exaggerated: a prospective budget deficit of no less than £120 million.

This was the shock-horror figure flashed around the world when the May Report was published on 31 July 1931. It came at a delicate moment; for two months banks had been crashing all over Europe; Germany stood on the brink of financial collapse; the May Report immediately imported the crisis to London. It demanded total cuts of £96 million, two-thirds to come from unemployment benefit. In a series of meetings during August, a majority in the Labour cabinet reluctantly agreed to cuts, though not on this draconian scale. MacDonald and Snowden, who had been empowered to talk to the leaders of the Opposition parties, briefed them all too fully: not just about the total agreed so far but about the further target at which they aimed. This ruled out compromise on any lower figure; yet consent to a higher figure was not forthcoming from the cabinet.

Here was a major political crisis; now it interlocked with a financial crisis that forced the pace. The pound was under strain; the Bank of England needed a loan from New York; its agent J. P. Morgan reported that the conditions would be an economy package which satisfied the Opposition parties. Since everything turned on confidence, a Labour Government which did not inspire confidence on Wall Street was not in a strong position. This was a fact of life, not a 'bankers' ramp' (which is how it went down in Labour mythology). It was not a precise figure of economies that mattered, still less one that the bankers specified: it was any total that would, in effect, satisfy the leaders of the Conservative Party. Since they believed in economy and knew the Government's breaking-point, it was hardly likely that they would let their opponents off a hook of their own devising. The only conspiracy was that bankers' instincts and Conservatives' prejudices naturally conspired together.

The real dilemma was MacDonald's. After a lifetime given to building up the Labour Party, he was not alone in his perplexity over how to build Jerusalem during an economic blizzard. He had never been in thrall to the axioms of sound finance, like Snowden; he had listened to the economists and made the Treasury respond to Keynes; he had explored the alternatives, albeit hesitantly. But in August 1931, what alternative was there to an orthodox emergency programme? The TUC came up with a package at the last moment, influenced by Ernest Bevin, whose scepticism about the gold standard had been tutored through his membership of the Macmillan Committee. The fact is that the Government now had to face the consequences of its policy of drift and this meant the trenchant logic of deflation. The alternative logic was devaluation, setting a lower parity against gold; this was not seriously considered, any more than it had been in 1925. The cabinet finally split down the middle. Since the economic imperative was clear to MacDonald, he was determined to do the right thing politically: to save the country, to salvage his self-respect and, he liked to think, to preserve Labour's credentials as a fit party of government.

The upshot was that when MacDonald had to tender the Labour Government's resignation on 24 August, he accepted the King's commission to form the National Government instead. The constitutional prerogatives of the King were actively used to promote this outcome, which George V welcomed, but the shots were called by the party leaders. For Labour, MacDonald knew that he could count on Snowden; Thomas and the Lord Chancellor, Sankey, were also in the new cabinet. For the Conservatives, Baldwin's decision to accept the Lord Presidency rather than insist on the premiership was crucial; and he accepted too that there would be only four Conservatives in the new cabinet of ten. This left two places for the Liberals, who had been led through the crisis by Sir Herbert Samuel, since Lloyd George was out of action with a prostate operation. (He thus missed his last big chance, in just the sort of crisis which had always brought out the best in him; and Churchill too was excluded.)

The initiative had passed to the Conservatives; but they were glad enough of the Government's National credentials to carry the dreaded economy proposals. Snowden's budget in September raised taxes; and a linked economy measure proposed a range of cuts in public salaries and 10 per cent off all unemployment benefits (not the 20 per cent of the May Report). True, the unemployed would feel this even more keenly than high-court judges, the lower ranks in the armed forces more than their officers. Indeed when able seamen at the naval base of Invergordon heard on the radio that they faced nominal cuts of up to 25 per cent (as against 7 per cent for admirals) they retaliated by refusing to muster. Again the news flashed round the world – mutiny in the British fleet! There were two main effects. The Government limited all its cuts to 10 per cent. While this was hardly likely to be popular among those affected, it should be remembered that one of the effects of the slump was a fall in the cost of living by 10 per cent since 1929. This may have helped account for subsequent public acquiescence.

The second effect of the Invergordon 'mutiny' was to trigger a sterling crisis. The credits from New York and Paris, which the National Government negotiated, were already under pressure; by mid-September they were being eaten up daily in a new run on the pound. At this point the Bank of England finally capitulated to brute facts by abandoning the gold standard. The National Government, which had been formed primarily to save the pound sterling, survived this collapse of its rationale. Instead, the crisis atmosphere seems to have rallied support to a Government which promised to take a grip on the situation. The ground was prepared for an imminent general election – the other eventuality which the formation of a National Government had been supposed to avoid.

On 21 September 1931 Britain left the gold standard. Like the Royal Navy, this had stood as a symbol of British pre-eminence; but no longer could Britannia rule the waves of currency speculation. At a stroke, the historic parity of sterling at $4.86 was no more; by the end of the year it was around $3.40. The consolation was that, once it had found its own level, sterling did not have to be supported by dear money; by June 1932 it was safe to reduce bank rate to 2 per cent. Confidence, moreover, had been restored by abandoning, not maintaining, the gold standard. By accident, the National Government found what the Labour Government had sought in vain: a policy which would allow the British economy to recover.

## CHURCH AND STATE

The rhetoric of politics still had a strong flavour of the Bible and the Book of Common Prayer. Philip Snowden's career had been founded on his 'Come-to-Jesus' style of oratory. In Lloyd George's case, this was the survival of form rather than substance, long after he had ceased to share the beliefs of the Dissenting preachers of whose art he remained a connoisseur. Churchill, likewise, had no real attachment to doctrinal Christianity: rather, a strong providential sense in his own and his country's destiny, for which the cadences of common worship were sometimes the right vehicle. The words for which Baldwin was most often remembered – 'Give peace in our time, O Lord' – were not just well chosen for the occasion but were the expression of a deeper and increasingly explicit Christian world view, underlying his familiar rural imagery. In opposition from August 1931, the Labour Party had three leaders in quick succession: first Arthur Henderson, who still carried the mien of a Methodist lay preacher; then George Lansbury, a pious Anglican High Churchman; finally Clement Attlee, whose undemonstrative manner (and taciturn agnosticism) gave little clue to the fervent attachment to a Christian Socialist ethic which his favourite brother Tom had been influential in fostering.

All these men, of course, were Victorians, brought up when Mr Gladstone stalked the land. They had all cut their teeth in the politics of a period when the Nonconformist conscience could not lightly be flouted and when Anglican opposition to the Liberals' Welsh Church Bill gave the language its longest, if most factitious, word (antidisestablishmentarianism). Even so, such survivals from the religious bedrock of Victorian politics are a warning against exaggerating the speed and extent of secularization in the twentieth century. Throughout the United Kingdom, older people continued to vote in ways that expressed the sectarian loyalties of the era in which they grew up. The religious affiliations of an earlier generation left a long-lasting residue.

Because population increased so fast throughout the nineteenth century, virtually all forms of organized Christianity could pride themselves on their ever-expanding numbers. This may have been statistically naive but it was psychologically important in reassuring the Established Church that theirs was not a losing battle and in encouraging sects which set a high value on proselytization that they were successfully spreading the word. There was, too, a straightforwardly competitive aspect to the numbers game, which had been fuelled by the only official religious census in 1851. This showed that about half the population of churchgoing age actually attended; and that those who did were split, again roughly half and half, between Anglicans and Nonconformists, with a small remnant of Roman Catholics. The shock at the time had been that there were so few attenders and so many Nonconformists – which may simply show that both Christianity and the Establishment were taken for granted. Subsequent statistics are not directly comparable, but figures for Church membership (a more rigorous threshold), calculated as a proportion of the population, give a measure of density from year to year. This is a sort of archaeological trench through time, bisecting the big dig through the strata of 1851, thus tracking the extent of subsequent change.

What is immediately apparent is that organized religion, and particularly the Church of England, held its ground more effectively than the literary evidence about a late-Victorian crisis of faith might suggest. True, the Nonconformists stopped expanding relative to population in the 1880s and their absolute numbers first teetered towards decline in the 1910s. But the number of Easter communicants in the Church of England formed as big a proportion of the (much increased) population at the start of the First World War as it had done at the beginning of Victoria's reign. Moreover Anglican density, measured as a proportion of the English population aged fifteen years and over, then declined slowly, from its peak of 12 per cent in 1910 to 10 per cent by 1940 and around 7 per cent until the 1960s. The nearest equivalent calculation for the Church of Scotland gives it a density of about 35 per cent in the 1930s, and still over 30 per cent in the 1960s. Putting the figures for the whole of Great Britain together, it is clear that the Nonconformists suffered the biggest and earliest losses; by 1966 they were little more than half as strong as in 1901, whereas it was after 1970 that the established Churches saw their sharpest decline.

In fact the only denomination to gain over the period was the Roman Catholic Church. It is hardly too much to say that during the twentieth century Great Britain lost its historic identity as a Protestant nation. Except in Northern Ireland, the old anti-popish bogeys (such as the flourishing Victorian mythology about convents) began to look like period pieces. Catholic France was no threat but an ally in two world wars against Germany; and when British propaganda told of Belgian nuns being violated by (Protestant) Prussian soldiers, people knew whose side they were supposed to be on. Francophile writers like Hilaire Belloc had already found a public, as in his charming travelogue *The Path to Rome* (1902), and later went in for some extravagant special pleading on behalf of an embattled reading of English history where, above all, the Reformation was not the Good Thing that generations of children had been taught. G. K. Chesterton, as Belloc's co-religionist and comrade-in-arms since the Edwardian period, shared much in his outlook: a large and flamboyant man of letters, who confronted the puritan ethic of industrial capitalism with romantic views about the superiority of pubs and peasants. His most memorable fictional creation, Father Brown, brought the insights of the confessional into the world of the whodunit.

If Chesterton and Belloc carried an essentially Edwardian air, there were now young Catholic novelists writing in a wholly different idiom: oblique, ironical, self-consciously modern, understated, flippant, worldly. It was in this guise that Evelyn Waugh made such a splash from the time of his first best-seller, *Decline and Fall* (1928). From modest origins in the professional classes, he reinvented himself after Oxford, with a conversion to Catholicism which showed him, from the time of *A Handful of Dust* (1934), championing the small recusant remnant of the English aristocracy who had clung loyally to the old religion since the Reformation. With beguiling deftness he showed their grace and stoicism – rising to fortitude later with Guy Crouchback in the *Sword of Honour* trilogy (1962) – as they maintained a way of life that was constantly threatened but constantly English too. A year younger than Waugh, Graham Greene, who was converted in 1926, was unavoidably stereotyped for many years as Waugh's left-wing counterpart. Greene waited longer for recognition as a major novelist, patently embarrassed by the success of his thrillers, or 'entertainments', like *Stamboul Train* (1932). Only with *The Power and the Glory* (1940) and *The Heart of the Matter* (1948) was the reading public properly introduced to 'Greeneland', with its sweaty torments of good and evil, argued into the night under foreign skies. His Catholicism was more a matter of cerebration than celebration.

Waugh's novels were literary artifice which deliberately distanced Catholicism from the real social roots of its revival in Britain. On one calculation, its density rose from 6 per cent in 1901 to 9 per cent in 1966; and the figures for attendance at Mass are congruent with this. Moreover, this growth parallels a rise in the proportion of Catholic marriages from around 4 per cent to a peak of over 10 per cent in England and Wales (10 per cent to 16 per cent in Scotland) though with a subsequent decline in the 1970s and 1980s. The difficulty here is to know exactly what we are counting. Estimates of the Catholic population, given in good faith by parish priests who were under no illusions about the devotional fervour of their flock, were often a function of the demographic impact of Irish immigration, sometimes one or two generations back. Such communities, through much of industrial England and Scotland, held together around the Church as a familiar haven in their adopted land, and propagated their sense of identity through Catholic schools. This was an extreme example of the way religion was imbricated in local subcultures, with their own lifestyles, loyalties – and feuds. In the inter-war period the politics of Liverpool, and to a lesser extent Glasgow, with their acute divisions on ethno-cultural lines, labelled people as Protestants or Catholics in a way that survived only in Belfast later in the century.

Most people used Churches, especially the Church of England, for rites of passage. Infant baptism or christening was common; and only late in the twentieth century did official forms start asking for 'first' instead of 'christian' names. Though civil marriage before a registrar was possible, it was not, as in much of continental Europe, necessary; the proper legal forms of marriage could take place in a church. In 1901 in England and Wales 85 per cent of marriages were religious; indeed, two-thirds of all marriages were conducted by the Church of England. To opt for a church wedding was to make an aesthetic as much as a doctrinal choice; little wonder that the words of the Anglican rite are among the most familiar in the English language or that they stacked the odds in favour of the Church. Even at the peak of Dissenting influence in 1906, when they claimed the election of no less than 180 MPs, their best since Cromwell, only one in eight marriages took place in the chapels of England and Wales. Moreover, here the Church retained its historic national role, solemnizing one in two marriages that took place in England into the 1950s, and still one in three in the 1980s. In Scotland, likewise, one in two of all marriages were still conducted by the Church of Scotland in 1960, as against one in four in civil ceremonies; at the beginning of the century as few as one in twenty marriages had been non-religious.[1]

The position of the established Churches, each with a different

---

1. Despite the traditional Scottish legal custom permitting couples to declare themselves married before a witness, such as, notoriously, the Blacksmith at Gretna Green, just across the border from England. The Scottish series of statistics is complicated by the fact that the Church of Scotland and the United Free Church reunited in 1929.

theology north and south of the border but each attended impartially by the sovereign, was not quite so anachronistic as it looked at first sight. At a low-pressure level it was accepted more placidly than in the Victorian period when insurgent Dissenters had hugged more keenly felt grievances. To many people the Church of England was a familiar, hierarchical and periodically useful national institution, like the Army; and in the Army recruits who expressed no other religious affiliation were routinely entered as 'C. of E.'. Great set-piece debates about Church and State, such as the Victorians relished, were rare after the First World War. True, the revision of the Prayer Book created a fuss in 1927–8. The revised Prayer Book simply brought it into line with the much higher level of ritual which many parishes now followed; it was permissive not mandatory; it would have legalized the Anglo-Catholics, with their newfangled smells and bells. This was too much for some of the evangelical Rip Van Winkles in parliament, which twice over rejected the revisions. Whereupon the Revised Prayer Book was published regardless and brought into use without statutory authority.

That there were some limits to what could be condoned was shown by the abdication crisis in 1936. George V died in January 1936, having celebrated his silver jubilee the previous year; not much of a speaker, he had nonetheless projected his gruff persona into millions of homes by broadcasting a Christmas message annually from 1932. King Edward VIII was quite a change from his dutiful father. He was a bachelor of forty-one, popular as the Prince of Wales, not least with a string of girlfriends from the smart set in which he moved. The plot could have been adapted from Waugh – all fast cars, expensive cocktails, brittle repartee, casual adultery, none of it to be taken too seriously. The trouble was that Edward's latest mistress, Wallis Simpson, proved difficult to ignore: not only was she the King's constant companion, she was American, she already had one divorce behind her, she was awaiting a second, and once the decree nisi came through, the King told the prime minister, Baldwin, that he wanted to marry her.

Through all this, it should be noted, the British media observed a complete news blackout: no compromising pictures from the King's Mediterranean yacht, no gossip or speculation, nothing even on the significance of the Simpson divorce hearing. This pregnant silence was broken in December 1936 by the Bishop of Bradford, who simply said that the King needed God's grace in his calling. The bishop had not even meant to cast the first stone; but it triggered the avalanche. Was this fitting conduct in a King? Most respectable people thought not; the King's cause was taken up by unreliable figures like Beaverbrook, Rothermere, Churchill, Mosley. Baldwin managed the whole thing neatly, insisting that if the King would not back off he must accept ministerial advice to abdicate; and Attlee agreed. Within days of the affair becoming public, Edward VIII had gone, and his brother had become King George VI.

How could the Supreme Head of the Church of England marry a divorcee when it was forbidden to its ordinary members? This was an issue which the Established Church was spared through Baldwin's speedy resolution of the crisis, and just as well. Its precept was still that of the marriage service: 'Those whom God hath joined together, let no man put asunder.' Although civil divorce had been instituted in the nineteenth century, there were in those days only a few hundred decrees annually. Not only did this represent, in effect, one law for the rich, since the process was prohibitively expensive, but also one law for husbands, another for wives, whose adultery was regarded more opprobriously. Since adultery remained the only offence for which a divorce action could normally be brought, it had first to be committed, or evidence to that effect manufactured, if a married couple decided to part. Hence the element of subterfuge – classically in Brighton hotel bedrooms – which was highlighted after the First World War by the growing number of divorce cases each year – up to nearly 5,000 by the mid-1930s. The 1937 Divorce Act made the law more honest and straightforward, notably by allowing desertion as an alternative ground.

It was, however, the Second World War which brought the significant change. In itself it disrupted marriages, separating wives from husbands who were in the forces, especially those serving overseas. The war also provoked concern to sort out those matrimonial difficulties likely to impair military effectiveness, which opened the way to legal aid, and thus made divorce courts genuinely accessible in the post-war period. There was a demobilization bulge of divorces as well as of births in 1947–8, when over 100,000 divorces went through – more in two years than in the whole period from 1900 to 1939. But the temporary effects of the war, and an easing of the law, can only explain so much; for deeper social changes were subsequently to have an accelerating effect on divorce rates.

The bishops of the Church of England (or rather a selection of them) continued to sit in the House of Lords and to draw stipends which enabled them to rub shoulders with the remnant of the landed interest. Only in the era of life peers (introduced in 1958) were the bishops dragged downmarket – sharing the fate of their clergy, once a gentleman's profession but in the mid twentieth century a shabby–genteel form of social work. Just as the post-war Conservative Party sought to generalize its Christian appeal in an ecumenical way, so the old notion of the Church of England as a pillar of Toryism was becoming out of date; wet parsons, agonizing about unemployment, symbolized its future stance. William Temple, son of an archbishop, could hardly be regarded as an unrepresentative figure, as he trod the path of preferment from Bishop of Manchester in the 1920s to Archbishop of York in the 1930s; yet he became the leading spokesman of a social Christianity which was plainly on the left of the political spectrum. It was Temple who was to establish the term 'welfare state'; and Temple – 'the only half-crown article in a sixpenny bazaar' – whom Churchill felt unable to pass over when the see of Canterbury became vacant in 1942.

## CULTURE AND POLITICS

The cult of 'Bloomsbury' has flowered too luxuriantly for many tastes in the twentieth century. The fact remains that a variously but indisputably talented group of writers – the work of the painters Vanessa Bell and Duncan Grant has lasted less well – thrived on mutual friendships originally formed among a group of (male) undergraduates at Cambridge. There was a homoerotic bond here, notably between Lytton Strachey, Duncan Grant and Maynard Keynes: this clearly helped reinforce the revolt against the respectable late-Victorian conventions, which Strachey's volume of biographical essays *Eminent Victorians* (1918) subjected to an exquisite literary assassination by a thousand digs. The book had an amazing success and inspired countless 'debunking' biographies in its wake. The marriage in 1912 of the high-minded Fabian socialist Leonard Woolf to Virginia Stephen (her sister Vanessa married the art critic Clive Bell) completed the Bloomsbury nexus, physically centred on this socially marginal area of London, between Euston Station and the British Museum, with the town houses in its fine squares then undervalued. Here, in the basement of their house in Tavistock Square, the Woolfs ran the Hogarth Press, which they had set up partly as therapy for Virginia's unstable mental state and partly as an outlet for new, young and – above all – modern authors.

Bloomsbury was already notable for championing the avant-garde: for example, London's first post-Impressionist exhibition, organized by Roger Fry, which created a highly satisfactory furore in 1910. The roots of modernism may have been pre-war but its cultural impact in Britain was felt in the 1920s, through a palpable change of generations. It was then, for example, that the sculptors Jacob Epstein and Eric Gill, though dogged by charges of obscenity, achieved public recognition for their stylized (and sometimes erotic) work – both had crucial commissions for the London Transport headquarters in the late 1920s, Gill later for the BBC at Broadcasting House too. In music, 1920 saw Elgar fall silent (after the great but initially under-performed cello concerto), and instead the young William Walton begin his association with the Sitwells which produced *Façade* (1923), the quintessence of the twenties, matching Edith Sitwell's recitation with Walton's high pastiche, drawing on the popular rhythms of jazz.

Modern art and modern music, like modern architecture and design, were nothing if not international; and these were fields in which Britain was famous for lagging – unlike literature, where a patriotic sense that the national heritage was at stake pervaded some ostensibly aesthetic judgements. E. M. Forster, though identified with Bloomsbury, worked within an established English literary tradition. In *A Passage to India* (1924) he used the novel almost as George Eliot had done, to illuminate the social relationships of a whole community through a multifaceted understanding of the misunderstandings between the British and the subjects of their Raj. This achievement simultaneously extended Forster's fictional range and exhausted his fictional oeuvre. Nonetheless it was in 1924 that Virginia Woolf proclaimed that 'we are trembling on the verge of one of the great ages of English literature'. Here modernism was nothing if not eclectic and, surely not coincidentally, often the literature of exiles.

Ezra Pound, an American poet who arrived in London in 1908, played an extraordinary role, something between entrepreneur and amanuensis. He was for a time secretary to W. B. Yeats, an Irish nationalist who actually chose to spend the larger proportion of his life in London. Yeats captured many of his countrymen's dilemmas and made them part of our twentieth-century sensibility: 'The best lack all conviction, while the worst / Are full of passionate intensity.' Yeats's spare images of the Easter Rising – 'A terrible beauty is born' – became central to its perceived role in creating the country which was to honour him as its most distinguished son by making him a senator.

The only honour that the Free State did for James Joyce was to stop his countrymen reading him. An Irish emigré, his stream-of-consciousness novel *Ulysses* made its hero's peregrinations around Dublin during 16 June 1904 into a modern myth, rendered with a mimetic fidelity – to both immediate experience and its imaginative recall – which held the power to shock. The struggle to get it published, in which Pound was instrumental, made *Ulysses* famous as a banned book; too scatological to be published in Britain (though it was offered to the Hogarth Press), it circulated in smuggled copies of the 1922 Paris edition for forty years. Joyce spent the rest of his life labouring on a gigantic further experiment in juggling words, myths and memories: *Finnegans Wake* (1939).

Pound's greatest literary coup was as midwife of T. S. Eliot's uniquely influential poem, *The Waste Land*, of which Hogarth published the British edition in 1923. Eliot was a fellow American exile; his was a talent which Pound had spotted years before, with its power of allusion and suggestion that Pound's blue pencil now rescued from simple parody. Eliot's original title for the poem was 'He Do the Police in Different Voices' – a clue to the modernist ambition to make poetry not by adopting a self-consciously elevated diction but by sending up the patterns of demotic speech, just like music hall, which had long had its own 'impressionists'.

> When Lil's husband got demobbed, I said –
> I didn't mince my words, I said to her myself,
> HURRY UP PLEASE ITS TIME.

Like *Ulysses*, which he admired, Eliot appropriated the epiphenomena of popular culture and the mundane trappings of industrial civilization for high art. 'We're not as good as Keats,' Virginia Woolf said to him. 'Yes, we are,' Eliot responded. 'We're trying something harder.'

Eliot, with his later conversion to Anglo-Catholicism and the conservative social views which emerged in the 1930s, may have been ideologically out of kilter with Bloomsbury; but aesthetically they were fighting the same corner. One extraordinary feature of *The Waste Land* was that it included textual notes, just like the references in a work of scholarship, giving the sources for its clever montage of literary borrowings. Thus: 'I had not thought death had undone so many (cf. *Inferno*, III, 57).' Eliot may only have been padding out the text to make a book of it and protecting himself against charges of plagiarism, but he was in danger of ponderously explaining his own jokes. All of this helped give *The Waste Land* some notoriety among people who did not normally take much notice of poetry.

Modernism was undeniably an elite movement, fostering a sensibility which only seemed accessible to a minority of self-conscious intellectuals. By the end of the century, Virginia Woolf was regarded as the great novelist to emerge in the 1920s – a perception which feminist perspectives enhanced – but during the 1920s she had a relatively modest following. Only with her historical fantasy *Orlando* (1928) did sales turn round, spurred here by the frisson of sexual ambiguity which the book purveyed. Unlike Arnold Bennett, whom she publicly made the butt of her scorn for 'materialist' fiction, Woolf found her own raw material in her own mind, tangling and occasionally disentangling a skein of memories and perceptions, heightened by a marvellous ear for the spoken word which she caught on the printed page in ways peculiar to herself. If *Mrs Dalloway* (1925) seemed relatively straightforward (at least after *Ulysses*), following two characters through the events of their very different days, the more complex vision of *To the Lighthouse* (1927) presented further challenges. Its portrait of the author's father, Sir Leslie Stephen, as Mr Ramsay was a joy for insiders. In *The Waves* (1931) multiple monologues allowed as many as half a dozen characters to interact (though action, in any strict sense, was hardly Woolf's forte).

Compared with Woolf, Aldous Huxley made a greater mark at the time as a coming novelist. Books like *Antic Hay* (1923) and *Point Counter Point* (1928) spoke in the idiom of the 1920s; like the fashionable plays of Noel Coward, they showed the 'bright young things', except that in Huxley they were just that much *brighter*, with intellectual pretensions which his own membership of a distinguished academic family made second nature. In *Brave New World* (1932) he went on to give a chilling vision of a post-industrial future where 'our Ford' was worshipped for the essentially empty satisfaction of induced wants. His parable extrapolated from emerging economic trends – mass production, consumerism, manipulation through advertising – just as George Orwell's *Animal Farm* (1945) would from political trends. They sketched rival visions of dystopia, neither of them faithfully borne out by subsequent history, but Huxley's insights arguably retaining as much pertinence today as Orwell's.

Alongside Huxley, and escaping his subsequent eclipse, D. H. Lawrence claimed a place in the sun – literally so as his precarious health drove him on a nomadic quest for fulfilment under southern skies. He died from tuberculosis in the south of France in 1930, only forty-five years old. In less than twenty years, since *The White Peacock* (1911) and *Sons and Lovers* (1913) had first made his name, he had taken Bennett-like provincial English settings and Wells-like autobiographical themes of educational aspiration and sexual awakening, and put his own stamp upon them. *The Rainbow* (1915), with its passionate sexual undertow, brought Lawrence's first brush with censorship (a foretaste of the difficulties over his far more explicit later novel, *Lady Chatterley's Lover*, which was not published in Britain until 1960). What informed *The Rainbow* was a densely realized response to the industrial realities of the Nottingham coalfield on which Lawrence had been brought up. Yet what he offered was no working-class novel with a programmatic political moral, but, especially in the sequel *Women in Love* (1920), a vision invested with Lawrence's virtually existential insistence on the authenticity of lived experience – not least sensual experience – personal affirmation and commitment.

Such a primacy of imagination over 'reality' goes some way to explain why Woolf found herself (to her chagrin) 'caged' with Lawrence, as well as Huxley, not to mention the inevitable Joyce, as modernist authors. But if these threatened to become stereotyped categories, they were ones which Woolf had helped establish through her open repudiation of Bennett, Wells and Galsworthy. She came to fear that mainstream, best-selling authors, like her contemporary Hugh Walpole, might 'dismiss me as an etiolated, decadent, enervated, emasculated, priggish blood-waterish 'ighbrow: as Arnold Bennett used to say'. Walpole's well-crafted historical storytelling is well represented in *Rogue Herries* (1930) and as an eminent book reviewer his opinion was golden. J. B. Priestley was another successful 'middle-brow' author, achieving fame with his picaresque account of a theatrical touring company, *The Good Companions* (1929); he wrote perceptively about his native Yorkshire, as did Winifred Holtby in *South Riding* (1936). These were reputable, serious authors who were read up and down provincial Britain. For all Woolf's literary recognition in her lifetime – she committed suicide in 1941 – her sales only posthumously exceeded theirs.

The fact is that modernism in literature, paralleling movements towards abstraction in art and music more common in Continental Europe, seemed foreign to a loyal reading public, schooled in the historic conventions of the English novel. In a more sophisticated idiom, the Cambridge critic F. R. Leavis was to write of *The Great Tradition* (1948) in which George Eliot (not Dickens) was a commanding presence. It can be argued that Leavis himself stood in a tradition of public moralists, whose tutelary role he sought to appropriate in the twentieth century through the propagation of English as a university discipline. His didactic definition of the canon was infused with his own affirmation of organic cultural values, as opposed to either shallow commercialism or introverted aestheticism. Though ready to defend Eliot and modernist poetry, Leavis despised Bloomsbury – but championed Lawrence. Plainly, it was not only 'modernism' which served to define and divide English writers.

By the mid-1930s, what put intellectuals in one camp or another was, above all, politics. This was most aggressively signalled by the commitment of many young artists, writers, poets – and scientists too – to Communism. The context was the apparent collapse of capitalism, or at least of prosperity throughout the capitalist world, in the early 1930s. At home the National Government looked like a put-up job by the old men, like a further betrayal of the now disillusioned young. There had been the culpable slaughter of the Great War, testified by the spate of anti-war literature which belatedly gushed from the press; and there had been a betrayal of the returning heroes, consigned to the dole queues. The extreme left was not the inevitable beneficiary of the perceived bankruptcy of bourgeois politics, still less of the new cry for action, which was, after all, virtually personified by Sir Oswald Mosley, who angled his British Union of Fascists towards ex-servicemen. Nonetheless, action usually meant Communism. Pacifism and Marxism offered obvious answers. Mass unemployment in the countries of the west tempted those brought up believing in progress to look east, to the great experiment of Soviet Russia, which purported to have banished such evils.

J. B. S. Haldane, a nephew of the Liberal and subsequently Labour statesman Richard (Viscount) Haldane, had proclaimed himself a 'scientific' socialist at the end of the First World War. Making his career as a biochemist at Cambridge in the 1920s, his major achievement was to re-establish Darwinian natural selection on the basis of Mendelian genetic theory. Moreover, Haldane showed a gift for popularizing science, in books like *Possible Worlds* (1927), which gave him a public platform. At this time, however, his transgression of prevailing sexual conventions – the university sought to dismiss him when he was cited in a divorce case – was more conspicuous than his political views. It was the Spanish Civil War which ultimately drew him to Marxism, initially as a supporter rather than as a member of the Communist Party. Haldane was not the only prominent scientist on the far left. Others included the biologist Lancelot Hogben, author of the best-selling *Mathematics for the Million* (1936), and the distinguished physicist J. D. Bernal, who became a lifelong party-line Communist.

It was not just that the slump discredited capitalism, it also discredited reformist attempts at tinkering with it. To the old Fabians Sidney and Beatrice Webb, the logic was to accept the bureaucratically controlled command economy of the Stalinist state as the fulfilment of their lifetime's agenda. Their vast tome, more widely cited than read, *Soviet Communism: A New Civilization?* (1935), was republished under the significantly different title *Soviet Communism: A New Civilization* (1937). And their friend Shaw, already a declared admirer of the brisk methods of Mussolini, was another fellow-traveller of Stalinism, admiring it from the privileged vantage point of a distinguished tourist. What gave verisimilitude to Communism was not so much the beauty of the actual Soviet alternative as the fact that Marxist theory had always insisted on the rottenness of the capitalist system, reformed or unreformed. Thus the promise of a better life, which was the foundation of liberal faith in progress, could only be redeemed by a more radical strategy – throwing over the attachment to private property which, as the slump now demonstrated, was the fatal flaw in the liberal prospectus. This is what the young poet Stephen Spender meant when he declared: 'I am a communist because I am a liberal.'

Spender, with his friends Christopher Isherwood and, above all, W. H. Auden, represents this generation of the literary left, who, in more than one sense, grew up in the 1930s. Auden's early work expressed, with a trenchancy of which he was later ashamed, the brutal choices sanctioned by a Communist morality which invoked the criterion of success – 'History to the defeated / May say alas but cannot help nor pardon.' In a polarized Europe, Communist discipline alone promised effective resistance to the rising threat of fascism. Liberals who clung to the niceties of their parliamentary liberties, rather than seeing that the class enemy must be beaten – and could only be beaten – at its own dirty game, were dismissed as 'objectively pro-fascist'. Though its determinist doctrine ostensibly rested on economic foundations, the appeal of Communism had a psychological underpinning: yoking an impulse towards action with the necessity of choice. This helped create the mood in which idealistic young Communists, as drunk on their own poetry as Rupert Brooke in 1914, found their destiny in Spain – 'that arid square, that fragment nipped off from hot / Africa, soldered so crudely to inventive Europe.'

The war broke out in 1936, with General Franco's armed challenge to the Popular Front Government of the Spanish republic, and dragged on until the republic's collapse in 1939. A knotty, messy, intractably Spanish conflict, with long historical roots, became a symbolic struggle between democracy and fascism. Seen through British eyes, it almost seemed a poets' war from the great literary outpouring it generated. This overlooks the diverse and widespread support for the republic on the left in Britain, ranging from liberal constitutionalists to Trotskyists, and the extent to which the battalions of the International Brigade were recruited from volunteers like unemployed members of the Glasgow ILP rather than articulate and well-connected Cambridge graduates, like the poets John Cornford and Julian Bell (son of Vanessa). Yet the deaths of Cornford and Bell are sufficient warrant of the authenticity of their own commitment. This was signalled in Cornford's lines, written as he faced 'the last mile to Huesca', even as he anticipated his own death: 'if bad luck should lay my strength / Into the shallow grave.'

Auden lived to become a greater poet, keeping his head down while he recorded 'the flat ephemeral pamphlet and the boring meeting'. His rhetoric was more powerful than his ideology (let alone his capacity to apply common sense to political judgements). Auden walked unscathed through the 1930s, like a short-sighted person who had been given a gun, his unawareness of its devastating firepower only matched by the uncertainty of his own aim. He met another gilded youth, the composer Benjamin Britten, through the Post Office film unit, then in its heyday under John Grierson, producing innovative documentaries with a progressive political slant. Britten and Auden were drawn to each other (both were homosexual) and their collaboration in the song cycle *Our Hunting Fathers* (1936) was the artistic fruit, with the political freight of an anti-fascist subtext. Auden ended 'a low dishonest decade' with a poem, simply called '1 September 1939', written in New York, where Britten and his partner, the tenor Peter Pears, shortly joined him. The poem was framed in the familiar ideological language, but in suggesting a personal and aesthetic resolution for such tensions it now signalled Auden's quest for a religious rather than a political panacea.

George Orwell, who fought in Spain under ILP auspices, came to recognize the machiavellian nature of the Communist Party's power politics, and memorably reprimanded Auden as blasé for writing of 'the conscious acceptance of guilt in the necessary murder'. Orwell's own account in *Homage to Catalonia* (1938) was perhaps the best book to emerge from the war, but not the easiest to get published. Its hard truths about Spain were politically inconvenient. It did not support the euphemistic cross-party line which held together the *bien-pensant* coalition of Republican supporters in Britain; it blew the gaff on the internal factionalism within the anti-fascist ranks; it showed Orwell's capacity for speaking out of turn, thus, as his friends kept warning him, 'playing into the hands' of political opponents who would use his unguarded words. These were warnings which Orwell, sometimes in an irritatingly self-regarding way, never learnt to heed; but his ephemeral writings have weathered rather better than those of most of his critics.

## NATIONAL GOVERNMENT

The National Government faced a general election in October 1931 with much better prospects than when it had been formed in August. It successfully pinned on Labour the charge of having run away from the crisis; Labour's own story about a bankers' ramp went down well enough with its own supporters but did not win it credibility or gain it support. Under Henderson's leadership, the Labour movement held together, opposing the National Government and its cuts, and expelling Macdonald, Snowden and Thomas, whose status as 'National Labour' was purely self-ascribed. The election was Labour versus the Rest; hence even on the same poll as in 1929, Labour would have lost seats. But its poll was also down by 6 per cent, to 31 per cent – almost exactly the same as in 1923 when this share of the vote had yielded nearly two hundred seats and put Labour in office. It was very different in 1931: little more than fifty Labour MPs were returned, even counting a handful of Scottish ILP members. Outside the coalfields, Labour was annihilated. Few ex-ministers were in the new parliament; what with the defection of the MacDonaldites and an electoral disaster which overtook Henderson and rising figures like Herbert Morrison, the parliamentary Labour Party turned to Lansbury as its leader, with the little-known Attlee as his deputy.

The National Government was like the Coalition returned in 1918 in that its majority was largely composed of Conservative MPs – 470 out of 554. It was unlike the Coalition in that it did not have Lloyd George. He now opposed the National Government, calling it a fraud, but could only rely initially on his own family group of MPs from North Wales, four in all (though other Liberals were to join them within twelve months). The Liberals had been swallowed up by the crisis. Sir John Simon led one group, thirty-five strong, who openly identified with the Government as National Liberals and were dependent on increasingly close electoral cooperation with the Conservatives. Able and chillingly ambitious, Simon revived his career as a cabinet minister, progressing through the great offices of state: Foreign Secretary under MacDonald, Home Secretary under Baldwin, Chancellor of the Exchequer under Neville Chamberlain, Lord Chancellor under Churchill. Worthy and chillingly scrupulous, Sir Herbert Samuel, supported by a comparable number of Liberal MPs, was clearly striving to do the right thing in challenging circumstances, rather like a preacher trying his hand as lion-tamer. Whereas the Simonites were swallowed whole by the National Government, the Samuelites were to be spat out.

Samuel as Home Secretary and Snowden as Lord Privy Seal constituted the Free Trade conscience of the newly elected Government. In the general election, everyone had tried to keep quiet about tariffs, since this would have driven the Free Traders back into Labour's arms, and MacDonald spoke only of 'a doctor's mandate'. But everything now pointed towards tariffs: the Conservative majority's prejudices and protectionist sentiment in the country alike. In February 1932 Neville Chamberlain, the new Chancellor of the Exchequer, had the satisfaction of introducing an Import Duties bill which, he claimed, finally vindicated his father. It brought in modest flat-rate duties on most imports, while on the hot issue of Imperial Preference it did what Snowden had done on the hot issue of economies a year previously – passed the buck to a small advisory committee under Sir George May (again). As a result steeper tariffs were imposed on some manufactures; and a British delegation under Chamberlain was sent to the Imperial Economic Conference in Ottawa.

Ottawa brought a double disillusionment, to Tariff Reformers and Free Traders alike. Chamberlain discovered that negotiating preferential duties did not unlock reserves of imperial goodwill and unity, as he had been brought up to believe. There was tough bargaining before the Ottawa Agreements came into effect in 1932; and their chief impact on Britain was to admit more food imports from the Commonwealth, not to help exporters overcome the protection which the Dominions were determined to keep for their own domestic manufacturing industries. Compared with the late 1920s, exports to the Dominions were over 20 per cent lower in the late 1930s, whereas imports from the Dominions increased, and their trade surplus with Britain doubled. Whoever got the best of the bargain at Ottawa, it was not British industry. But it may have suited British financial interests, with their spokesmen in the Treasury and the Bank of England, rather better.

The crisis marked the beginning of the sterling area, as a group of countries based on the Empire (with the notable exception of Canada) though also including others like Denmark, heavily dependent on trade with Britain. When Britain went off gold, so did they; and they used sterling instead for their international trade. Rather than floating freely, sterling became a managed currency, with an exchange rate which (following the US devaluation in 1933) settled down until 1939 at just under $5. Britain's imports from the sterling area cost no more than before 1931, since everyone had devalued together; and the Bank of England, no longer able to run the gold standard, was at least able to run the sterling area, with everything scaled down to imperial measures. The Dominions remained astonishingly loyal customers of Britain. If they bought less in the 1930s, it was because they could not afford to, because they had been hit worse than Britain by the slump; three-quarters of New Zealand's and South Africa's imports still came from the UK, and over half Australia's.[1] They had heavy sterling commitments in London, for all kinds of debts and invisible charges: commitments which they were enabled to meet only by their privileged access to the increasingly buoyant British consumer market. The

[1]. Not, perhaps, the best moment to provoke a crisis in Commonwealth relations; yet this is what the English cricket team did during their 1932–3 tour of Australia. Failing to check the prodigious career of Donald Bradman, Australia's leading batsman, by ordinary means, the English fast-bowlers were instructed to use 'body line' – a tactic which duly succeeded in winning the Ashes (appropriately named in this instance).

British people sucked the dried fruit of Empire to save the sterling area.

None of this amounted to the 'producer's policy' of which old Joe Chamberlain dreamt. But if Imperial Preference amounted to less than the Tariff Reformers had hoped, Ottawa was still too much for the Free Traders to swallow. For several months the cabinet had practised the constitutional innovation of an 'agreement to differ', which allowed Snowden and Samuel to oppose their own Government's tariff proposals. In September 1932, following the Ottawa conference, they resigned. Snowden turned on the National Government for its betrayal with all the venom with which he had denounced Labour a year before, while the Samuelites now joined forces with Lloyd George in opposition. All of this ostensibly turned on the great issue of tariffs, which for thirty years had caused one political crisis after another; yet as soon as tariffs were implemented they apppeared less important, either for good or ill.

It was not protection so much as cheap money which opened the door to economic recovery. Bank rate could hardly go lower than 2 per cent, its level from June 1932 until November 1951 (except for two months at the outbreak of war in 1939). To measure real interest rates, of course, the annual change in the value of money has to be allowed for, which means adding the falling prices of the slump to the nominal rate quoted. The cost of living continued falling, if less sharply than in 1929–31, until some time in 1933; but the sort of industrial prices crucial to investment decisions had already bottomed out in 1932. Thus interest rates really were low and, moreover, they were stable – ideal conditions for investment, once confidence returned.

Here the Government could play a good hand. Its personnel and its avowed policies both inspired confidence among the bankers and industrialists who had been unhappy with Labour. Even protection helped in this sense. The Treasury was able to take advantage of cheap money to effect a massive conversion of the war debt to a lower-interest-rate structure. Total debt charges had claimed over 40 per cent of every tax pound in 1929 but this fell to under a quarter by the mid-1930s. This was another measure of how much it had cost to stay on the gold standard. The Treasury made the best of a situation in which gold had gone and Free Trade had gone, and at least maintained the principles of sound money by insisting that the Budget be balanced. Chamberlain looked the part of an iron chancellor, but was lath painted to look like iron, and his measures avoided making the deflation worse. Ignoring the sinking-fund provision, the only year between 1921 and 1939 when there was an actual budget deficit (albeit a small one) was 1933. It did not matter, since it did not disturb confidence.

The housing boom was the most important stimulus to the revival of domestic investment. New industries were often associated with it, supplying consumer durables literally for the home market, from electric irons to radios, which revolutionized work and recreation alike. There were, for example, 1 million telephones in the United Kingdom in 1922, 3 million by 1938. Science-based industries exploited new technologies, often electrical, and new materials, like plastics, with an increased emphasis on styling in marketing their products. The British motor industry became big business behind a tariff wall; compared with the 1920s, imports halved; exports meanwhile doubled, and so, above all, did the number of private cars on the road. A town like Oxford, the headquarters of Morris Motors, was yanked out of the Middle Ages into a Fordist brave new world (the reverse of what an earlier William Morris had hoped for). The dismay which this transformation caused Evelyn Waugh has been eloquently recorded in *Brideshead Revisited* (1945); but the perspective of a car worker's family, able to afford a house on a new estate in Cowley, was somewhat different. In 1934 Oxford had 5 per cent unemployment, Abertillery 50 per cent.

The statistics show how economic recovery gathered pace. The official unemployment figures touched 23 per cent in January 1933 and thereafter maintained a virtually uninterrupted fall, briefly dipping below 10 per cent in the summer of 1937. Money wages of those in work did not fall as fast as prices during the slump; the result was that by 1933 real wages stood 10 per cent higher than in 1929 (17 per cent higher than in 1926). It could be argued that these gains had been bought at the expense of all those who had meanwhile lost their jobs. But this higher average real income was maintained during the revival of employment – as workers came off the dole queue, they were cut in on their share of the new prosperity.

This provided a serviceable platform for the National Government when it came to fight a general election. In June 1935 Baldwin, who had patiently served as Lord President of the Council under MacDonald, changed places with him, bringing the premiership into line with the preponderantly Conservative complexion of the Government. MacDonald had tried to maintain its National credentials, even after the Free

Traders had departed, but he was now, in every sense, a sad and lonely figure. Not that Baldwin wanted a rabidly partisan approach, since the fact (or fiction) that this was a National Government allowed him to keep in check the diehard elements in his own party whom he had always fought (most recently over moves towards Indian self-government). In the general election of November 1935 Baldwin was triumphantly returned at the head of 429 MPs, of whom 387 were Conservatives and 33 Simonite National Liberals. Despite some slippage since 1931, the Government won over 53 per cent of all votes cast in 1935.

There was now a proper opposition, led by Attlee, who had done a decent enough job as Lansbury's deputy to be given a chance as his successor. Labour took over 100 seats from the Government and bounced back to 38 per cent of the vote, fully as good as in 1929. But in a two-horse race this was not good enough. If the 1935 results are compared with those of 1929, the net effect of the 1931 crisis becomes apparent; Labour had stayed level, while the Conservatives had put 10 per cent on their vote, almost entirely at the expense of the Liberals, who ended with less than 7 per cent of the vote and only 21 MPs. The change from a three-party to a two-party system thus put the Conservatives into a commanding position, from which it took a world war to dislodge them.

All that Labour did in the mid-1930s was recover to the level of 1929; and much the same is true of the economy. In 1929 unemployment was already a problem, concentrated in appalling black spots, and even in 1937, at the peak of recovery, it was a problem still. Politically, it might be said, the Government was able to ride out a crisis of capitalism, counting on the haves outnumbering the have-nots, the prosperous south of England outvoting the depressed regions of industrial Britain. Yet this is too simple. Wales had a clear majority against the Government, both in seats and votes, but in Scotland the National vote was not much less strong than in England. True, the Labour vote held up best throughout the 1930s in constituencies where unemployment was highest; but these were also heavily unionized areas where pre-existing Labour loyalties ran deepest. In London, conversely, where a purely economic interpretation would predict support for the Government, Morrison's formidable Labour machine was going from strength to strength; having won the LCC in 1934 Labour started picking up parliamentary seats well outside the deprived core of the East End that had withstood even the 1931 debacle.

The Conservatives made a more effective, broad-based appeal to the public – not least women voters – than an opposition which still lacked credibility. Where the Government had to be careful was not so much over its record on unemployment but over its treatment of the unemployed. The cuts in benefits were restored in 1934; in real terms benefits were now higher than ever. But what drew blood was the proposal in 1935 for a new Unemployment Assistance Board to take over the long-term unemployed from local Public Assistance Committees (the residual agency of the old poor law) with standard scales of payment based on a household means test. This was a typical measure in the Chamberlain tradition, confident that administrative reform could take the issue out of politics. Instead, when responsibility for those who had been on transitional payments was transferred to the new UAB in January 1935, an unprecedentedly widespread political protest erupted, not only in parliament but spilling into the streets. In Hitler's Europe, this was a potent warning. The Government backed off; it deferred the changes and bought off the protest with higher scales.

By contrast, policies for tackling unemployment did not achieve such a high profile. To be sure, Lloyd George was talking of a British New Deal, Keynes was advocating a counter-cyclical economic strategy, the Labour Party began talking a Keynesian language, and middle opinion was mobilized behind *bien-pensant* manifestos, notably *The Next Five Years* (1935). The Treasury, however, moved cautiously, acknowledging the pragmatic force of some of these arguments, but always constrained by Chamberlain's overtly political handling of the issue – his announcement of new road-building during the 1935 election campaign, for example. One difficulty, which Keynes acknowledged, was that of dealing with unemployment through a general stimulus of demand when the forces of recovery were already creating bottlenecks. The peaks of structural unemployment in the regions, masked for a time by the enveloping economic blizzard, were now visible.

This provoked a Government initiative ostensibly aiding the depressed areas – or special areas, as they were named – notably the derelict coalfields of Durham and South Wales, the deserted shipyards on Tyneside and Clydeside. The unemployed men of Jarrow, where up to two-thirds were out of work, undertook a well-disciplined march to London in 1936, which provided a stark image of the problem. It was less clear whether the solution was to move the workers to the jobs, by assisting transfer to more prosperous parts of the country, or to move the jobs to the workers, by encouraging inward investment. Little was done, let alone achieved. Lancashire was not classified as a special area, yet in Wigan one-third of the workers were registered unemployed; and if Orwell's *Road to Wigan Pier* (1937) is not quite the documentary record it purports to be, it is still a fitting literary monument to the darker side of Baldwin's beloved England.

The sharply different impact of prosperity and impoverishment which people experienced during this period coloured their sharply different perceptions and memories of it. In retrospect the National Government was doubly damned, from left to right, on domestic and international counts. Had such feelings been widespread at the time, the Government could not have polled over half the popular vote, and Britain might have been more susceptible to the extremist politics on offer from the British Union of Fascists (BUF) or the Communists. Mosley, emulating Mussolini in his black-shirted uniform, made a splash with his eye-catching demonstration at the Olympia arena in 1934. But this bubble, temporarily inflated by favourable publicity in Rothermere's *Daily Mail*, soon burst. The BUF's only mass following was recruited by exploiting populist resentments against the longstanding Jewish community in the East End of London; and even here the attempt to reinvigorate BUF support in 1936 backfired when anti-fascist activists forced Mosley to call off the Blackshirts' march at Cable Street. The impotence of the police was promptly remedied by a change in the law, which, by banning political uniforms, effectively undercut Mosley's theatrical appeal – in the end the reason why his Blackshirts were to remain so memorable.

The Public Order Act of December 1936 was one of the last measures of Baldwin's premiership, his twinges of anxiety allayed by some cause for satisfaction. If, at its peak, the BUF could claim forty thousand members, this was more than double the number in the Communist Party; but it was the Conservative Party, with a membership of up to 1.5 million, that clearly had more proletarian adherents than either. Baldwin's last months in office, before he chose to retire in May 1937, also saw the abdication crisis neatly defused and a new King and Queen crowned, amid traditional patriotic symbolism, endorsed by protean signs of social solidarity and popular rejoicing (faithfuly recorded on coronation day by the amateur anthropologists of Mass Observation). It did not seem a bad legacy for a Conservative leader to leave.

# 6

## Guilty Men
### 1937–45

### APPEASEMENTS

The succession to Baldwin as Conservative leader had long been debated, by press lords and others; but since 1931, at latest, it had been clear that Neville Chamberlain would take over, sooner or later. Rivals had come and gone. One fancied candidate in the 1924–9 Government, Sir Douglas Hogg, had instead settled for the Lord Chancellorship.[1] That left Chamberlain – unless, of course, anyone thought Churchill worth running. After all, the two of them together had provided the dynamism in the second Baldwin Government, just as Churchill and Lloyd George had in the Asquith Government; though ever since the Carlton Club meeting in 1922 everyone knew Baldwin's opinion that a dynamic force could be a terrible thing. It is a myth, however, that Churchill, like Lloyd George before him, was excluded as a man of decision by a conspiracy of mediocrity. His own bad decisions were decisive.

In the Baldwinian Conservative Party Churchill simply had too many strikes against him: ambitious, untrustworthy, impetuous, adventurous and tainted with unworthy associates, from Lloyd George to Birkenhead and Beaverbrook. Not only had he clung to Free Trade on rejoining a basically protectionist party, his Chancellorship was subsequently regarded as an electoral disaster. When Churchill withdrew from the shadow cabinet at the beginning of 1931, he was not wantonly throwing away a great chance that would otherwise have come his way in the ordinary course; but his detachment surely sealed his exclusion from the National Government. Once out, Churchill was kept out.

---

1. As Lord Hailsham in 1928. Hailsham was to have the reversion to this post once the MacDonaldite Sankey could be eased out of it in 1935. His son renounced the hereditary peerage in 1963 in order to run for the Conservative leadership but later took a life peerage, also as Lord Hailsham, to become Thatcher's Lord Chancellor.

The issue on which Churchill broke with the Conservative leadership, and on which he campaigned throughout the early 1930s, was India. He emerged as the most forceful spokesman for the diehard wing of the Conservative Party, which saw an all-party front-bench conspiracy to sell the British Raj down the river. This was a plausible charge. The commission which the Conservative Government had set up in 1926 to report on Indian government sat under the chairmanship of Sir John Simon, still a Liberal, and included the still obscure Clement Attlee as one Labour member. The Viceroy, Lord Irwin (later Halifax) was a prominent Conservative, a pious High Churchman and a close friend of Baldwin. Irwin's declaration in October 1929, dangling Dominion status before Indian eyes, was not only agreed with the Labour Government but initially supported by Baldwin in opposition, much to the fury of many of his backbenchers. The Simon Report in 1930 bore the stamp of its chairman, famous for sitting on the fence, with cautious tactical proposals for enlarging the scope of representative government, seeking a consensus that would propitiate not only the Indian princes but Gandhi's nationalist supporters in the Congress Party, while safeguarding the essentials of British control and calming down the diehards.

Following the report, in 1930 MacDonald convened a round-table conference in London which squeezed concessions out of the princes but was vitiated by the refusal of Congress to participate. In 1931 he tried again. This time Irwin tried direct talks with Gandhi: two holy men foxily striking a deal. Their pact secured Congress's attendance; Gandhi himself was an unforgettable spectacle amid the London rain in his distinctive white robe and sandals, mocked with racial condescension by the intemperate Churchill. The political crux was that, although MacDonald had, by the time the conference convened, become dependent on Conservative support, his Government would not significantly modify its stance on India. Appeasement remained their strategy for removing causes of avoidable friction and thereby salvaging as much as possible in a changing world where, as the 1931 crisis brought home, Britain could no longer call the shots. Together MacDonald and Baldwin pressed on with their Indian policy, issuing (after a third round-table conference) in the Government of India Act of 1935 one clear testimony to their Government's National credentials.

In India the provisions in the bill for increased self-government were to some extent undercut by the reluctance of the princely states to join the proposed all-India federation; though once the princes' stance became clear at Westminster it actually eased the passage of the bill by making it seem less cataclysmic. Throughout, Churchill put himself at the head of the 100 or more Conservative MPs who regularly voted against the Government; the debates occupied 4,000 pages of Hansard. Churchill, moreover, was the main voice in the country of the right-wing India Defence League. Although some of his utterances, warning of intercommunal violence if Britain were to quit India, could be read as prophetic in the light of the bloodshed following independence (and partition) in 1947, Churchill's perspective was not really forward-looking; it looked back to the imperialist assumption 'that we are there for ever'. Picking up where the press lords had left off, he made an unmistakable challenge to – if not for – the leadership, reaching a high point at the party conference in October 1934 when the diehards came within a handful of votes of success. Little wonder that Baldwin showed a steely determination not to admit this man into his last cabinet, despite Churchill's belated overtures of reconciliation; nor that he was ignored when the torch passed smoothly to Chamberlain.

By the time Chamberlain, already sixty-eight years old, finally came into his inheritance it had gone sour. He retained his keen appetite for government business, prodding his ministers relentlessly and poking his nose into their departments. His whole training, however, had been in the administration of complex matters of domestic policy, of which he had an unrivalled grasp. It was his brother Austen, the ex-Foreign Secretary, who had recently told him: 'Neville, you must remember you don't know anything about foreign affairs.' Yet the only Chamberlain to get to 10 Downing Street was to be swamped by an all-embracing international crisis, only resolved in 1945, which saw him off and saw him out. To an extent unparalleled in twentieth-century history, what British politics were about in these years was foreign policy. If Chamberlain was found wanting, it was not on ground of his own choosing.

Chamberlain, however, never asked for sympathy, never acknowledged fallibility. Instead he threw himself into mastering the new brief and, unlike Baldwin, made the prime minister's office the hub of decision-making in foreign affairs. A favourite civil servant, Sir Horace Wilson, nominally chief industrial adviser to the Government, sat in the office adjoining the prime minister, walked daily with him in the park, and was more of a confidante than any of Chamberlain's cabinet colleagues. Mistrustful of the career diplomats, Chamberlain used the Downing Street press office for briefings that at times contradicted the Foreign Office, and his evident determination to show who was boss became apparent to foreign ambassadors. It was this sort of friction, rather than acute policy differences, which soon led to a crisis at the Foreign Office.

Good-looking and well-dressed, Anthony Eden had been only thirty-eight – barely into his job as Minister for League of Nations Affairs – when Baldwin found that he desperately needed a new Foreign Secretary at the end of 1935, in place of Sir Samuel Hoare. Eden, with his fastidious mind and grasp of languages, was always a diplomat's diplomat; he had clean hands and was the darling of the liberal pressure group, the League of Nations Union, which in June 1935 declared the results of its house-to-house 'peace ballot', showing massive support for League sanctions against an aggressor – even for military measures. This was fine in principle; but Mussolini's designs on Abyssinia brought a more practical test. The trouble with Hoare was that the Government, elected in November mouthing pledges of support for the League's measures to protect Abyssinia, was caught out in December simultaneously planning to partition it instead (the Hoare–Laval plan). Hoare had to go. Eden's dazzling promotion succeeded in freshening the Government rather than saving Abyssinia. By June 1936, with the League's credibility in tatters, Chamberlain was openly calling sanctions 'the very midsummer of madness'. The left-wing press and the League of Nations Union might fume, but their invocations of 'collective security' as the means of resisting aggression had a hollow ring in the absence of a willingness to back words with British firepower.

None of this was much to the taste of the new Foreign Secretary; but he was content to describe the substance of his policy as 'the appeasement of Europe as a whole', by which he meant what liberal opinion had endorsed since Versailles – the removal of the causes of war by the remedy of justified grievances. Thus Eden acquiesced in Germany's remilitarization of the Rhineland in 1936. True, it was a violation of the Versailles Treaty – but who now defended its one-sided and obsolescent provisions, denying Germany full control of its own territory? True, it had been achieved by force – but who wanted war to take back from Hitler what would otherwise have been conceded to him across the conference table with a handshake from a smiling Eden? Eden's quarrel was not with appeasement as such, but the advent of a new prime minister meant that Eden was no longer free to play the poor cards in his hand in his own way. Humiliated by the manner in which Chamberlain took the conduct of diplomacy into his own hands, Eden resigned in February 1938, to be replaced by a more compliant successor.

The appointment of Lord Halifax, famous for his conciliation of Gandhi, marked a new phase in the policy of appeasement; but he found one familiar opponent still against him. 'It is not that our strength is seriously impaired,' Churchill had said about India. 'We are suffering from a disease of the will.' Churchill's reading of the European situation can be seen in similar terms. Bark at Gandhi, bite Hitler! Yet, it can be argued, a different imperative applied if the maintenance of the British Empire were to be ruthlessly regarded as the top priority by a nation in straitened circumstances. For in that case the logical course was to conclude a deal with the dictators in Europe so as to leave each master race free to exercise its own hegemony, with no questions asked, least of all the tedious questions about freedom and democracy which the League of Nations Union kept maundering on about. This was not, however, the line which Churchill took. Instead, from 1936 he started working with bodies like the Anti-Nazi Council, with its Jewish, left-wing and trade-union supporters, in seeking to rally effective opposition to Hitler's Germany.

Mussolini's Italy remained a puzzle. It was harder to know if it should be conciliated, as a realistic strategy for isolating Germany, or opposed as another fascist dictatorship, which was the more ideological response of the left. Both Churchill and the Government wobbled between the two courses.

Rearmament had been Churchill's consistent theme since 1934. Initially, in a climate where pacifism was often well-regarded if ill-defined, it was possible to dismiss him as a belligerent imperialist. His estimates of relative British and German air strengths, however, were sufficiently well-founded to cause the Government embarrassment, for the reason that Churchill was leaked official secrets by sympathetic public servants. Indeed Baldwin was at one point forced to climb down in the House of Commons. The truth was obscure; with access to the archives historians have suggested that Baldwin's retraction was itself in error, and that Churchill's figures were incorrect all along. The fact is that the rearmament programme was seriously begun under Baldwin, pushed along more slowly than Churchill wanted, but more quickly than the Opposition advocated. Defence spending, pegged at about 2.5 per cent of GNP until 1935, increased to 3.8 per cent by 1937.

Labour was only converted by stages to the practical necessity of rearmament. One step came at the Labour Party conference in 1935, when Ernest Bevin, with all the authority of his union's block vote behind him, reprimanded the sweet-natured pacifist Lansbury for 'hawking your conscience round from body to body asking to be told what to do with it'. At seventy-six, Lansbury was ready enough to resign. Bevin's shocking remarks signalled an altogether more tough-minded approach; in 1937 he became chairman of the TUC and Dalton chairman of the Labour Party. Together they went a long way in removing any real resistance to rearmament (though parliamentary support for the hated Chamberlain was another matter).

The Government's perception of Britain's relative weakness actually made it less likely to take a strong line of the kind that Churchill advocated. Chamberlain, with his long tenure at the Treasury, was acutely aware of the real economic constraints on British rearmament, especially when seen through the spectacles of economic orthodoxy. Simply stepping up orders for aircraft was no good unless there were factories with capacity to produce them; and even so this would divert resources from productive uses – an echo of the old 'Treasury view' ('crowding-out'). Likewise, raising taxes might throttle recovery in the economy, which was Britain's real strength if war should come. Conversely, borrowing raised the awkward political question why it was right to unbalance the budget for armaments but not for investment in public works; and when the Government launched a defence loan in 1937, it met Labour criticism. In the event, rearmament gave a favourable stimulus to the economy, by increasing demand just when recovery was faltering.

Chamberlain, however, could not be expected to regard defence spending as other than a burden and a waste. Moreover, his sombre mood was reinforced by the Imperial Conference, which made clear that the Dominions had no more stomach for a fight than himself. After all, why should the Australians, with their bitter memories of being sent to Gallipoli by Churchill some twenty years previously, be ready to offer themselves as cannon fodder again? Backed by the Empire and the USA, Britain had only just survived against Germany last time. Without either, how might it turn out next time?

The League of Nations retained a ghostly presence at Geneva but after Abyssinia talk of collective security was meaningless. If Britain and France were to preserve the Versailles settlement, they would have to act themselves. Their failure to do so over the Rhineland was a boost for Hitler; his annexation of Austria into the Reich in March 1938 was another violation of Versailles, another bloodless coup, another blow to the prestige and morale of the western powers. Whatever next? The obvious answer was Czechoslovakia. Hitler's demands on behalf of the ethnic Germans of the Sudetenland, incorporated into the Czechoslovak republic after Versailles, became the all-absorbing issue during the summer of 1938.

Chamberlain acted desperately to forestall the impulsive Hitler, literally preparing the ground for concession by sending a British mission under Lord Runciman to intervene in the German–Czech border negotiations. Runciman's findings became the basis of an Anglo-French plan, on the Hoare–Laval model, for the partition of Czechoslovakia, giving Hitler those areas of Bohemia where ethnic Germans were in a majority. After all, was not this in line with the principle of self-determination? And anyway, what could Britain and France do to defend Bohemia? Justifications of Chamberlain's course were not hard to find, and sympathetic newspapers, notably *The Times*, warmed to the theme. The alternative was a European war, if Czechoslovakia should resist, backed by its guarantees from France, which would in turn expect support from Britain, just as in 1914. Hence Chamberlain's crucial role; hence his offer to fly out to meet Hitler in September 1938.

In the jet age, this initiative may seem commonplace. At the time, when a man of seventy who had never been in an aeroplane made his flight to Berchtesgaden, it made a dramatic impact, even on Hitler. Chamberlain, supported by his rolled umbrella and the constant presence of Sir Horace Wilson, now had the bit between his teeth, pioneering not just summit meetings but shuttle diplomacy. Twice Chamberlain flew back and forth, reporting on Hitler's terms to his colleagues in London, keeping the French Government under Daladier in line, roping in Mussolini, and browbeating the reluctant Czechs. Still Hitler asked for more; war seemed imminent. The prime minister, observing the military precautions in London – trenches and gas masks – went on radio to express his incredulity at the idea of war 'because of a quarrel in a faraway country between people of whom we know nothing'. Then, in a further dramatic stroke, while Chamberlain was addressing the House of Commons on 28 September, a message from Hitler was brought to him, with an invitation to fly to Germany for a third time – to Munich.

The name Munich has become synonymous with a pejorative sense of appeasement, and with some reason. The two jackbooted dictators received the two western prime ministers for four-power talks (excluding Czechoslovakia itself). The terms were no better than before; but Chamberlain, having undermined any French will to resist, now closed on the deal and presented the bill to the Czechs. They had no option but to cede the Sudetenland to Hitler. Chamberlain thus succeeded in his immediate aim of averting war. Thereby, as Sir John Simon chose to argue, he saved Czechoslovakia; and it is a melancholy fact, cited by later historians, that far more of the Poles for whom Britain ostensibly went to war in 1939 perished in the Second World War than Czechs who were betrayed in 1938. This does not, though, mean that the Czechs were not betrayed. At Munich the fine arguments for appeasement as a process of mutual concession involved Chamberlain in making the necessary sacrifices, not on his own behalf, and not at his own expense, but that of the Czechs.

There was to be no war in 1938 – but what about 1939? Chamberlain took what comfort he could from the written undertaking, which he waved on the tarmac at Heston airport, promising that Hitler would now mend his ways. So Chamberlain quelled his own doubts, believing what he wanted to believe. The cynical idea that he was buying time at Munich, put around by some later apologists, had no part in Chamberlain's thinking. Instead he invested his policy with his own sense of self-righteousness, seeking a moral as well as a political triumph over his opponents; and this, in a temporary spasm of relief, he achieved. His promise of 'peace for our time', which impressed Church leaders, was one which he had to live up to – or rather Hitler had to, or Chamberlain was finished.

What snapped the credibility of appeasement was Hitler's conduct after Munich, when every point had been stretched in his favour. At the end of 1938 Kristallnacht was a demonstration of the full inhumanity – not yet the full horror – of the Nazi regime's treatment of the Jews. Then in March 1939 Hitler's occupation of Prague made a nonsense of all his promises to respect the new (and undefended) Czech frontiers. Even now Chamberlain stumbled deeper into the mire. But Halifax at the Foreign Office showed that he appreciated the difference between Gandhi and Hitler. Halifax saw that appeasement was holed below the waterline and was determined that the whole Government should not go down with the sinking ship. The result of this tension was an extraordinary lurch in policy. Prompted by (ambiguous) signs of Polish will to resist and by (misleading) reports of an imminent German attack. Chamberlain offered a guarantee of Polish independence.

If Czechoslovakia was a faraway country, Poland was further; if Bohemia could not be defended by British troops, no more could Danzig; if the democratic Czech republic had its flaws, the Polish regime was far more suspect. What had changed was the context in which even the prospect of war no longer seemed the worst evil. But Poland made one further issue unavoidable: what about Russia? The left had long called for alliance with the Soviet Union against the fascist powers. The Government had reason to doubt whether the Red Army, still reeling from Stalin's purges, could so easily be enlisted in defence of the western democracies; but negotiations were belatedly opened in Moscow, only to be pre-empted in August 1939 by the amazing news that Stalin had concluded a pact with Hitler instead – a sort of eastern Munich.

One effect in Britain was to disabuse many people on the left of their simplistic belief that Communists could be relied upon to combat fascists. At the same time the mutual suspicion between the different groups of anti-appeasers was easing. Eden and his admirers, young men mindful of their future in the Government, had initially kept well clear of Churchill; so even Chamberlain's Conservative critics were not united. Moreover Churchill's links with the anti-fascist left were complicated by his stance on Spain, where his anti-Communism initially made him wary of supporting the republican cause; and only late in the day did he modify his position. It was one sign that he was ready to generalize his appeal, subsuming his own nostalgic nationalism in a wider ideological conflict. Conversely, on the left, there was talk not only of a popular front as an alternative to the National Government, but even of bringing in Churchill, whose scenario on the Nazi menace had a new verisimilitude. By the summer of 1939, therefore, Chamberlain's policy was in ruins and his own position was no longer unassailable. The Conservatives now had an alternative leader in Halifax; and Churchill, rising sixty-five, no longer looked ripe for retirement.

## FINEST HOUR

Unlike the summer of 1914, few doubted that war was on the way in 1939. Even Beaverbrook's *Daily Express*, with its determinedly optimistic view of appeasement, dropped the regular streamer from its front page offering readers a contrary assurance. On 1 September, with the Nazi–Soviet pact in place, Hitler felt free to commit his troops against Poland. A flurry of diplomatic moves momentarily suggested a revival of appeasement, alarming its opponents in all parties; in the House of Commons Chamberlain came under pressure. It was the Tory Leo Amery who called out to Arthur Greenwood, acting as Labour leader while Attlee was ill: 'Speak for England!' Chamberlain failed to strike the right note, even in speaking for a country now united on the necessity for war with Germany (not Italy yet). For this was actually his achievement – perhaps the only one, certainly his final achievement – in pursuing his policy to the bitter end. It served as an object lesson to all those who had been sceptical about the need to fight: the bulk of the Conservative Party who had pined for a businesslike deal with Hitler, the Simonite National Liberals with their Nonconformist scruples, those advocates of collective security in the Labour Party who had supposed rearmament dispensable, even fellow-travellers of the Soviet Union who had thought it the vanguard of the struggle against Hitler. Moreover, the Dominions – including South Africa – each decided to enter the war alongside Britain.

This was the second world war for Britain in a generation. Painfully acquired experience, barely twenty years previously, suggested what needed to be done. There would be food rationing, there would be convoys, there would be air-raid sirens and a blackout; moreover, there would be conscription – Labour's support was now ensured. There would be new Ministries of Food, Economic Warfare, Shipping, Home Security, and (jointly) Labour and National Service, all marking administrative lessons learnt from the First War. But would there also be a coalition government? Not under Chamberlain, the Opposition parties declared. So the reconstruction of the Government was confined to bringing in the dissident Conservatives. Eden went to the Dominions Office. Churchill was the big catch, his own eyes long set on the post of Minister for the Co-ordination of Defence which had been created in 1936. This proved too much for the National Government to swallow and Churchill had to be content with returning, twenty-five years on, to the Admiralty. He sat in a war cabinet of nine, otherwise stuffed with familiar Chamberlainites like Simon, Halifax and Hoare. Like Asquith's coalition in 1915, this attempt to pack the Government with the prime minister's cronies turned out to be less clever than it first looked, since it set them up as whipping boys for subsequent failures.

So began the 'bore war' – the American term 'phoney war' came later – its spirit captured by Evelyn Waugh in *Put Out More Flags* (1942). Eerily, life went on as normal for many people. To be sure, men of military age started to be called up; some anticipated by enlisting voluntarily; and they had to be trained and equipped. But, when plans for the evacuation of mothers and children from the great cities were hustled into effect, most of them soon returned, with or without authorization, since the threatened bombardment had failed to materialize. There was a sense of anti-climax, which fed the thought that not enough was being done. The 'old gang' were still in office; Treasury priorities prevailed; income tax remained at 5s 6d in the pound (27.5 per cent). In fact some big changes were under way. Under the new Ministry of Supply, modelled on the old Ministry of Munitions, production of armaments was stepped up, especially aircraft. Defence spending, which had previously not exceeded 7 per cent of GDP, changed its trajectory in 1939, when it reached 18 per cent, rising in 1940 to 46 per cent – a higher proportion than in Nazi Germany.

The Nazi claim to put guns before butter seemed more plausible at the time. Conversely, the distortions produced by the Nazi war economy were seen as a reason for confidence in Britain's staying power. Chamberlain had some ground for arguing that 'the Allies are bound to win in the end and the only question is how long it will take them to achieve their purpose'. But whereas it took years to vindicate this assessment, it took only months to make it seem culpably complacent. Yet a sense of urgency awaited a sense of danger to instil it. For most British people the war was happening off-stage; distraught messengers reported battles in the east – Poland duly overrun by Germany, Finland defeated by Russia. Britain's first major military intervention did not come until April 1940.

The Norwegian expedition, aimed at ousting German forces from the port of Narvik, was primarily the responsibility of the First Lord of the Admiralty, Churchill. Yet its failure brought immense pressure to bear upon Chamberlain, whose recent claim that Hitler had 'missed the bus' seemed to miss the point. Subterranean discontent in parliament, suppressed for six months, either patriotically or tactically, now erupted – most dangerously for the Government among its own backbenchers. A number of known critics, old men like Amery, younger figures like Harold Macmillan, were now ready to vote with the Opposition, which steeled Labour to move a censure motion. This was Chamberlain's moment of truth: would the open confrontation consolidate his wavering support or would the defections be so great as to undermine him?

It was one of very few occasions when a vital issue was settled on the floor of the House of Commons. Amery spoke his lines, cribbed from Cromwell: 'In the name of God, go.' This was predictable; what was unpredictable was how many former loyalists would now abstain. Churchill was duly wheeled out in defence of the Government; whereupon Lloyd George, in his last decisive intervention, warned his old colleague not to be 'converted into an air-raid shelter to keep the splinters from hitting his colleagues'. This nicely distinguished between two potential targets, exonerating the First Lord at the expense of the prime minister. In Chamberlain's entourage, suddenly taken aback by the hostility they encountered, it was still thought that the Government would be safe if its majority, normally 250, kept above 100. In the event it fell to 80, because 40 rebels voted with the Opposition and 80 others abstained. Thus over a quarter of Chamberlain's 'friends' (the word he used in his final appeal) spurned him.

This was a moral defeat, entailing the reconstruction of the Government, as everyone recognized; yet it should also be remembered that the Chamberlainites were, and remained, the majority. The Opposition leaders refused to enter a coalition under Chamberlain. Halifax, however, would not have encountered the same objection. Churchill knew that he was less welcome to Conservative MPs, but that he had more widespread support across party lines, not only in the House but in the country. He was ready and able, therefore, to force the issue, by silently refusing to support Halifax when Chamberlain convened a meeting between the three of them. It was Churchill who was summoned to Buckingham Palace on 10 May 1940. His own image, later made famous through his war memoirs, was that he was 'walking with destiny'. But although he was free to form his own Government, he was not free to act exactly as he chose.

Chamberlain stayed. In the new war cabinet of five, he was Lord President of the Council, in effect responsible for coordination of domestic policy, the more so since his protégé, Kingsley Wood, the new Chancellor of the Exchequer, was left outside. Churchill's war cabinet was initially like Lloyd George's in its size and in its exclusion of departmental ministers; but unlike it in personnel, including party bigwigs rather than brilliant outsiders. Thus Chamberlain, still party leader, was joined by Halifax, the second man in the Conservative Party; while the two Labour places went to the party leader, Attlee, and the deputy whom he had beaten for the leadership, Greenwood. Churchill had learnt the lesson that a coalition worked best if it was stuck together with party loyalties rather than pitted against them. Hence whenever the Churchill Coalition threatened to fracture, it was along party lines; and it was to come apart cleanly at the end of the war.

Churchill had some room for his cronies, notably Beaverbrook, who was given the new Ministry of Aircraft Production, and for ex-ministers who had fallen foul of Chamberlain. Amery got the India Office; Duff Cooper, who had resigned over Munich, was brought back as Minister of Information; Eden had to be content with the War Office – for the moment. The centre of gravity in politics had shifted, with long-lasting effects. The record of a rising Conservative minister like R. A. Butler was blighted, while the prospects of Harold Macmillan, a persistent critic of the National Government on both unemployment and appeasement, were transformed. For the time being, Chamberlain retained the party leadership, and did his best to bring his own back-benchers around to accepting Churchill – who was at first only cheered by Labour. When Chamberlain, gripped with cancer, had to resign in the autumn of 1940, Churchill at last became leader of the Conservative Party. And, once Halifax was eased out of the Foreign Office, the way was clear for Eden's return, which recognized him also as the heir apparent.

By the end of 1940 the leadership of both the Conservative and Labour parties was settled for the best part of twenty years. Clement Attlee had been lucky to be elected leader of the Labour Party, as rivals like Herbert Morrison and Hugh Dalton never ceased to reflect. Attlee represented Labour's first generation of upper-middle-class recruits, faithful to his social background in everything except his politics; edu-cated at public school and Oxford, he had served in the trenches and was known as Major Attlee in the inter-war years. Notoriously a man of few words, he had no personal charisma and was easy to under-estimate. Yet Churchill had to accept him in his war cabinet and came to appreciate his mettle; so that, with increasing responsibilities, Attlee's gift for ruthless chairmanship gave him oversight of the domestic policy of the Coalition, notably through the Lord President's Committee.

Labour's other big figure, in every sense, was Ernest Bevin. The leader of the Transport and General Workers' Union, which he had virtually created, Bevin became Minister of Labour and National Service in 1940. This striking appointment signalled a new era, when the integrated control of the country's manpower resources – so contentious during the First World War – could be put in the hands of this strongly class-conscious union boss, who had no parliamentary experience. Bevin quickly had to be jobbed into a safe Labour seat, though, already nearly sixty, he never really became at home in the House. Instead he relished the exercise of power, bringing the resources of his capacious experience and his intuitive intellect to bear upon a whole range of political issues, not just those of his department. Within months he had been brought into the war cabinet. The axis which he formed with Attlee was fundamental in running the Labour Party until Bevin's death. So long as the war lasted, his weight was likewise thrown behind that other fat man, Churchill, 'representing you might say the other half of the English people and English history', as the broadcaster J. B. Priestley put it.

The task facing the Coalition, though simple, was hardly easy – hardly possible, some thought in May 1940. Churchill's strength was that he did not pretend otherwise. Victory was the sole aim which he declared in his first speech to the Commons; 'blood, toil, tears, and sweat' the sole means of achieving it. His own contribution to winning the war (as Attlee once put it) was mainly to talk about it. Radio meant that Churchill's voice could reach virtually the whole nation – nine out of ten people were glued to the news – and he read this speech again on the BBC after the 9 o'clock news: the first of several that summer. Something between a growl and a lisp, his distinctive delivery was much imitated in the affectionate retailing of Churchill stories, many of them apocryphal. This was one sign of how effectively, despite his own lingering resentment against the BBC, his personality was projected through radio. In the heightened atmosphere of this crisis his elevated rhetoric, the only sort he knew, was happily matched to the level of events, saving Churchill from the bathos which his style had courted. In the 1930s his set pieces had often sounded dated; in 1940 his words sounded historic.

Or so enough people thought to give him a chance, against any rational assessment of the odds. Not that ordinary people were defeatist; indeed, according to opinion polls, never fewer than three-quarters of the population professed to expect victory. This stubborn populist mood, whether it is called instinctive or bloody-minded, was closer to Churchill's outlook than the ostensibly better-informed views of sceptics in his own Government, faced with the snowballing collapse of the allied front in Europe, not to mention Mussolini's entry into the war as Hitler's jackal. From 10 May 1940 the German blitzkrieg swung into top gear, moving with breathtaking ease through the Low Countries and into northern France, where the British forces found their lines of supply – and retreat – under imminent threat. The swift collapse of France was both a cause and a consequence of the decision at the end of May to withdraw the British expeditionary force, a quarter of a million strong, to the channel port of Dunkirk. This was a humiliating reverse, redeemed only by the success of evacuation in saving almost all the British army (and 100,000 other troops, mainly French). Most troops were transported by the Navy, but this was supplemented by a flotilla of volunteers in small boats, which helped turn Dunkirk into a myth of national deliverance by plucky amateurs when mere professionalism had failed.

Churchill made desperate efforts to induce France to fight on, even talking of constitutional union between the two countries; but the spirit of the hour was *sauve qui peut*. For the French Government, this pointed to negotiating a peace which left the north under German occupation but the south under the collaborationist Vichy regime; only the stiff-necked General de Gaulle stood out with his Free French followers. For the British Government, Dunkirk demonstrated that defence of Britain was the priority. The next logical step in damage limitation was a negotiated peace which, however unpalatable, might salvage something from catastrophe. In the war cabinet Chamberlain and Halifax both wanted to explore this option; Churchill allowed that it might become necessary, under some other leader, at some other time. His own decision was to fight on; in this he was supported by the two Labour members. The war cabinet did not go back on this commitment, which was indeed the rationale of the Churchill Government.

If Germany were to mount a successful invasion, it would need to establish air superiority over the English Channel before the end of the summer. The relative strength of the two sides was largely determined by what was in the pipeline when Chamberlain left office. But Beaverbrook's piratical methods in spurring greater efforts in aircraft production, seizing supplies as he needed them in violation of carefully laid plans, yielded short-term results in a situation where the short term might be decisive. He too was brought into the war cabinet.

In the decisive struggle for mastery in the air, Britain had two secret weapons. One was the crucial role played by superior British intelligence, which only came to be publicly appreciated well after the war. The other was what became known as radar. Originally the brainchild of the electrical engineer, Robert Watson Watt, this was a means of using short-wave radio signals to detect the approach of enemy aircraft. From 1935 the system had been developed by the Air Ministry, prompted by its scientific adviser, Sir Henry Tizard, the Rector of Imperial College, London. By September 1939 a chain of radar stations protected the south-eastern flank of Great Britain, thus allowing Fighter Command in 1940 to economize on reconnaissance patrols and to concentrate every available aeroplane on effective interception.

At the time the heroism of young fighter pilots in engaging the Luftwaffe, day by day above the fields of Kent, was what captured the imagination. It was Churchill's best-remembered speeches which focused these images of 1940 and invested them with his own thrilling sense of history in the making. Rather than minimizing the threat of invasion, he had dramatized it, talking of fighting on the beaches. Once France was lost, it was his term, the Battle of Britain, which made sense of the strategic contest; and he had already projected himself into the future in telling his fellow members of 'the British Empire and its Commonwealth' that this would stand as 'their finest hour'. Certainly many worse ones were yet to come.

In July an opinion poll showed popular approval of Churchill standing at 88 per cent; this figure never fell below 78 per cent until May 1945. He was accepted with all his idiosyncrasies, ostentatiously smoking cigars big enough for any plutocrat, guzzling too much brandy – points which German propaganda fruitlessly put to the British people, who instead joked about Winston as a folk-hero. National unity, in the face of the grimmest threat the country had ever faced, pushed aside ordinary party politics; yet it is hardly too much to say that 1940 brought a political revolution.

The decision to fight on under Churchill, even though Britain and the Dominions now stood alone, was a standing repudiation of Chamberlain and the National Government, its policies and its personnel alike.

Three left-wing journalists from the Beaverbrook stable – one was Michael Foot, a later leader of the Labour Party – seized their chance to publish a polemic of genius, *Guilty Men* (1940), which gave the indictment its classic form. The eponymous guilty men were held responsible for the country's present peril: Baldwin for putting electoral popularity ahead of the need for rearmament; Chamberlain for truckling to Hitler; others of the 'old gang' for supporting them – Halifax, Simon, Hoare and the rest. Beaverbrook's role was passed over in silence; so were the inconsistencies of Churchill and the left. This was, in short, a piece of selective myth-making about appeasement, condemned in retrospect as it had never been at the time, providing a story on which supporters of Churchill and the left could complicitly settle for the next twenty years.[1]

## BLOOD AND TEARS

How could Churchill think victory possible? Nobody supposed that this war would be over by Christmas – except on Hitler's terms, of course. A negotiated peace of any other kind was a chimera, attracting only isolated individuals at the time and a few revisionist historians later; it was simply not on offer from the Nazis. In the mid twentieth century, there was no way of preserving the British Empire on the cheap (Chamberlain's illusion at Munich); or indeed at all (Churchill's ultimate disappointment). Instead Britain's stand in 1940 was to be the means of checking what Churchill, surely accurately, called 'a monstrous tyranny, never surpassed in the dark, lamentable catalogue of human crime', and of rallying a worldwide coalition against it. Newspaper readers were in for a six-year course in elementary geography, learning to find on the map a string of place-names, milestones to a reshaped world: Narvik, Dunkirk, Placentia Bay, Pearl Harbor, Singapore, El Alamein, Stalingrad, Anzio, Arnhem, Yalta, Belsen, Hiroshima.

First, defeat had to be staved off. The line was held in the Battle of

---

1. This can clearly be seen from the treatment of Baldwin's self-confessed 'appalling frankness' in November 1936. What he said in the Commons was that *if* he had called a general election in 1933–4, when Labour had recently won a by-election at East Fulham, campaigning against 'war-mongering', the National Government could not have secured a mandate for rearmament. *Guilty Men* represented this as referring to the actual general election of 1935; in Churchill's war memoirs Baldwin, as he appeared in the index, 'confesses putting party before country'.

Britain; by mid-September it was clear that Hitler would not launch an invasion. He really had missed the bus, though Churchill refrained from putting it that way. Next it was a matter of holding on until, as in the First World War, the USA was brought into the conflict. This hardly looked likely so long as the war was seen as a defence of the British Empire; though there were signs that the reporting of the courage which ordinary British people showed in response to the Nazi threat was producing a more favourable and – above all – democratic image. British propaganda obviously stressed this theme. Roosevelt's re-election as president in November 1940, for an unprecedented third term, was a hopeful sign; he was ready to give Britain sympathy, though hard cash, let alone armed assistance, was another matter.

Financial caution was now thrown to the winds, the sterling balances were raided, overseas investments were sold off. The vital support of the USA was assured when Britain traded her remaining assets, strategic as much as economic, for war supplies. Churchill called the Lend-Lease agreement of March 1941 'the most unsordid act in the history of any nation', but it was not, as it turned out, the most unprofitable. Since they held most of the cards, the Americans inevitably got the best of the deal economically.[1] Churchill was surely right to be gracious about it, however, not only because this was tactful, but because Lend-Lease was simply essential to British survival. It secured an open-ended guarantee of supplies. Churchill and Roosevelt met aboard a warship off the Newfoundland coast (Placentia Bay) in August 1941 and issued the Atlantic Charter. Common post-war aims were stated in vague and lofty terms; the telling point was that the USA, though non-belligerent, was hardly neutral.

Britain's traditional wartime role was as the paymaster of allies who actually shouldered the biggest share of the fighting. In the American century, this was one of many roles usurped by the USA, and it was Britain which became the client state. With Lend-Lease able to substitute imports from the USA, ordinary British production could be run

---

[1]. This was shown by the way they prospered in their role as the arsenal of democracy. Lend-Lease can be seen as a division of labour between the teeth and the tail of the military behemoth which the Anglo-American alliance became. Britain provided more of the fighting teeth: the USA more of the tail of vital supplies. This kept Britain in the war, which was what mattered in 1940–41, but at the cost of a gross distortion of its whole economy. By 1945 Britain had far too many teeth, far too little tail, for economic survival.

down, or diverted into war uses, enabling a high level of military mobilization to be achieved (at a price to be paid later, of course). Until 1938 British armed forces had totalled under 400,000. By 1940 over 2 million men were serving (some women too): by 1942 4 million, and in 1944–5 around 5 million – about two out of five men of military age. These were larger numbers, and for longer, than in the First World War; and more of them lived to tell the tale. In exposed positions the carnage was terrible enough – for fighter pilots and the aircrew of bombers, for sailors escorting convoys, for soldiers storming the Normandy beaches. A total of 360,000 British nationals died; but this was markedly fewer than Germany suffered, while the Russian losses were to run into unnumbered millions, leaving traumatic scars which were simply not part of the post-war British experience.

In the first three years of the war, indeed, more British civilians were killed than soldiers, a telling demonstration of the contrast with the First World War, when slaughter was largely confined to the trenches. Now Blighty itself was in the front line. Everyone was issued with a gas mask. Bombing of the great cities had long been expected. This was the aspect of modern warfare which made its prospect so terrible, with predictions of a total breakdown of civilized life. The ports of Plymouth and Portsmouth suffered first. What hit London on 7 September 1940, when the Germans began fifty-eight consecutive nights of bombing, was thoroughly unpleasant for all, fatal for some, devastating for those who lost their families and homes. But it did not lead to general demoralization, still less a quick collapse. 'The Blitz' was thus a misnomer; it did not work like lightning at all. The real lesson was that a strategy of bombing relied on attrition as much as trench warfare had. In mid-October a Luftwaffe officer told Goebbels: 'London is going to be our Verdun of the air.'

As in the First World War, however, deadlock did not inspire a magic remedy; and the defiant sentiment that 'London can take it' was not made to yield a strategic insight about the ineffectiveness of indiscriminate bombing. The RAF's role thus shifted by stages from defence, through fighters in the Battle of Britain, to offence through bombers. Air Marshal Harris was one vigorous champion of a bombing strategy, which simultaneously enhanced the importance of Bomber Command and offered the only means of hitting back against Germany. 'Bomber Harris' thus appealed to Churchill's instincts rather than his intellect. Though both sides denied it, simple revenge was one motive – Cologne for Canterbury – and though London largely escaped the attention of the Luftwaffe after the winter of 1940–41, other British cities were hit. They too showed that they could take it. This did not prevent Britain squandering resources – precious materials, even more precious men – on perilous 'thousand-bomber' raids on German cities. US intervention was to reinforce not only allied airpower but the same line of thinking on strategic bombing. The destruction of Dresden at the end of the land war in 1945, wreaking death and destruction in an inferno disproportionate to any military objective, posed a disturbing moral dilemma.

The Navy took up where it had left off in 1918, fighting off U-boats to keep the Atlantic shipping lanes open. Churchill adopted the Germans' phrase, Battle of the Atlantic, in March 1941, when shipping losses had reached half a million tons a month, approaching 1917 levels. Already Britain was dependent on supplies from the USA – if they could get through. In fact American neutrality gave some shield and by the end of 1941 Atlantic losses had been halved; whereas once the USA became a belligerent the U-boats were uninhibited. Merchant seamen faced terrible odds; 30,000 died in all. During the month of March 1942 over 800,000 tons of shipping were lost – an unsustainable haemorrhage. The left-wing *Daily Mirror* published a cartoon of a seaman on a raft, with the caption: 'The price of petrol has been increased by one penny – official.' It is a mark of the Government's jumpiness that this sobering comment was the excuse for a threat to ban the *Mirror*. As late as November 1942, total allied losses again exceeded 800,000 tons in a month, before the rate was halved in the spring, and halved again by the next autumn.

Unlike the war in the air or at sea, British troops had it easy – for the moment. True, once Italy was in the war, it launched an attack on Egypt. The Italians were repulsed by British and Australian troops under the command of General Wavell, who promptly retired to Cairo – leaving an Australian garrison exposed at Tobruk. This sweeping victory at Benghazi at the end of 1940 was was not to be matched throughout the next two years, in any theatre of operations, much to Churchill's impatience.

Churchill was not only prime minister, chairing a defence committee of the war cabinet which on the whole left the conduct of the war to him: he had also appointed himself Minister of Defence, which bypassed the departmental responsibilities of the three service ministers, and gave him a seat on the joint chiefs of staff committee, alongside the military commanders themselves. In this role, Churchill was not really the architect of British strategy: more like an irrepressibly restless and opinionated patron of a succession of hand-picked architects whose professional judgement he would, at the end of the day, respect. But first he needed to be persuaded in the cut and thrust of argument, preferably deep into the night. The literate but inarticulate Wavell, who would not enter into this game, was found wanting, and was eventually packed off to India, clearing the way for other generals to make their mark in the North African desert. By contrast, from 1941 the prime minister found the perfect foil for his over-bright ideas in Sir Alan Brooke, the (frequently exasperated) chief of the general staff for the rest of the war.

There was little that Britain could do to turn the course of the war in 1941, except hope that its enemies would make mistakes. Luckily they did. Thwarted in the west, Hitler turned east and invaded Russia in June, bringing the Soviet Union into the war. Churchill opportunely seized upon this windfall, ready to welcome any ally and let bygones be bygones. At home the ideological implications were resolved with a little discreet trimming of the official line; and the Communist Party of Great Britain was happy to call off its internally divisive denuciations of an imperialist war, only to begin insistent demands for a second front in western Europe. Meanwhile it was left to the Red Army, in a blood-soaked rearguard action, to hold the line against the hitherto irresistible German forces. Britain's other stroke of luck was undoubtedly the surprise Japanese attack upon the US naval base at Pearl Harbor, bringing American involvement in a Japanese war, which Britain promptly entered; and as a bonus prompting Hitler and Mussolini to declare war on the USA.

Some kind of Japanese attack had not been wholly unsuspected by British intelligence, which – in one of the war's most effectively guarded secrets – had achieved partial access to the German system of codes (known as Enigma). This does not mean that Churchill knew in advance of the strike at Pearl Harbor, still less that he risked compromising himself by concealing vital information from Roosevelt. No British deception could have succeeded so well as that of the Japanese. Once allied with the USA, Britain shared the Enigma secret. The code-breakers at Bletchley Park in Buckinghamshire provided daily decrypts which captured the amateur enthusiasm of the prime minister and in the hands of more expert analysis allowed enemy intentions to be read.

At many critical points this gave the allied commanders an advantage which may well have shortened the war by a year. Another Anglo-American secret, which was to have a similar effect, was the joint development of a technology for nuclear weapons, which could now be pursued in the safety of the New Mexico desert.

By December 1941, with the two superpowers committed against Germany, Churchill knew that his faith in final victory had been vindicated. But not, of course, at once or on the terms he would have liked. Churchill spent the rest of the war making the best of a bad job, which was at any rate better than the worst-case situation he had inherited. Relations with Stalin were henceforth important. The insistent Russian demand was that their allies open a second front in western Europe. Though the Americans showed some interest, any thought of a landing in France seemed premature to those with memories of the Somme. The ill-conceived Dieppe raid in August 1942, in which Canadian troops were massacred in attempting to storm well-defended beaches, reinforced caution. For the rest of the year, the Red Army's bitter resistance at Stalingrad – their Somme, their Verdun – became the focus of vicarious awe and anxiety. If Russia had to bear the brunt of the war, it was no surprise that it would claim the rewards in eastern Europe, once the Germans were thrown back. By the end of the year this had been achieved, and thereafter, with Stalin increasingly able to call the shots, Churchill had to swallow more than one lesson in appeasement, especially over Poland.

Churchill's relations with Roosevelt were more than important: they were crucial. Churchill invested his own eloquence and charm in winning Roosevelt's friendship, but knew it could not be an equal friendship. Decisions on the conduct of the war, now that it was winnable, slipped increasingly into American hands, with the British gamely talking of a special relationship as their claim to a privileged, albeit subordinate, position. With Germany out of the way, Britain's position as the greatest wholly European power was assured. Other allies, with their exiled governments in London, had a nuisance value, especially France, with its national honour jealously guarded by de Gaulle and his Free French and Resistance supporters. Lecturing de Gaulle (fruitlessly) on the appropriate demeanour for ex-Great Powers to adopt, Churchill confided that he woke up every morning thinking of how he could please President Roosevelt. Stalin, Roosevelt and Churchill might be spoken of as the Big Three; it was really Two-and-a-Half.

The USA agreed to giving the European war priority over the defeat of Japan. This was good news for Britain, not so reassuring for Australia, which was painfully discovering that a direct Pacific partnership with the USA was the future path of realism. Japan's blitzkrieg replicated the successes of Germany's. The fall of Singapore in February 1942 was as traumatic in this theatre as Dunkirk had been – and without the compensation of evacuation of the British and Australian defenders, left to suffer in Japanese prisoner-of-war camps. If this brought humiliation for the British, for the Australians it brought the prospect of invasion and a revelation of the impotence of imperial defence.

Churchill held himself to blame – and he was not alone in doing so. Moreover, following the loss of Benghazi to the German Afrika Korps under General Rommel, Tobruk fell in June 1942, again with prisoners. This was the low point of Churchill's leadership; as many people were now dissatisfied with the conduct of the war as satisfied. Yet his own popularity was hardly dented; what he needed, as he well knew, was a victory in the field. This is what General Montgomery, in command of the Eighth Army, provided at El Alamein in October. Rommel was decisively defeated, and his crack German troops finally shown to be no more capable of holding North Africa than the Italians whom they had reinforced. Montgomery did not snatch victory against the odds, that was not his style; instead he had husbanded superior resources until he was confident of maximum success – with minimum casualties. The fact that he was no chateau general, instead living among his men, dressed like them in a beret, was one reason why 'Monty' became the British military hero. Coinciding with Stalingrad (the real turning point in the east) and preparing the way for Anglo-American landings against the Vichy position in North Africa, El Alamein had a decisive impact on morale. In England the church bells were suddenly ringing, while Churchill could now stop wringing his hands.

'It is not the beginning of the end but it may be the end of the beginning,' Churchill declared in November 1942. With the Mediterranean cleared, landings in Sicily began an Italian campaign in the summer of 1943. The fall of Mussolini, and Italy's change of sides in September, still left Italy stubbornly defended by German troops. In January 1944 the allied landings at Anzio, behind enemy lines, took the war to mainland Europe but brought no quick or easy results. It was now Germany which stood alone and defiant in Europe. While Stalin controlled the eastern front, a second front in the west was finally opened with the allied landings in Normandy in June 1944. Montgomery, leaving the Eighth Army fighting its way from Italy to Austria, was given command of the British ground forces but was (uneasily) subordinate to the American commander, General Eisenhower, reflecting the fact that the USA provided most of the troops. Indeed, over $1\frac{1}{2}$ million GIs had been stationed in England, sometimes for prolonged periods, in preparation for D-Day.[1]

Eisenhower succeeded in landing 2 million troops by the end of June, initially on the beaches, later through the channel ports. But his forces had no easy passage. Moreover D-Day signalled new dangers for British civilians, since the Germans had now developed the V1, a flying bomb; and in August 1944 came the V2, a rocket. Whereas the V1 was not too difficult to bring down, at least in daylight, the V2 could not be intercepted, thus increasing the pressure on the allies to capture the launching sites in the Low Countries. The airborne operation at Arnhem in September 1944 was a gamble for quick victory, aimed at securing a bridge on the Rhine; but it proved to be, as one British officer presciently put it, 'a bridge too far'. There were to be no short cuts. Attempts to force the pace of the allied advance brought a bloody reminder of the tenacity of the German Army, shown in early 1945 by its ability to sustain a counter-offensive in the Ardennes against the Americans – to Montgomery's personal glee, but to the geopolitical benefit of Stalin, who thus had his chance to reach Berlin first.

When the Big Three met at Yalta, in the Crimea, in February 1945, to settle the shape of the post-war world, the war was not yet over, even though its final outcome was no longer in doubt. Any decisions about the fate of Poland had to be premised on the fact that Stalin already dominated eastern Europe. As long as he kept his hands off other countries, especially Greece, Churchill had shown himself ready to wink at a fairly cynical carve-up of spheres of influence. Free elections were the subject of free pledges, to be honoured later (or not at all, as it turned out, in the Soviet-dominated satellite countries). The ambiguous

---

1. On the eve of D-Day there were over 1.65 million US troops in the UK, more than ten times as many as a year previously. But there had been at least 100,000 in every month since August 1942 – including by D-Day 130,000 black GIs, at a time when the total black community in Britain was only 8,000. The GIs made a considerable impact on the natives they met: not least, of course, on personable young women – with war babies and 'GI brides' as two after-effects.

agreements concluded at Yalta thus left obscure which countries were, in the end, to be 'betrayed' and which 'saved'. While the Big Three (shortly to be depleted by Roosevelt's death) played old-world power politics, in the new world the more appealing side of the allies' war aims was displayed through the foundation of the United Nations Organization at a conference in San Francisco, where Eden traded in his League of Nations credentials for the new model. But only in the spring did the allied armies finally close on the Reich – the allied advance from the west, the Red Army from the east, the British Eighth Army from the south. Hitler committed suicide in his bunker and the German forces surrendered in May 1945.

Victory in Europe had been achieved; the flags were hung out in streets up and down Britain. Two sobering developments clouded the jubilation of VE Day. One was the revelation of the horrors of the Nazi concentration camps. The starving inmates were a spectacle for which British troops liberating Belsen had not been prepared; but soon the images of these gaunt survivors became all too familiar through press photographs and newsreels. And many, above all the Jewish population, had not survived at all. The rumours which had first seeped out about a systematic extermination policy had been difficult to credit, especially in view of the overblown atrocity stories which the British had put about in the First World War. From the end of 1942, however, British propaganda was presenting specific, authenticated allegations about Nazi extermination camps. For all that, seeing was believing.

A second shock that came soon enough lay in the way the Japanese war ended. At VE Day in May 1945 it was still estimated that the war in Asia might last another eighteen months. For Britain's 'forgotten army' in Burma this was galling; for prisoners of war life-threatening; though for the Government it meant some practical relief through a period of phased transition from war to peace. All of this was blown away by the decision to use the nuclear device, which was now ready, against Japanese cities. When a new American president, Truman, consulted with a new British prime minister, Attlee, there was no disagreement on using the new weapon. On 6 August 1945 Hiroshima was bombed, with a devastating loss of life; a few days later a second atomic bomb hit Nagasaki. The immediate result was a Japanese surrender. The Second World War was over and the nuclear age had begun.

## WHOSE GOOD WAR?

There was general agreement that this was a 'good war'. No one now defended the Nazis; no one thought Britain guilty of starting the war – guilty of not starting it sooner, if anything. Few saw how Hitler could have been stopped otherwise; many pacifists in the First World War took a different line in the Second, though conscientious objectors to conscription felt both less impassioned and less persecuted. Moreover many individuals had a good war. The camaraderie of the forces was, for most men who served, not seared by the sordid traumas of trench warfare; equally, fewer took their medals or joined the British Legion afterwards. The war was a significant force for social mobility; for the lucky ones, it was an induced career-break, with opportunities to develop new skills, and allowances made for returning soldiers in achieving professional recognition. Furthermore, it was a good war for those institutions which adapted to its pressures: for Whitehall and Westminster, for the monarchy and the BBC, for the TUC and the Labour Party.

Whether it should be called 'a people's war' – a term that came into use in 1940–41 – depends on how ambitiously that claim is meant. It was partly a description of the blurring of obvious class distinctions brought by a sense of shared crisis. Appeals to 'the Dunkirk spirit' were subsequently debased by reiteration; but in the summer of 1940 the authenticity of this emotion can hardly be dismissed. Few stood on their dignity when crammed together in air-raid shelters; queues were a great leveller; there was a common topic of conversation in war news; smart clothes were hardly patriotic in the make-do-and-mend atmosphere. Evacuation of deprived inner-city children, sometimes displacing the comfortable classes from spacious homes, was a shock all round. For the upper classes – Harold Nicolson's diary brings this out nicely – a whole way of life collapsed; and some of them ruefully welcomed it. Locking the iron gates to the gardens in privileged London squares was suddenly intolerable – and impossible once the iron had gone as scrap for munitions drives. Saving for victory, digging for victory, sewing for victory – this was a war in which everyone could 'go to it' and do their bit on 'the home front'. This went a long way to bridging the gulf in experience and memories which was a legacy of the First World War.

'A people's war', in a more ideologically ambitious sense, meant a radical agenda, seeking to fulfil dreams of a popular front, to win the war by and for socialism. This was the domestic implication of the repudiation of the guilty men and their regime of outdated privilege. Conversely, the left's indulgence towards Churchill in 1940–41 was based on his obvious readiness to subordinate all other considerations to winning the war. He had not been afraid of 'war socialism' in the First World War; nor was he now, though he demanded that every collectivist measure be justified as genuinely for the war. Taunted about his anti-communist record by his private secretary on the eve of the invasion of Russia, Churchill 'replied that he had only one single purpose – the destruction of Hitler – and his life was much simplified thereby'.

It is not too paradoxical to say that, while the patriots became unexpectedly left-wing, the left became unexpectedly patriotic. George Orwell, whose tract *The Lion and the Unicorn* (1941) captures this moment well, wrote that the people had picked a leader in Churchill, 'who was at any rate able to grasp that wars are not won without fighting', and that later they might pick another, 'who can grasp that only Socialist nations can fight effectively'. England, 'the most class-ridden nation under the sun', was nonetheless a family, with 'its private language and its common memories', and ready enough to close ranks at the approach of an enemy – it was 'a family with the wrong members in control'. The people's war did not effect the radical changes which people like Orwell anticipated in the winter of 1940–41, but for him Britain was still 'my country, right or left'.

What happened was that the groundswell making for a people's war was captured and contained – not simply thwarted – by the surprising resilience of famous British institutions, shaken rigid in 1940, flexible under pressure subsequently. *The Times*, for example, a newspaper so august that it had often been quoted as the voice of the Government, started printing leading articles about social justice as a British war aim, prompting one Tory MP to call it 'the threepenny edition of the *Daily Worker*'. Orwell was one of many left-wingers used by the BBC (an ambiguous phrase, not lost upon him). Whitehall weathered the advent of new masters and new imperatives; Labour ministers eventually became the biggest fans of Britain's impartial and efficient civil service. There was an affinity of interest here since Labour's statist policies required more bureaucrats; the post-war civil service, at around 400,000, was three times as big as pre-war.

Big government – of the people, for the people, but not actually by the people – was the theme of the Second World War. Government took on an emergency welfare responsibility with far-reaching effects – milk for babies, a vitamins scheme which gave children concentrated orange juice and cod-liver oil. The effect is difficult to quantify; but the fact that the indices for infant mortality maintained their long-term improvement in the later years of the war is indicative. The claim by Lord Woolton, the businessman brought in as Minister of Food, that the nation had 'never been in better health for years' was not nonsense. This seems paradoxical in an era of shortages and queues and regimentation. True, food rationing was the most obvious sign of privation – yet also of 'fair shares' in allocating scarce resources. Woolton's success was built upon sound administration but also a shrewd grasp of public relations (which later made him a very successful chairman of the Conservative Party). He thought that the public would either laugh or cry about rationing; the publicity campaigns of the Ministry of Food therefore enlisted wry humour to leaven the unappetizing national loaf. 'Points' in ration books provided a fairly sophisticated alternative currency, capable of substitution on a range of purchases. Those who could afford higher quality goods were better able to manipulate this system, and likewise to buy meals in restaurants, where restrictions were less onerous; but the rich actually experienced a bigger drop in their standard of living than the poor, who had always been rationed by price.

Moreover, the grosser inequalities in purchasing power were eroded at both ends, partly spontaneously, partly by design. More steeply progressive taxation of incomes brought a standard rate of 10s in the pound (50 per cent) from 1942–6, double the pre-war level. For those on lower incomes, a basic diet – albeit humdrum – was not priced out of their reach once food subsidies had been introduced in 1941, stabilizing the official cost-of-living index at 30 per cent above its level at the outbreak of war (20 per cent for food only). Manual workers who were earning £3.50 for a 48-hour week in 1938 were earning £6 pounds for a 53-hour week by 1943. Even allowing for the intervening price rises, this was a big improvement – for those in work. Those who missed out were now the men on military pay, and their families on separation allowances, rather than the unemployed. The number out of work in the UK, still 1 million in 1940, subsequently plummeted to 100,000.

What had transformed the economy was the enormous growth in

government expenditure, from £1 billion[1] in 1939 to £4 billion in 1941 and £6 billion in 1945 – at its peak around two-thirds of the national income. This mopped up unemployment, just as Keynes had always said it would. Indeed, with a stimulus to demand far greater than he had ever envisaged, the macroeconomic problem had dramatically changed its character – not mass unemployment but inflationary pressure. His *General Theory* (1936), however, in principle allowed for both. Keynes, as usual, had a plan, initially proposed in his pamphlet *How to Pay for the War*. He proposed using the fiscal system as a makeweight or balancing factor, adjusting the level of total disposable income to the level of the total resources available for it to purchase, and thus avoiding the inflation caused by an excess of spending power. This was a macroeconomic approach to policy-making, essentially symmetrical in its application, either for stimulating demand or restraining it.

The difference 1940 made was that Keynes was suddenly *persona grata* at the Treasury, where he was installed for the rest of the war as adviser to the Chancellor of the Exchequer. An adaptation of his strategy for restraining the inflationary effects of excess demand was adopted in the 1941 Budget: through food subsidies and through tax increases, both disguised and undisguised. The disguise was the scheme of 'post-war credits', used to withhold compulsory savings. The extension of income tax to newly prosperous workers soon brought the innovation of a pay-as-you-earn (PAYE) system to collect it. Above all, the 1941 Budget was the first to disclose its macroeconomic impact, by presenting experimental national-income estimates, not just accounts for the Government's own revenue and expenditure. These were tools of economic management on which the Treasury, under Sir Richard Hopkins, adroitly seized. In danger of sinking with the guilty men, widely accused of penny-pinching which had left Britain unprepared, the Treasury instead strapped on a Keynesian lifebelt which took it buoyantly into new waters.

Other historic British institutions regained esteem, partly through a flattering contrast with the evils of totalitarianism. Did not a constitutional monarchy hold together the British Commonwealth, which alone had defied Nazi Germany? The new King, George VI, was a shy

1. In this book the word 'billion' has been used to mean '1,000 million' (rather than '1 million million').

man, a heavy cigarette smoker at a time when this showed the common touch (though it shortened his reign). He was much fortified by the strong personality of his consort, Queen Elizabeth; with their two teenage daughters, the royal family projected a wholesome and dutiful image. The King was a family man with his own ration book; by comparison, his elder brother, now Duke of Windsor, was just an exiled playboy. The royal family stayed in London during the Blitz and visited the bombed-out residents of the working-class East End; when the opulent West End was eventually bombed too, and Buckingham Palace itself hit, the Luftwaffe unwittingly reinforced the social solidarity of the capital and completed the rehabilitation of the British monarchy.

Parliament, often dismissed as a mere talking-shop in the 1930s, was treated with elaborate deference by Churchill, who exploited its sense of theatre in his ripe orations. The medium was the message in conveying the primacy of democracy, Westminster-style, as a war aim. Again, Nazi bombing helped fix an image, when the chamber of the House of Commons was destroyed in 1941; a famous photograph, showing Churchill brooding over its smouldering ruins, was worth more than anything staged by the Ministry of Information.

The BBC had a good war. Reith, who had already left before the outbreak of war, found his tenure as Minister of Information terminated in 1940 by Churchill, who resented his own exclusion from broadcasting in the 1930s. Now Churchill made up for lost air-time; his broadcasts after the 9 o'clock news were listened to by half the adult population in 1941. But so were the 'Postscripts', given in the same slot by J. B. Priestley, whose reputation was transformed from that of a solid north-country writer to that of a major media personality. He offered a vernacular, populist and broadly left-wing counterbalance to Churchill – with such impact that the BBC's failure to renew his contract in 1941 provoked an outcry from the left. Though it is true that Priestley's gift for raising war propaganda to the level of patriotic myth was little appreciated by the Government, the decision does not seem to have been the result of political pressure, as was alleged at the time. The BBC's reputation for impartiality brought it wide – indeed worldwide – prestige, as listeners tuned in to London to hear the truth about the war. The whole truth? Of course not; and there was more Government pressure behind the scenes than legend had it. Still, it was not a bad record for the official news service of a country at war.

Moreover, the popular appeal of radio was secured by a further relaxation of severe Reithian standards of taste, when the single Home Service of 1939–40 was supplemented by the Forces (later Light) Programme. The singer Vera Lynn, 'the Forces' sweetheart', acquired an enormous following. The misgivings of the Corporation's Board of Governors – 'How can men fit themselves for battle with these debilitating tunes in their ears?' – had to be overcome before the BBC was enabled to make its biggest contribution to the war effort: that of cheering up overworked people already stuffed with overworked propaganda clichés. It was *ITMA*, the anarchic, fast-paced comedy programme inspired by Tommy Handley, which did this best. It created a cast of characters – like Mrs Mopp, the charlady, asking, 'Can I do you now, sir?' – whose catchphrases everyone knew. These became national institutions of a sort, albeit not the sort Reith had planned.

The BBC also found that its audience for classical music and drama doubled. Beethoven, a German, posthumously provided the V-for-Victory theme in the first bar of his Fifth Symphony, much played. At the National Gallery in London, the pianist Dame Myra Hess gave lunchtime recitals which proved a big draw. This incipient interest in the arts was fostered bureaucratically through the establishment of the Council for the Encouragement of Music and the Arts, later the Arts Council, with Keynes as its part-time chairman, wheedling modest grants from the Treasury even during the years of greatest economic stringency.

There was a parallel wartime demand for all kinds of literature, which was met partly by public libraries and partly by publishers, especially of paperbacks. Penguin was the name to conjure with. The brainchild of Allen Lane, Penguin Books had since 1935 tapped a new market both for reprints from hardback editions and for specially commissioned paper-bound books – usually sold at sixpence in a wide variety of outlets. Penguin Specials, quickly published on current topics, exploited the interest in politics and international affairs; the bias was generally towards the left, though free of the (ill-dissimulated) party line of the Left Book Club. Penguin negotiated a good deal with the Government under wartime paper restrictions, and its publications circulated widely, not least in the armed forces by arrangement with the Army Bureau of Current Affairs, with which Penguin personnel were closely associated. ABCA's mission to stimulate discussion of current affairs encountered occasional accusations of left-wing bias, not to mention indifference from cynical troops; but once reconstruction became a live topic, it played an important role in shaping informed opinion.

The established institutions of the Labour Movement became the beneficiaries of the increased economic bargaining power of labour and the political salience of progressive ideas. War expanded trade-union membership by 50 per cent, to over 9 million by 1947. The unions gained a wholly new power and status: signalled by the pre-eminence of Bevin. His achievement was the extraordinary effectiveness of British mobilization, monitored through an annual 'manpower budget'. Bevin used conscription not simply to raise big armies but to put the right men in the forces and keep the right ones working in the mines and at the factory bench; moreover young single women were used as a mobile reserve in filling vacancies, while married women were brought into jobs near their homes. Bevin met criticism early in the war for the sparing way in which he exercised his powers for direction of labour; he appealed to his record in vindication. It is true that until 1944, when a dispute broke out in the Kent coalfield, industrial disputes accounted for only one-third as many days lost as in the First World War and, despite a tight labour market, had been held to the same level as the slump years of the early 1930s. The Ministry of Labour would only issue essential work orders once it was satisfied that factories met welfare criteria along trade-union lines. It was Bevin's Catering Wages Bill in February 1943, presented as necessary to the war effort, resented by backbench Tories as another piece of socialism by stealth, which occasioned the second significant parliamentary split in the Coalition.

The first – to which it was retaliation – had been in the previous month, when the Commons debated the Beveridge Report. What Beveridge deliberately did in his official report, *Social Insurance and Allied Services*, was to provide a comprehensive blueprint for post-war welfare policy. What he accidentally achieved was an impact granted by lucky timing, for his report was published on 1 December 1942, within weeks of the victory at El Alamein which so relieved British anxiety about the course of the war. Vague, uplifting rhetoric about war aims was not the point; all the evidence suggests that people wanted something practical and achievable, consolidating the welfare gains of the war. This Beveridge offered. With thirty years' experience as a social administrator behind him, he showed how poverty could be abolished through a comprehensive and integrated scheme of social insurance. To this he added a plan for child allowances; and he made two further assumptions, necessary to his scheme but not part of it. One was that a national health service would be created; the other that mass unemployment would not be permitted to recur.

The Beveridge Report became an unexpected best-seller, selling over 600,000 copies; a short version was prepared for the forces (though then temporarily withdrawn). Nineteen out of twenty people had soon heard of the Beveridge Plan; it was widely noted abroad; its author became a major public figure; all talk was suddenly focused on post-war reconstruction. Meanwhile, the Government grumpily observed – Attlee and Bevin as much as Churchill – the war had to be won. Hence the cautious reception which the Government gave the Beveridge Plan in the Commons; hence a backbench revolt by nearly a 100 Labour MPs, demanding a more urgent commitment to it. This proved to be a political watershed. Thereafter support for a post-war coalition dropped away; and opinion polls showed Labour well clear of the Conservatives if there were to be an election. The effect of Beveridge was to channel the force for domestic change behind a plan for remodelling the existing National Insurance scheme, as first instituted in 1911.

In the last part of the war, the Labour Party gave institutional form to the unfocused radical impulses of 1940–41. The electoral truce between the parties had not eliminated all contests in by-elections. Labour MPs were replaced with little trouble, most without a contest (though Labour lost Motherwell to the Scottish Nationalists in April 1945). But from 1942 Conservative vacancies produced a crop of unofficial left-wing challengers; not only did they take four seats from the Conservatives between March and June 1942, which could be blamed on Singapore and Tobruk: the subsequent improvement in the war news did not, post-Beveridge, translate into a revival of Conservative fortunes. Candidates of the Common Wealth Party, set up by an idealistic ex-Liberal MP, Sir Richard Acland, achieved by-election upsets during the last two years of the war – clearly because it offered the only opportunity to vote against the now discredited Conservative Party. The full significance of this was not appreciated at the time, and opinion polls were largely ignored; but the signs of a widespread leftward shift are unmistakable in retrospect. The Communist Party, with its close links to the Soviet Union, enjoyed a limited revival; but the impressive successes of the Red Army were read as a more general vindication of planning – both a catchword and a catch-all at this time. Whatever its diverse origins, virtually all this support fell into the lap of the Labour Party, the residuary legatee of Priestley, Beveridge, Keynes, Acland, Stalin and other distinguished non-members.

VE Day signalled the victory which Churchill had promised. His own suggestion of continuing the Coalition until VJ Day was unacceptable to Labour, and the Coalition came to an end in May 1945, its mission completed. Churchill formed a Conservative Government, which he hoped would be returned at the forthcoming general election. Such expectations were widely held, since many people remembered Lloyd George's triumph in 1918; Labour relied on voters remembering what happened next, a constant theme in its propaganda. Churchill reverted to type as a narrowly partisan campaigner. Afterwards, one of his extravagant claims, that the same Labour colleagues with whom he had worked for five years against Hitler were about to introduce their own Gestapo into Britain, was blamed for losing votes. But, according to the opinion polls, the Conservatives actually gained support during the campaign; in the spring of 1945 they were 20 per cent behind Labour and closed the gap to 8 per cent on polling day in July.

The fact was that, in retrospect, the Conservative Party's pre-war record on unemployment and appeasement inspired little confidence in their professions of support for the Coalition's reconstruction agenda. Churchill's reception suggests that he remained personally popular at home – as a great war leader, at least. The reactions of some members of the armed forces may well have been more sceptical. All the indications are that their votes, cast in special polling stations around the world under better arrangements than in 1918, went heavily to Labour. But the breadth of Labour's constituency, putting a clear 10 per cent on its pre-war share of the vote, was the key to victory. In London Morrison had courageously staked his credibility on an appeal for cross-class support by standing for the socially mixed suburban seat of Lewisham East, which he won for Labour. The Liberals polled under 10 per cent nationally; even Beveridge failed to win a seat. As the results came in – three weeks after polling day to allow for the forces' participation – it became clear that Labour had gained nearly 250 seats from its opponents, giving it a clear majority for the first time.

# 7

## Let Us Face the Future
### 1945–55

### CRADLE TO GRAVE

On 26 July 1945 the election results showed that Labour would have nearly 400 seats in the new parliament, the Conservatives just over 200. To the world's astonishment, the mighty Churchill, freshly garlanded with the honours of war, was suddenly out of office. With Bevin's forthright support, Attlee went ahead with the formation of a Labour cabinet. It was (1931 aside) the most experienced ministry ever to take office. Labour may have run as the Opposition in the recent election, but the Party had it both ways in simultaneously benefiting from the credibility with which high office had endowed its new Big Five.

Morrison became Lord President of the Council, with wide responsibilities in domestic policy. Perhaps for that reason, Attlee decided at the last moment, and with the King's approbation, to send Bevin not to the Treasury – where friction between him and Morrison was all too predictable – but to the Foreign Office. Conversely, this meant that Hugh Dalton, for all his pre-war apprenticeship in foreign affairs and his wartime stint at the Ministry of Economic Warfare, had to be switched into the vacancy as Chancellor of the Exchequer. Finally, a suitable berth was found at the Board of Trade for Sir Stafford Cripps. Cripps, a polished barrister who had been a left-wing rebel in the 1930s, starting the weekly paper *Tribune* to champion a popular front, had ridden a surging red tide during the war, notably as ambassador to the Soviet Union. The steely integrity of his Christian socialist convictions impressed Attlee, who now gave Cripps his big chance.

Though Dalton was later eclipsed by Cripps, it was really this constant inner core – Greenwood, replaced as deputy leader by Morrison in 1945, was fading fast and left the Government in 1947 – which saw the Government through its first parliament. In those five years the Labour Party had the unusual satisfaction of seeing its election manifesto, *Let Us Face the Future*, carried out with remarkable fidelity, at least in domestic policy. Legislation to create a welfare state was high on the agenda.

There was one statutory monument to the short period of office of Churchill's 'caretaker' administration from May to July 1945: the Family Allowances Act. This fulfilled an objective set in the Beveridge Report, by making an allowance of five shillings a week (25p) for the second and subsequent children in all British families. The idea of 'family endowment' had been publicized for thirty years, notably through the tireless campaign led by one of the early women MPs, Eleanor Rathbone. Herself from Liberal stock, she had support from Labour, and the fact that the bill was put through by the Conservatives speaks for the strong cross-party consensus on this issue. Motives were mixed. Some saw it as an attack on the poverty associated with large families through the redistribution of income; others as a feminist advance since it was the mother who received the allowance. But if these were typically tender-minded arguments, invoking a New Jerusalem to be built regardless of cost, there were also tough-minded arguments for this particular welfare measure that spoke a rather different language of national (even 'racial') efficiency.

After the revelations of the Nazi treatment of the Jews, in particular, this sort of talk came to sound suspect, racist and reactionary; but concerns about 'eugenic' improvement of the nation's offspring had, in earlier decades, often been intertwined with the conventional progressive arguments for welfare reform. Some of this was lazy thinking or ambiguous rhetoric. Thus Edwardian references to 'breeding an imperial race' might be nothing more sinister than a tactic for diverting imperialist enthusiasm into social reform; and it should be remembered that the term 'racial' was long used as a supposedly elevated synonym for 'national'. Still, there was a strong eugenic undertow to discussion of demographic trends in the twentieth century. One taunt directed at birth control early in the century was 'race suicide'. Fears of population decline seized public attention in the period between the two world wars – both of which were wars of attrition between mass armies, recruited from dwindling cohorts of men of military age.

The census gives a crude indication of the pivotal change that took place. In 1911 it showed that the population of England and Wales, which had quadrupled in the previous century, was still increasing at over 1 per cent a year. The next census in 1921 showed that this rate of increase had been halved – to an annual rate at which it was to remain for the next half century.[1] The Registrar-General's statistics for births and deaths show why this was happening. Continuing a trend which commenced in the late 1870s, the annual number of births dropped from about 30 per thousand of population at the turn of the century to about 20 per thousand by 1920 (ten years later in Scotland). This fall of about 10 per thousand compared with a fall in the number of deaths per thousand, over the same periods, of little more than half as much. So the death rate and the birth rate were both falling, but births much faster. One result was a decreasing rate of population growth. Another was an ageing population – produced not so much by the fact that more people were living longer but by the smaller proportion of young people in the population, caused by a lower birth rate. In 1901 almost a third of the British population was under the age of fifteen, while only 5 per cent were over sixty-five. By 1951 less than a quarter was under fifteen, but more than 10 per cent over sixty-five.

Where had all the babies gone? Someone reaching seventy in 1945 had been born at a time when there had been fifteen births each year for every hundred women of childbearing age in England and Wales; in 1911 this figure fell below ten, and by the 1930s it was stuck at around six. The initial fall was associated with a progressive postponement of the age of marriage, as shown by the four censuses after 1871; yet the proportion of women who were married crept up steadily during the first half of the twentieth century, which hardly accounts for the further fall in fertility. Births outside marriage contribute little to the explanation; the proportion of illegitimate babies declined from a shade over 5 per cent to a shade under 5 per cent of all births between 1870 and 1940.

The main explanation of the fall in fertility, as contemporaries were quick to note, lay in the deliberate restriction of births within marriage: a trend which was already clear by 1911 but which only revealed its full dimensions over the next quarter-century. Women who got married during the first decade of the century produced an average of 3.4 live

1. In Scotland, where the annual rate of increase was already down to 0.6 per cent in 1911, the population increased subsequently by a only quarter of a million, before stabilizing at around 5 million in the mid twentieth century. But the difference north and south of the border was due to migration rather than a radically different pattern of births and deaths. The natural rate of increase in Scotland was marginally higher than in England and Wales.

births. This figure conceals a wide spread, with over 25 per cent of them still having more than five children – compared with fewer than 10 per cent among those who got married thirty years later. By the 1930s the two-child family was not only the average but normal; more than half of all new marriages produced either one or two children. Extrapolation of this trend suggested that the British population would fail to replace itself by the end of the century; and proposals for encouraging young couples to rear families found a readier hearing.

Initially this decline in fertility was more pronounced in certain occupational groups, like textile workers, whereas miners continued to rear large families until the coal industry fell on hard times after the First World War. Among the better-off classes, families with two children were already commoner than those with three in early-twentieth-century marriages – at a time when four or five children were normal for manual labourers. Hence the chorus, often ideologically inspired, of eugenic apprehension (or misapprehension) about the detrimental effect on the national stock. Indeed such concerns helped to generate the Registrar-General's official classification of the British social structure.[1] In fact the fertility gap between various classes was later narrowed. Among couples married in the 1920s, agricultural labourers now produced fewer children than farmers had done twenty years previously, and manual wage-earners fewer than non-manual wage-earners had done previously. Between 1931 and 1951, fertility apparently increased by 10 per cent in the Registrar-General's two highest socio-economic classes, while it held fairly steady in the lower occupational groups. On the face of it, this should have allayed eugenic alarm.

Family planning, in any strict sense, relied on confidence that children would survive, which gains in infant and child mortality after 1900 steadily assured. It became a strategy which couples chose to adopt in a context of changing expectations about the costs and benefits of large families. The costs were increasing with restrictions on child labour,

---

1. The Registrar-General's model was used from the 1911 census onward. It identified a linear social hierarchy with professionals at its apex as Class I, and unskilled manual workers as Class V. Not everyone who used the model subscribed to eugenic theories, but it made them easier to test. There was subsequent reclassification, notably an expansion of Classes I and II, which means that comparisons over time need to be treated with caution.

better enforcement of school attendance, and the requirement to keep children at school longer. Conversely the benefits which folk wisdom attributed to children as a hedge against aged penury – whether relying on filial duty or, as the Poor Law claimed, on legal obligation – were questionable. Rowntree's social survey of York at the turn of the century found that only one in seventy households harboured three generations. Old-age pensions after 1908 increased the bargaining power of aged parents, either in getting their families to take them in, or in maintaining their independence. None of these relationships was simple; but the indications are that changing expectations about the parental role militated against the burden of large families.

Compared with this sort of motivation, the availability of mechanical means of contraception, like condoms, was secondary. Knowledge of the process of conception was more important, eroding a barrier of deliberately fostered ignorance about sex and reproduction. Keeping young girls 'innocent' was one side of late-Victorian sexual propriety and almost a test of respectability among rich and poor alike. There is now abundant evidence, even in this essentially private area, that couples who wanted to avoid conception practised abstinence and age-old techniques of coitus interruptus. Such methods were not foolproof but, backed up by abortion if they failed, they were demonstrably effective in achieving a general fall in fertility. The propaganda for birth control, especially by women doctors like Marie Stopes, author of the best-seller *Married Love*, helped break down some taboos in the 1920s; and, more informally, it seems clear that putting 10 million young men into uniform during two world wars served to disseminate a good deal of rough-and-ready sexual and prophylactic information.

Demobilization had its own demographic consequences. In 1920 there had been an upward kink in the number of births – at well over 1 million, the highest ever recorded. Nationally, this was a demographic compensation for the war dead; while for the new parents here was a compensation for babies forgone during the war. The effect was temporary and within five years the birth rate was lower than ever. The same thing seemed to be happening at the the end of the Second World War. In 1946–8 there were over half a million excess births above the established trend – a post-war 'bulge' which can hardly be attributed to the sole motivation of the new family allowances.

But the birth rate did not then fall back to the low level seen before the Second World War; instead of six births annually for every hundred women of childbearing age, there were at least seven in the early 1950s, rising to nine in the following decade – levels not sustained since the years just before the First World War. In 1963-5 there were more births than in 1946-8. Yet married women in the early 1960s were bearing only two children for every three borne by married women fifty years previously. What had happened was that more women were getting married – almost two out of three of those aged fifteen and over, compared with barely half at the beginning of the century. Above all, people were getting married younger. For England and Wales as a whole, in 1911 less than a quarter of women aged 20-24 were married; by 1951 half were, and by 1971 60 per cent. In the long term, therefore, a fall in fertility which was initially associated with a postponement of marriage (sometimes indefinite) was maintained in an era when it became normal to marry at relatively young ages. Not until the 1970s was this pattern again significantly disrupted.

The welfare state of the 1940s offered, as Churchill put it, 'national compulsory insurance for all classes for all purposes from the cradle to the grave'. This was what the Beveridge Plan was all about. Child allowances were a necessary buttress, using general taxation to supplement incomes in families with several children. Otherwise the assumption was that a (male) breadwinner would earn enough to support a wife and one child; and out of his earnings a single weekly deduction would be taken as his contribution towards a comprehensive scheme of social insurance, also financed by an employer's contribution and a state subsidy. What Beveridge's tidy mind achieved was a consolidation of all the previous schemes, established haphazardly and incrementally, safeguarding the insured person from the hazards of injury at work, disability, sickness, unemployment, old age and even death (in the form of widow's pensions).

Beveridge provided, broadly if not in every detail, the basis of the National Insurance legislation of the post-war Labour Government. Standard levels of benefit were established, based on the subsistence income necessary for the conventional household unit of husband and wife and child, thus implementing the poverty-line strategy set out by Rowntree half a century earlier. The whole employed population was covered, not just manual workers or those on lower incomes, as in the pre-war National Insurance scheme. A further provision was that those who fell through the cracks of this tessellated insurance mosaic would nonetheless receive National Assistance. This fulfilled the residual obligation, which the Poor Law had always recognized, for the community to relieve destitution. It did so by generalizing the function of the Unemployment Assistance Board, as implemented in 1935 to howls of Labour indignation about its means-tested benefits; but Labour's National Assistance Board helped claimants not as of right but on discretionary grounds of proven need, which amounted to much the same thing.

The (contributory) state retirement pension was now made available to all – even to those who were too old in 1946 to have paid the contributions. The age limit of seventy for the original old-age pension meant that 3 per cent of the population had been eligible in 1911. By 1951, what with increased longevity and the reduction in the age limit to sixty-five for men and only sixty for women, nearly 14 per cent of the population were eligible. This was an expensive commitment, and bound to become more so.

What Beveridge did not disclose was how his airy assumption of a national health service could be implemented; and though the Coalition accepted the principle, it had not resolved either the administrative difficulties or the conflicts of interest with which health-care proposals bristle. There had been enormous difficulties in bringing the British Medical Association round to participating in the Health Insurance scheme in 1911–13. As formidable a civil servant as Sir Robert Morant had found his abilities taxed in the effort; and Lloyd George had required all his Welsh guile and pertinacity. After 1945 the doctors were to get another dose of the same medicine. ·

The Minister of Health in the post-war Labour Government was Aneurin Bevan. The son of a coal miner, Bevan had himself gone down the pit in South Wales before making a career in the Labour movement, initially through his education at the (Marxist) Central Labour College, and rapidly entering Parliament in 1929 as MP for his native Ebbw Vale. His eloquence and free-ranging mind made him an attractive figure on the backbenches, where he remained during the war as a gadfly critic of Churchill, whom in many ways he emulated: not only predictably (as a parliamentary orator) but also, more provokingly, in affecting a disdain for mere 'bourgeois' politicians. In the cabinet Bevan represented youth, radicalism, wit and charisma, marking him out as a predestined future leader of his party if he could only harness these gifts to a consistent political strategy, inspiring trust and support. As a minister he made an excellent start, showing a sure grasp of administrative technique for all his lack of previous experience in office.

Bevan knew how to walk softly, charming the BMA out of their largely self-induced anxieties about being reduced to the status of state employees; but he also carried the big stick of a decisive parliamentary majority, which he used to enforce his own priority of nationalizing the hospital service. At a stroke this imposed a simple principle on the inherited anomalies between ancient charitable hospitals, old poor-law infirmaries which had passed to municipal control, cottage hospitals, tuberculosis sanatoria established under Health Insurance auspices, and other diverse institutions. Once the hospitals were brought under state control (exercised through regional hospital boards) the general-practitioner service could be organized in a more decentralized fashion, through capitation fees paid by the state on behalf of every patient registered with a participating doctor's practice.

Still this was not enough to allay the professional fears of the British Medical Association, speaking for the general practitioners and seeking to mobilize a boycott of the new scheme. It was here, in the two years between the passing of legislation and its implementation in 1948, that Bevan faced essentially the same trial as Lloyd George before him and it was to be resolved in essentially the same way – not only by cajolery (though that helped) but by buying off the doctors. The consultants were Bevan's first target. Their opposition melted once they were promised the right to continue private practice within the NHS hospitals, thus getting the best of both worlds. The President of the Royal College of Physicians, Lord Moran, whose own best-known private patient was Churchill, was opportunely turned (some said twisted) into an agent of Bevan's grand design. Outflanked, the leadership of the BMA persisted in its proposed boycott; but a referendum in May 1948 showed that half the country's GPs were now in favour of cooperation, and the BMA capitulated.

The fact was that the NHS, like the panel doctor system before it, simply channelled more resources into medicine than doctors, especially in poorer districts, had previously commanded. The participation of over 90 per cent of doctors was assured by the 'appointed day' in July 1948, when the NHS came into operation. In the first two years expenditure exceeded the estimates by 40 per cent, provoking alarm that spending was out of control, though the real reason was an under-estimate of what needed to be done for patients who had previously lacked adequate attention. For insured persons, under the National

Insurance Act of 1911, panel doctors had already provided medical benefits, albeit of a more restricted kind. But these were overwhelmingly for men in the prime of life – the very social category which was least in need. For women, for dependent children, for the elderly, the NHS established a right to a quality of medical service which had previously been a narrow privilege, hedged by costs which cast a shadow over many unlucky households.

What Bevan did was to transform the National Health Service from a pipe-dream into an enduring British institution. It was to become Labour's best card with the electorate for the rest of the century. In the short term, however, it became the vehicle of Labour's worst party crisis for twenty years, which in turn permitted a Conservative resurgence on a scale unanticipated in 1945.

## THE POST-WAR SETTLEMENT

The Attlee Government's economic policy sought to reconcile two objectives. One was to take a number of enterprises into common ownership, the other to maintain full employment. Labour suggested that through 'planning' – whatever that meant – the one could be made the tool of the other. Indeed some on the left, like Aneurin Bevan, went so far as to dismiss the Keynesian claims of the Coalition's White Paper on Employment Policy in 1944, with its commitment to maintaining 'a high and stable level of employment', on the ground that only a socialist regime would be able to do this.

In practice, of course, it was not so simple. The socialist goal of common ownership had been enshrined in Clause IV of the Labour Party constitution for a generation, but the means by which this would be secured had received little attention – except from Morrison. His creation of London Transport under a largely autonomous public corporation provided a model, which he did not impose on others – he did not have to – but which became the template for the nationalization measures of the Attlee Government. In fact Morrison's programme owed a good deal more to pragmatism than ideology: that is one reason why, at Labour's pre-election conference in December 1944, he had resisted calls for a hard-and-fast 'shopping list' of industries to be nationalized, which he saw as an election-loser. The left had their victory on this occasion, and since the subsequent election was not lost, their faith in the popular appeal of public ownership was reinforced. But Morrison's expertise put him in the driving-seat, where he steered almost the whole programme through Parliament, with skill and caution; and applied the brakes before approaching one particularly awkward corner. It was the nationalization of the iron and steel industry which spelt political danger for Labour.

By contrast, putting the Bank of England under public ownership in 1945 moved few people – and arguably changed little in the already close cooperation between 'the authorities'. The remodelling of the British Overseas Airways Corporation (BOAC), as created by the Chamberlain Government, caused even less of a stir. Even the nationalization of the coal mines in 1947, though emotive for all who identified with the miners' unavailing struggle in 1926, had been on the political agenda since the end of the First World War; and had been preceded by the nationalization of coal royalties (by the National Government) in 1938. When the gas industry, still closely linked with coal before natural gas was discovered, was nationalized in 1948, this was more a measure of centralization than of extending public ownership, at least so far as it affected the third of the industry which had long been in municipal hands (in Birmingham, for example, since Joseph Chamberlain's day). This did not stop the Conservatives putting up a great show of opposition in parliament, largely to revive their own spirits; but they found themselves more compromised the next year in arguing against extending public ownership to electricity supply (or rather to the third of it not already municipalized) since it was a Conservative Government which had established the national grid as a public utility twenty years previously. Nor was Churchill, that ancient proponent of railway nationalization, the best leader of the opposition to the amalgamation of the four oligopolistic companies into British Railways, part of an integrated British Transport Commission.

In all of these examples, a strong pragmatic case existed, in line with classical principles of free competition, for eliminating private monopoly by taking essential utilities into public ownership. This was not, however, the case which appealed to socialists, who preferred to dwell on the abolition of the capitalist system through dispossession of the tsars of big business. This raised the ideological temperature, in ways that generally helped the Conservatives, by subsequently making the perceived failings of the undercapitalized rail network or the played-out coal industry into object lessons in the inefficiency of nationalized industries. It also raised the stakes in the set-piece confrontation over iron and steel, the only major manufacturing industry on Labour's list. Landed with this unwanted commitment, Morrison's approach was half-hearted Fabianism: delaying until the moment appeared ripe, then, when it failed to ripen, delaying again, and finally striking anyway. The Iron and Steel bill was at last introduced in 1949, coupled with a measure to shorten the period for which, under the Parliament Act, the House of Lords could obstruct legislation (from two years to one). Even so, this left insufficient time to complete the process before a general election had to take place – and it kept an issue which was now hurting Labour on the boil. Though the Act eventually came into force in 1951, it was an easy matter for the subsequent Conservative Government to engage in their one centre-stage piece of 'denationalization' (though intermittent noises-off from the wings indicated the similar fate of the road-haulage industry).

The finance of nationalization proved the least of the problems. The Government issued public stock as compensation to the shareholders of the companies taken over.[1] Most of them got a good deal, initially through a favourable valuation and subsequently through a perverse effect of Government monetary policy upon capital values. When, as Chancellor, Dalton tried to enforce 'cheaper money' than the already low interest rates which prevailed, he savoured Keynes's dictum that a declining rate of interest – if it could be enforced – would bring 'the euthanasia of the rentier'. The crunch, however, came with the failure of the issue of Government stock in 1946–7 ('Daltons') which attempted to fund part of the long-term national debt at the unprecedentedly low level of 2.5 per cent. The fact was that the markets could not be bullied into buying this kind of stock at par, and it had to be unloaded at a knock-down price. So much for 'cheaper' money – though cheap money, signalled by a bank-rate fixed at 2 per cent, persisted. The perverse consequence came through an appreciation of the value of

1. The gilt-edged public debt which Labour inherited was £13 billion and a further £2 billion was added by 1951, almost entirely in compensation for nationalization. Since gilt-edged bonds bore a fixed interest rate, based on the nominal value of the stock, the actual price at which they traded would slump if the nominal rate of interest were lower than market expectations. Thus £100 of stock, bearing an interest rate fixed at 2 per cent in a market where the market expects a return of 2.5 per cent, would actually change hands at £80; since the annual payment by Government on this stock is fixed at £2, the actual return on £80 works out at 2.5 per cent.

assets with a prospective annual return higher than these rock-bottom official interest rates. Capital gains, which escaped the attention of the Inland Revenue until 1965, thus gave rentiers a tax holiday at Dalton's unwitting expense. One effect was to question the wisdom of cheap money itself; another to expose the limitations of high income tax as a means of redistributing wealth.

This was one indication of the limits to which Labour could get its own way within a mixed economy. Yet the alternative was a fully articulated command economy, on the Soviet 'Gosplan' model, which held little charm for any of the ministers who successively held economic portfolios – and no appeal whatsoever for the Government's American paymasters. The fact is that the UK had become dependent on economic assistance from the USA in the winter of 1940–41 and was to remain so for the rest of the decade. This was not through choice, on either side, but necessity, which each side had difficulty in recognizing. Hence the three phases of American support: each a generous shot-in-the arm for the exhausted British economy but each storing up horrible withdrawal symptoms.

First to come (and go, of course) was Lend-Lease. The strategic impact was decisive; quite simply it allowed Britain to win the war. The economic impact was equally decisive; it meant that Britain's distorted, fully mobilized command economy was no longer independently viable or competitive in post-war markets. The financial burden of the Second World War for Britain was twice that of the First, wiping out 28 per cent of the country's wealth, leaving a net deficit in overseas assets; in particular, a debt of £3 billion to the rest of the sterling area had been run up (the 'sterling balances'). Above all, the war had reduced the export industries to a fraction of their pre-war capacity. True, domestic food production had been increased; but the prospective deficit on the balance of payments in 1945 approached £1 billion. Plans for a move by stages towards equilibrium, in the breathing-space between VE Day and VJ Day, when Lend-Lease was due to end, were blown sky-high at Hiroshima. The Japanese surrender was a mixed blessing for Attlee, in the first month of his premiership; within days President Truman innocently cut off Britain's lifeline. If the beginning of Lend-Lease was the most unsordid act, its ending was surely the most unsettling act in Anglo-American relations. Though transitional arrangements were pieced together by sympathetic American officials, the alternatives now facing Britain were desperate – to beg, borrow or starve.

Keynes was sent to Washington, confident of his mendicant skills. When begging got nowhere, the haggling began over the terms on which the UK could borrow. In the end a loan was negotiated totalling $3,750 million, which was topped up by a (proportionately much larger) loan of $1,250 million from Canada. The terms were easy – or impossible, according to which way one looked at them. For American assistance depended on an undertaking to make sterling freely convertible with the dollar on a fixed timetable, set for the summer of 1947. The whole thing was delusive, outrageous, humbling: or so a discordant chorus from both the socialist left and imperialist right maintained. The alternative remained starvation, hardly less, since a siege economy would have required severe reductions in the already meagre British diet. As it was, bread went on the ration for the first time in 1946.

Keynes's judgement prevailed; the North American loan was accepted. Thus began the second phase of dollar dependency, which virtually encompassed Dalton's Chancellorship. The calculation was that Britain's balance of payments could be turned round within a couple of years or so, bringing an equilibrium with the USA which would allow all obligations to be met. A fiscal squeeze was maintained on domestic consumption to allow resources to flow into exports. This is how the young Keynesian economists, concentrated in the Economic Section and later the Central Economic Planning Staff, conceived the problem; meanwhile the old hands in the Treasury were content that high taxation was moving the budget back towards surplus. From either point of view, the analysis pointed towards a tough budget in April 1947, when Dalton maintained income tax at its peacetime record level of 9s (45 per cent) and doubled tobacco duties – to save dollars rather than the people's health.

For the 'dollar gap' was by now the crucial problem. British exports as a whole had already regained their pre-war volume and, despite difficulties in reconciling these estimates, it is now clear that the overall balance of payments was no worse than had been anticipated, though errors in the figures published at the time gave cause for general alarm. Britain's problem, however, was specifically a dollar shortage. Crudely, the war had enriched the USA, making it essential to put enough dollars into the hands of its trading partners to finance their imports of American goods. Britain's markets in the sterling area and other soft-currency countries were now as incapable as Britain of breaking into the hard-currency markets dominated by the dollar; so the traditional means of financing a British deficit with the USA, through multilateral settlements, did not work. Instead, through the sterling area in particular, the UK was piling up new investments to a value not far short of the dollar loan – which was meanwhile draining away to pay for essential imports (which included Hollywood movies and Virginia tobacco). It took two crises, in 1947 and 1949, to resolve the dollar paradox.

First, however, the Government faced another crisis of even more traumatic dimensions. Coal was still the source of over 90 per cent of British energy supplies, employing 700,000 miners to cut 200 million tons in a good year, which 1947 was not. It saw the worst winter of the century, with a prolonged freeze-up from January to March, followed by severe flooding in the thaw. This was unforeseeable; but a fuel crisis was not unpredictable – except, as he hubristically said himself, by the Minister of Fuel and Power, Emanuel Shinwell, Shinwell's manifest lack of grip was the worst possible advertisement for nationalization as a cure-all. The energy shortage meant that the country was virtually shut down for weeks. The public's honeymoon indulgence towards the new Government was replaced by a sense of having lived for two years in a fool's paradise.

And the dollars were trickling away, month by month. In July 1947, as agreed, it became possible to convert sterling into dollars, which many people promptly did, turning a trickle into a torrent. The sterling crisis exposed the nakedness of the Government's pretensions to be in control of a planned economy. Dalton, his nerve badly shaken, stumbled on; it was Attlee's worst moment, his normal decisiveness temporarily lacking. The economic outcome was a suspension of convertibility in August, with American acquiescence; the political outcome, a cabinet reshuffle in September. Cripps, who had had a good crisis, boldly told Attlee that he thought it was time for a change of prime minister (preferably to Bevin). The prime minister checked with Bevin by telephone and told Cripps that he thought otherwise. But Cripps was adroitly shifted into a new post as economic supremo; and in November, when the hapless Dalton inadvertently disclosed the austerity measures in his emergency budget to a waiting journalist – an old-fashioned scoop which spelled resignation by the old-fashioned code of ministerial integrity which prevailed in that era – Cripps became Chancellor himself.

The names Cripps and austerity became synonymous. He imparted into his stewardship a stern sense of purpose which was almost providential, captured in Churchill's quip: 'There, but for the grace of God, goes God.' But what actually paid the bills were more dollars – a third phase of subventions from the USA. In June 1947 the American Sec-retary of State, George Marshall, gave a suitably uplifting commence-ment address at Harvard, asking that the European nations take an initiative over reconstruction of their devastated continent. Ernest Bevin pounced. Encouraging noises from Washington emboldened him to organize a concerted response from western European governments which resulted in the handsome offer of Marshall Aid. These grants from the USA can be called a form of enlightened self-interest and were not, it now seems, the beginning of European recovery, which was already under way. Even so, enlightenment of this order was rare enough, reconciling reconstruction with post-war social as well as eco-nomic expectations. Seemingly, the welfare state was made possible by Marshall Aid; and the growing warmth of social-democratic attitudes towards the USA needs to be understood in this context.

The final dollar-based crisis in 1949 was Cripps's last. In only three years as Chancellor he established a new regime at the Treasury, remov-ing much ambivalence about the adoption of a Keynesian approach. Rather than 'Gosplan', a liberal conception of planning now carried the day, relying on the budget as the main tool of demand manage-ment. Big surpluses were piled up in his three budgets, producing the required shift into exports. The overall balance of payments moved into a healthy surplus; estimates vary, but on any reckoning it was over £150 million in both 1948 and 1949. But with the dollar area, although the deficit of £500 million in 1947 was subsequently reduced to a net figure under £100 million, this was after Marshall Aid had been counted. Without it, the deficit with the dollar bloc in 1949 would have ap-proached £300 million. The solution was not too difficult for an economist to see: a devaluation of sterling (and other soft currencies) against the hard currencies of the dollar area, to bring the pattern of settlements into balance. There were by now enough economists, not only in Whitehall but in key ministerial posts, to ensure that this option was discussed.

The three young ministers who were left with this problem in the summer of 1949, while Cripps sought to regain his health in a Swiss sanatorium, were all professional economists. Hugh Gaitskell, the Minister of Fuel, was the most senior; he was joined in his advocacy of devaluation by the youngest member of the cabinet, Harold Wilson, President of the Board of Trade, and by Douglas Jay, Financial Secretary to the Treasury. Cripps thus became the agent of this policy; it was agreed by the cabinet at the end of August, then put on ice for three (leak-free) weeks while Cripps and Bevin visited Washington (by sea), with carte blanche to settle on a new parity, radically lower so as to be lasting. Instead of $4.03, which had prevailed since 1940, the pound was devalued by no less than 30 per cent, to $2.80. There was a determination to impose wholly different priorities in this crisis than in 1931. No longer did the authorities carry the day in their overriding anxiety that Britain should not repudiate its obligations; and it was, of course, true that the sterling balances would be worth 30 per cent less in dollars. The course adopted inevitably (and painfully) involved Cripps in denying the imminence of devaluation to the House of Commons: which he did to such good effect that the markets were taken by surprise, allowing Britain to reap the full advantage. This was considerable, and it was already apparent before Cripps, now fatally ill, was replaced at the Exchequer in October 1950 by Gaitskell.

Backed by a wages freeze at home, reinforced by physical controls to suppress inflation, and building on the existing strength of Britain's trading position, devaluation finally corrected the chronic dollar deficit. So much so that in 1950 Marshall Aid to Britain was cut off early. British exports in 1950 were 50 per cent higher by volume than in 1937, at the peak of pre-war recovery; and the UK's share of world trade in manufactures produced by industrial countries had now bounced back to nearly 25 per cent, compared with 21 per cent in 1937. Admittedly, the real competition from other European countries was still to come through. All told, though, there is some plausibility in the judgement, privately recorded by a Conservative cabinet minister a couple of years later, on the record of his political opponents: that 'the story was one of achievement – a picture of substantial recovery from 1945-50, succeeded by a period of difficulty due mainly to circumstances beyond our control'.

## ONE WAR TOO MANY

The strength of the British armed forces in peacetime had normally been under 400,000. With demobilization at the end of the Second World War the total dropped from 5 million in 1945 to 2 million in 1946; but in 1948 it was still nearly 1 million. A system of National

Service was instituted in 1947, putting all eligible eighteen-year-olds into uniform for up to two years. This was to keep the strength of the armed forces at around three-quarters of a million until 1957, and only from 1961 did the numbers fall below half a million, with the phasing-out of National Service. Virtually every man born between 1880 and 1940 had been eligible at some time for military service, which gave three generations a taste of military discipline and an insight into what was meant by the term military efficiency – a common culture of reference which, for better or worse, a later generation, growing up from the 1960s, simply missed. For Britain, peculiar in its insular tradition, post-war National Service was a unique period of conscription during peacetime – if that is what this period was.

It hardly seemed so. In 1947 defence spending took nearly 18 per cent of gross national product (GNP); still 6 per cent in 1951. Some of the costs followed from the way the war ended. An army of occupation in Germany had to be maintained; moreover, the hapless German population in the British zone had to be fed – the main reason for bread rationing in Britain. Such were the spoils of victory. Britain behaved like a great power and offered a broad back for such burdens. The reality of dependence on the USA took time to sink in, just as its counterpart – the inescapability of opposition to the USSR – took time to be acknowledged. In Germany the result was an effective amalgamation of the British and American zones in 1947, as their common aims (if unequal resources) in rehabilitating the west diverged increasingly from Soviet policy. The British Army of the Rhine (BAOR), which had gone to hold down the Germans, stayed on to hold off the Russians.

Churchill supplied two images which nicely capture British perceptions of the post-war world. One was that of an iron curtain descending across Europe, the other of Britain standing at the intersection of three overlapping circles: Europe, the Empire, and a transatlantic partnership. When the apprehensions generated by the first perception drove the grandiose ambition of the second, the result was an over-extension of Britain's role in all directions simultaneously. No more than Churchill did Bevin, the most masterful Foreign Secretary of the century, regard Britain's great-power status as a matter for debate: simply as a given end to which the exertion of will and skill supplied the means. When he told the miners that he would give them a new foreign policy if they would give him more coal, his realism did not extend to cutting back commitments ruthlessly in line with resources.

Although his efforts were prodigious and his achievements not inconsiderable, they did not, of course, permanently reverse the trajectory of British decline. Indeed, the question which seems obvious fifty years later is how much Britain was weakened by fighting above its weight. A few people asked this at the time – Keynes, for example, in his advice to the cabinet in the closing months of the war (and of his life) or the chief scientific adviser (Sir Henry Tizard) with his prophecy: 'We are a great nation, but if we continue to behave like a Great Power we shall soon cease to be a great nation.'

It is, however, inconsistent to applaud the bloody-mindedness which was responsible for 1940 while expecting a wholly different gut reaction to the challenges of the post-war world. Hitler cast a long shadow. A whole generation of British statesmen resolved not to become guilty men, whatever the price exacted by a show of resolution. Signs of Soviet intransigence were interpreted, not by extending the benefit of the doubt to the country which had suffered most from the war, but on a worst-case scenario, intent on checking the march of another totalitarian regime bent on expansion. On the left, there had been talk of a socialist foreign policy, which Bevin himself was misinterpreted as entertaining at the end of the war. In fact he needed few lessons in scepticism towards the Soviet Union from the Foreign Office mandarins. Instead, anecdotal incidents from Bevin's career as an anti-Communist trade-union leader, wearyingly reiterated, clothed his guiding insights – giving some ground for the gibe that he treated the Soviet Union like a breakaway branch from the TGWU. Bevin's suspicion of Communist activities in Greece in the aftermath of the war was an early example of his equal determination to resist both Soviet influence and the vocal left wing of his own party. While Churchill, freed from responsible office, made widely reported speeches pitched at 'the English-speaking peoples', Bevin took practical steps to create an Anglo-American axis.

Labour's policy was clearly different from Churchill's, however, when it came to India. Attlee himself, a veteran of the Simon Commission, took charge here. He did what he thought necessary with a good grace and an iron nerve, moving beyond the endless talk about Dominion status by conceding the case for independence, even at the price of partition of the subcontinent between a Muslim state (encompassing West Pakistan and, in the east, what later became Bangladesh) and India itself, a non-sectarian state but a predominantly Hindu society. The last Viceroy was sent out: Admiral Lord Mountbatten, the former allied commander in south-east Asia. Immaculately well-connected and relentlessly self-promoting – Noël Coward's wartime film *In Which We Serve* talked up his naval exploits – Mountbatten behaved like minor royalty, which he was, but with a provoking radical twist. It was Attlee's policy, however, which was implemented: to withdraw expeditiously while securing the goodwill of the leadership of the successor states. Faced with prevarication, Attlee reacted by bringing forward a firm deadline for the transfer of power; meanwhile the Mountbattens hobnobbed with the Congress leaders, especially with Nehru. Delhi was the backdrop for the most piquant chapter in a glittering career: In Which We Scuttle.

It was Churchill, as leader of the opposition, who introduced the term 'scuttle'. True, the dark side of withdrawal was the intercommunal bloodshed which accompanied partition in 1947. But the loss of life – Gandhi's too, indirectly – which accompanied the end of the British Raj at least saw the realization of Indian independence without open war – and (under a formula designed to accommodate the new republic) without severance from the Commonwealth. This seemed the greater prize, since Labour set great store by fostering the conception of a multiracial Commonwealth. The old Dominions, which had shown themselves Britain's only real friends when the chips were down in 1940, would in due course be augmented by other peoples, set on the path to self-government under the tutelage of the inventors of the parliamentary system. In this sense the new Commonwealth rhetoric can be seen as updating the old paternalist approach – imperialism with a human face. Scuttle had served well enough in India but there was no plan to work on such a timetable in Africa. In Tanganyika an ambitious neocolonial plan was conceived for promoting the cultivation of groundnuts for vegetable oils, and all within the sterling area – the sort of thing Joseph Chamberlain went in for. Its failure became a frequent taunt against the extravagance and waste of socialism, at home or abroad.

The central achievement of post-war British foreign policy was to yoke the USA to the future security of a renascent western Europe, once eastern Europe had fallen under Soviet domination. Bevin's role in making a reality of the Marshall Plan pointed the way; and the fact that, as expected, in July 1947 the Soviet delegation walked out of the talks about implementing Marshall Aid merely confirmed that Europe was now divided into two camps. Bevin now worked on a further plan of his own. The initial stage involved the creation of a Western European Union in March 1948, pledging Britain, France and the Low Countries (the future Benelux) to create an integrated defence system. The completion of the grand design depended on its transatlantic dimension. As in 1939, Canadian help was forthcoming but it took longer to bring the USA round to the view that its security was bound up with that of the touchy and unreliable French or the importunate and stubborn British. Far from leading an anti-Soviet crusade, at this point the USA had cold feet about its cold-war allies.

Bevin's vision of what needed to be done received persuasive corroboration from Soviet behaviour. In February 1948 there was a coup in Prague, overthrowing again the democratic government of Czechoslovakia. The effect on social-democratic opinion was decisive; Bevin's firm line met with little further dissent within the Labour Party. Four months later, the Soviet Union cut off the land corridor to west Berlin. Rather than simply acquiesce or simply jump into a conflict on the ground, a third option was chosen – an airlift of all necessary supplies. This was a mammoth operation, successfully accomplished, month by month, until Stalin finally called off the blockade in May 1949; and the political effects, in establishing the US Air Force in British bases, were long-lasting. In this context smoother progress of the negotiations for an alliance became possible, and the North Atlantic Treaty (soon to become known as Nato) was signed in April 1949.

But where did Britain stand in the third circle, Europe? Bevin had furthered western European integration through his initiative in responding to Marshall and his Plan; the Committee of European Economic Cooperation (CEEC) was the result. Yet the British ignored the Europeans when they decided to devalue the pound, instead taking the Americans and the Canadians into their confidence. This snub to CEEC was characteristic of British condescension towards European countries which, generously enough, did not quickly forget who had liberated them. The trouble was that the British too had forgotten nothing – and learned nothing either, at least about their changing international role. Britain pursued a foreign policy which threw sops to European initiatives – this was how Bevin treated the Council of Europe in 1948 – with an overriding anxiety not to compromise Britain's independent status in the eyes of the USA (though the Americans, unimpressed, favoured Britain's involvement). Churchill's lush oratory in opposition gave him a reputation as a good European; but the fine print already hinted at what his return to power clearly disclosed – that his high-sounding notions for European unification did not embrace actual British participation. So it was that, when France came up with an invitation (or ultimatum) for Britain to join a new European Coal and Steel Community in 1950, the cabinet was unanimous in its refusal.

Declining its opportunities to shape the new Europe, the British Government persistently looked to a world role. This explains the decision to build a British atomic bomb; that Britain was capable of doing this in turn flattered pretensions to global influence. The development of a nuclear capability, under the leadership of the brilliant mathematician William Penney, and without the benefit of US cooperation, was certainly a tribute to the high calibre of British scientific expertise in nuclear physics. The Cavendish laboratory at Cambridge, with the New Zealander Lord Rutherford as its head from 1919 to his death in 1937, had pioneered research on nuclear fission. It was here that two of Rutherford's 'boys', the young physicists John Cockcroft and E. T. S. Walton, had developed the high-voltage particle accelerator with which they had succeeded in disintegrating lithium nuclei in 1931. In an experiment which created worldwide interest, the atom was thus 'split' for the first time by artificial means; and twenty years later the two men split the Nobel prize for physics.

It was a long scientific journey from the lab-based possibilities unleashed at the Cavendish – Rutherford had called the idea of harnessing nuclear energy 'moonshine' – to the capacity to explode an atomic bomb at Hiroshima, let alone the first British test at Monte Bello, Australia, in 1952. Moreover politics inevitably jumped into the driving-seat. The moral dilemma of making such terrible weapons had been largely resolved by the even more terrible prospect that the Nazis might get there first. It was the British Maud Report in 1941 which had initially persuaded the Americans of the feasibility of nuclear weapons, and in a wartime context the practical problems of pooling allied expertise were overcome. A group of Cambridge physicists under Cockcroft became the core of an Anglo-Canadian team based in Montreal, and other British scientists were integrated into the 'Manhattan Project' at Los Alamos, New Mexico. Thus the British stake in making the first atomic bomb reinforced a commitment, at least at the top level in government, to maintaining a nuclear presence after the war; and once it became clear, in 1946, that the USA would cease further cooperation, this meant deciding whether to mount an independent weapons programme. The decision to do so, basically taken by Attlee and Bevin, was belatedly acknowledged in Parliament in 1948. This may have been secretive but it was hardly furtive.

Labour ministers had a robust sense of rectitude about their international stance, feeling that, at any rate, Britain had met successive international challenges more effectively than in the late 1930s. The higher level of defence spending was an affordable if onerous price to pay. Whether the British people would pay any price, or could bear any burden, was shortly to be tested by another quarrel in a faraway country of which they knew little – Korea.

Following a general election in February 1950, the Attlee Government found itself on a knife-edge. It had maintained the extraordinary record of never having lost a by-election. In this it was aided by some luck, since swings against it in double figures had been recorded in several previously safe seats, like the north London suburb of Edmonton in November 1948. Still, Labour's hold among its traditional supporters remained strong; and the 1950 general election showed that Labour support had slipped by only 2 per cent since 1945, while the Conservatives increased their share of the poll by 4 per cent. There were, however, major boundary changes which not only corrected Labour's previous over-representation in depopulated urban areas but created a new bias against it. Thus the Conservatives' small gains in votes were magnified into an impressive gain of 200 seats, putting them only 17 MPs short of Labour. Since there were 9 Liberals, this cut the Government's majority to single figures. Though the Liberal vote held steady at 9 per cent nationally, this was achieved by putting up far more candidates than in 1945: a total of 475, of whom two-thirds lost their deposits, thus virtually bankrupting the Liberal organization. It was with this much-reduced majority that Labour hobbled through twenty months of crisis, facing a now rejuvenated Conservative opposition, baying for blood.

Why, at this juncture, an assault by the corrupt, repressive North Korean regime upon the corrupt, repressive South Korean regime should have enlisted such concern was a function of the cold war and of a cold-war mentality. The fact that Russia now had the atom bomb raised the stakes. Revelations of Soviet aggression made for a plausible scenario in which North Korea was simply a cat's-paw in the onward march of international Communism, masterminded from Moscow and (following the Chinese revolution) Peking.

Here was a theatre where the US strategic interest had been much disputed; but for Britain the preservation of Nato was the crux. There was also the leverage exerted by the United Nations, an organization thwarted in its early years by constant exercise of a Soviet veto, but opportunely freed (through temporary Soviet withdrawal) to act as the conscience of the world community in resisting aggression. Again, remorse over the failure of collective security in the 1930s brought belated overcompensation. The call for action in defence of South Korea, formally under UN auspices, but effectively as part of an alliance with the USA, met a weary and reluctant, but impressively unanimous, response from Britain. By the end of August 1950 British troops had landed in Korea, where they remained embattled in a messy conflict, prolonged by Chinese intervention, for the next three years.

Yet again, Britain was at war. A small war, to be sure, distant too; but one with implications of the first order for the economy and domestic politics. The painfully achieved economic recovery was halted in its tracks. Part of this was unavoidable, given that the US war machine was bidding up commodity prices in world markets, in ways that were bound to be unfavourable to British trade. The marginal cost of the war itself, it can be argued, was not very great, given the immense stockpiles of obsolescent supplies left over from 1945. But general rearmament now became a priority. In January 1951 Attlee announced a three-year defence programme for 1952–4 estimated at £4.7 billion. With the GNP standing at about £13 billion, the implication was that well over 10 per cent per annum would be spent on defence. It had been done before, of course – with American assistance. This time, despite encouraging hints, the USA's profuse support for British rearmament was to be verbal, not financial.

Hugh Gaitskell faced the problem of finding the money in his first Budget in April 1951. Only forty-five when he succeeded Cripps, suddenly challenging Bevan as Labour's rising star, Gaitskell was well fitted to be Chancellor by his previous career as an academic economist. He was, however, no mere technocrat, juggling the figures, but, for all his upper-middle-class background, a strongly egalitarian social democrat, with a passionate undertow of emotion lurking beneath the cold polished surface of his lucidly articulated arguments. Given his implicit support for Bevin, Gaitskell set about willing the means to achieve the agreed ends. His budget piled up taxation to shift resources out of private consumption into defence production. The standard rate of income tax went up to 9s 6d (47.5 per cent); with surtax, the top rate was 97.5 per cent. The political flashpoint was not here but in the accompanying proposals to levy charges for false teeth and spectacles supplied under the NHS.

This was the occasion – hardly the full reason – for the resignation from the cabinet of Aneurin Bevan. The NHS was his creation; though no longer Minister of Health, he took a proprietorial interest in it and stuck by the principle that there should be no charge at the point of use. The sum at stake was £13 million within an expenditure totalling over £4 billion. The issue was not well handled. Bevan had made cogent criticisms of the impossible scale of the rearmament programme, given the real resources available – on which Gaitskell could profitably have taken a lesson in economics – yet Bevan chose a peripheral point on which to leave the Government. Harold Wilson, whose surprise resignation came the following day, took his stand squarely on the scale of the defence programme. No doubt Bevan was egged on by his left-wing friends, to whom 'Nye' was an inspiring if volatile hero; and no doubt he felt sore about being fobbed off with the Ministry of Labour when a younger man was catapulted over his head into the Chancellorship. For the poor handling of this crisis betokened an imminent changing of the guard in Labour's leadership. Bevin died in office – as Lord Privy Seal, having become too ill to continue as Foreign Secretary in March 1951 – only a week before Bevan resigned; Cripps had gone; Attlee was in hospital. Bevan and Gaitskell were locked in a struggle about the leadership and identity of the Labour Party which was to last for most of the next decade.

Bevan's resignation in April 1951 signalled the outbreak of a kind of factionalism which Labour had previously escaped under Attlee's leadership; indeed his strength as prime minister was as the executor of an agreed programme. Now the Bevanites voiced a left-wing alternative to the Government's cautious consolidation, with renewed pressure for nationalization and a persistent tinge of anti-Americanism. A minority in the parliamentary party, but able to carry the constituency activists, the Bevanites challenged not only the official leadership but its reliance on the trade-union block vote as its means of controlling the Labour Party conference.

When the inevitable further general election came in October 1951, however, Labour's resilience was surprising. The party split proved less damaging than might have been imagined. Propaganda against nationalization was hurting Labour; its proposal in 1950 to add sugar to the next shopping list provoked the industry into a particularly effective campaign based on the cartoon figure, 'Mr Cube', whose message was projected from every sugar packet. But Labour had hard-hitting lines of its own, playing on fears that the Conservatives might dismantle the welfare state or bring back mass unemployment. Moreover, the Conservatives did not enjoy their customary advantage on defence and international issues, and a scaremongering campaign against Churchill in the *Daily Mirror* simply asked, 'Whose Finger on the Trigger?'

Opinion polls had forecast a Conservative lead of between 4 and 8.5 per cent; yet Labour, though it won fewer seats, narrowly outpolled the Conservatives nationally, both breasting 48 per cent. This left under 3 per cent for the Liberal Party, now unable to finance much more than 100 candidates. The result was a boost for the Conservatives in the hundreds of constituencies where Liberal voters – left-leaning in 1945, but now leaning towards the right – had no candidate of their own. That they did not usually abstain is evident from the high turnout figure of 83 per cent. The Conservatives had a narrow but workable overall majority of 17. This was the apogee of the two-party system; and had the half-dozen Liberals in the new parliament accepted Churchill's offer of participation in the new Government, their party's history might easily have ended at this point.

## CHURCHILL (AGAIN)

Housing, along with jobs and social security, had been a key issue working in Labour's favour in 1945. It was one plank in Labour's platform which was not effectively nailed down by the Attlee Government, thus giving the Conservatives an opportunity to prise it away from their opponents. During the war about half a million houses had been destroyed or made unfit for habitation, while the construction of new houses, which had been running at 350,000 a year in the late 1930s, totalled fewer than 70,000 in the last five years of the war. Put together with the war-related blip in the marriage rate (with peaks in 1940 and 1945) and the post-war bulge in the birth rate, this spelt out the need. Ex-servicemen starting families in shared or inadequate accommodation would not have been impressed to learn that, measured by the statistics of persons per room, overcrowding declined slightly between the census of 1931 and that of 1951. Post-war expectations were judge and jury.

Under Attlee, legislation was passed giving government new powers over town and country planning – indeed a new ministry was created – but housing remained the responsibility of the Ministry of Health (and Housing, as it now became). Since Bevan was preoccupied with the creation of the NHS, this lent colour to the joke that the Government kept only half a Nye on housing. But the real problem was a shortage of resources: materials for construction, labour in the building industry, room for investment within an overstretched economy. The Government's first priority was industrial reconstruction; housing lagged. Admittedly the housing stock was increased by the rehabilitation of war-damaged dwellings as effectively as by new houses; and prefabricated houses, using aluminium and asbestos, were introduced as a temporary expedient, which lasted long enough for many children to grow to adulthood knowing only a 'prefab' as home. Moreover, Bevan made it hard to achieve high quantitative targets by setting high qualitative standards for council houses, which produced fine homes but frustratingly few of them. Even so, in 1948 the total number of houses built approached 250,000, only to be cut back to under 200,000 in each of the next three years.

This was the Conservatives' opportunity. Grassroots pressure at their party conference forced a target of 300,000 a year upon the leadership and this claim became central to their election campaign in 1951. As prime minister, Churchill created a separate Ministry of Housing, to which he appointed one of his cronies, Harold Macmillan. A left-wing rebel in the Conservative Party in the 1930s, Macmillan had found his career transformed by the Churchillian takeover of the party. Churchill had sent out Macmillan as minister-resident in North Africa, where he worked cheek-by-jowl with the Allied commander, Eisenhower, and, on a more elevated plane, with the leader of the Free French, de Gaulle. This was heady promotion at the time (and was to be the basis of useful, though also delusive, personal contacts in the late-1950s) but it did not make Macmillan into a front-rank political figure at home. The hot seat at the Ministry of Housing did that.

Macmillan had an able junior minister, Ernest Marples, who understood the industry and proved his efficiency in the execution of the big plan. Macmillan's role was, first, to make it all much easier by scaling down the building standards for council houses; secondly, to secure the claim of housing upon the Government's allocation of resources; thirdly, to trumpet the achievements of his Ministry once they came through. In 1953 the famous target was reached; Macmillan handed over the keys to the 300,000th house, to the accompaniment of exploding flashlight bulbs; and the totemistic number was maintained for five years. In economic terms this was not so difficult, given that similar levels had been commmonplace twenty years previously. It followed from a shift in priorities, which was at the expense partly of defence, with the ending of the Korean war, and partly of industrial investment. Over-commitment of resources to housing in Britain, and a parallel failure to invest in production, is the other side of Macmillan's success.

Although private housebuilding was now moving towards parity within the programme, the expansion of council housing was the distinctive post-war development. In the ten years 1945–54 over three-quarters of all new dwellings were built by local authorities, compared with less than a quarter during the 1930s. So Macmillan's achievement was to beat Labour at its own game; only later, during his premiership, did the strategy change. Accommodation rented from private landlords still accounted for nearly 60 per cent of British housing in the immediate post-war period. But with rent control this was economically unprofitable for the landlords, while it was politically unprofitable for the traditional landlords' party to defend them. The Rent Act of 1957 was to bring a measure of decontrol, at a disproportionate political price, which demonstrated to the Tories that the 'property-owning democracy' of which they had talked might be a better bet. The abolition of Schedule A followed in 1963, giving a tax subsidy to owner-occupiers.[1] Well over half the new houses built between 1955 and 1964 were owner-occupied; and by this time mortgage offers came to exceed half a million a year, twice the pre-war level. While owner-occupied properties were of all ages, council houses and flats were obviously

1. The Inland Revenue taxed property incomes under Schedule A (cf. self-employed earnings under Schedule D, incomes from employment under Schedule E). The whole system was based on archaic assumptions. When an owner-occupier filled out a return, he (seldom she) was assessed on the notional rent he received as owner from the occupier (himself). But if he had a mortgage, the interest paid was allowed against tax. The abolition of Schedule A removed the tax liability but continued the general tax allowance for interest payments – an allowance restricted to mortgages alone in 1968. Since British owner-occupiers also escaped capital-gains tax, they henceforth enjoyed an internationally unparalleled position of fiscal privilege.

newer – indeed in Scotland over 85 per cent of all dwellings built since the First World War were owned by local authorities in 1965. In the twenty years after the war, the net result was to extend owner-occupation to half of the housing stock, while simultaneously lifting the local authority share to over a quarter.

If housing gave the Conservatives something to crow about, so did the abolition of controls and, above all, the ending of rationing. Much of this had been in the pipeline in the late 1940s, but Labour had undoubtedly become identified as the party of rationing which, after ten years, was increasingly unpopular. The use of controls to suppress inflation in a high-pressure economy inevitably gave rise to a black market in which that quintessentially mid-century figure, the spiv, found his niche. The ending of the Korean war brought a peace dividend which allowed the Conservatives to end rationing of sugar and sweets, eggs and bacon, margarine and butter, cheese and meat. Here was the 'red meat' which Churchill had promised.

In what was obviously his last premiership, Churchill wanted nothing more. Though he had growled about the enormities of the Attlee Government, he had no intention of undoing its work. If he promised to 'set the people free' in 1951, this was good politics, not a commitment to the full rigours of traditional sound finance, of which he had had a bellyful thirty years previously as Chancellor. Still less did Churchill, pushing seventy-seven when he took office, propose to learn new tricks. While he was busy writing his war memoirs and composing great speeches to world audiences, he had taken a fitful interest in leading the Opposition, and had been content to leave the hard task of reconstructing his own party in more capable hands. Lord Woolton, the post-war party chairman, had been charged with making the Tory Party palatable to the British people, just like wartime food. The party machine had been democratized and its fund-raising made more purposeful; it was no longer possible for a rich amateur simply to buy the Tory candidature in a somnolent constituency. Policy too, especially under the reign of R. A. Butler at the Conservative Research Department, had come to terms with the welfare state. Well and good, smiled an inattentive Churchill; but when it came to mouthing appreciative remarks about his party's new policy document, *The Industrial Charter*, he had privately expostulated, 'I do not agree with a word of this.'

Sure enough, little more was heard of these airy commitments once the Conservatives were in office. To be sure, there was a short-lived innovation in the cabinet system, with the appointment of three 'over-lords', senior ministers charged with coordinating departmental responsibilities in key areas – but not the most crucial of all, the economy. Otherwise, like the Republicans after the New Deal in the USA, the Tories were content to live down their reputation as the party of unemployment by adopting 'me-tooism'. Churchill's approach to industrial relations signalled a wary acceptance of the enhanced status of the trade unions, now with nearly 10 million members, with whom he was determined not to pick a fight. The Ministry of Labour was given to Sir Walter Monckton, a lawyer who had negotiated a settlement of the Abdication crisis; his emollient skills earned him the name 'the oilcan'. Especially in the nationalized industries, where the Government was the ultimate paymaster, industrial trouble was bought off. Conversely, although the unions would not deliver to a Conservative Government the formal commitment to wage restraint which they had given Cripps, settlements were reached which did not unleash serious inflation. One reason why retail prices did not race away was that wholesale prices actually fell by 10 per cent in the years 1951–4. There was a shift of the terms of trade in Britain's favour. The same imports into the UK required 12 per cent less exports to pay for them in 1954 than three years previously. So long as there were customers for British exports at the prevailing prices, this was a real windfall.

Not that Butler, as Chancellor of the Exchequer, inherited a bed of roses. The finance of the Korean war was his main headache. Defence costs absorbed almost 10 per cent of GNP and 30 per cent of total government expenditure. But the sheer size of the programme set its own ceiling. The Churchill Government was forced to concede what the Bevanites had said all along, that it could not be done. Commitments were trimmed accordingly. The persisting problem here was the ratchet effect upon the defence estimates which, once Korea was out of the way, showed no reversion to their previous level. Still, the buoyancy of the national income – 40 per cent higher by 1955 than five years previously – made such burdens easier to bear. This permitted Butler to make cuts in the standard rate of income tax, first from the crisis level of 9s 6d (47.5 per cent) to a Crippsian 9s (45 per cent); but more tellingly, with an election pending in 1955, to a new post-war low of 8s 6d (42.5 per cent), which was to set the norm for a quarter of a century.

It was in 1954 that the *Economist* coined the term 'Butskellism' to describe a supposed continuity of policy at the Treasury. Perhaps it would be fair to say that broadly the same policy instruments were used by Gaitskell and Butler, but to different ends. The limits of divergence between them are shown by one actual and one abortive departure in policy. The modification that was implemented – though even here Gaitskell had toyed with this idea – was to use bank-rate as a tool of economic management. In November 1951, in the first peacetime change for nearly twenty years, bank-rate was raised, as was by then expected: from 2 to 2.5 per cent initially and to 4 per cent the next year. From this point, manipulation of bank-rate became the classic means of exerting a credit squeeze, or applying disinflationary pressure, in a way that became thought of as Keynesian. In fact it owed much more to the traditional techniques which the authorities had developed in the days of the gold standard.

Moreover, the authorities' discreet campaign for a further policy departure – or reversion – was only narrowly thwarted. What was proposed here was a scheme (code-named Robot) for solving the balance-of-payments problem by letting the pound float. The implication was that the necessary defence of sterling by the traditional methods would introduce a salutary discipline, automatically triggered, into financial policy. What this meant in practice was that full employment might well have to yield to other priorities. Butler himself went a long way with this line of thinking, and Robot was only quashed by the mobilization of an informal coalition against it. Eden, in line with his reputation as a thoroughly modern liberal Conservative, was primed to tell Churchill that this would be like the return to the gold standard all over again. And that, for Robot, was that. It took twenty years for such ideas to gain a serious hearing.

Anthony Eden was becoming restive as crown prince, a role which he had already occupied for more than a decade. His tenure of the Foreign Office, he hoped, would be brief, his move to Downing Street swift. Churchill did not see it that way; he was determined to savour fame and power while he could, and believed that he could perform one last irreplaceable service: as healer rather than warrior. At home, he watched King George VI dying before his eyes; but the succession of the young Queen Elizabeth II in February 1952 encouraged his romantic fancy of playing Melbourne to her Victoria, and the Coronation in 1953 was a pleasing festival, uniting the Commonwealth. The aged Churchill had learnt to call Nehru 'the light of Asia'. This irenic vision was one which Churchill was determined to translate into international détente, preferably through a dramatic personal initiative, following up on his campaign promise in 1950 to seek 'a parley at the summit'.

Eden, a highly professional Foreign Office man, was apprehensive about where all this might lead. Though his immediate predecessor had been Morrison (a brief and unhappy interlude for all concerned), the shoes Eden really filled were, of course, Bevin's. Not for the first time – one gibe about Bevin was that Anthony Eden had got fat – a substantial continuity was observed in foreign policy. On Korea, the United Nations, the Commonwealth, Nato and relations with the USA, the Conservatives followed much the same line. So too on nuclear weapons; the development of the atom bomb under Labour was now openly acknowledged and a hydrogen bomb was authorized. Moreover, despite some Europhile noises in cabinet from Macmillan, Eden prevailed in his scepticism about moves towards integration; and barely a peep was heard from Churchill, for all the expectations he had aroused. There was indeed something like a left–right split on one issue, the proposed rearmament of the German Federal Republic, formed from the three zones occupied by the western allies and now ready to enter Nato. Even here, however, the front benches were united, and the fracture line ran through the Labour Party, where the Bevanites took up the anti-German cry.

For Churchill, pursuit of a summit became what Home Rule had been for Gladstone: an ever-receding goal, solely sufficient to prolong his leadership. Churchill's lack of grip on ordinary business was becoming embarrassing even to those of his colleagues whose names he could remember; and he was lucky that routine exposure by television came just too late for him. When he had a stroke in 1953, and was out of action for months, his luck held – Eden too was ill, very unluckily for himself, undergoing major surgery which left him permanently less robust. Churchill sought to use personal links forged in wartime: with Stalin, who died, with Eisenhower, now American President, who was not interested. By the time of Churchill's eightieth birthday in November 1954, everyone wanted the party to go well – and the prime minister to go soon. When he finally resigned in April 1955, Eden's impatience was at last rewarded. He called an immediate general election, seeking a mandate in his own right.

In the Labour leadership too it was clearly time for a change of generations. The fact was that Morrison's moment had come and gone; hanging on as deputy leader in hopes of the reversion, he had no more insight than Attlee into what the party should do next. Attlee had been a fine chairman, an adroit conciliator, a trusted captain of a united team; such skills were no longer enough to hold Labour together in opposition, still less to present it as an effective alternative Government in 1955. His retirement soon followed. For fifteen years – longer than Gladstone and Disraeli – he and Churchill had been rival party leaders.

# 8

## Never Had It So Good
### 1955–63

### A CONSUMER CULTURE

Economics and politics aside, in the post-war years the British people had a 'special relationship' with American popular culture, disseminated by Hollywood. Even in the extremes of the dollar shortage, attempts to restrict imports of American films, whether by taxes or quotas, did not work. The Second World War reinforced Hollywood's pre-existing dominance in the British market. It was a prime example of an American industry stepping in to supply consumer demand while British resources were diverted to supplying war priorities. Making feature films did not generally qualify as such – especially not films like Michael Powell's and Emeric Pressburger's *The Life and Death of Colonel Blimp* (1943), in fact a very gentle satire but one which, like the *Daily Mirror*'s populist campaigns, touched a raw nerve with the war cabinet. There was no such objection, of course, to *In Which We Serve* (1942), a nicely orchestrated anthem to the stiff upper lip, directed jointly by Noël Coward and David Lean, with a propaganda value that was the more effective for remaining implicit. Almost at the close of the war, it was clearly worth demobilizing Laurence Olivier, the most thrilling actor of his generation, to make his heroic version of *Henry V* (1945), which surely spoke for others, still awaiting 'demob', in saying that 'there ne'er arrived from France more happy men'.

Not that Hollywood was ideologically unsound. Even before the USA became an ally, the ingenuous democratic message of a film like *Mr Smith Goes to Washington* (1939) was clearly directed against the dictators, and *Casablanca* (1943) became a classic partly because the romantic entanglement enacted between Humphrey Bogart and Ingrid Bergman tugged against the primacy of an anti-fascist struggle. It is a safe bet, however, that the millions who attended cinemas during the blackout or under conditions of post-war austerity were seeking escape, not least from propaganda. Hollywood showed them a new world where there was no food rationing and no shortage of nylons: often an opulent lifestyle, yet not that of the status-bound upper classes in Britain, but one in which automobiles and refrigerators were as much of a common culture as smoking cigarettes (the other irreducible drain on post-war dollars).

The sheer firepower of Hollywood should not obscure the fact that, during and after the war, British films acquired a reputation for quality, not just a cynical notoriety as cheaply made 'quota quickies'. There had, of course, been isolated successes previously. The young British director, Alfred Hitchcock, made his reputation as a master of suspense with a notable adaptation of Buchan's *The Thirty-Nine Steps* (1935) and went on, in *The Lady Vanishes* (1938), to evoke a sinister sense of the Europe of the dictators, cross-cut with a quintessentially English comic sub-plot about the latest score in the test match. The best British films succeeded by offering something subtly different from Hollywood. David Lean's *Brief Encounter* (1945) turned a one-act play by Noël Coward into a beautifully realized account of a potentially adulterous passion, thwarted by social constraints. Understated in its playing by Trevor Howard and Celia Johnson, set in the buffet of a British railway junction, its matter-of-fact manner was belied by a Rachmaninov soundtrack. The other enduring classic, financed by the new National Film Corporation, was surely Carol Reed's *The Third Man* (1949). It was set in post-war Vienna under allied occupation, literally opening the lid on the sewers of an exploitative black market in drugs which compromised personal loyalties as well as official regulations. The beguiling zither theme which cleverly signalled the appearance of Harry Lime (Orson Welles) worked with Graham Greene's economical screenplay to build suspense and imprint some memorable images.

Pre-war British comedies had often relied on putting a stage comic, like George Formby, on to the screen. In the late 1940s and early 1950s the Ealing film studios created a niche for a much more subtle genre, built around rather whimsical plots but with many well-observed satirical shafts which found their mark. It was here that the versatile talents of Alec Guinness, an actor whose anti-heroic style transferred more easily to film than Olivier's, found full appreciation, notably in *Kind Hearts and Coronets* (1949), where he played all those members of an aristocratic family who stood as heirs between a distant relative and his succession to the estate. The black comedy of their successive demise, which inevitably required a suitably moral ending, was sustained to the last frame. The same sort of tension between a conventionally urbane format and more subversive social comment animates Alexander Mackendrick's *The Man in the White Suit* (1951), notably when the meritocratic and public-spirited inventor is checked by a combination of management and unions against a perceived threat of innovation – a parable for British industry reiterated a decade later in the Boulting brothers' production of *I'm All Right, Jack* (1959). *Passport to Pimlico* (1949), with its populist celebration of an idealized local community in London, dates from Ealing's prime, as does *The Lavender Hill Mob* (1951), with its innocent portrayal of British bobbies and villains playing their allotted parts in a battle of wits. But *The Ladykillers* (1955), though not the least, was almost the last in this genre. The British film industry, sustained neither by effective state subsidy nor by a buoyant home market, was disproportionately hurt by a decline in the cinema habit.

The peak of cinema attendances (1635 million) was reached in 1946, which implies an average not far short of once a week for everyone over the age of fifteen. Ten years later British cinemas still had seating capacity for 4 million, but actual attendance had slipped by a third. The real avalanche, however, was just beginning; by 1962 cinema attendance had collapsed to less than a quarter of its peak level. This major change in social habits was both complemented and explained, of course, by the growth of television over the same period. By the 1960s a third of the population would normally be watching television in the evening, whereas fewer than one in five adults attended a cinema once a month.

When the BBC resumed its television service in 1946, there were only 15,000 licence-holders, concentrated in London; by 1956 there were over 5 million, and by then 98 per cent of the country was able to receive television. This represented a major investment by the BBC, sheltered by its monopoly, in making a leap towards a mass audience for the new medium. It was a shift of priorities not much to the taste of the BBC's post-war director-general, Sir William Haley, who initially refused to have a television set at home and kept his office in Broadcasting House rather than the Television Centre.

Haley's monument was the creation of the Third Programme, as a highbrow radio channel with a varied menu of classical music, drama and talks. It succeeded partly because it was satisfied with an audience of a quarter of a million on a good night. T. S. Eliot, with his frankly elitist view of culture, was one happy contributor. There was much to admire in the output of the Third – Dylan Thomas's voice-play of small-town Wales, *Under Milk Wood* (1954), was one highlight. But there was too some feeling that the Third's forbidding format did not reach out to the public whom it might have attracted. Its programming was premised on a listener who would transcend the division of labour within high culture by patronizing opera, drama, and 'talks', all in one evening. Though the proposal which came in 1970 to turn it into Radio Three, concentrating on a 'stream of music', aroused vociferous regrets from faithful listeners, the new channel was to fill a more distinct and – with Promenade Concerts, for example – more appealing slot.

There was no escaping the fact that the golden age of radio lay back in the 1940s. The Light Programme had had a vast audience in a pre-television era, and its comedy shows continued to provide stock national catchphrases. *Educating Archie* was a radio show in which the eponymous hero was a ventriloquist's dummy – an extraordinary illustration of suspension of disbelief on someone's part. Moreover, there was still innovation within this format in the early 1950s, and *The Goon Show* stands in an apostolic succession between the mildly anarchic forays of *ITMA* and the fully fledged surrealism which *Monty Python's Flying Circus* later brought to television. The two media were bridged, until his early death, by Tony Hancock, whose evocations of the lower-middle-class proprieties of Railway Cuttings, East Cheam, were perfectly conveyed: creating 'ancock as a projection of himself, with aspirations as elusive as aspirates. By the 1960s the Light Programme was dying on its feet, a bygone idiom in entertainment; its relics were embalmed in the new Radio Two, whereas Radio One was frankly pitched at the teenage audience. Finally, the BBC's Radio Four, child of the Home Service, became the surviving descendant of Reith's original National Programme.

In a television age, the BBC made its reputation all over again in its coverage of major national events, which reinforced its image as the most august of public corporations and the voice of the establishment. The Queen's Coronation in June 1953 showed the way. Here was a pageant of national renewal, spoken of as inaugurating a new Elizabethan age, presented for the first time as a television spectacular. With more than a year to prepare, this provided a unique sales pitch for new sets and was the moment when the television audience started to leap into the millions. It showed how the monarchy could be projected through the new medium, with a smooth voice-over from the doyen of commentators, Richard Dimbleby, who became little less than a national institution himself.

Even so, the BBC was not safe; the Conservatives' zeal to introduce market solutions into the public sector was denied other outlets under Churchill, but, still mindful of Reith's power to keep him off the air, he had little time for the BBC. A committee on broadcasting under Beveridge had advised against commercial broadcasting; but a dissenting report from a Conservative backbencher, Selwyn Lloyd, kept the issue open and in 1954 legislation was passed setting up a rival television network, financed through advertising. This was, however, by no means complete deregulation. The Independent Television Authority (ITA) had powers to control the output of the commercial stations and to limit advertising; sponsorship was not to be introduced for another thirty years. In many ways this concept of 'independent' television was an extension rather than an outright repudiation of the ethos of public-service broadcasting.

Commercial television, indeed, at first had a hard time in generating profits. Sir Kenneth Clark, the urbane art historian who became chairman of the ITA, had to talk up its prospects in 1957 with claims that over 70 per cent preferred the new channel – which only meant that this was the proportion of new television sets which were equipped to receive both it and the BBC. Even in 1960 only 6 million sets out of the current total of 10 million could receive ITV. Once over this hump, the companies benefited from the fact that this was a tightly regulated market; the Canadian newspaper tycoon Roy Thomson, who bought Scottish Television at the bottom of the market, was shrewd as well as candid in calling a television franchise 'a licence to print money'. The popularity ratings of television programmes could not be disregarded by ITV once they were selling this time to advertisers, nor by the BBC once it was locked into competition for viewers to justify the licence fee.

ITV won the initial battles in the ratings war. Nearly two-thirds of the population over sixteen claimed to watch it regularly in 1961; the only snag was that its viewers were more likely to be C2s (skilled workers) rather than more affluent middle-class customers. The big draws were game shows – *Double Your Money*, *Take Your Pick*, *Beat the Clock* – of a kind which the BBC had previously disdained; its own pre-eminence in drama and documentaries was hardly challenged. Yet it would be unfair to say that ITV simply debased standards. Granada, with a Manchester-based franchise, was notably creative among the early commercial companies. Independent Television News, a central service which the companies were forced to support, brought innovative techniques of presentation to Britain, making newscasters like Robin Day and Ludovic Kennedy into a new sort of television personality. Imitation by the BBC was the most ratings-conscious form of flattery. The fact is that during the 1960s competition and cross-fertilization between the networks revitalized the BBC, which claimed its market share back from ITV, once the appeal of novelty wore off.

With two popular networks, television simply became *the* mass medium. In 1964 BBC2 was opened as a third channel, with a more highbrow pitch (though hardly a televised Third Programme) and in 1967 it began broadcasting in colour. In 1969, by which time nine out of ten households held a licence, television occupied nearly a quarter of the leisure time of both men and women in England and Wales, more than twice as much as gardening, its greatest single competitor. Significantly, both were home-based activities. On the whole, television was not introduced into pubs in England (as in Ireland, for example) but provided a private setting for the enjoyment of a range of leisure pursuits which had previously taken place outside the home. Thus people did not watch fewer films, but more; they simply stopped going out to the cinema and started watching older films at home on television. Soon new releases were to become more quickly available in a routine way, which altered the financing of films.

Likewise television did not kill commercial sport; but whereas in 1949 the English League soccer clubs had had over 40 million paying customers on the terraces of their grounds, within twenty years a third of them had disappeared. Again, what had happened was that television stole the show – or rather had to pay the Football Association for the rights. When England staged (and won) the World Cup in 1966, the popularity of television soccer was confirmed. Moreover, the Cinderella spectator sport of Rugby Union came to benefit from the televising of international matches; the Wimbledon tennis championship proved well suited to the small screen; and as new camera techniques were developed for showing test cricket, armchair spectators were given a privileged view of the action at the crease. When England at last won the Ashes from the Australian tourists in 1953, viewers who had missed Bradman at least had a chance to catch the last stand of the great England batsmen, Hutton and Compton. Even sporting contests which presented less obvious opportunities – golf, snooker, sheepdog trials – came to acquire a mass following through television.

At the time of the debate over commercial television, fears of the Americanization of the medium had been widespread, the more so since competition from Hollywood was currently throttling the British film industry. It is obviously true that the new British franchise-holders picked up many tricks from the longer experience of commercial television in the USA; true too that screening old Hollywood movies was a cheap way of filling the slots between the advertisements. Yet, though the small relative size of the British market may have provided an inadequate base for its film industry to rival American productions, the same was not true in television. On the small screen far more of the output was home-produced.

Above all, the impact of television was to emphasize the importance of the private household. To some extent this was directly at the expense of older face-to-face contacts. Richard Hoggart achieved a deserved success with his book *The Uses of Literacy* (1957), a sensitive (and learned) evocation of the street-based, northern working-class community in which he grew up. Writing on the eve of the introduction of commercial television, he castigated the (virtually synonymous) Americanization and trivialization of popular culture; the world we had lost, with all its failings, was one fit for this eloquent elegy. In this vein, it might be held that the immensely popular television soap opera, *Coronation Street*, which Granada introduced in 1962, with its sepia-tinted portrayal of a traditional Lancashire working-class community, came to provide a vicarious substitute for the real thing. Yet the remaking of the English working class was a long and continuing historical process, one hardly confined to the sudden advent of consumerism in the 1950s.

Resuming the trend of the inter-war period, newly affluent households were buying not only television sets but a range of appliances which made homes more attractive and convenient to run: vacuum cleaners, washing machines, electric heaters and cookers. In real terms consumer expenditure rose by 45 per cent between 1952 and 1964. The largest items were food, drink and tobacco; but whereas they naturally came to take a smaller proportion of a larger income, the share of consumer durables more than doubled, with most of the increase in the years up to 1959. In 1952 there were 2½ million private cars on the road, barely more than in 1939; by 1959 there were 5 million, since consumer spending on cars and motor cycles had meanwhile quad-rupled. A snapshot at this point might suggest that car ownership remained a middle-class status symbol in a way that television owner-ship no longer was. In fact, from the time of the Coronation the increase in vehicle licences tracked the increase in television licences, but at a lower level – at virtually any moment until the end of the 1960s two out of three households which had a television also had a car. Moreover 1959 saw a record jump of 200,000 in motor-cycle registra-tions, giving a 1¾-million total which did not decline until the late-1960s. This was the golden age of the motor bike, poised between the artisan image of the bumbling family sidecar and a shockingly fast youth culture based on new teenage affluence.

It was inescapably apparent that more people could now afford a decent standard of living. Average weekly earnings, which had been £7 10s (£7.50) a week in 1950, had climbed to over £11 pounds by 1955; this was a rise of 50 per cent over a period in which the cost of living rose by 30 per cent. By 1964 average wages were to be over £18 a week, rising at an annual rate double that of prices. Moreover, unlike the situation before the war, these gains were not restricted through mass unemployment, since there was now a tight labour market where almost everyone of working age could find a job. From the introduction of the new National Insurance scheme in 1948 until 1970, in only eight years out of twenty-three did the number of registered unemployed average as much as 2 per cent. Full employment was, as Beveridge had said, the real underpinning of social security, providing against want not through state benefits but by letting people benefit from their own exertions. For those with bitter memories of the prolonged slump before the war, this marked an epoch. 'Let's be frank about it,' Harold Macmillan told a meeting in 1957, 'most of our people have never had it so good.'

## EDEN'S WAR

The Conservatives had thought themselves lucky to get back into office in 1951 and were accordingly content to acquiesce in a political agenda largely set by their opponents. For a year or two there were by-election swings against the Government which underlined the precariousness of its position, though only one seat was actually lost. By the time Eden took over, the prospects looked much brighter, with swings towards the Government in recent by-elections in comfortable London suburban seats like Sutton and Cheam, Orpington and Twickenham. The general election in May 1955 was one of the most predictable of the century. Its novelty lay in being the first television election, though the politicians had yet to learn how to handle the medium effectively. The Conservatives, fighting on the slogan 'Conservative Freedom Works', never looked like losing. The Gallup Poll slightly exaggerated their advantage, showing them with over half of the popular vote, whereas although they came close (49.7 per cent) they narrowly failed to achieve this elusive distinction. They made net gains of about twenty seats from Labour, almost entirely in England, and continued to benefit marginally from redistribution, thus increasing their parliamentary majority to over sixty.

Yet Labour was still polling impressively, only 3 per cent behind the Conservatives. With a margin as narrow as this, it is hard to accept that the Labour Party's own self-inflicted wounds were unimportant in denying it office. Splits in the party seemed endemic and were impossible to conceal. Bevan remained the darling of Labour's left-wing constituency parties which consistently elected his supporters to the party's national executive committee, where they ritually confronted the power brokers of the big trade unions, whose block votes ultimately controlled the party. Arthur Deakin, Bevin's successor in the Transport Workers, emerged as a key figure, mobilizing an alliance between the mineworkers (NUM), his own union (TGWU) and the other 'General Workers' union (GMWU), later supported by the engineers (AEU). They appeared to the Bevanites simply as right-wingers, intent on betraying Labour's socialist aspirations; the Bevanites in turn were regarded at best as wild, at worst as fellow-travellers – a potent charge in the cold-war atmosphere (especially given the large number of Roman Catholics in the Labour movement). Bevan himself, though critical of the Soviet Union, was not enamoured of the USA either. German rearmament, supported by the leadership as a means of strengthening Nato, found its loudest opponents among the Bevanites; and it was Bevan's opposition to the official line of support for the South East Asia Treaty Organization (Seato) which caused him to lose the party whip as an MP, and almost provoked his expulsion from party membership – all this only two months before the 1955 general election. The fierce disciplinarians in the party were clearly intent on imposing trade-union norms of solidarity; they had found, moreover, a capable agent in Gaitskell.

It may have been convenient but it is hardly accurate to call Gaitskell a right-winger too. His vision was that of a social democrat seeking a relevant role for Labour once it had exhausted its historic mission by mid-century – an analysis that was to be developed by his disciple Anthony Crosland in *The Future of Socialism* (1956). It sketched a strategy for furthering social equality through managed growth in a mixed economy rather than identifying socialism with further measures of nationalization. What Deakin saw in Gaitskell, however, was simply a politician of Bevan's generation (eight years younger indeed) who was prepared to stand up to him – and to stand against him, initially for the Treasurership of the Labour Party, which Gaitskell won, thanks to the block votes in 1954. Following Attlee's retirement and Morrison's eclipse, Gaitskell defeated Bevan for the party leadership in December 1955.

Gaitskell did not want a continued feud with the Bevanites – why on earth should he? – but the rifts in the party were difficult to heal. The policy differences were slight but the personal animosities between Bevanites and Gaitskellites ran deep. Harold Wilson, whose resignation with Bevan in 1951 had identified him as a Bevanite, in fact had little patience with the ideological posturing of either side and had already made his peace with the leadership. Bevan too was now welcomed back into the shadow cabinet, where he somewhat uneasily tried to reconcile himself to working under, or at least with, Gaitskell. Within a year they had established a surprisingly effective partnership – brought together this time, rather than driven apart, by a defining crisis in foreign policy.

Eden, of course, was intent on running his own foreign policy, a field where his credentials were backed by cabinet experience stretching back twenty years. His problem, it was generally supposed, would not lie abroad but in putting his stamp upon domestic policy. Here he could fairly claim that his subordinates let him down. Butler's spring Budget in 1955, reducing income tax before the general election, had to be followed by an autumn Budget, to stave off a renewed sterling crisis through a fiscal squeeze, which clawed back double the amount of revenue disbursed only months previously. Whether seen as sharp practice or incompetence – Butler was deeply shadowed by bereavement following his wife's death – this meant that he would have to be moved. Eden's own interventions were driven more by social conscience than free-market ideology. Having scotched Robot, he still vetoed the abolition of bread subsidies, in his efforts to establish his authority over his cabinet.

Willy-nilly, the make-or-break issues of Eden's premiership lay in foreign affairs. Churchill's notion of Britain standing at the intersection of three circles – and refusing on principle to choose between them – still provided the guiding assumption in British foreign policy. Macmillan had become Foreign Secretary, following his brief tenure of the Ministry of Defence: a difficult man to place, with too many big ideas, not least about his own role. If he was the most serious Europhile in the cabinet, this says a lot about the lack of seriousness of the rest, for Macmillan was no more ready than them to give Europe real priority. 'The Empire must always have first preference,' he still proclaimed: 'Europe must come second.' There was to be no challenge, therefore, to the ingrained scepticism which the Foreign Office manifested towards the developing process of western European integration.

The Coal and Steel community which Britain had refused to join in 1950 had meanwhile done wonders for its six continental members. In June 1955 they held a conference at Messina, at which an agenda for establishing a wider economic union, and devising appropriate European institutions, was accepted. Britain was warmly invited to participate in the negotiations which ensued, but first hesitated, then prevaricated, and ultimately withdrew. The other six pressed ahead despite the empty chair. The problem for Britain did not come from the USA, with which a specially rocky relationship currently prevailed, encapsulated in Eden's distate for the moralistic Secretary of State, Dulles. It was, indeed, US policy to encourage British participation; and it was the Foreign Office which kept up the constant disparagement of the European initiative in its communications to the State Department. The Commonwealth was a more serious obstacle. As late as 1948 the four Dominions accounted for 25 per cent of British trade; Australia took half its imports from Britain. These were bonds forged in peace and war. If they now shackled Britain, however, it was surely because the sterling area was regarded as a viable means of maintaining British interests into the late twentieth century. By comparison with these global, great-power pretensions, symbolized alike by sterling's role and by a concomitant geopolitical strategy, what was on the table after Messina seemed pitifully inadequate. The Foreign Office thus succeeded in catching the mood of the British public in watching with sceptical condescension while the six European countries set about pooling their inferior resources in a common market.

Eden had bigger fish to fry. A month after the British withdrawal from the Messina process, in December 1955, he moved Macmillan to the Treasury and in his place appointed the hitherto obscure Selwyn Lloyd as Foreign Secretary. Lloyd, with his tidy legal mind, proved an excellent henchman: not only a loyal lieutenant (with a loyalty that was as unflagging as it was unrequited) but a meticulous staff officer who would implement the orders from above. High policy, as he realized, would be made by an inner circle increasingly concentrated around the prime minister – ironically reminiscent of the policy-making methods of Neville Chamberlain, the first prime minister whom Eden had served.

But the content of that policy, at all costs, would be different. Stung by taunts in the Tory press about his lack of decisiveness, Eden was determined to appear as Churchill's successor in a full sense, with no taint of appeasement. Eden's personal staff knew all about his fierce temper, recently exacerbated in the aftermath of unsuccessful surgery, which made him feverish at times of stress. In the summer of 1956 the stress duly came when the Egyptian leader Nasser nationalized the Suez Canal, Britain's historic route to the east. Blowing hot and cold alternately, Eden responded testily to a frustrating course of events, involving France, Israel, the USA and the United Nations. Soon the prime minister's staff observed that he was 'violently anti-Nasser, whom he compares to Mussolini'.

It may not have been a very apt comparison but Eden was not alone in making it; Gaitskell used similar language in the House of Commons in August. Determination to learn the lessons of appeasement had run through every post-war crisis. It may not have shown deep historical insight to invest Stalin with the potential territorial ambitions of Hitler; but it was surely plausible, as a rational response prompted by caution. To cast Nasser in the same role, however, seems either unimaginative or over-imaginative; and Eden's constant ruminations about a Russian link look paranoid rather than prescient. The fact was that Egypt wanted to build a dam on the Nile at Aswan and did not much care whether it was paid for by dollars or roubles – or canal dues. The real issue was what response from Britain was appropriate.

There had been an earlier Middle East crisis in 1951, in the dying months of the Labour Government. The assets of the Anglo-Iranian

Oil Company (better known after 1954 simply as BP) at Abadan had been nationalized. A student of nationalization measures himself, Morrison considered that the appropriate response for a socialist Foreign Secretary was to send a gunboat. Gaitskell was one of those in the cabinet who stopped this, on the grounds that lack of British resources or of American support made it deeply unprofitable to antagonize the Arab world for no good reason. This was not very glorious, and the Tories duly made political capital out of Abadan – another reason why they were moved to behave differently over Suez in 1956.

The long British occupation of Egypt had recently been terminated, the canal zone evacuated in favour of the base in Cyprus. With the treaties governing the canal running rapidly towards extinction, Britain's legal rights were at best a wasting asset. The cabinet meeting held immediately after nationalization in July 1956 was advised that Britain would be on weak ground in claiming that Nasser had acted illegally. What occupied the prime minister for much of the next three months was the attempt to find a respectable public reason for the use of force, to which, in private, he increasingly inclined. The more Eden used diplomacy to clear the ground for intervention, the more the situation deteriorated. Initially it took time to formulate contingency plans for military operations to be launched from Cyprus, but, once the armed forces were prepared, there was an inbuilt momentum for action. Those who were bent on intervention were increasingly impatient over the time-wasting pantomime at the United Nations, ostensibly aimed at a diplomatic settlement. Macmillan, in whose diary Nasser and Hitler became indistinguishable, was a crucial voice for intervention. Forced to dissimulate his real feelings when dealing with the Americans, because of their insistence on maintaining a line of high moral rectitude, his own cynicism led him to a gross misjudgement of the likely American response. 'I know Ike,' Macmillan assured his colleagues. 'He will lie doggo!'

At the United Nations Lloyd's line, innocently enough, was all about protection of the rights of international canal-users. While he was away, however, Eden concocted a war plan with the French, who were already in touch with Israel (and not ashamed of it). When Israel attacked Egypt, Britain and France would have their excuse to intervene, in the guise of peacemakers; the backstairs collusion which engineered this was largely designed to secure the acquiescence of the United States in a British 'police action'. At first it went according to plan.

Israel duly attacked Egypt on 29 October; Eden promptly announced an ultimatum, addressed to both sides, backed by a threat to intervene, thus pre-empting action through the United Nations. The United Nations, unimpressed, lumbered into action with a resolution branding Britain and France as aggressors, backed by the threat of oil sanctions. The support of a united Commonwealth was lacking; Australia was in favour, Canada against. Moreover, President Eisenhower, running for re-election in the USA, flexed his muscles. Not only did Ike fail to lie doggo; he even failed to suspend his critical faculties when asked to believe the British fairy story. Macmillan's cheerful predictions were quickly forgotten, at least by their author, now a beleaguered Chancellor of the Exchequer, counting the cost of his fine words. Once US support for the pound was withdrawn, there was a devastating drop in the sterling area's currency reserves, which a chastened Macmillan certainly did not minimize in his reports to his colleagues.

By now Suez had become a divisive political issue in Britain. Nasser, to be sure, had few open defenders. His enemy, Israel, evoked more mixed feelings. The Foreign Office, despite its traditional pro-Arab line, simply acted on the maxim that my enemy's enemy is my friend. The real friends of Israel in Britain had obviously been those Zionists, especially strong in the Labour Party, who had campaigned for a Jewish national home in the first place. Only eight years old, Israel owed its creation not to Britain but to the activities, including terrorism, of the Jews themselves. The way that Bevin had operated the post-war UN mandate in Palestine had satisfied nobody: neither the victims of the Jewish holocaust who wanted to immigrate freely, nor the Palestinians who were displaced, nor the UN, nor the left-wing Zionists, whose frustration at the whole drift of Bevin's foreign policy was vented on this issue. Declining to serve any longer as whipping boy, Bevin truly did execute a policy of scuttle in 1948, leaving the Jews free to make their new state by force of arms. Israel, as the living symbol of atonement for the Jews' historic sufferings, was still a great left-wing cause; few yet acknowledged that the atonement was at the Palestinians' expense. Many people in the Labour Party remained emotionally committed to Israel's success, and the British Government's fervent denials that the two countries were acting together made it easier to maintain a distinction between them.

Whatever their other shades of difference, virtually the whole of the opposition in Britain condemned Eden's unilateral use of force. It was the moment when middle-class liberal opinion turned anti-Conservative, promising the Liberal Party a political future after all. One symbol was the anti-Suez stance of the Sunday newspaper, the *Observer*, at the price of a significant slice of its former Conservative readers. By contrast, there are few signs that Labour's working-class supporters were much moved by an issue so redolent of the middle-class politics of conscience of an earlier era. Eden and Gaitskell each thought that the other had misled him; now they were bitterly at odds, Eden accused of betraying a lifetime's commitment to the United Nations, Labour more straightforwardly branded as unpatriotic. Bevan unleashed his oratory in a great open-air protest meeting in Trafalgar Square. Gaitskell successfully claimed the right to reply on television to the prime minister's broadcast announcing hostilities, thus provoking not only another internal crisis over the autonomy of the BBC but also allegations from Conservatives of its lack of loyalty. The party was almost solid for Suez, sceptics like Butler quelling their doubts once the adventure was begun.

The Conservatives, however, were to become divided once the cabinet abruptly decided to quit. The tension between the actual and the avowed aims of the British Government was not just a moral flaw in its case: it became a disabling inconsistency in its strategy. Its purported *casus belli* disappeared within days, since Israel achieved an inconveniently quick victory and Egypt stopped fighting. Eden's story, such as it was, now collapsed. Having pretended to go to war for this reason, Eden had to pretend to be pleased with this result when it was agreed to withdraw British troops in favour of a UN force. Meanwhile, on the ground, none of the real military objectives had been secured by the time of the ceasefire. The canal itself lay immobilized by Egyptian blockships. Above all, Nasser lived to fight another day. British war aims, never very clear in the first place, had been wrapped in the layers of ambiguity necessary to sustain the subterfuge, with damaging effects on Anglo-American relations. Once the cover story was blown, the British appeared doubly guilty – not only of aggression against Egypt but guilty too of calculated deceit of their great ally.

As a military operation Suez was a sideshow. There was little loss of life on the Egyptian side and even less on the British – the offstage death of a British soldier at Suez in John Osborne's *The Entertainer* (1957) had a significance that was clearly not statistical. Nonetheless it is surely a mistake to play down the importance of Suez. Great powers can no doubt get away with actions far worse than anything Britain did in 1956, which is hardly the most infamous date in its long history of international self-assertion. At exactly the time of Suez the Soviet Union sent in its tanks to crush a struggle for self-government in Hungary, and did so with an impunity which is only partly explained by the opportune diversion staged by the western imperialist nations. What Suez demonstrated with brutal frankness was that Britain was no longer in the great-power league, was no longer capable of playing by its rules, and simply looked absurd when it tried to cheat.

This was a sad conclusion to Eden's long career as an international statesman. The crisis finished him; his precarious health gave way. While the withdrawal of British troops was taking place, the prime minister himself withdrew to the West Indies for recuperation. During his absence, Butler, who had always doubted the wisdom of Suez, sought to minimize the damage through tact and conciliation. As an old appeaser, these had always been his methods – or so too many Tories, still smarting from their reverses, came to think. The real beneficiary of Suez was Macmillan who, like his hero Churchill after Narvik, walked away unscathed from a disaster that was partly of his own making. What Macmillan grasped was that retreat was certainly necessary; but that it should take place under cover of a mien of effrontery. The anti-American right wing on the Conservative benches, who thought the only mistake lay in calling off the operation, liked Macmillan's style. When it became clear, on Eden's return in January 1957, that he could not continue as prime minister, the expectation was still that Butler would succeed. But the informal processes used to sound out the cabinet, in supplying advice to the Queen, showed strong backing for Macmillan. He became prime minister of the United Kingdom in January 1957, just two months before the Treaty of Rome was signed by the six countries which established a European Economic Community (EEC).

### 'SUPERMAC'

Against the odds, the succession had passed to an older man and it was to be Macmillan rather than Butler who set his stamp on the late 1950s. The two of them worked warily together. Butler, as Home Secretary, took the title of deputy prime minister, which was accurate in that he was the second man in the government, only inaccurate in implying that he would automatically get the reversion. At the Home Office he was a reassuring figure, capable of blandly defending his department from the authoritarian instincts of many grassroots Tories, as ritually displayed at party conferences. Faced with a social rather than an economic agenda, he was actually more of a Butskellite at the Home Office than at the Treasury.

It was Butler, more than anyone else, who had given Conservative domestic policy its post-war facelift; Butler whose liberal credentials had worked against him in the aftermath of Suez, while Macmillan was initially acclaimed by the imperialist, anti-American right-wingers of the Suez Group. Yet there was little real difference of outlook between the two rivals, and the right wing was to find itself marginalized once more as Government policy unfolded, at home and abroad. Since Macmillan's *métier* was dissimulation it took time for this to become apparent. Prime minister was a part which Macmillan had long wanted to play, and play it he did, returning at intervals to a favourite author, Trollope, for inspiration as well as recreation. His Edwardian grand manner teetered on the edge of self-parody but proved a highly effective mask for a fine intellect, cynically weighing the odds. Though acutely nervous before some of his parliamentary appearances, in public his air of 'unflappability' became part of his legend.

The first priority was to rebuild the alliance with the USA. Macmillan shamelessly exploited his old friendship with Eisenhower, fortunately a man of cool temperament who did not bear grudges. A well-managed conference at Bermuda effected a public reconciliation. This reliance on personal diplomacy was to become characteristic; and it was loyally accepted by Lloyd, who remained as Foreign Secretary since Macmillan shrewdly judged that it would look too much like an apology for Suez if he were to be removed. Macmillan took up where Churchill had left off in his pursuit of a summit conference, at which, it was still assumed, Britain would be represented. His visit to Moscow in 1959 may have played some part in reaching an agreement on banning nuclear-weapons testing but its main impact, shortly before a general election, was in enhancing Macmillan's own image as world statesman. His white fur hat made for good pictures.

Britain's own nuclear capability, with its hydrogen bomb now being tested in the Pacific, was given high priority. Following Bermuda, it was to be made operational through US cooperation; and US missiles were in turn to be granted the unrestricted use of British bases. Indeed, a nuclear strategy became the basis of the White Paper which the Defence Secretary, Duncan Sandys, presented in 1957, declaring a doctrine of massive retaliation in the event of a Soviet invasion of western Europe. The attraction of such a policy, despite its appalling risks, was that it enabled a significant reduction in Britain's conventional defences, the cost of which remained onerous. The ending of national service was foreshadowed and, when this was implemented a couple of years later, it resulted in a halving of the number of British armed forces. It is sometimes claimed that this retrenchment did not materialize over the next five years, but in real terms there was a significant economy. All told the claim of defence spending, which had pre-empted almost 10 per cent of GNP in the mid-1950s, was cut back to 6 per cent by 1964. There is a political paradox here; for despite the Conservatives' rhetoric about their unique commitment to defending the country, it was a Labour Government which had put guns before butter – a priority which was now reversed. The simple appeal of this shift in resources is not hard to see when, out of every £100 of total national earnings, three or four pounds which had previously gone in taxes to pay for arms were left in the taxpayers' own pockets.

In this major reassessment, Britain's independent nuclear deterrent became a (relatively) cheap substitute for the imperial ambitions which had proved so expensive at Suez. Sterling had proved to be Britain's weak link; cutting overseas commitments would reduce the strain on the balance of payments. Cyprus was an obvious example. The agitation for union with Greece had been unequivocally resisted by the British, who pleaded that they could 'never' leave because of the likelihood of communal violence between ethnic Greeks and Turks, and who sought to implicate the Greek orthodox archbishop, Makarios, in the terrorist campaign that was raging. But Suez showed that the game was up. In 1957 Makarios was released from gaol; in 1960 he became leader of an independent state, and the British base was run down.

In Cyprus 'never' turned out to mean six years; and Britain's African empire was soon switched to the new timescale. Learning from Attlee's experience in India, Macmillan put a good face upon an accelerating transfer of power to well-disposed successor regimes. This strategy had originally been the brainchild of Sir Andrew Cohen, a highly influential colonial administrator and diplomat. Here at least the British could read the writing on the wall, and acted more adroitly in winding up their empire than did other European countries like France, Belgium or Portugal. Nkrumah in the Gold Coast, like Nehru before him, in an almost complicitous process, first earned his nationalist credentials in gaol and subsequently became leader of an independent state. Thus in 1957 Ghana became the first black African republic in the Commonwealth; but such an outcome was easier to achieve in west Africa than in colonies with a higher density of white settlement.

That the transition was not free from conflict and bloodshed was shown in Kenya, where the British attempt in the early 1950s to demonize the Mau Mau movement, and link it to the imprisoned nationalist leader Jomo Kenyatta, had left a legacy of brutality which was exposed by the death of a number of prisoners at Hola Camp in 1959. It was the old story of colonial racism and irregularities, instinctively covered up by the men on the spot lest tender consciences in faraway Westminster become carried away by the horror of it. The scandal was a bad moment for the Government, not a major setback. Macmillan was determined to speed up the process of decolonization and appointed Ian Macleod as Colonial Secretary in 1959 with this brief. Macleod was a tough operator, the rising star of the liberal wing of the party, and in a couple of years he effectively worked himself out of a job. Nigeria went in 1960; Sierra Leone, Gambia, Uganda soon followed. With Kenyatta duly transformed from terrorist to responsible leader, Kenya became independent in 1963.

Only in central Africa did the policy of scuttle falter. Rickety federations across the globe had become a temporary monument to geopolitical schemes scribbled on the backs of Colonial Office envelopes – in the West Indies, in Malaya, above all the Central African Federation, set up in 1953. This lumped together Nyasaland and Northern Rhodesia, both overwhelmingly black, with (Southern) Rhodesia, where a white supremacist government on the South African model had long been firmly entrenched. But by 1960 it was apparent that the tail could not wag the dog in this way. Macmillan, in a widely reported speech to the South African parliament in Cape Town, spoke of 'a wind of change'. When Monckton ('the oilcan') was sent as elder statesman to report on the viability of the Central African Federation, it was reminiscent of sending Runciman to report on the viability of Czechoslovakia; it signalled to the white settlers that a sell-out was imminent, albeit one implemented in accordance with the wishes of the majority in the disputed territories. Monckton's recommendation that

Nyasaland and Northern Rhodesia be free to secede spelt the doom of the Federation. It was left to Butler to preside over its obsequies in 1963, which he did with his inimitable lugubrious charm, thus paving the way for the independence of Malawi (Nyasaland) and Zambia (Northern Rhodesia). Apart from the intractable problem of Rhodesia, decolonization might be considered appeasement's finest hour.

Such imagery held no appeal, however, for Macmillan, whose diary reveals a man whose vision had been decisively formed in a previous era. On his visits to the Dominions he still talked of 'the old country' – even in South Africa. No wind of change was going to blow South Africa out of the multiracial Commonwealth which had emerged from his own policies, not if he could help it. Macmillan may have thought the doctrinal attachment to apartheid misguided, but when the crunch came in 1961 he bitterly reproached Canada for breaking ranks with the 'Whites' in the moves to expel South Africa from membership. In the Middle East, it was the same story, with little comprehension of the authenticity of Arab nationalism, which spelt the end of docile client relationships with the west (or the east). The refusal to admit that Suez was misguided, symbolized by the prolonged attempt to cover up the collusion with Israel, was not just an understandable, disingenuous, face-saving piece of rigmarole for the benefit of his more dimwitted supporters: it was indicative of Macmillan's own outlook. He still stereotyped Nasser as Hitler in a fez.

Macmillan's deep ambiguity was a priceless political asset. It helped him quell the Conservative right wing, which was rarely confronted with the fact that the prime minister's policies were out of kilter with his rhetoric. There is little evidence that Suez as such hurt the Tories electorally, since they were already well behind Labour before it happened. Still, the by-elections were bad for the Government, which lost the socially marginal London suburb of North Lewisham to Labour in February 1957. Twelve months later, the Conservatives lost the old cotton town of Rochdale to Labour, not because the Labour vote increased but because, boosted by the candidacy of the television star Ludovic Kennedy, the Liberals, who had not even stood in the previous general election, took 36 per cent of the votes, almost all from the Conservatives. Only a month later, when Mark Bonham Carter, Asquith's grandson, captured the Devon seat of Torrington from the Conservatives, it looked like a Liberal revival, or at least an exhumation. By midsummer 1958, the Conservatives had lost a total of four seats, two to the Liberals and two to Labour.

This sort of collapse in the mid-term Government vote was to become a commonplace of the electoral cycle; but it had not been an early feature of post-war politics; until 1957 only one seat had changed hands in a by-election – and that had been a Government gain.[1] Macmillan thus needed all his sang-froid in his first two years as prime minister. His achievement was first to impose his authority on his Government as Eden had never succeeded in doing; then, with an increasingly sure touch, to capture public opinion.

Faced with rising unemployment – albeit within a range where 2 per cent began to look high – Macmillan chose to jettison his Chancellor of the Exchequer rather than his own broadly Keynesian priorities. Memories of dole queues in Stockton, his pre-war constituency, not only animated Macmillan: they became familiar to the Treasury knights, who had served him while he was Chancellor, as a code word for expansionary measures, whatever the inflationary risk. In January 1957 the vacancy at the Treasury was filled by Peter Thorneycroft, whose attachment to sound money was well known, backed by two junior ministers of even more severe outlook, Nigel Birch and Enoch Powell. Perhaps Macmillan saw this as a manoeuvre to calm anxieties, especially in the City, about inflationary pressures – the retail price index in 1957 showed an increase of nearly 4 per cent over the previous twelve months. At all events, so long as the trade figures remained reassuring, with exports currently at record levels, the Treasury was content to take a relaxed view.

In the summer of 1957, however, a sterling crisis arrived out of the blue, fuelled by fears that Government spending was out of control, and prompting talk of devaluation. Fortified by Birch and Powell, Thorneycroft staked out a strategy for controlling the money supply and for pegging the level of public spending. He got his way to the extent of a two-point jump in bank-rate, to 7 per cent, the highest level since the Lloyd George Coalition turned to deflation in 1920. In the cabinet, however, Macleod, who had been a free-spending Minister of Health and currently nursed the sensitive Labour portfolio, led the resistance to measures which might increase unemployment to 3 per

---

1. Sunderland South, Labour to Conservative in May 1953. I do not count the two university seats and one Ulster seat in which there were contests in 1946; nor Glasgow Camlachie in January 1948, since it had been won for the ILP in 1945.

cent, recently accepted as the official definition of full employment. Thorneycroft's proposal to end the allowance payable for a second child in a family was opposed by Macleod on political grounds, since this had been the one part of the welfare state enacted by a Conservative Government; and he was to remain a champion of family allowances.

If Macleod made the running, he had crucial support from Butler – who had either forgotten about Robot, or perhaps remembered, it was difficult to be sure – and, above all, from the prime minister, who manipulated the agenda so that, by January 1958, Thorneycroft was left isolated; the final difference was a matter of £50 million of cuts, which most people found trivial. Like Bevan, he had failed to broaden the issue of his resignation; like Bevan, he took two other ministers with him. Unlike the Bevanite crisis, however, the departure of the entire Treasury team did not signal the onset of damaging consequences for a divided party. Thorneycroft went quietly; both he and Powell were to return to office a couple of years later. Macmillan, flying off on a Commonwealth visit, paused at Heathrow to deliver a patiently rehearsed throwaway line about 'little local difficulties'.

Derick Heathcoat Amory, an easygoing west-country squire, became the next Chancellor. He inherited a plum situation, which he simply allowed to ripen. The modest curb on public spending and the credit squeeze had reined in any inflationary pressure; the cost of living was to rise by barely 1 per cent in either of the next two years. The terms of trade, moreover, again sharply tuned in Britain's favour with a 7 per cent drop in import prices in 1958, thus easing the balance of payments. By November 1958 bank-rate was down to 4 per cent, by now a sensitive point for those with mortgages, and in the 1959 Budget Heathcoat Amory felt justified in making sweeping tax cuts, notably a reduction in the standard rate of income tax from 8s 6d (42.5 per cent) to 7s 9d (38.75 per cent), a new post-war low, not reduced further until the Thatcher era. The economy, which had been stagnant in 1958, grew in real terms by 4 per cent in 1959 and by nearly 6 per cent in 1960.

It was on this tide of consumer prosperity that Macmillan's reputation was buoyed up. In November 1958 the London *Evening Standard* printed a cartoon; its economical draughtsmanship and its distinctive sharp brush strokes proclaimed it as by Vicky, whose left-wing stance, like that of Low before him, was licensed on grounds of sheer talent by a tolerant Beaverbrook. Was it a plane, was it a bird? It was, of course, 'Supermac', with the bravura of Macmillan's padded torso countered by the bathos of his penny-round spectacles, dangling from one out-stretched hand. It was a memorable image, brilliant propaganda – not, as it turned out, against Macmillan but, with a steady shift of percep-tions in his favour, decidely to his advantage. His apparent mastery of the political situation meant that, within three years of Suez, he was able to claim a convincing mandate from the electorate. Folk myth has him campaigning on the slogan, 'You've never had it so good.' The phrase which actually appeared on the hoardings was: 'Life's better with the Conservatives. Don't let Labour ruin it.'

The 1959 crop of by-elections held few terrors for the Conservatives; the opinion polls showed them moving into a narrow but fairly steady lead over Labour, and once more, in an era of stable party loyalties, the polls were proved right. In the general election which Macmillan called in October, the Conservatives maintained their share of the vote, again just short of 50 per cent, with Labour now a clear 5 per cent behind. The Liberals' by-election advances fell away, though with over 200 can-didates they doubled their vote to 6 per cent (and kept their six MPs). As in 1955, the Conservative gains came in England, notably in the prosperous west Midlands, the home of the booming car industry. Conversely, they lost ground not only in Lancashire, where the cotton industry was on its last legs, but also in Scotland – the beginning of a political divergence which was to become increasingly significant.

Purely political explanations for Labour's defeat focused on Gaitskell's last-minute pledge not to increase the basic rate of income tax; but, like Churchill's supposed gaffes in 1945, the effect is difficult to discern in the polls. Up to polling day, the general view was that Labour had fought a good campaign, with more professional presenta-tion of its broadcasts on television by rising centrist politicians like Anthony Wedgwood Benn, who had worked in the medium. It could be claimed that Labour now looked like an alternative government, with Bevan as a responsible shadow Foreign Secretary, no longer easily dis-missed as a left-wing bogeyman, and Harold Wilson, no longer quite so disgracefully young, a highly competent shadow Chancellor. The Bevanites were now working to a Gaitskellite brief which played down nationalization in favour of other interventionist measures on the supply side, while sketching a social programme to be financed through economic growth, and promising no great upsets in foreign policy.

There was little enough here to lose an election for Labour; yet lost it was. The Conservatives had now advanced in four general elections running; the electoral pendulum had ceased to swing. The revisionist right of the Labour Party sought to turn the techniques of market research to political advantage, and a widely cited analysis appeared under the significant title, *Must Labour Lose?* Had affluence under a bipartisan welfare state simply robbed Labour of its constituency? With the benefit of hindsight, this does not seem a silly question but it may imply a premature answer. Sociological trends were indeed against Labour, eroding its traditional working-class bedrock, but such geological processes are slow to show their full effects. For example, it should be remembered that the miners who, more than anyone else, had pioneered labour representation still numbered 660,000 in 1959, a decline of only 5 per cent since 1951. Trade-union membership held steady at just over half the male workforce and just under a quarter of the women. Such symbols of the traditional working class as cloth caps, whippets, brown ale, even the TUC's own *Daily Herald*, all survived the 1950s and only subsequently yielded, cohort by cohort, to shell-suits, rottweilers, lager and Murdoch's *Sun*. It is simplistic to regard Labour's electoral decline as predetermined, least of all by sociology.

A crude economic explanation works somewhat better, since organized workers, notably in the currently prosperous motor trade, could become affluent under the free collective bargaining which the Government offered. This did not transform them into members of the middle class, still less convert them overnight into loyal Conservatives. Instead they remained militant in their commitment to their unions, which were viewed instrumentally as the means of securing fatter pay packets. Government was increasingly judged by the same criterion: whether it held out the prospect of a better standard of living, through its impact on jobs and prices (in that order).

The idea that there was a trade-off between unemployment and inflation, which was given academic respectability with the 'Phillips curve' in 1958, had important implications for the workings of the democratic system. Government, it seemed, could control the economic cycle through doses of reflation; and, given the British prime minister's prerogative of choosing an election date, such stimulation might be coordinated with the electoral cycle. As the issue of economic management became increasingly central to electoral behaviour, two readings of the situation were plausible. One was a piece of economic determinism, reassuring for a party already long established in power: to wonder how on earth a decently competent Government could ever lose an election again. The other reading allowed more for the role of immediate political contingency: to wonder whether even Supermac could continue – as was now required by a more fickle electorate – to provide unfailing proofs of his irreplaceable virtuosity.


## ANGRY

The consumer society, which had seemed to nourish mere relief and complacency in the mid-1950s, in turn fed its own restless dissatisfactions, once its comforts came to be taken for granted. The title of J. K. Galbraith's book *The Affluent Society* (1958) introduced a subsequently inescapable term, a reminder that Europe was now going down a road already familiar in North America – with a disjunction between private affluence and public squalor as the unappealing feature which Galbraith highlighted. Earlier, Crosland's *The Future of Socialism* (1956) had offered a congruent message: that 'Keynesianism', let alone 'Butskellism', was not enough; within the new framework of consensus, there were stark choices to be faced about the priority given to social spending as against ever-increasing private consumption. This was a revisionist interpretation of socialism, which Crosland offered as a social-democratic strategy for a modernized Labour Party (though his opponents in the party certainly had a point in saying that it was hardly traditional socialism at all). These two books were widely influential in shaping attitudes on the left.

There were more strident voices which caught the current mood. In John Osborne's play *Look Back in Anger* (1956) Jimmy Porter's impassioned cry is that there 'aren't any good, brave causes left' – as though affluence had robbed the rising generation of the fine opportunities for expressing their moral indignation that Jarrow or Spain had provided in the 1930s. Osborne's work, dramatically powerful but ideologically incoherent, was seized upon by journalists as typifying a generation of 'Angry Young Men', who were hastily parcelled together as a literary movement. Colin Wilson, with a beard and sandals, obviously looked the part; and his philosophically pretentious literary study, *The Outsider* (1956), enjoyed an otherwise inexplicable hour of heady fame. It was savaged in a review by Kingsley Amis, whose down-to-earth satire on academic life, *Lucky Jim* (1954), had already won a following a couple of years previously; but that did not stop the media from conscripting Amis too as an 'AYM' Other supposed members – the poet and novelist John Wain, and John Braine, with his north-country romance of upward social mobility, *Room at the Top* (1957) – were even more disparate.

How angry were they – and about what? Osborne became notorious for challenging the stifling social mores of upper-middle-class England. In this he was abetted by his influential champion, Kenneth Tynan, the young dramatic critic of the *Observer*, who directed his fire at the 'well-made play', long the vehicle of West End successes for Noel Coward and, above all, Terence Rattigan. For example, in *The Winslow Boy* (1946), both in the theatre and in Anthony Asquith's smoothly directed film (1950) – one of his many happy adaptations of Rattigan's plays – the conventions of courtroom drama had rarely been exploited to such good effect, gripping audiences who knew that this was what they liked. Goaded by Tynan, Rattigan jumped to the defence of his public, appealing to his mythical 'Aunt Edna' as against a supposed avant-garde.

These contrasting aesthetic stereotypes obscured the fact that it was hardly *literary* innovation which distinguished the Angry Young Men. After *Look Back in Anger*, Osborne went on to stage a brilliant evocation of British decline through exploiting the idiom of the music hall in *The Entertainer* (1957). 'Don't clap too hard – it's a very old building,' quips the ageing star, Archie Rice, who could easily have stood in for Macmillan, as Vicky quickly spotted in another inimitable cartoon. But had Osborne really strayed far outside the range of Coward's dramatic conventions – *Cavalcade* (1931), for example – or only his social and political conventions?

Kingsley Amis, who was to write a string of versatile novels, nothing if not well-made, found his oeuvre even more easily assimilated over the next forty years by an establishment he had once scorned. By stages the conventionally left-wing asperities of *Take A Girl Like You* (1960) were subtly modulated. In *Girl, 20* (1971) facile *marxisant* stereotyping – 'You are an imperialist racist fascist' – is observed with wry disdain. By the time of *Stanley and the Women* (1984), fashionable feminist nostrums come to supply the sand in Amis's oyster. Politically this represented a sharp shift to the rebarbative right. In the public persona which he projected, Amis ended up as a latter-day Evelyn Waugh, albeit without the religion, offering his public an impeccable performance as Exasperated Old Buffer. Amis self-consciously reached out, if not to

Aunt Edna, then to a 'middlebrow' reading public, exhibiting his own virtuosity by publishing one novel, *The Riverside Villas Murder* (1973), in the idiom of the classic whodunit, and another, *Colonel Sun* (1968), in the style of Ian Fleming, creator of James Bond.

Dorothy L. Sayers and Agatha Christie were long the big names in detective fiction, a staple of the now struggling commercial libraries, like Boots the Chemist, and later of the burgeoning paperback imprints. Sayers, who died in 1957, had quit the genre twenty years earlier when her fictional sleuth, Lord Peter Wimsey, solved the last of his baffling cases. Several had been set against backdrops Sayers, the thwarted academic, knew well from her own career: the advertising agency in *Murder Must Advertise* (1933) or the Oxford college in *Gaudy Night* (1935). Nonchalant, aristocratic, scholarly, and accompanied by his faithful manservant, Lord Peter had outshone plodding professional policemen like the true amateur he was; but he could hardly have survived in post-war Britain.

By contrast, Agatha Christie maintained an astonishing popularity from her first thriller, *The Mysterious Affair at Styles* (1920) until her death in 1976 (by which time her play *The Mousetrap* had completed the first quarter-century of its run in the West End). Her books showed her perfunctory about characterization, instead opting to pit her wits against her readers in solving the finite puzzles of her tightly constructed plots. For her purposes, such stylized settings as country houses isolated by fresh snow supplied the necessary rules of the game, not a whimsical, sub-Brideshead social context. Her detectives – whether Hercule Poirot, the retired Belgian policeman, or Miss Marple, the underrated little old lady – were not easily pigeonholed in the conventional hierarchies; and the relatively classless nature of Christie's appeal kept her wide readership comfortable.

The popular success of James Bond, secret agent 007, did not rest on blurring status distinctions. From the moment when *Casino Royale* (1953) instantly made him a best-selling author, until his death in 1964, Ian Fleming annually produced a new Bond adventure, sizzling with 'sex, sadism and snobbery', as one unfriendly review complained (counter-productively, of course). But, in so far as it was indeed snobbery that helped sell the books, this was not old-fashioned, pedigree-conscious social stuffiness so much as – like John Braine's novels – a deft manipulation of brand-name snob appeal, fit for a consumer society with the promise of room at the top. After *Dr No* (1958) became the first Bond book to be filmed, 007 lost any remaining English public-school inhibitions in his transition to dazzling international stardom.

Bond was to become the basis of some of the most profitable British films ever made, replete with gadgets, gloss and glamour. Conversely, it was 'kitchen-sink' realism which originally heralded a 'new wave' in British cinema, paralleling that in France. The film version of *Room at the Top* (1959) put a sharper edge on Braine's social comment on the class system, as well as introducing a frankness in its treatment of sex hitherto lacking in British films. Alan Sillitoe's novel *Saturday Night and Sunday Morning* (1958) was another class-conscious account of the industrial north, juxtaposing the alienating experience of Arthur Seaton's workday week with his wild weekend binges of booze and sex. Under the direction of Karel Reisz, and with a fine performance from Albert Finney, there was a faithful translation in the film version (1960), which was produced by Woodfall Films, a new company formed by John Osborne and Tony Richardson. The Woodfall film of *The Entertainer* (1960), directed by Richardson and keeping Olivier in the starring role, eventually succeeded in getting Osborne's own work across to cinema audiences, after an initial disappointment with the filmed *Look Back in Anger* (1958): its choler, bile and spleen dissipated on celluloid, despite having Richard Burton in the leading role.

The anger welling up irrepressibly in Osborne was as difficult to miss as its target was difficult to identify. Sometimes called the new Shaw, Osborne lacked the coherence of the Shavian political vision: instead Osborne's was a highly visceral, highly polemical impulse which led him to proclaim his hatred as much for Gaitskell as for Macmillan.

The cause which most effectively appealed to this inchoate, unfocused mood of frustration and protest was surely the Campaign for Nuclear Disarmament (CND). Its rise came not only post-Suez but post-Hungary, since the consequent exodus of many intellectuals from the 'old-left' Communist Party saw the inception of a 'new left'. The Communists, of course, applauded the Soviet bomb, as a workers' bomb; but the new left was comprehensively anti-bomb – Soviet, American, but above all, nearest to home, against the British bomb. The proliferation of nuclear weapons in the early 1950s caused widespread anxiety about their capacity to devastate and pollute the world; and with good reason. As Macmillan well appreciated, there would have been even greater alarm about nuclear contamination had he not suppressed reports of more than one accident at the plutonium-processing plant at Windscale (Sellafield) in Cumbria.

The orthodox argument exploited the paradox that, precisely because its use was unthinkable, the bomb's deterrent effect would be able to preserve peace, through a balance of terror and a mutual assurance of destruction (MAD). The Defence White Paper of 1957 brought this debate to a head, not least at the Labour Party conference that autumn at Brighton. Many of the old Bevanites were by now pressing for Labour to repudiate a nuclear strategy altogether; but they had to suffer the public defection of their erstwhile hero. Bevan, speaking as shadow Foreign Secretary, declined the prospect of going 'naked into the conference chamber'; when he summarily dismissed his old comrades' motion as 'an emotional spasm', it was a thrilling piece of theatre. It consolidated the post-Suez axis at the top of the Labour Party; it killed some of Bevan's oldest political friendships; but it did not kill CND.

After Brighton, CND emerged as a pressure group outside the ordinary party political structure, with the support of big names like Bertrand Russell, J. B. Priestley, A. J. P. Taylor and (of course) John Osborne, as well as Bevanites like Michael Foot and the trade-union leader Frank Cousins. Where CND initially succeeded was through the simplicity of its message – 'Ban the Bomb' – which used the language of protest rather than calculation. In reposing such faith in the worldwide moral effect of a British renunciation of nuclear weapons, the unilateralists surely harboured their own great-power illusions. At Easter 1958 there was a march from London to Aldermaston, the weapons research station in Berkshire; the next year the march made even more impact on public opinion, partly because it now started out from Aldermaston and picked up vast numbers on its last leg into Trafalgar Square. Pacifist in inspiration, the Aldermaston marches remained pacific in method, notable as good-tempered annual festivals for all the family. The distinctive CND logo soon became familiar through lapel badges and graffiti.

The popular support which the movement for unilateral disarmament gathered was enough to alarm the Government, which visibly redoubled its efforts for a test-ban treaty, partly so as to show the feasibility of multilateral measures to control nuclear weapons. It was, however, the Labour Party which had most to fear politically. The fact that Gaitskell was firmly identified with Nato and its nuclear strategy meant that his leadership was clearly at stake, so that the issue of unilateral disarmament became intermeshed with a broader struggle between left and right over the identity of the party.

This was brought out by the Labour Party conference in 1959. In the aftermath of electoral defeat, Gaitskell made the radical proposal to amend Clause IV of the party's constitution, which had defined its rationale in terms of common ownership. In Germany the SPD (the social democrats) had done essentially the same thing at their Bad Godesberg conference earlier that year. In Britain, however, revisionism was not so easy to accept. Bevan, now a stricken man, within months of his death, sought reconciliation within the party, but could not save the leadership from a rebuff. The support of the big unions, which had been Gaitskell's mainstay, had come adrift. In particular he could no longer rely on the TGWU once Deakin's right-wing regime had been replaced (after a short interregnum) by the election of the left-winger Cousins as general secretary. Gaitskell had to accept their rejection of his revisionist agenda, moreover, because within months he was faced with a bigger crisis.

By 1960 the unilateralists had won enough union support, as well as left-wing constituency parties, to carry their policy motion at the party conference, in the face of Gaitskell's impassioned plea that this was incompatible with British membership of Nato. He isolated this commitment (rather than Britain's own bomb) as the crucial issue in imploring his supporters to 'fight and fight and fight again to save the party we love'. The Parliamentary Labour Party was now at odds with conference decisions but Gaitskell succeeded in getting conference to reverse itself the following year. This was partly the product of a grass-roots campaign in the constituencies; but chiefly it was due to the fact that three out of the six biggest unions changed sides between 1960 and 1961 – voting for the status quo, just as they had over Clause IV. The effect of these vicissitudes on Gaitskell's own position was potent, partly because his role had been dramatized by television coverage of the party conferences, at time when moves to broadcast parliament had not yet been successful. By 1962 his public image was incontestably that of a strong and decisive leader – whereas it was Macmillan who was by now reeling from crisis to crisis.

The basic trouble was the economy. The boom which peaked in 1959 and 1960, with growth between 4 and 5 per cent, was unsustainable. Heathcoat Amory's measures had stimulated domestic consumption, so that imports were growing nearly twice as fast as exports.

Macmillan, belatedly recognizing the symptoms of overheating, once more sought a new Chancellor and drafted in Selwyn Lloyd, who had served him faithfully at the Foreign Office. (The appointment of the Earl of Home as the new Foreign Secretary seemed less significant at the time.) Lloyd began cautiously, showing understandable reluctance to choke economic growth through dear money, and bank-rate wobbled for over a year, before the weakness of sterling dictated the full severity of a 7 per cent rate in July 1961.

This time round, though, a monetary squeeze was not left to work alone. In his 1961 Budget Lloyd had armed himself with new powers to vary revenue duties; these 'regulators' permitted a new flexibility in the fine tuning of the economy. Thus in July Lloyd was able to reinforce his monetary squeeze with an immediate fiscal squeeze. Moreover, he backed this package with a 'pay pause' – the first attempt since Cripps to devise direct controls on inflationary wage settlements.

The outcry was enormous, not least because of the anomalies the policy created. In particular, it froze new settlements in the public sector while merely subjecting the private sector to restraint by exhortation. Partly to cope with such issues, the Government now moved to set up a National Incomes Commission, but, since it was boycotted by the TUC, this did little to win assent for the new policy. TUC cooperation was secured, however, for the creation of another tripartite body, representing unions, employers and Government: the National Economic Development Council (NEDC). The Treasury was steadily abandoning its 'hands-off' approach to economic management, and this sort of coordination of information was a tentative exercise in indicative planning, if hardly dirigiste.

Not only was the language French but both the inspiration and the stimulus were likewise European, and with good reason. The fact was that the EEC had proved successful despite its lack of British participation. Indeed it was Britain's attempt to organize a rival grouping of seven countries within a European Free Trade Area (EFTA) which already looked sad. The Seven, which included countries like Denmark and Ireland, overwhelmingly dependent on the UK market for their food exports, was a loose free-trading association of the kind which Britain could easily accept; but it failed to get access to the common market established by the Six, which – inward-looking, corporatist, cartelized, over-regulated, protectionist, or whatever – was now the dynamic force.

In 1953 the Six between them had accounted for only 10 per cent of British imports, compared with 14 per cent from Australia and New Zealand, which in turn took over 12 per cent of British exports, slightly in excess of the European share. By 1960, however, nearly 15 per cent of British imports came from the EEC, only 8 per cent from the antipodean Dominions; and the EEC now took 16 per cent of British exports, while Australia and New Zealand took only two-thirds as much. Commonwealth preferences simply meant that the British economy was now facing the wrong way, with its back turned on the expanding markets it most needed if it was to keep pace with the growth of international trade. British exports had claimed around 16 per cent of world trade in manufactures in the mid-1950s; by 1960 this share was under 13 per cent (and it was to drop below 10 per cent by 1966).

Macmillan, who had always professed a sneaking sympathy for European integration, decided that there was nothing for it but to swallow his pride and sneak no longer. In the summer of 1961 he persuaded the cabinet to apply for membership of the EEC. The Community structures which Britain might have hoped to mould after Messina were instead naturally setting in a shape not much to Britain's liking; in particular, the Common Agricultural Policy, with its petty protectionism and gross farm subsidies, flew in the face of Britain's historic bias towards free trade in food. Special arrangements to ease the transition for Australia and New Zealand were clearly necessary; Canada, long since in the dollar area, did not pose the same problem. These were difficulties which Edward Heath, as Minister for European Affairs at the Foreign Office, was commissioned to resolve. Heath, a former chief whip, was an able recruit to the cabinet, a committed Europhile ever since his entry to Parliament in 1950, and an obviously appropriate figure to represent Britain's new commitment in the protracted negotiations which now began in Brussels. The real obstacle to British membership was not in Brussels but in Paris, where President de Gaulle took a lofty view of his duty to judge the European credentials of the Anglo-Saxons, with whom he had always experienced such difficulties. But Macmillan felt confident that he could exploit a long-standing personal relationship here, just as he had with Eisenhower.

Macmillan's difficulties were compounded by the fact that he had launched his European initiative, not from strength but to retrieve an already weak position. The Government's popularity, following the pay pause, had plummeted. The Liberals had been picking up votes in the

1961 by-elections. In March 1962 they almost toppled the mountainous Conservative majority in Blackpool North; the next day, they fulfilled their wildest dreams in capturing Orpington in Kent, a byword for deepest Tory suburbia. This was the biggest by-election upset since the war; the spectre of Orpington Man suddenly stalked the Conservative benches in parliament. Macmillan's response was designed to give his Government a new lease of life by removing the main target of its unpopularity – Selwyn Lloyd. But in executing this piece of selective ruthlessness, he lost his nerve, and sought to cover it with a major reconstruction of the cabinet in July, in which no fewer than six other ministers were also sacked. This 'night of the long knives' stored up further resentments, without turning the tide in public opinion.

Though there was no repetition of Orpington, Liberal intervention was now clearly helping Labour, which snatched three seats from the Conservatives before the year was out. The prospect of a Labour Government, unsettling in itself, had a particular European dimension since the party seemed generally sceptical about the whole idea. The Liberals were the only party straightforwardly in favour of entering the common market, but they would not be calling the shots. Formally Labour reserved its position, but in October 1962 Gaitskell again baffled observers who thought that he lacked emotion, this time by telling the Labour Party conference that entry to the EEC would mean 'the end of a thousand years of history'. This passionate stand may have been inspired by concern for the Commonwealth, and it did not commit a future Labour Government, but it hardly made for a pro-European atmosphere.

Just as the Bevanites had felt betrayed by Bevan five years previously, so the younger Gaitskellites like Roy Jenkins, among the keenest of Europhiles, were now discomfited. Conversely, Gaitskell received unwontedly warm tributes from the left wing whom he had so recently worsted. In January 1963, however, after a routine illness had suddenly taken a critical turn, Gaitskell died, aged fifty-six. There were sufficient doubts about the personal qualities of his deputy George Brown to provoke another Gaitskellite, James Callaghan, to stand as well for the leadership; and the result was the election of neither, but of Harold Wilson, the ex-Bevanite.

By the time Wilson took over as leader of the Opposition, the Government was in deeper trouble than ever. Macmillan had raised the stakes over defence policy by insisting that Britain keep its own independent nuclear weapons, even though it had become totally dependent on the USA for any means of delivering them. This was the problem, largely self-imposed, which confronted him in his dealings with President Kennedy, whom he met at Nassau in December 1962. The British had relied upon a half-promise that the American Skybolt rocket would be supplied; but when the Kennedy administration decided to cancel it as operationally unsound – 'pile of junk' was one expression used – Macmillan was left politically exposed. He played the few cards in his hand with brilliant finesse, invoking his recent support for the USA in the Cuban missile crisis in one breath, his memories of the Somme in the next. What he got from a reluctant Kennedy was an agreement to supply the UK with the Polaris-submarine missile-launching system, which could be duly armed with British nuclear warheads. Whether this strike force could be called independent of the USA, which supplied the indispensable technology, was disputable; but the Nassau conference undoubtedly proclaimed a strong symbolic message about the 'special relationship'.

How far Macmillan had calculated (or miscalculated) on de Gaulle's response (or lack of response) is not clear. De Gaulle might well have blocked British entry in any event; but Nassau provided him with an object lesson in Britain's preference for a transatlantic relationship over a European commitment. Macmillan had proved strategically mistaken in supposing that he need not choose. De Gaulle's veto, announced in Paris in January 1963, effectively ended the negotiations over British entry to the EEC, and Heath sadly made his way home.

Ruefully, secretly, Macmillan recognized that this rebuff removed the keystone in his policy arch; yet there is every sign that he fully intended to fight another election. Nor was his resolve broken by the eruption of the Profumo scandal in the summer of 1963. Though provoking a riot of colourful rumour and innuendo, as it gradually came out that the Minister of War had been sharing a girlfriend with (among others) an attaché at the Soviet embassy, it led only to Profumo's resignation, not the prime minister's. The reason for Macmillan's departure in October was not, therefore, the debilitated state of his Government, but his own misdiagnosed medical condition. A prostate operation temporarily laid him low; and before he turned the corner – which he shortly did, to such good effect that he was to remain a public figure for the next quarter-century – he had set the wheels in motion for resignation.

Since the drama was played out at just the time the Conservatives were assembling for their party conference, the leadership struggle was conducted in the glare of publicity, importing some of the razz-matazz of an American party convention into the incongruous setting of Blackpool. Once more the Tory Party turned towards Butler; once more they turned away – or, as critics like Macleod maintained, were purposely turned away from Butler in favour of less-qualified candidates, through the operation of a 'magic circle'. Under recent legislation, permitting hereditary peers to renounce their titles, two new candidates emerged. One was obviously Lord Hailsham, whose flagrant bid for the premiership, however, lost him the support of the bedridden incumbent, who inclined instead towards Lord Home, the Foreign Secretary, whom almost everyone had forgotten. Macmillan advised the Queen that the majority of the cabinet preferred Home. Macleod and Powell not only decided that they would not serve under him: they told Butler so, thus, in Powell's image, handing Butler a loaded revolver, which, characteristically, he chose not to use. Thus Macmillan had his way to the end; Lord Home became prime minister as Sir Alec Douglas-Home, and Butler yet again took second place in the new Government, this time serving as Foreign Secretary during the tail-end of a parliament which now had only a year to run.

# 9

# In Place of Strife
## 1963–70

When Butler looked back on a long parliamentary career – which he finally relinquished after 1964 to ply his inveterate political skills before a more appreciative audience as Master of Trinity College, Cambridge – he saw that his real monument was the 1944 Education Act which, so he liked to think, had opened the door of opportunity to all. The Butler Act remained for forty years the basis on which local authorities were responsible for maintaining state schools and assisting denominational schools. It finally took the heat out of the disputes over religious schooling which had bedevilled educational reform for more than a century. The practical result here was that the number of Church of England schools fell over the next twenty years to one in three of all primary schools, while Roman Catholic schools rose to one in ten of all secondary schools. The Act also gave substance to the aspiration of secondary education for all – before the war four out of five children had stayed in elementary schools till they entered the labour market at fourteen – by making a break at the age of eleven when children would move on for at least four more years' schooling, once the long-postponed raising of the school-leaving age to fifteen was implemented in 1947.

The administrative genius of the Butler Act, explaining its longevity, was that, while it implicitly expected a selective basis to be generally adopted for the provision of secondary education, it left it open for local education authorities (LEAs) to institute multilateral or comprehensive schools. The result was that, in most areas of England and Wales, three types of school were provided for selective 'eleven-plus' education: grammar schools with an academic curriculum, designed to satisfy matriculation requirements for universities through the General Certificate of Education (GCE); technical schools with a vocational emphasis; and secondary-modern schools for the rest.

In 1944 it had been thought that the school population might divide in the proportions 5 : 15 : 80, implying a sharply tapered skills pyramid. By the mid-1950s it turned out that over 25 per cent of eleven-plus pupils in England and Wales were at grammar schools, fewer than 5 per cent at technical schools, and the remaining two-thirds at secondary-modern schools (with a further 1 per cent at a dozen or so comprehensive schools). Thus the grammar schools took a larger and the technical schools a smaller proportion of the population than had been envisaged. The perceived pedagogical advantages, or simply the social cachet, of a grammar-school education drove local authorities, under electoral pressure from parents, in this direction. In Wales grammar-school places were available for over 30 per cent of the age group. This was reflected in a correspondingly higher number of Welsh children staying at school beyond fifteen; in the early 1950s the proportion staying until eighteen in Wales was double that in England, and so was the proportion going on to some form of higher education. Scotland, with its much longer tradition of encouraging the democratic intellect, already had a school system which was more broadly based.

The fact was that in Britain – England worse than Wales or Scotland – education remained solidly class-bound. In England and Wales, two out of five children born in the professional and managerial classes in the early twentieth century had had a grammar-school education, rising to three out of five for those born in the late 1930s (the first cohort to benefit fully under the Butler Act). By contrast, children of unskilled manual workers, whose chance of secondary education had been one in a hundred before the First World War, had a one-in-ten chance of passing the eleven-plus after the Second. The best that could be said about this was that it was progress in the right direction. Moreover, once this post-Butler cohort was in grammar (or equivalent) schools, the initial social bias was progressively accentuated since many more children from a professional background stayed on beyond age seventeen. Such statistics indicate a complex of intractable social influences, as much a product of cultural aspirations as of economic inequalities. The easiest target, however, for those in search of an immediate remedy was the inequity of eleven-plus selection.

The idea that carefully designed tests could – regardless of prior tuition or home background – accurately measure a child's intelligence quotient (IQ), was one which the work of the educational psychologist Sir Cyril Burt (1883–1971) had done much to propagate. Educational selection based on IQ-testing had a plausible progressive pedigree; after all, it could be seen as a way of challenging existing social privilege in the name of sheer ability, to be found impartially among all classes. When the sociologist Michael Young introduced the term 'meritocracy' – in his book *The Rise of the Meritocracy* (1958) – he was pointing (with some misgivings) to this new sort of legitimation for social elites. But his worries about the chilling efficiency of a meritocratic hierarchy were premature at a time when the crass inefficiency of eleven-plus selection was more apparent. Not only was its social bias evident in the disproportionately high success rate of middle-class children: even among the privileged classes it was a poor indicator of academic apti-tude, as shown by the good GCE results subsequently achieved at independent schools by children who had previously failed the eleven-plus. In due course, too, the integrity of Burt's pioneer research was impugned, thus shaking the intellectual foundations of IQ-testing.

The post-war euphemisms about parity of esteem between different kinds of secondary schools were belied by social realities. The fact was that secondary-modern schools ended up preparing working-class-children for working-class jobs – or rather, instead of preparing them, simply conditioned them. Here was the nub of the case for comprehen-sive schools, which moved from being the policy of a few maverick (again mainly Welsh) councils to the status of a defining progressive nostrum. It remained an issue to be resolved through LEAs, not through the imposition of a single model from the centre. Butler de-lighted in the fact that this was so under his 1944 Act; and before the Conservatives left office in 1964 200 comprehensive schools had opened. Alongside Wales, the other early breakthrough for comprehen-sives came in Greater London, where Labour likewise dominated local government.[1] What the incoming Labour Government did was to put its influence behind secondary-school reorganization, notably in the circu-lar 10/65 which Crosland issued after he took over the Department of

[1] Labour controlled the London County Council for thirty years – one reason for its abolition by the Conservatives' London Government Act of 1963. This Act extended the metropolitan area to the suburbs under the Greater London Council (which Labour still won more often than not). The LEAs were formed from the borough councils in the outer ring of suburbs; but the Inner London Education Authority (ILEA) inherited these functions within the inner-city boroughs. Since the ILEA was controlled by whichever party was stronger within the old LCC boundaries, it is not surprising that it continued under Labour control.

Education and Science in 1965. This influence, albeit without statutory sanctions, pushed open a door which was already ajar. There were over 1,000 comprehensive schools with over 30 per cent of secondary-school pupils by 1970; and 2,000 comprehensives with 60 per cent of pupils by 1974 – despite a change of government which put Margaret Thatcher in charge of education. By 1980 comprehensives had reached 90 per cent coverage, with only a few LEAs under firm Conservative control, like Kent, keeping their grammar schools.

At the time, pro-comprehensive rhetoric was commonly pitched against the grammar schools – Crosland's self-ascribed mission 'to destroy every fucking grammar school' in the country was only unusual in its vernacular force. Yet grammar schools had generally done a good job, not least in educating the rising generation of meritocratic leaders like Wilson, Heath, Jenkins and Thatcher. It was the failings of the secondary-modern concept, and the puny resources devoted to technical education, which seem culpable in hindsight. The planned raising of the school-leaving age to sixteen was designed to remove some long-standing disparities in educational experience; but it was postponed in the economic crisis of 1968. The fact was that the gains for the majority from Labour's policy were largely prospective; whereas the losses were immediate, through the disruption of reorganization and the loss of locally respected grammar schools. Such apprehensions were often to help the Conservatives electorally, as well as fuelling a (selective) movement by middle-class parents into the private system, leaving state secondary schools in this respect less comprehensive than before.

Crosland's own passion for social equality need not be doubted, since this was wholly in keeping with the priorities of Labour revisionists (conventionally called 'right-wing'). The fact that Crosland had himself attended a 'public school' had hardly made him tender towards this form of education. Yet the effect of Labour policy in the 1960s was curious. State grammar schools were shut down on the argument that otherwise a truly comprehensive system could not be created. Fee-paying schools in the independent sector, by contrast, though arguably the most socially divisive way of perpetuating privilege, were let be.

Independent schools of various kinds continued to educate about 5 per cent of all children, a drop from 9 per cent since the Second World War. This sector may have become smaller but it also became more efficient (the term used in granting recognition by state inspectors). The grotesque private-school incompetence memorialized by Eveyn Waugh in *Decline and Fall* (1928) steadily gave way to the businesslike approach of the top public schools, which made a hard sell in a tough market by emphasizing, on the demand side, tax-efficient ways of meeting school fees, and on the supply side, good teaching in small classes. In a league of their own stood a group of schools with a hybrid status, receiving a direct grant from the state, yet often members of the Headmasters' Conference (the traditional definition of a public school). These 180 direct-grant schools were, for the most part, ancient endowed grammar schools which admitted a substantial proportion of children on scholarships funded by LEAs. Academically strenuous, with little more than 2 per cent of secondary schools entrants, they nonetheless accounted for about 8 per cent of those staying on to age eighteen, and half their school leavers went on to university. Over the years, many schemes for dealing with the prestigious 'public' schools had been mooted, some designed to abolish them, others to prop them up financially. Independent schools were not touched by the comprehensivization of the 1960s; but in 1975, the direct-grant schools – the crème de la crème of meritocratic selection – were abolished, though public schools still survived.

England's selective school system had long been married to an even more selective university system, where likewise academic selection reinforced social discrimination. At the beginning of the century there had been 20,000 university students in Great Britain, about one-third of them undergraduates at Oxford and Cambridge. Indeed Oxbridge maintained its numerical domination of the academic profession until the Second World War. In the post-war years, with scholarships more widely available under the Butler Act, the proportion of university students for the first time went above 2 per cent of the relevant age group, rising to 4 per cent by 1962. By then there were thirty universities. Oxford and Cambridge, each with about 10,000 undergraduates, were dwarfed by London, with constituent colleges, like University College, King's, Imperial and the London School of Economics, which were largely autonomous. Moreover, the five provincial colleges which London had spawned (Nottingham, Southampton, Hull, Exeter and Leicester) had in turn become universities in their own right, reinforcing the ranks of an earlier generation of civic or 'red-brick' universities (like Manchester, Birmingham and Leeds). In Scotland the four ancient universities (Edinburgh, Aberdeen, Glasgow and St Andrews) had all expanded; and the University of Wales, under its 1893 charter as a federal institution, had fully constituent university colleges in Aberystwyth, Bangor, Cardiff and Swansea (later Lampeter too).

This was a story of expansion; but also still of restriction. For example, the proportion of students whose fathers were in manual occupations remained stuck from 1920 to 1960 at more or less a quarter. Whereas at least one in eight middle-class children eventually gained university places, fewer than one in a hundred working-class children did so. Perhaps surprisingly, the position in Scotland was not very different from that in England; and only in Wales were there significantly larger numbers of university entrants whose fathers were manual workers. By international standards, the proportion of the relevant age group in higher education was low – only 8 per cent in 1962, including all those in teacher-training and other colleges.

Here was the problem which confronted the Committee on Higher Education under the chairmanship of the economist Lord Robbins. The solution proposed in the Robbins Report in 1963 was to create an altogether bigger system of higher education. Since the Government had already committed itself to providing grants for all students admitted to university, this further commitment was not only expansive but expensive. The result was that the total number of students in higher education doubled by 1970. The number in universities, around 120,000 at the time of the Robbins Report, was to reach 370,000 by 1990.

The expansion which Robbins proposed over a twenty-year period was supposed to be geared in favour of science. At the time this was a fashionable plea. In 1959 C. P. Snow had created a notable stir in identifying 'two cultures' – those of the literary intellectuals and of the natural scientists – between whom there subsisted a gulf of mutual incomprehension. It was an updated form of the 'gap' which had worried Wells forty years previously; and one perennially advocated remedy was to improve scientific education. Robbins found that students taking degrees in scientific and technological subjects in 1962 were not far short of half the total in universities; and it was hoped that they would form a clear majority during the next twenty years. Instead, although the number of science students nearly doubled by 1980, the number of students in the arts went up by 160 per cent – by then including as many women as men. By contrast, for every two women taking medicine in 1980 there were still three men; in pure science, five men; and in technology, eighteen men.

Stubbornly, science thus remained, if not the male preserve it had once been, still unfriendly to women, at all levels. There was, of course, great distinction in British scientific research, with a haul of Nobel prizes, proportionate to population, which was internationally outstanding. It remains piquant that the most notable breakthrough of the post-war period, the discovery of the structure of the key genetic substance DNA at the Cavendish laboratory in 1953, resulted in Nobel prizes ten years later for all but one of the scientists most closely involved: for James Watson and Francis Crick, for their Cambridge colleagues Max Perutz and John Kendrew, and for Maurice Wilkins at King's College, London. There could be nothing, however, for his colleague Rosalind Franklin, whose X-ray work had provided a crucial link: a magnificent role model for women in science, robbed of due recognition by her tragic death four years before the awards.

In the post-Robbins era, it was the new polytechnics which set the pace in opening up higher education to first-generation students. By the time he left the Education and Science Department in 1967, Crosland had commissioned thirty polytechnics, to be jointly controlled by his department and by local government. The aim was to provide a wider range of courses than universities, and to concentrate on teaching rather than research. Often regarded as a comprehensive form of higher education, some of them experienced similar problems in amalgamating existing institutions, with diverse objectives and incompatible traditions, operating on a shoestring on scattered sites. Many polytechnics, however, were immediately successful in carving out a new role, while others chose to follow an existing academic model, competing for students with universities.

Robbins gave an enormous boost to the clutch of new universities, already under construction, which received their own charters at once, with no tutelary attachment to existing institutions. Sussex was a notable success and was soon followed by East Anglia, York, Essex, Kent, Warwick and Lancaster, all built on greenfield sites in England. In Scotland, Stirling followed this model, but Dundee, Heriot-Watt in Edinburgh and Strathclyde in Glasgow each developed on an existing urban base. Indeed Strathclyde, formed out of the Royal College of Science, had some affinities with the nine English colleges of advanced technology which were given university status after Robbins; it may be significant that only Bath and Loughborough retained the word technology in their titles. By 1968 the total number of universities had reached fifty-six. But it should not be forgotten that London and the older red-brick universities were themselves expanding, sometimes almost out of recognition.

The most striking development in mass higher education was qualitative as well as quantitative. The Open University was very much the brainchild of Harold Wilson, and as prime minister he ensured that its launch received adequate resources. Using radio and television in innovative forms of distance learning, it recruited a student body, largely of part-timers, with a wholly different social profile from that of the traditional British undergraduate. Mature students, women students, disadvantaged students – for many people with thwarted educational aspirations the Open University became a lifeline. It was given broadcasting facilities on BBC networks at unsocial hours, which initially served to test the devotion of its students until the advent of cassettes and videos eased this particular rigour. The rigour of academic standards, however, was maintained in a highly traditional way. The Open University's offer of the challenge of intellectual adventure, amid distracting human predicaments, irradiates Willy Russell's play, and later film, *Educating Rita* (1979 and 1981).

Perceptions of academic life were palpably changing. In his day C. P. Snow had captured the nuances of a Cambridge college nicely in *The Masters* (1951); Kingsley Amis had rendered the post-war academic career pressures in a Welsh university college into high comedy in *Lucky Jim* (1954). But Amis's own later prognostication that 'more will mean worse' did not have to be accepted to recognize that more certainly meant different. The proud civic university which Chamberlain had founded in Birmingham was to become a stylized backdrop for David Lodge's witty exploration of Anglo-American academic interpenetration in *Changing Places* (1975). Above all, though Robbins himself would hardly have liked it, the post-Robbins ambience of a social-science department in a new university was unmistakable in Malcolm Bradbury's *The History Man* (1975), with its easy-come, easy-go, *marxisant* rationalizations of sexual irregularity between staff and students.

Students – even at Oxbridge this term was increasingly used – had become news by 1968. Beards and anoraks, placards and banners, chants and loud-hailers, served to mark the end of Britain's exemption from the sort of student demonstrations in the streets which happened abroad. The Vietnam War provided the great focus for this kind of agitation; but in 1968 it was turned on targets nearer home, with occupations of college and university buildings which partly mimicked parallel events in France and the USA but also directed attention to more immediate student grievances. The fashionable Marxist claim was that students had a natural affinity with an exploited working class, though their links with organized labour rarely transcended this nebulous rhetoric. Some theorists even argued that, with an apathetic working class smothered by consumerism, the eternally renewed discontent of the young could itself bring about radical change in society.

Though few students perceived themselves as the shock troops of the revolution, their lifestyle was often a shock to parents, teachers, taxpayers – in short, to older people. The sexual behaviour of young people was escaping traditional controls, not least among students living away from home. This stereotyped impression of the 'swinging sixties' was often linked with the introduction of the new birth-control pill for women. But there is evidence indicating that changes in conduct in fact preceded – by as much as a decade – the widespread availability of the pill in the late 1960s, a development which was more a response to new sexual mores than their cause. Certainly the deterrent of unwanted pregnancy became less feared and artificial means of contraception more widely employed. Whether there was as much sexual activity among the young as talk about a 'permissive society' suggested is not easy to establish; but there was a new openness. The poet Philip Larkin, in his adopted role as professional curmudgeon, was to make himself the spokesman of the view that 'sexual intercourse began in 1963' – a poetic truth perhaps. Moreover, the use of drugs by young people achieved widespread prominence, provoking – as was sometimes intended – a backlash of disapproval. Thus the 1960s raised timeless issues of inter-generational conflict to new levels, partly because, with growing prosperity, economic independence was more quickly achieved by teenagers in a tight labour market. Students, too, were well provided for, with not only their fees paid from public funds but maintenance grants that were generous by international standards.

A conspicuous and noisy youth culture, which had been hotting up for years, came to the boil in the 1960s. Pop music became its most obvious bond, whether live or on records or radio. Since the war the USA had dominated this market; suddenly British groups acquired worldwide fame. The Beatles, whose spectacular career took off in 1962–3, were from Liverpool, as songs like 'Penny Lane' never let anyone forget. They had in John Lennon and Paul McCartney songwriters of genius, achieving deceptively simple effects which created an unparalleled number of enduring classics. 'Yesterday' was to be recorded in several hundred versions over the years. Apart from the Queen and the aged Churchill, the Beatles became instantly the most famous Britons alive, with a string of hits which all young people knew, even if some subcultures preferred the raw suggestiveness of the Rolling Stones. In their wake came dozens more groups, seeking to exploit the 'Mersey sound'.

Here was the market tapped by pirate radio ships, broadcasting pop music almost non-stop on unlicensed frequencies. The Wilson Government, with its heavy-handed attempts to enforce the BBC's monopoly, struck many young people as out of touch and foolish; and whether Wilson retrieved or compounded this folly by recommending the Beatles for the MBE is a moot point. Belatedly, the BBC launched Radio One – on dry land, but its own exercise in piracy nonetheless. No longer did the family cluster round the wireless in the sitting room to share a favourite programme; instead the car radio and the transistor set flourished – especially among young people, who had their own channel. Thus developments in technology and changes in consumer demand, which had once pioneered the crystal set, ultimately produced the Walkman – headphones to headphones in three generations.

In dress, too, Britain was surprisingly successful in catching an international idiom, marketed with panache from Carnaby Street, just off Regent Street, which temporarily became the young fashion centre of the world. Informality was the keynote, with protean uses of denim and bold floral fabrics, for men and women. The long skirts of the post-war decade were not simply shortened; the mini-skirt of the late-1960s hitched the hemline to the mid-thigh, which in itself made this a style which young women could best carry off. The big names here, like Mary Quant and Biba, were new names, reaching out to a young clientele. The power of popular culture to override, or at least mask, long-standing social distinctions was shown in many ways, setting styles which marked off generations rather than classes. Even a privileged education offered little insulation; the public-school accent, once a reliable indicator of social class, went into irreversible decline among teenagers, for whom it became just one of many funny voices they could do. It was more than an old fogeys' joke that young men and women were indistinguishable in their long hair and jeans; young people of all backgrounds were indeed starting to look alike, and to feel at least a skin-deep affinity. Stumbling in the wake of such changes, the political parties began fumbling for the youth vote; there was little coherent opposition to the lowering of the voting age to eighteen in 1969.

## CONSENSUS POLITICS

The twelve-month premiership of Sir Alec Douglas-Home in 1963–4 was dominated by Harold Wilson. No previous leader of the Opposition, without the authority of being an ex-prime minister himself, had enjoyed such an ascendancy. Moreover, it was deserved since Home may have been a stopgap but he turned out to be no pushover; though Wilson naturally made great sport at the idea of a fourteenth earl seeking to run a great modern country. Home's riposte that, after all, his opponent could be called the fourteenth Mr Wilson, was nicely judged, but it could hardly remove the sting from a disadvantageous contrast in their backgrounds and experience. Home was unused to the House of Commons, where Wilson had perfected a punchy despatch-box style, partly by observing the methods of Macmillan. It was in these years that prime minister's questions, normally a couple of times a week, became elevated into a gladiatorial contest. Home came across as a decent and honourable Tory of the old school; it was Wilson, with his common touch, who captured the public ear.

Wilson, at forty-six, seemed young in an era that had become used to statesmen of pensionable age: Churchill, Adenauer, Eisenhower, de Gaulle, Macmillan. But youth was now on his side. The sort of under-graduate send-up of fuddy-duddy politicians that had long been the staple of the Cambridge Footlights created a sensation when it hit a late-night television audience in *That Was the Week That Was* in 1962–3 (a sign of the new freedom which the BBC claimed under its director-general Sir Hugh Greene). Macmillan and Home were satirized as figures from the past. By contrast, the vigorous image of the Kennedy presidency seemed attractive. In November 1963 Kennedy's assassination was widely mourned in Britain and – an even more sincere tribute – his political legacy was appropriated by Labour. Wilson, too, talked of getting the country moving again. His own pitch was to make a rhetorical link between science and socialism, projecting himself as the hero of meritocratic, technocratic middle managers whose energies would be released by a Labour Government in a purposive plan to regenerate Britain. This was a 'classless' appeal which put the Tories on the defensive in the class struggle, suggesting that it was their vested interest in maintaining ossified social distinctions, such as fourteenth earls, which was holding the country back.

If this sounded like Lloyd George reincarnated, it was hardly surprising in view of Wilson's roots in north-country Nonconformist radicalism; yet his political career since 1951 had been founded on his image as a Bevanite; his role as champion of the left and of the party conference had been reaffirmed as recently as 1960, when he had stood against Gaitskell for the leadership. In fact Wilson's priority all along had been party unity; he was no fundamentalist believer in nationalization or unilateralism; he was, like his colleague Crossman, really a Bevanite revisionist, working with the Labour left, but not of it. Here, too, Wilson aspired to be the Labour Macmillan, leading his party towards the middle ground under cover of traditional partisan slogans. Wilson set his agenda in a series of well-publicized speeches, hammering away at the need to create a new Britain, which would be able to afford higher social spending out of the increment of higher economic growth. This gave Labour a sharp image, though the content of the policies which would achieve this happy state was less distinctive.

The fact was that for at least a couple of years much of this agenda had been shared by the Conservatives, stirred from complacency about so-called affluence, and urgently moved to experiment. Heath, fresh from observing the new Europe, was given a wide brief in an expanded Board of Trade, where he pushed through his own pet scheme for freeing the economy from antiquated restrictions on competition. Resale price maintenance, a practice obliging shops to sell goods at standard prices set by the suppliers, was declared illegal – much to the fury of the small shopkeepers who were a vocal element in local Conservative associations. This was a brave move by Heath, which did him no harm once the dust had settled: it helped mark him out as an effective rival to the easygoing Maudling, should the Tories soon require a leader of Wilson's age and aptitude.

As Chancellor of the Exchequer since 1962, Reginald Maudling had been faced with the problem of reviving an economy in which unemployment averaged 2.6 per cent in 1963, the worst annual figure since the post-war welfare state had come into effect. The 'stop–go' cycle therefore entered its pre-election go phase, with a low bank-rate and a sufficient stimulus from consumer spending in the 1963 Budget to lift the growth rate from 4 per cent in 1963 to nearly 6 per cent in 1964 – though with the familiar mounting side-effects of overheating and a strain on the balance of payments. Maudling was determined to maintain his 'dash for growth', hoping that the balance of payments difficulties would be solved by an induced dynamism in exports, which were indeed rising. By 1964, however, with exports just over 10 per cent higher than in 1961, imports were nearly 20 per cent higher, sucked in by higher consumer spending.

It was politically impossible to do anything about this before a general election; and, since the opinion polls and the by-elections both indicated a big swing to Labour, Home decided to hold on until the last moment. His own inclination was to focus on the nuclear issue, where Wilson's record was suspect, rather than on economic management, where the Government was on the defensive. It had to maintain that the roaring pre-election boom could be translated into a permanently higher growth level of 4 per cent: a claim which pushed Labour into bidding even higher. Labour's insistent talk of 'thirteen wasted years' of Tory Government succeeded in catching a mood for change. Wilson's poll ratings remained way ahead of Home's; the fact that this was a matter of generalized image is shown by Wilson's lead not just on competence but on sincerity too. Yet Home's performance, in a modest register very much his own, should not be disparaged. After all, he inherited a demoralized party, facing the pit of electoral oblivion. To many people's surprise, the general election in October 1964 turned out to be a close-run thing.

Labour only just squeaked home, with 317 seats out of 630. With 44 per cent of the popular vote, it was less than 1 per cent ahead of the Conservatives. Nonetheless the shift since 1959 was appreciable, with the Conservatives dropping 6 per cent in their share of the vote and losing 60 seats. More than half of Labour's gains came from tightening its existing hold over traditional areas of support in London, Lancashire, Yorkshire and Scotland. But overall it did not win as much as the Conservatives lost, partly because the Liberal vote was underestimated; only nine Liberal MPs were returned, but the party's share of the poll was 11 per cent, the highest since 1929. These were mainly anti-Conservative votes, many attracted by Jo Grimond's strategy as Liberal leader in proclaiming the need for a realignment on the left. Plainly this was not achieved in any formal sense; but Liberal support indicated a reservoir of centre–left voters, distributed fairly evenly through all classes, which Labour might well pick up – a clear moral for Wilson in thinking ahead, as the close result made prudent, towards a further election at no distant interval.

Wilson's Government, with a majority in single figures, was unusually dominated by electoral considerations, a fact which played alike to the prime minister's skills and his inclination. He foresaw 1966 as the moment when he would form his 'real' cabinet, once his interim administration had improvised its way to a more convincing electoral victory, through adroit tactics and clever compromises, designed to keep everyone guessing. This end was duly achieved, but at the price of making the means into a way of life, from which it was subsequently difficult to escape. Wilson was the master but he accommodated his rivals for the leadership by making the stolid Callaghan Chancellor of the Exchequer and creating an entirely new economic ministry for the volatile Brown. Apart from the prime minister, only James Griffiths, Labour's elder statesman at the new Welsh Office, and Patrick Gordon Walker, the Foreign Secretary, had previously held cabinet posts.[1]

Wilson's political balancing act allowed him to reward his two closest allies from Bevanite days: Richard Crossman and Barbara Castle (the only woman in the cabinet). Each had to come to terms with a new role as minister, not least in relation to formidable civil servants. It took time for Dame Evelyn Sharp, confronted with the intellectual bully Crossman (self-described) as her minister at Housing and Local Government, to get him house-trained in the ways of Whitehall. The compensation was that this eye-opening process was recorded for posterity in his diaries, which later inspired the television series, *Yes, Minister*: the most successful seminars ever staged on the workings of the British constitution. Conversely, Castle got off on the right foot with the corpulent Sir Andrew Cohen in forming a high-profile partnership ('Elephant and Castle') bent on shaping the new Ministry of Overseas Development. The problem there was to reconcile Labour's

---

1. The supposed experience of Gordon Walker, a dowdy Gaitskellite, actually counted for little, since he had lost his seat at the general election – in a racialist campaign at Smethwick which made it a debt of honour to go through with his appointment – and he went on to lose the by-election which was engineered as an attempt to get him back into the Commons in February 1965. Michael Stewart, with equal lack of charisma, became the obvious man to take over the Foreign Office at short notice after this false start.

rhetoric about more aid to developing countries with the many competing claims on resources. In fact, Castle only lasted a year before being promoted, and the commitment to increase the level of overseas aid lasted hardly longer.

To the countries of the new Commonwealth, especially in black Africa, it made little difference that a Labour Government was now in office, as its handling of Rhodesia, the residual legacy of decolonization, was to show. Southern Rhodesia (or Rhodesia as it became after Northern Rhodesia achieved independence as Zambia) had enjoyed effective self-government, though without Dominion status, for forty years. By the 1960s, it was apparent that this gave Britain the worst of both worlds: a moral commitment to safeguard the rights of the black majority before granting independence, but no means of implementing this policy short of external coercion. It was obvious that the white supremacist government, under the wily and stubborn leadership of Ian Smith, was ready to make a unilateral declaration of independence (UDI). British policy, under Home as subsequently under Wilson, was to head this off if possible, or at any rate for as long as possible. In 1965 there was still bipartisan support for the British Government's statement of the five principles which were regarded as preconditions of independence – not an immediate move to majority rule, but guarantees that it would be expedited. The Smith regime, unmoved, declared UDI in November 1965.

At this stage Wilson's confidence was impressive, if misplaced. In domestic politics, it was the Rhodesian lobby in the Tory Party which continually threatened to make trouble, unreconciled to the liberal consensus between the two front benches. The Government, for its part, had ruled out the use of force, which was naturally urged by some African states. Instead it relied on economic sanctions, especially an oil embargo, enforced under UN auspices. This was just enough to keep the Commonwealth Prime Ministers in line at their meeting in January 1966, with Wilson optimistically foreseeing a Rhodesian capitulation 'in weeks rather than months'. Notoriously, this failed to happen. One reason was Britain's avoidance of conflict with South Africa, which was left free to siphon off supplies to Rhodesia. As the weeks lengthened to months, Commonwealth pressure mounted for Britain to harden its stance by accepting the principle of no independence before majority rule (NIBMAR). Wilson's compromise was to hold the threat of NIBMAR over Smith's head to induce him to negotiate a settlement, within the terms of the five principles, but not going so far, so fast. The two men met on HMS *Tiger*, off Gibraltar, for three days of talks in December 1966. Wilson thought that he had gained Smith's agreement to a sophisticated package of constitutional reforms; but Smith simply played for time by going home to consult his cabinet, which rejected the plan.

The *Tiger* terms would have been difficult to sell to Labour back-benchers and Commonwealth leaders alike, with their moral and emotional commitment to NIBMAR. The case for them depended on a rational calculation that this was the best settlement available. Since it was not available anyway, Wilson was relieved of the political odium but at the price of continued impotence. Worse, the failure of oil sanctions, vaguely blamed on the French at the time, ought not to have been such a puzzle since the Government was made aware of the swap agreements between the big oil companies which, in effect, allowed them to main-tain supplies to Rhodesia. In any case, short of confrontation with South Africa, which rightly saw Rhodesia as the front-line rampart of white supremacy, economic sanctions could not exert sufficient press-ure to achieve a settlement on the basis of NIBMAR, which was now official policy. There was thus an element of charade in Wilson's fur-ther assignment off Gibraltar in October 1968. This time it was HMS *Fearless*; otherwise things were much the same – much the same old terms, much the same old weather, much the same old Smith, much the same old excuses. All that Wilson finally achieved was to show that further negotiation was fruitless and thus to hold together a world-weary political consensus about Rhodesia. As a potential electoral issue, it was a problem averted.

The central issue for the Wilson Government, from its first day, was the economic crisis. The balance of payments turned out to be in even worse shape than Labour's partisan gibes at the hustings had sug-gested: a deficit of nearly £400 million on current account in 1964, the worst figure since the Second World War. In fact the deficit amounted to 1.3 per cent of GDP, compared with a deficit of 2.3 per cent which the Conservatives had inherited in 1951 (and a deficit of 4.4 per cent in 1989). It was nonetheless a real crisis, which the new Government, determined to pin the blame on their predecessors, initially made worse by including capital movements too, with the result that talk of a deficit of £800 millions spread further alarm in the markets. The two classic means of correcting such a deficit were deflation and devaluation.

Deflation worked by cutting back economic growth, which duly cut back exports; but Labour had denounced this option as 'stop–go'. Devaluation was a clear economic alternative, since signs that the pound was overvalued, not only against the US dollar (at $2.80) but even more strikingly against the German mark (still at a parity over 11 DM), were mounting with every sterling crisis. This option, however, was immediately ruled out by Wilson, in consultation with Brown and Callaghan.

The reason was partly economic – Wilson had an essentially micro-economic approach which predisposed him towards directly inter-ventionist measures – but it was mainly political. Wilson's view, which none of his colleagues challenged, was that Labour, the party of devalu-ation in 1949, simply could not afford to be cast in this role again: the more so since its parliamentary position was so precarious. So the Government was reluctant to wield either of the economic weapons in its hands. This left it at the mercy of events – and of the USA. For the critical importance of dollar support for sterling, with its overstretched role as a reserve currency, could be in no doubt; it was when US support was withdrawn that Suez had ended in tears. Macmillan had drawn the lesson that in future the UK should tag along with the USA, as a junior partner; this was the basis of his nuclear defence policy, maintaining Britain's great power pretensions with a show of 'independence' which Wilson had derided. The irony was that Wilson pursued an economic strategy which was, in reality, similarly dependent on US support, and subject, therefore, to conditions determined by the Americans.

In November 1964 sterling was saved by concerted action on the part of a number of central banks, including the Bank of England, which raised its rate to 7 per cent, by now the conventional crisis level. A temporary surcharge on imports was imposed, despite being against GATT rules; and income tax went up to 8s 3d (41.25 per cent). The Treasury relied on this package doing the trick, by squeezing the econ-omy back into balance. Meanwhile the new Department of Economic Affairs continued as though nothing had happened to disturb its plans for economic expansion. It was, like Lloyd George's Ministry of Muni-tions before it, basically a vehicle for the unruly talents of one idio-syncratic individual. The way that Brown drove the vehicle, however, made for an unsteady if exciting ride. Brown's instability – drink was one obvious problem – made him a mercurial colleague, prone to tender his resignation when he felt thwarted, but capable at his best of striking intuitively to the heart of a problem and of coaxing agreement against all odds.

The National Plan, to which Brown devoted long months of effort, was fashioned in this way. Published in September 1965, after elaborate consultations with both sides of industry and the NEDC apparatus, it set the goal of sustained growth at 4 per cent per annum – levels which were not wholly unrealistic, since they had been exceeded in 1963 and 1964, but which, even as the Plan was sent to the printers, were being rendered unattainable by Government decisions. There had been talk of 'creative tension' in the making of economic policy between the DEA, representing the real economy, and the Treasury, representing finance. The grip of the Treasury, with its massive expertise and its hold over the entire Whitehall machine, was never really loosened. Given the chronic weakness of sterling, Treasury policy was bound to prevail. Moreover, it is now known that in the summer of 1965, in order to secure US support of sterling, Callaghan gave assurances that the Government would maintain a tight policy. How deeply this compromised the National Plan was not immediately clear.

In all of this, Wilson's position was crucial: not just in arbitrating between Callaghan and Brown, nor in insisting that nothing be done to spoil the Government's election chances, but in reaching a package deal with the Johnson administration in Washington. What Johnson, with the escalation of the Vietnam war dominating his presidency, really wanted was British support in south-east Asia. He was forced to accept that he would not get British troops in Vietnam, only general expressions of sympathy for US aims from Wilson and Stewart (punctuated by specific dissociation from some later US military measures). There was, however, an indisputable linkage between sterling and Vietnam, often as this was officially denied at the time. The terms of the deal which Wilson was able to strike, therefore, were governed not only by how much the Americans wanted his help, but by how much he would pay for theirs in avoiding devaluation. If they perceived that he might easily devalue sterling – a step which they wished to avoid because it would in turn make the dollar vulnerable – they could not exact as high a price as they could if Wilson himself seemed prepared to do anything to avoid devaluation. Since the latter was in fact Wilson's position, as the Americans correctly gathered, he had almost as few cards in his hand as Macmillan had had at Nassau. None of this was glorious; but at least Wilson avoided miring British troops in the swamps of Vietnam.

Wilson's ascendancy was little impaired, either in his own Government or in the eyes of the public. Whatever economic difficulties the Government faced, they could for the time being be blamed upon the Conservatives, who remained in no shape to make an electoral comeback. Home, poor chap, would have to go, that was widely accepted. But Wilson used rumours of an imminent election to stall moves to select a more formidable Conservative leader; only in July 1965 did Home bow out, leaving the party to implement its new electoral procedure for the first time. Macleod was back in the shadow cabinet but was now suspect in the party: Powell even more so, as his action in standing for the leadership and his showing as a poor third in the ballot of Conservative MPs both served to confirm. The outcome was that Heath narrowly but decisively defeated Maudling. But the honeymoon effect on the Conservatives' popularity was short-lived; despite the Government's deflationary package in the summer of 1965, it was ahead again in the opinion polls by September.

In terms of presentation, the Wilson Government was doing magnificently. The National Plan went down well. Bank-rate had been eased; the economy was still growing, albeit not so fast; despite some fears about job losses, unemployment averaged only 1.5 per cent throughout 1965–6; in 1966 prices may have been 9 per cent higher than two years previously – but earnings were 11 per cent higher. As the more perceptive members of the cabinet recognized, Labour needed to capitalize on its popularity while its luck lasted and while its opponents were still in disarray. This was where Wilson's leadership was seen at its most effective, in passing off a makeshift holding operation as the prelude to a period of constructive government. He was taken at his word in the country, meaning that the Labour campaign could, to an unusual extent, be built around him, since he was running ahead of his party.

The signal came with the Hull by-election in January 1966. The Government opportunely intervened by announcing that a suspension bridge over the River Humber would be built; at the time the intervention was hardly more necessary than the bridge itself, but Labour's opinion-poll lead was comfortingly buttressed by a strong pro-Government swing. The general election followed and duly produced a Labour majority of 100 – a mirror-image of what the Conservatives had achieved in 1959. Like Gaitskell before him, Heath found himself politely ignored in his sober warnings about an economic fool's paradise. The Conservative vote held up fairly well, only 1.5 per cent lower than in 1966; this compared with a drop of 2.7 per cent in the Liberal vote (which was, however, consolidated where the party needed it most, with the result that the number of Liberal MPs increased from 9 to 12). So Labour won two votes from the Liberals for every one from the Conservatives in increasing its share of the poll to 48 per cent, a level virtually identical with that of 1945. The Labour gains were much more evenly spread across the country than in 1964, with modest further increments from its old urban and industrial bastions, but now augmented with a broadcast scattering of support in mixed suburban constituencies, new towns, university cities and cathedral cities. Bristol North-West and Croydon South, Harrow East and Portsmouth West, Bebington and Billericay, High Peak and Chislehurst, Bedford and Exeter, Lancaster and York, Oxford and Cambridge – all went Labour for the first time since the constituencies were redrawn in 1949. Wilson's dream of making Labour into 'the natural party of government' seemed to be well on the way to fulfilment.

## SOCIAL POLICY

When the welfare state was created in Britain after the Second World War, it was often said to be the envy of the world. The Labour Party certainly took pride in having implemented it; and the Conservatives forswore any notion of dismantling it. Based on the Beveridge Plan, which in turn looked back to the poverty-line concept established by Rowntree at the beginning of the century, it aimed to slay the giant of Want, if not with a single blow then in a concerted and lethal attack. Full employment was itself the best means of tackling the sort of poverty that had been widespread throughout the old industrial areas between the wars. Concomitantly, the National Health Service alleviated the economic burden of family sickness, while child allowances channelled direct support to larger families. These measures cleared the ground for social insurance to require and assist everyone to cover themselves against the normal contingencies of life: the residual incidence of frictional unemployment, essentially while people were between jobs; sickness of a breadwinner; injury at work; old age. And just in case anyone still could not negotiate the tightrope of economic viability, there was the safety net of National Assistance, granted to individuals (like poor relief before it) once their genuine destitution had been established.

'Poverty has been abolished,' proclaimed the Durham miners' leader, Sam Watson, to the Labour Party conference in 1950. This was no mere partisan claim. When Rowntree returned to his native York, half a century after his pioneer study, to direct a final social survey, published as *Poverty and the Welfare State* (1951), he revealed a less sombre, more gratifying picture than ever before. The headline story here pointed to a fall in the proportion of the working class living in poverty from over 30 per cent in the 1930s to under 3 per cent. *The Times* called it 'the virtual elimination of the sheerest want'. Yet a decade later such judgements looked like period-piece complacency, and the talk now was of the 'rediscovery of poverty'. Partly this was a matter of more sophisticated analysis of the empirical data, as Rowntree's methods came to look crude beside the expertise developed in new university departments of sociology and social administration. But the achievement of Professor Peter Townsend, in particular, was to move the goalposts.

The concept of a poverty line had been radical in its day. By establishing a scientifically valid subsistence level, with a price-tag attached, it challenged those who were sceptical about poverty to explain how the poor could possibly get by on an income less than this. But its objectivity was spurious in that it reflected a middle-class expert assessment of what the poor needed, not an actual pattern of working-class expenditure. The poor were often to be criticized for 'wasting' their money on 'non-essential' items which nonetheless seemed important to them. The truth here was that necessities were, to a large extent, socially conditioned; they were what real people felt they needed to participate fully in the life of their own community. By the 1960s, this did not mean clogs and shawls, if it ever had. It could now be argued that if people could not afford access to television – at a time when television had become a conventional social bond – they were marginalized through their poverty. Introducing such subjective elements into the definition of poverty inevitably turned it into a relative concept, with implications for the political economy of welfare that were to be far-reaching.

It should not be supposed that the Conservatives had cut back on welfare expenditure. They may have harboured ideas of making savings on the NHS through eliminating waste; but the Guillebaud Report in

1956, largely guided by two specialists, Richard Titmuss and Brian Abel-Smith (both policy advisers to the Labour Party), suggested that the NHS was efficiently run. Spending on it rose, first under Macleod, and later (more surprisingly) under Powell, whose period as Minister of Health in the early 1960s saw a notable expansion of the hospital-building programme. Social expenditure in fact broadly maintained its share of the national income during the 1950s. Then came a sharp and sustained acceleration.

An upward momentum here, putting increasing strain upon the Budget, was already apparent before the Wilson Government came to office. Its policies made things worse – or better, according to which way one looked at it. Labour was committed on principle to higher public expenditure, on the grounds that this had a bias towards disadvantaged social groups. Hence Crosland, the theorist of this strategy, could express satisfaction that during Labour's period of office, 1964–70, public expenditure rose.[1] Moreover what drove this process was the rise in social expenditure. Public spending on education, health, pensions and unemployment grew by 5 per cent a year in real terms in the period 1960–75. In fifteen years these programmes increased their share of GDP from just over 11 per cent to nearly 19 per cent – a major shift of resources, probably double what was achieved under the Attlee Government. Yet it did not produce the same sense of satisfaction, either among its supposed beneficiaries or among the electorate.

The reasons for the increase in social spending, which was common to other OECD countries, are complex. A relatively small part can be atttributed simply to demography, especially more old people and dependent children in the population. Most was due to real benefit increases, though here demography exerted a secondary influence since an ageing population brought not only an inexorably higher pension bill to be met by the state, but also a growing constituency for whom higher state pensions were a priority. Whereas in 1951 14 per cent of the population were eligible for state pensions, over the next thirty years the proportion increased to 18 per cent (and rising). The assumption that the problem of poverty in old age could be met through a universal

1. Such statistics need particularly careful interpretation. Crosland cited a growth of public expenditure from 41 per cent to 48 per cent of GNP, which was in line with current Treasury definitions. In 1977, however, the basis on which the British figures were calculated was brought into line with international conventions, producing an apparent fall in public expenditure by about 7 per cent of GDP.

state pension had been unrealistic from the outset in 1948, since this was set at a level too low to be adequate in itself and was too seldom supplemented by cover from private sources. So many pensioners applied for National Assistance, and old people constituted one of the largest pockets of poverty for persistent rediscovery. In opposition, the Labour Party had worked out a new approach under Crossman, with a plan for a fully funded national superannuation scheme. This was one of Labour's most prominent proposals in the 1959 and 1964 general elections. The aim was to give everyone the prospect of a secure and adequate pension, related to previous income.

The response of the Conservatives, who favoured private provision, was to give palliative increases to existing state pensioners. This succeeded in buying time for the expansion of occupational pension schemes, which came to act as a vested interest against radical change. Once Labour was in office, instead of going ahead with its big plan, it resorted to similar hand-to-mouth measures. One intractable problem, as in introducing any scheme which relied on long years of contributions to build up a self-financing fund, was how to deal with the generation who were too old to have contributed. Instead of the plan that had been prudently worked out in opposition, a pay-as-you-go scheme, financed from current contributions, was introduced in 1970, too late in the parliament to have any chance of passing. This meant that those soon approaching retirement would see an immediate benefit; it also meant that taxpayers were faced with a virtually open-ended commitment. The State Earnings-Related Pension Scheme (Serps) finally came into operation in 1978, much amended over the years, but retaining one feature that went back to the wholly different plan of twenty years previously: pensions that were linked to earnings.

Earnings-related supplements had been introduced for sickness and unemployment benefits in 1966; and the right to redundancy payments, established in 1965, was likewise geared to the lost earning-capacity of different individuals. The introduction of these indexed benefits signalled a consistent move away from the flat-rate principle, dependent as it was on a concept of subsistence which was now discredited. Instead, the poverty line was increasingly redefined as the level of National Assistance payments (renamed 'supplementary benefits' in 1966). In effect the poverty line itself had become index-linked – to average living standards – pushing up expectations to levels which were simultaneously difficult to satisfy and difficult to afford.

Measured by these relative standards, plentiful and well-publicized evidence emerged about the number of households with incomes below the (constantly rising) threshold. *The Poor and the Poorest* (1965) by Abel-Smith and Townsend became a peculiar kind of Christmas best-seller, tapping the seasonal market in compassion to raise popular consciousness of the problem. Nobody now dared say that poverty had been eliminated. Indeed, how could it be, failing the elimination of all relative disadvantage? Thus issues of income distribution became more closely intermeshed with those of poverty as such, once the new methodology framed the agenda in this way.

One immediate political implication was that a Government which sought to reduce the number of people living in poverty by simply raising the level of welfare benefits would be making a rod for its own back – by thus raising also the level of income on which the number living in poverty was calculated. The Wilson Government certainly encountered vocal criticism of this kind. Some statistics, which purported to demonstrate that it left more people living in poverty than ever before, in fact demonstrated that it had increased benefit levels in real terms, or else pointed to a much more deep-seated problem of relative inequality in wealth and incomes.

The 'poverty lobby' was now an active force, keeping up a barrage of well-informed propaganda on behalf of disadvantaged groups whose case had previously gone by default. A wholesome development in itself, this correspondingly created interest groups with their own axes to grind. The bureaucratization of a burgeoning social-administration community, whether employed by the state, local government, universities or voluntary organizations, meant that a growing number of experts had a professional interest in increasing the welfare budget. There is no need to demonize the welfare bureaucracy to acknowledge that in the process its own status and rewards were sometimes enhanced more tangibly than the living standards of its clients. Simply spending more public money was coming to be queried as a simplistic approach to complex issues of social justice.

An increased role for voluntary agencies – towards which the Labour Party had often been hostile – can be seen as one symptom of a growing reaction against statism. To be sure, mutual-aid associations, like those which ran playgroups and similar schemes for young children, look like an example of self-help; but often they sought and gained support from public funds, notably local authorities. Help the Aged

(1961) was an example of a philanthropic care-giving organization which also raised popular consciousness about the inadequacies of public provision for old people. The best-known voluntary organizations in fact acted so as to prompt rather than obviate state action. Shelter (1966) took up the cause of the homeless, not by providing homes itself but by campaigning on the issue, with a panache that produced favourable publicity. As its director, Des Wilson, put it: 'It was for the government to come up with the solutions.' Likewise, the Child Poverty Action Group (1965) was effective in keeping the case for child allowances in the public eye, notably by seizing on survey evidence to show that large families remained a major cause of poverty.

These lobbyists were a radical influence, stirring the Wilson Government to action and chastising it when it fell short, especially the latter. The Government's record in welfare policy was perceived as a disappointment not only because of its inability to find the necessary economic resources but also because of its inability to meet expectations which it had helped arouse in the first place. In housing, there was a cutback after the devaluation crisis, and the Government's target of 500,000 new houses a year was abandoned; yet in 1967 and 1968 over 400,000 houses were built, a new record, well ahead of what Macmillan had achieved in the era before Shelter raised the stakes. Likewise the Government got little credit for its ingenious scheme to help poorer families, which was finally pushed through the cabinet against Treasury opposition in 1967. A substantial increase in the child allowance, paid to all, was matched by a fiscal 'clawback' which would only affect better-off families paying income tax, thus targeting help to the poor without requiring either an initiative on their part or a means test. If Labour expected any political reward from such measures, it was to be disillusioned by the reproaches of the Child Poverty Action Group during the 1970 election campaign.

Better received, less costly to implement, and more durable in its social impact was the legislation sponsored by the Home Office, notably during the two years after Roy Jenkins became Home Secretary in December 1965. As a backbencher Jenkins had been instrumental in introducing the Obscene Publications Act (1959), which introduced literary merit as a possible defence, and thus paved the way for Penguin Books' successful legal battle over the publication of *Lady Chatterley's Lover* in 1960. This measure signalled Jenkins's concern about censorship, which he was to follow up as Home Secretary by insisting, against pressure from Buckingham Palace, that the Lord Chamberlain's historic role in licensing stage productions should be ended. The form taken by the obscene-publications legislation, moreover, provided a model for subsequent measures in sensitive areas which were controversial but non-partisan, through private members' bills which would subsequently be given the cover of Home Office support.

The death penalty had been abolished in this way in 1965. In 1966 Jenkins tried to persuade the rising Liberal MP David Steel, who had won a high place in the ballot on private members' bills, to introduce a measure on homosexual-law reform; since Steel thought this too outré for his Scottish Border constituents, he opted for abortion reform instead. This proposal, for the first time permitting legal abortions, proved surprisingly popular, with opinion polls giving it over 70 per cent support, probably because both the prevalence and the dangers of illegal or 'backstreet' abortions were common knowledge. Homosexual-law reform soon followed, since in October 1966 Jenkins induced the cabinet to provide government time in the Commons for a private member's bill, already introduced. The proposal to legalize homosexual acts between adults in private, which had been stalled since the Wolfenden Report had recommended it ten years previously, became law in 1967.

Similar libertarian moves were common in other western countries in this era; so was the backlash of self-proclaimed 'moral majorities' later. It was a sign of a new determination to assert personal and civil rights, of which 'women's liberation' and 'gay liberation' were conspicuous examples; conversely it was a sign of the erosion of traditional norms of social behaviour and deference, which was making Britain a less easy nation to govern. The measures on hanging, censorship, abortion and homosexuality were not Labour manifesto pledges; in the Commons they attracted the cross-bench support of liberally minded MPs while encountering resistance from traditionalist (often Catholic) Labour members. Nonetheless they would not have been passed but for the existence of a Labour majority, aided during the years 1965–7 by a Labour Home Secretary prepared to mobilize it. It was understandable, therefore, that Labour should have been associated with the 'permissive society' – an association which Callaghan later tried to repudiate after he had succeeded Jenkins as Home Secretary.

Jenkins himself preferred the term 'civilized society' and was happy to nail his colours to this mast. The son of a Welsh Labour MP, with grammar school leading on to Oxford, he lived up to the Balliol myth of effortless superiority, with an enviable reputation (duly provoking envy among less talented colleagues) as an accomplished biographer. He was undeniably able to reach out to liberal public opinion more effectively than he projected himself in the class-bound confines of the Labour Movement. Along with his contemporaries, Tony Crosland and Denis Healey, he had been a committed Gaitskellite (at least until the Common Market issue erupted at the end of Gaitskell's life). Healey at the Ministry of Defence and Crosland at the Department of Education had both entered the cabinet ahead of Jenkins, who initially made his mark in Whitehall as a tough-minded Minister of Aviation, unafraid to cancel expensive projects like the TSR-2 strike aircraft (though the Anglo-French Concorde supersonic airliner survived). His promotion to the cabinet had been an expected step upwards; but the Home Office was notoriously the graveyard of political reputations. Jenkins's achievement was to make himself the agent of policies which pleased most Labour supporters, at a time when they were getting tired of apologizing for their Government. By the end of 1967, Jenkins's growing ministerial stature gave him a position which came to rival that of a now fading Wilson: a point not lost upon either of them.

## RECOVERY

Wilson was famous for his adroit tactics; it was the strategy that was less apparent. The hopes which he had inspired, of using the big majority gained in March 1966 to carve out a coherent long-term policy, were soon jolted. The initial problem, or at least excuse, was a strike by the National Union of Seamen, which not only threatened the norms for wage settlements under the prices and incomes policy but also temporarily distorted the flow of imports and exports during the summer of 1966. Wilson chose to regard this as an overt challenge to his authority, making MPs' flesh creep with allusions to a 'tightly-knit group of politically motivated men' (in the union, not the Government). This may have helped achieve a speedy settlement, though it also talked up the crisis, which was bound to be bad for sterling. Callaghan had tried to avoid overt deflation in his post-election budget by introducing the selective employment tax (SET), a bright idea of his adviser Nicholas Kaldor, as a means of giving incentives to the whole of the manufacturing sector by penalizing employment in the whole of the service sector of the economy. Whatever the long-term structural merits of such a plan might have been, the fact that any fiscal restraint from SET would not be felt for six months left the economy vulnerable in the short term (and in the long term SET was not to survive anyway).

It was the short term which mattered in the sterling crisis of July 1966. Wilson said the seamen's strike had blown the Government off course. What the crisis revealed was that it had never been on a course likely to reconcile the existing exchange rate with economic growth. The case for devaluation had hitherto been plausibly resisted for political reasons; but the General Election removed and reversed this argument – there could be no better time to push it through than at the beginning of a parliament, with an impregnable majority at the Government's back. Callaghan, a political animal to his fingertips, decided in mid-July that devaluation was now the only option. This left Wilson vulnerably isolated. Virtually all the big guns in his cabinet were now pointing the other way. His most important allies on the left, Crossman and Castle, were now ready to support devaluation, which was already advocated by right-wingers in the cabinet, with Brown to the fore, and they were now much reinforced by the arrival of Crosland and Jenkins. This was a powerful combination. Yet not only was Wilson unpersuaded: he made the grounds of his own scepticism into the means of rallying the cabinet once more behind the existing parity of sterling.

First Wilson squared Callaghan, face to face, to re-establish their axis before meeting the full cabinet. Here, what made all the difference was Europe. It was generally accepted – certainly the French Government was ready to say this – that the British economy could not be integrated with that of the EEC while sterling remained overvalued at $2.80. There were thus grounds for suspecting – and suspicion was deeply ingrained in Wilson's temperament – that those who advocated devaluation had Europe in mind. Now support for British membership of the Common Market was not only growing: it was growing in a pattern which was to have far-reaching effects on the unity and effectiveness of the Labour Party for the next twenty years. By and large, the pro-Europeans were on the right of the party, especially the revisionists or social democrats who had once identified with Gaitskell (except on this issue). And by and large, the opposition came from the left, many of them with old Bevanite loyalties. It was on these factional allegiances that Wilson now played. Seeing – or at any rate depicting –

devaluation as a plot by the pro-Europeans in the cabinet, he called in his political debts. When Brown personalized the issue as one of leadership, Wilson knew that he was safe. Moreover, he adroitly seized on the point that some deflationary measures would be needed to make devaluation work. If this were so, he suavely argued, agreement on a deflationary package should surely precede a decision on the exchange rate. Having secured this agreement, Wilson progressively pushed devaluation into a hypothetical future, in a masterly display of prime ministerial power.

The July package amounted to a major squeeze: bank-rate at 7 per cent, cuts in Government spending (both at home and overseas), hire-purchase restrictions, and a complete freeze on wage and price increases. The immediate casualties were Brown and his National Plan. Brown's credibility was critically sapped. His resignation from the cabinet – not his first, not his last, but one of the few actually in writing – though subsequently withdrawn, became public knowledge; he was pensioned off as Foreign Secretary, a much diminished figure. The National Plan was now dead. Michael Stewart, displaced from the Foreign Office, went to the DEA to pick up the pieces, especially over prices and incomes policy. A voluntary incomes policy had been sold to the unions in exchange for economic expansion; now they bristled at the threat of statutory restraint in an era when expansion had been sacrificed to the maintenance of the exchange rate.

Incomes policy set a conundrum during the Wilson Government similar to that set by conscription during the Asquith Coalition: how to appease the tender consciences of its backbench supporters by giving an ostensibly voluntary policy the force of law. In a replay of the Derby Scheme of 1915, the 1966 wage freeze was initially voluntary, but backed by a statutory requirement to notify proposed increases to the Prices and Incomes Board. Once this pantomime had duly proved ineffective, the freeze itself was finally given legislative backing for twelve months, creating the further problem of what to do when the twelve months were up. The short-term impact of these measures was impressive. The rise in industrial earnings was halved. Brute economic forces, of course, reinforced the policy, since the economy grew by little more than 2 per cent in either 1966 or 1967 (half the rate envisaged in the National Plan).

Such policies could be justified if the unpalatable medicine proved efficacious. A wage freeze, in particular, was a once-for-all emergency measure, staking all the Government's remaining goodwill with its supporters in the trade unions upon one great gamble against the currency markets. Wilson was well aware that his decisive intervention needed vindication from results, especially on exports, by allowing a healthy pattern of growth to be resumed. True, the balance of payments for 1966 finished in the black, for the first time in three years, but it then plunged back into heavy deficit. The reason was a jump in imports at a time when exports were stagnant. The visible trade gap in 1967 touched £600 million, even wider than in 1964. Within a year of the July package it was obvious that more needed to be done.

Signs of a reorientation in Government policy began to emerge during the winter of 1966–7. First there was a defence review. Denis Healey was an intellectually masterful Minister of Defence throughout the Government's period of office. In 1964 he had gone along with Wilson in presenting the continuation of the Polaris submarine-building programme as a fait accompli to a surprisingly complaisant cabinet. While maintaining Britain's pretensions as a world power, Healey was tough-minded in seeking to achieve such ends only if the appropriate means were available, which they were not, as the July 1966 crisis demonstrated. Serious defence cuts, especially overseas, were now needed, and the obvious target was Britain's presence east of Suez. Yet this was exactly what Wilson had promised the USA to maintain in exchange for support for sterling, which was more necessary than ever. So the Government's difficulties went full circle.

Vietnam may have been President Johnson's problem, but whenever he sneezed, Wilson caught a cold. His own domestic standing, especially with his old constituency on the left, was increasingly prejudiced by his complicity in this increasingly messy and unpopular war. Wilson had more than one reason, therefore, to wish it could be brought to a dignified conclusion – or any other kind. When the Soviet leader Kosygin visited Britain in February 1967, Wilson went into action as a mediator, using all his arts in negotiation to wring grudging concessions from Washington so as to enlist Kosygin's good offices in dangling them before the Communist regime in Hanoi. Wilson was carried away by the drama of this personal summitry, relishing his hotline access to the Johnson administration. He imagined that he teetered on the edge of peace, while he anxiously waited for his calls to be returned, only to find that the line had gone dead, since Johnson was in no mood to settle, least of all in this manner. A comment recorded in a White

House transcript – 'we don't give a goddamn about Wilson' – captures the reality of the special relationship, which thereafter resumed its steady decline.

In the early months of 1967 Wilson seems to have had a change of heart, not only about Britain's essentially ex-imperial role in the world but also, by implication, about its relations with Europe and the USA. He now rejected a further deal offered by the USA, explicitly linking support for sterling with a continued British presence in the Far East. Instead plans were made for a phased withdrawal east of Suez. Meanwhile the Government sought to seize the political initiative by launching a bid to enter the EEC. Brown's move to the Foreign Office had pushed the matter up the agenda; by November 1966 the Government announced its intention to apply, which provoked relatively little dissension in the Labour Party; and from January to March 1967 Brown and Wilson made a series of exploratory visits to European capitals. They discovered only what they could have expected to discover: that five member states were well disposed but that de Gaulle was still adamant. Nonetheless, at the beginning of May the cabinet decided to make a formal application, without this entailing the resignation of the handful of sceptics, like Castle. Since entry was strongly favoured by the Conservative Party under Heath, not to mention the Liberals, the Government won overwhelming backing in the Commons, though with 36 Labour MPs voting against. All of this may have been symbolically important; but it cut no ice with de Gaulle, who immediately declared his continued opposition; and, despite cheerful noises from Brown, it was only a matter of time before the formal rejection of the British application came through in November.

By then there was a new situation, or rather an old situation (a sterling crisis) with a new outcome (devaluation). This was not a policy decision so much as a capitulation to events. Callaghan's persistent reading of devaluation as a political catastrophe became self-confirming; a shaken man, he left the Treasury in the aftermath. By the end there was little dissension since there was little alternative, barring an International Monetary Fund (IMF) rescue under onerous conditions. The pound was devalued by 15 per cent against the dollar, to a new rate of $2.40 (and 9.5 DM). Wilson, as usual, had an excuse; this time it was the Six-Day War in the Middle East, and the consequent closure of the Suez Canal, that was to blame. Indeed, unlike Callaghan, Wilson bounced back with a resilience bordering on effrontery, appearing on television to tell the British people that this gave them the chance to make a new start, and adding a folksy reassurance that 'the pound here in Britain – in your pocket or purse or bank' had not been devalued (presumably in case anyone thought they would only receive change from seventeen shillings the next morning).

For Wilson, it may have been a new start; it certainly meant starting all over again, with little to show for fifteen months of fruitless economic sacrifice. The next exercise in deflation would therefore be heavier to bear – economically, psychologically, politically. Bank-rate now stood at 8 per cent. The Government was already in serious difficulties, losing by-elections on swings of up to 18 per cent in the biggest turnover of votes between Labour and Conservatives since the war; and the Lanarkshire seat of Hamilton was lost to the Scottish Nationalists. The opinion polls told the same story; despite the lacklustre leadership of Heath, the Conservatives were way ahead.

Wilson needed a new Chancellor of the Exchequer. The two obvious candidates were Crosland and Jenkins, economically literate ministers who had long urged devaluation. Wilson chose Jenkins, feeling that he had the better political grasp, while Crosland remained at the Board of Trade. Balancing the advance of the Labour right, Wilson made sure his cabinet was buttressed with the support of old friends on the left. Crossman became Lord President of the Council and Leader of the House of Commons, responsible for the handling (and sometimes mishandling) of the Government's legislative programme. Castle, following a forceful stint at the Ministry of Transport, where she stepped up the campaign against drink-driving, was again promoted in April 1968, acquiring the resplendent title of First Secretary of State at the Department of Employment and Productivity. This gave her a wide-ranging brief in shaping industrial policy, on lines which had fateful consequences for the Government.

If these were all ministers on the way up, Brown was on the way out. At the beginning of 1968 he resigned once too often; it was another late-night, highly public row, another next-morning repentance. This time Wilson could afford to let him go; Stewart, who had obligingly made room for Brown at the Foreign Office, now obligingly went back. The incident came opportunely in the wake of a cabinet crisis (plot, said Wilson) largely engineered by Brown and Callaghan, over whether to resume arms sales to South Africa – an episode which allowed the prime minister to show himself still master in his own cabinet and thus cleared the air. Apart from the rumbling threats of the eclipsed Callaghan, now in exile at the Home Office, this became a more united and more collegial Government, with more input from other strong ministers, and relatively less from Wilson's intensely personal 'kitchen cabinet', in which his personal secretary Marcia Williams remained a controversial figure. The cabinet was held together by common adversity, which notably cemented an effective working relationship between Numbers 10 and 11 Downing Street. Both Wilson and Jenkins had the strongest interest in making devaluation work.

To do so, more cuts were necessary, in order to release resources for exports and stop the immediate drain through overseas spending. In a series of meetings in January 1968, the cabinet eventually accepted Jenkins's demand that withdrawal from military commitments east of Suez be accelerated. A deadline of late 1971 was agreed. Other cuts included cancellation of US fighter aircraft, emphasizing the symbolic importance of a reordering of priorities which the US Secretary of State feelingly called the 'end of an era'. Defence spending, which had been stuck at about 6 per cent of GNP, was to fall to 4 per cent within seven years. The other cuts in government spending, though less contentious in cabinet, fell on commitments nearer to the hearts of Labour supporters, notably the postponement in raising the school-leaving age to sixteen and the abandonment of the target of 500,000 new houses. In his first Budget in March 1968 Jenkins piled on tax increases all round, not only duties on petrol, drink and tobacco, but also a once-for-all levy on high incomes, to the tune of £900 million. This drastic budget was well received on the Labour benches in the Commons, but in the country the Government's deep unpopularity was testified by record swings against it in a string of by-elections.

Jenkins had promised 'two years' hard slog' but he did not foresee the unremitting difficulty of the struggle to turn the balance of payments around. The deficit in 1968 was practically as bad as in 1967. The Basle agreement was negotiated in July 1968, providing for the run-down of sterling as a reserve currency; but in the meantime there was inadequate support should the pound face a renewed onslaught. Desperate plans were secretly prepared – first 'Brutus', then 'Hecuba' – for a further devaluation. In November 1968 the trade figures still seemed so unresponsive that an emergency scheme for import deposits was pushed through. Moreover, the Government's prices and incomes policy was now disintegrating, with increasing anomalies in framing it, increasing difficulty in enforcing it, and increasing reluctance by Labour MPs to vote for its renewal.

It was in this context that Barbara Castle's proposals for trade-union reform became so highly charged. She called her White Paper 'In Place of Strife' in homage to her hero Bevan's political testament *In Place of Fear* (1952); but critics had a point when they said it was really In Place of Incomes Policy. A Royal Commission on the trade unions had recently endorsed the traditional British view that the law was best kept out of industrial relations; but the Conservatives had undoubtedly struck a popular chord in saying that a legal framework was now necessary. Trade unions could no longer count on a benign image, dating from the Bevin era; though 70 per cent of the public claimed to think them generally a good thing in 1964, and only 12 per cent bad – proportions similar to ten years previously – by 1969 only 57 per cent said good, and 26 per cent now said bad. Membership, at around 10 million, was virtually unchanged in a decade; but the days lost in industrial disputes, after five years of quiescence, were steadily rising. Moreover it was the ill-disciplined nature of spontaneous walkouts, led by shop stewards rather than sanctioned by the official union structure, which was highlighted as a problem. Castle's aim was to create order out of chaos, on good socialist principles, by balancing new rights for trade unions against a new legal obligation to observe proper procedures.

The grand strategy of 'In Place of Strife' was overtaken by more pressing political priorities. Wilson was attracted by the idea of outflanking the Tories, as so often before; and trade-union reform made an appeal to ministers worried about the economy, both in itself as a means of promoting efficiency and through its effect on foreign confidence in sterling. Yet the very idea of arming government with powers to require strike ballots or impose a cooling-off period went against the grain in the Labour movement. Not only were the unions predictably hostile, but backbench Labour MPs threatened to withhold their support, and even in the cabinet a group of ministers, led by Callaghan, were clearly determined to wreck the measure. Wilson's tactics were to speed up the whole process, so as to pre-empt opposition. A short bill was therefore prepared in April 1969, excluding compulsory strike ballots but giving government powers to intervene in disputes. Yet this too fell foul of the combination against it at all levels in the Labour Party. Eventually the Chief Whip told Wilson that he did not have a Commons majority to ensure the passage of such a bill. Wilson and Castle, locked in negotiations with the TUC, were left to devise a face-saving formula to cover their retreat.

There can be little doubt that the Government got the worst of both worlds in first ostentatiously bringing forward, and then ignominiously abandoning, trade-union legislation. Labour thus conceded the case for reform – and showed itself incapable of implementing it. What is remarkable is not that the Government was left in such poor shape in the summer of 1969 but that within a year it appeared to have staged such an impressive comeback. Just as economic weakness had spurred it to promise action on industrial relations, so economic recovery released the pressure upon it.

During 1969, unsteadily at first but then with compelling momentum, the monthly trade figures at last moved into the black. The balance-of-payments surplus for the year turned out to be nearly £500 million; in 1970 it was to touch £800 million. What had happened was that British exports in 1969, now priced more competitively in foreign currencies, were over 25 per cent greater in volume than before devaluation, whereas the increase in the volume of imports was only half as much. But since the increase in imports had come through first, and at the higher sterling prices which devaluation entailed, it took a couple of years for the net advantage to show.

So far as the Government's electoral prospects were concerned, the economic recovery had come in the nick of time. Yet once Jenkins had achieved the balance-of-payments surplus, which had proved so elusive for so long, he was determined not to let it slip away again. Not only was the 1969 budget fairly severe, there was to be no electioneering budget in 1970 either – or rather it was a pre-election budget of a more sophisticated kind. Instead of a tax-cutting bonanza, which Jenkins thought would be a give-away in more than one sense, he instead sought to project a mood of confidence in continued prosperity through an exercise in fiscal and monetary prudence. Moreover this went down surprisingly well, not only in the markets but with the electorate. The swing back to Labour in the local-government elections in May 1970 encouraged talk of an early general election, which suddenly looked winnable for a Government which, only months previously, had been reeling from by-election rebuffs. Wellingborough had been lost on a swing of 10 per cent as recently as December 1969, the last of fifteen seats lost.

By June 1970, however, the sun had come out. Wilson, from his garden seat at 10 Downing Street, announced that he was going to the country and proceeded to spend a succession of cloudless days walking around shopping centres, chatting about the chances of the England soccer team in the World Cup in Mexico. In place of politics, one might say. It was the Conservative Party under Heath which sought to disturb the voters' complacency, just as in 1966; but all the polls suggested that Wilson had correctly gauged the public mood. At the close of the campaign, however, there were disquieting signs for Labour – an anomalously bad set of trade figures, a break in the weather, England's defeat in Mexico, a rogue poll showing a narrow Tory lead – which proved ominous. The swing to the Conservatives throughout the UK was the biggest since 1945. In England, where the anti-Labour swing was over 5 per cent, there was a fall in turnout to 71 per cent, 13 per cent lower than in 1950, nearly 5 per cent lower than in 1966. The fact was that a lot of people who might well have voted Labour had stayed at home. Worse was to follow.

# 10

# Winters of Discontent
## 1970–79

### BRITONS?

Foreigners were naturally quicker to recognize the reality of Britain's changed world status than were most Britons. Dean Acheson's much-quoted remark in 1962, that Britain 'has lost an empire and not yet found a role', pointed to an obvious truth which was equally obviously unpalatable to Macmillan, busy as his Government was in winding up the British Empire. This process could be represented, in a flattering but not wholly false light, as an enlightened transition to the creation of a multicultural Commonwealth. The Commonwealth was in many ways a fine concept, enlisting some more admirable features of an imperial ideology of service behind a relationship among equals who freely chose to sustain many peculiar traditions, from cricket to the common law. Commonwealth universities, for example, had close links, based on mutual affinity; the London School of Economics exemplified this, both in its high intake of Commonwealth students and the prominence of its alumni in elite groups in many Commonwealth countries. Since the Queen was accepted, even by republics, as Head of the Common-wealth, the monarchy was given a useful symbolic role, distinct from that of the British prime minister (as became apparent more than once during the 1980s). But whereas the Empire had been like a family busi-ness (maybe one run by the wrong members, as Orwell had it), the Commonwealth was at best an institutionalized family reunion, after all its members had gone into business on their own account.

In its day British imperialism had had a coherent political economy, presented as the timeless truths of Free Trade, but in fact premised on British naval supremacy and London's financial hegemony; thus using both gunboats and the gold standard to enforce a discipline which generally benefited the metropolitan country (and sometimes the dependent territories too). One mistake was to swallow this ideology whole and suppose that Britain could complacently go on in this way, as though the twentieth century had no nasty surprises in store. Conversely, the Chamberlainite imperialists, though alive to this problem, proposed a solution, based on preferential tariffs, which also led nowhere. This was demonstrated by the increasingly divergent imperatives of a declining great power and those of the developing countries which chafed under its yoke. The Commonwealth, in short, lacked either the political commitment or the economic rationale to satisfy those British statesmen who thought imperially.

Politically, the 'Old Commonwealth' of white settlement had shared Britain's finest hour in 1940, just as Churchill had said; but he was to be proved wrong in thinking that this kind of relationship had a future. Economically, the preferential trading pattern of the Ottawa agreements, and the sterling area which was its financial counterpart, proved hardly more viable in the post-war world. Sterling, encumbered with historic external debts (sterling balances) which showed how over-stretched the pound had become as an international currency, stumbled from crisis to crisis. The devaluation of 1967 was the final blow, demonstrating a divergence between domestic economic priorities and the international credibility of sterling – of a kind that would have been unthinkable in the prime of the gold standard. Likewise, Britain now belatedly wound up its historic imperial defence commitments; and though the Conservatives naturally blamed all of this on Labour, in fact the Heath Government was to reinforce the new priorities. Contrary to Tory election pledges, it did not reverse the evacuation east of Suez; it let the pound sink rather than abandon domestic economic growth; and it took Britain into the European Community.

It was a full twenty years after the Second World War before the post-imperial reckoning came. Moreover, the question of Britain's identity raised social and cultural issues of identity for individual Britons. The United Kingdom, as a political creation, had been predicated on an international economic and political supremacy of which the British Empire was the highest expression. It was often remarked that the end of empire did not produce in the United Kingdom the sort of traumatic domestic effects apparent in some other ex-imperial powers. Albeit with some British understatement, such effects were nonetheless surely apparent in the conflicts and doubts which surfaced over neglected issues of immigration, race and nationalism, with unravelling implications about the identity of the United Kingdom itself.

It would be wrong, of course, to suppose that British society had previously been unaffected by patterns of migration. Outward migration on a heroic scale had been common before the First World War. Though emigration from the United Kingdom to the Old Commonwealth was temporarily reversed during the 1930s, it resumed its outward flow after the Second World War. British immigration into Australasia was the biggest factor: it reached a level of over 50,000 a year in the early 1950s, and touched 80,000 in 1965. But these net statistics are a product of the fact that the number of British emigrants to Australasia, rising to 100,000 per annum throughout the late 1960s, was offset by a lagged rise in the number of antipodean immigrants into the United Kingdom, approaching 40,000 a year during the early 1970s. These were not, for the most part, Australian and New Zealand citizens (though there were a few thousand a year, such as the writers Germaine Greer and Clive James) but British nationals, returning home for a variety of reasons, from disappointment to family ties. Still, net emigration from the United Kingdom exceeded immigration in every year from 1946 to 1979 – albeit very narrowly in 1960 and 1961, because of a sudden surge of immigrants from third-world countries in the 'New Commonwealth', chiefly the West Indies and the Indian subcontinent.

What these aggregate net statistics for the United Kingdom do not reveal, however, is that the real pressure-points of immigration were at bottom an English problem. In Scotland, as late as 1966, only two out of every thousand people had been born in the New Commonwealth, compared with an English figure six times higher. In England this was part of a net flow of inward migration which had been apparent since the 1931 census. In Scotland, by contrast, emigration intensified in the inter-war period. Whereas, in each of the first two decades of the century, a quarter of a million Scots left home, in the 1920s the total reached nearly 400,000 – one in twelve of the population – and this outflow continued in the post-war period.

Scotland had obviously lost the economic magnetism which, at the turn of the century, had drawn immigrant labour across the Irish Sea, producing an Irish immigrant density three times greater than that in England. While the Irish rediscovered the attraction of England after the Second World War, Irish immigration into Scotland tailed away. But Scots continued moving south of the border, as they always had, though now in larger numbers. In the 1981 census the population of England was 30 per cent higher than sixty years previously; that of Scotland only 5 per cent higher. These national contrasts in demography, themselves the result of economic disparities, echoed the divergent experience of Britain and Ireland which, a century previously, had resonated so deeply in the national consciousness. Perhaps it is not surprising that, by the 1960s, Scottish nationalism had acquired a new salience.

Hitherto, Scottish politics had followed much the same trend as in the United Kingdom as a whole. In 1931, for example, the National Government virtually swept the board both north and south of the border; in 1945, conversely, the balance was reversed. The 1959 general election was a little-noticed turning point in the decline of Unionism (the name Scots Conservatives still used). For it left them, for the first time since 1950, with fewer Scottish seats than Labour. In 1970 the swing to the Conservatives in England was not replicated in Scotland, where Labour held 44 seats to the Unionists' 23. Moreover the Scottish National Party (SNP) had now emerged as a significant third party, just as the Liberals had south of the border. Indeed the increase in the SNP share of the vote in Scotland from 1959 to February 1974 was broadly similar to that of the Liberals, except one general election in arrear. In October 1974 the SNP polled over 30 per cent of the Scottish vote, 5 per cent clear of the Unionists, only 6 per cent behind Labour. Whereas Labour and Conservatives were now level-pegging in England, Scotland was represented by 41 Labour, 16 Unionist, 11 SNP and 3 Liberal MPs.

By-election upsets had signalled this surge, notably the SNP's stunning gain of the Lanarkshire seat of Hamilton from Labour in 1967. This seemed the more ominous since it followed a by-election gain by the Welsh Nationalists (Plaid Cymru) the previous year in Carmarthen. Given that the Conservatives, the historic champions of the Union, were now a permanent minority in Scotland and Wales, Labour relied increasingly on its Celtic fringe to redress its weakness in England. Was even this base to be undercut by Celtic nationalism? Carmarthen, admittedly, was in the Welsh-speaking heartland; and Labour expedited the passage of the Welsh Language Act (1967), if only to draw the political sting from cultural nationalism through concessions on bilingualism. But Plaid Cymru's achievements in the 1967 Rhondda West by-election, with 40 per cent of the vote in a predominantly English-speaking constituency, and similarly in the 1968 Caerphilly by-election, together with local election victories, showed that the nationalist impulse was not confined to a linguistically defined cultural base.

Indeed the SNP, with no linguistic constituency, nonetheless went on to mount a stronger political showing than Plaid Cymru after 1970. In the general election of that year, each had secured just over 11 per cent of their respective national polls; but whereas the SNP doubled this in the next general election, and nearly trebled it in that of October 1974, Plaid Cymru failed to make a broad advance (though it still secured three MPs). The fundamental reason for the SNP's second surge surely resides in the economic rather than the cultural purchase of its appeal. By 1974 the discovery of large-scale reserves of oil under the North Sea, combined with an equally dramatic increase in the international price of petroleum, transformed the economic outlook for Scotland. True enough, within five years production of crude oil in the United Kingdom was to rise from 87,000 tons to over 75 million – with each ton now fetching several times its previous price. The prospect of no less than a thousandfold increase in this 'black gold' was a heady stimulus to nationalist thinking, summed up in the SNP slogan, 'It's *Our* Oil'. Here was the means of translating historic grievances about the growing economic gap between north and south into a political challenge to the Union itself.

Most sophisticated English politicians regarded nationalism as a bore – other people's nationalism, of course, for they affected to have none themselves. Not so Enoch Powell, who emerged as a lonely prophet of trenchantly expressed views which simultaneously brought him an influential moment of fame and a permanent exclusion from office. He was idealistic: his ideal still one that thrilled to the lost chords of empire, his hero Joseph Chamberlain, whose biographer he became. Powell's intellectual brilliance was in no doubt, nor his readiness to make principled stands at the expense of his career, as shown by his resignation from the Macmillan Government in 1958 on the ground of its financial prodigality and his refusal to serve under Home in 1963. Back on the Conservative front bench for the third time, Powell finally ensured his dismissal with an apocalyptic speech in April 1968.

When Powell addressed the issue of immigration, juxtaposing anecdotes about 'wide-grinning piccaninnies' with a vision of 'the River Tiber foaming with much blood', he was transformed overnight into an unlikely popular tribune, the hero of London dockers as much as of his Wolverhampton constituents, as the one established politician ready to articulate widespread anxieties (or prejudices) about racial issues. Repudiated by the Conservative leadership, Powell nonetheless found a wide constituency for his views, though he did little to exploit it beyond revelling in the applause for speeches which grabbed attention with their vivid warnings. His proposals for action, however, notably on repatriation, often turned out to be less extreme (or more fraudulent) than they seemed at first sight. The disproportionately strong Conservative showing in the West Midlands in the 1970 elections was commonly attributed to Powell; he was applying a political torch to a highly combustible heap of social grievances which others had swept into a corner.

It could be said that, since over 92 per cent of the population of England and Wales were English or Welsh by birth at the time of the 'River Tiber' speech, immigration was statistically a marginal issue; and within this margin, rather over 2 per cent were born elsewhere in the United Kingdom, chiefly Scotland, whereas just under 2 per cent were Commonwealth immigrants, followed closely by the Irish, who were in turn just ahead of the proportion of people born in foreign countries. But overwhelming though this proportion of natives seems, it was a full 4 per cent lower than the figure of around 96 per cent native-born which had held steady in England and Wales until 1931. Not only had the number of incomers doubled in the span of a generation: within this total the fact that there were twice as many Irish as thirty years previously was practically invisible, compared with the effects of burgeoning immigration from the West Indies and the Indian subcontinent.

It was the visible presence of 'dark strangers', concentrated in some English towns and cities, which gave immigration statistics a racial edge. The newcomers had their own distinctive habits and conventions, from cooking to religion; and, of course, their own distinctive skin colour. English people rarely talked about 'niggers' – despite the electoral slogan, 'If you want a nigger for a neighbour, vote Labour'[1] – and at the time it was considered polite to avoid speaking of a black population by using the term 'coloured': a convention that was soon to be

1. This was not, of course, sanctioned by the Conservative Party, and Heath's treatment of Powell showed that he was determined to see that his party had clean hands on racial issues. But this slogan, which was reported during the 1964 campaign in Smethwick, was, to the author's knowledge, used in the 1968 local elections in the London borough of Haringey, a borough with a high concentration of New Commonwealth immigrants.

reversed. But few white people were wholly unprejudiced or showed the understanding of street relationships between the immigrant 'spades' and the native 'Jumbles' (from John Bull) which Colin MacInnes displayed in novels such as *City of Spades* (1957) or his short stories, *England, Half English* (1961). Conversely, the novelist V. S. Naipaul, settled in London since the early 1950s, returned to the Caribbean, imaginatively at least, for the settings of books like *A House for Mr Biswas* (1961).

Economically, immigrants were sucked in by the needs of an over-stretched labour market in recruiting unskilled workers for a range of low-paid jobs, of which those in public transport and the NHS were particularly conspicuous. Whereas the 1951 census had shown a population of 100,000 born in the New Commonwealth, ten years later this total had quadrupled. Amid difficulties in reconciling divergent estimates – the product alike of differing criteria, methodology and motivation – the Institute of Race Relations put the size of the coloured population at 1 million in the late 1960s.

Such growth, however, was no longer the product of current immigration; the abiding problem was instead one of race relations between British citizens. In 1962 the Government had passed, against Labour opposition, a Commonwealth Immigrants Act which for the first time restricted the right of Commonwealth citizens to settle in the United Kingdom, notably by making employment vouchers necessary. The number of vouchers was further restricted to 8,500 in 1965 by the Labour Government, which sought to compensate for the hard face it now turned on prospective immigrants with a smile of welcome for those already settled – the first Race Relations Act (1965), declaring racial discrimination illegal. This dual policy had a lot to be said for it, since it was difficult to argue that the United Kingdom, virtually alone in the world, should exercise no control over entry and citizenship; while even those who considered the open door to have been a historic mistake generally flinched from systematic revenge on a new generation of black Britons. Holding this consensus together, however, was no easy matter. In trying to monitor fair practices, the new Race Relations Board met with a lot of sniping (for example, the folk myth that an unspecified doctor had been denied the right to engage a specifically Scots housekeeper to make his morning porridge). Moreover, the attempt to arrest a dynamic process of family migration initially exacerbated as many anxieties as it alleviated, and thus licensed racially motivated agitation under the cover of criticisms of the supposed laxity of immigration control.

For immediately before the Commonwealth Immigrants Act came into force in 1962, no fewer than 230,000 immigrants had arrived from the New Commonwealth, virtually doubling the immigrant population in the space of eighteen months. To a large extent this was a once-for-all movement, to hustle through the door before it closed. But the level of Commonwealth immigration, in the first three years under the Act, remained above 50,000 a year; nor was this level significantly reduced by the cutback on vouchers in 1965. The reason was that the dependent wives and children of the male workers who had already been admitted were now exercising their right to follow the breadwinner to the host country. This too could be seen as a once-for-all effect, albeit on a timescale of a decade or so, not just a year or so. Nevertheless, in 1968 immigration controls were once more tightened, this time in a way that made a racial bias in the process unmistakable. The effect was that one category of British passport-holders (the Asian community in Kenya, and later Uganda) was denied what had hitherto been considered a full legal right of entry; while another category of prospective immigrants, who did not hold British passports, was nonetheless to be admitted on the basis of 'patriality', or British ancestry. This was justified by Callaghan as Home Secretary on the grounds of what the public would stand for; and he mollified liberal critics by combining the new checks with a strengthening of the race-relations legislation. The upshot was that immigration from the New Commonwealth fell by half over the next ten years and then stabilized.

It was in this context, with a rather shaky front-bench consensus seeking to suppress the racial issue, that Powell started huffing and puffing. The paradox was that immigration hit the headlines at just the moment when its tap root had already been severed; so that little more needed to be done – or could be done, short of denying legal immigrants the right to reunite their families. 'Send them home' was one cry; but voluntary repatriation was at best a humanitarian measure for a tiny minority; and compulsory repatriation bristled with difficulties over human rights, over the attitude of other Commonwealth countries, and, above all, over the meaning of 'home'. The much-discussed 'immigrant' population actually comprised a number of ethnically distinct communities, the growth of which was henceforth a matter of demography and culture rather than immigration, since they contained an ever-increasing number of children born in the United Kingdom.

Already by 1966, four out of five children with Jamaican parents had been born in Britain – no fewer than 70,000 black Britons – reflecting the fact that Jamaicans had been longest settled. By the 1980s a majority of the half million West Indian community were British-born. More recent immigrant groups, like Pakistanis, subsequently entered the same family life cycle, since their age structure was skewed towards high reproduction.[1] Moreover, during the 1960s immigrants (not least the Irish) were having bigger families than natives – their average family size was about the same as that of English families half a century previously.

The demographic implication was that there would for a time be a period of growth in the size of Britain's non-white population. But how long a period, and how much growth? In fact the first census to ask about colour was to show a total non-white population of under 3 million in 1991. But an official estimate that it would reach 3.5 million as soon as 1985 had been given to the House of Commons in 1967; and even higher extrapolations were derived from the disproportionately high numbers of children in immigrant families, especially in inner-city maternity wards and schools. The supposition about an immigrant burden on the welfare state was also based on false inferences. The fact was that in the course of this generation, immigrants would make heavy demands on child-welfare services and schools, but little on old-age pensions and geriatric care; that in a subsequent generation this balance would be reversed; and that immigrants' claims on unemployment benefits would, in the presence of discrimination against them in the labour market, be unusually sensitive to any rise in the overall level of unemployment. Meanwhile, there was plenty of scope for misconception about the total extent of immigration because it was concentrated in certain areas.

Concentration of immigrant communities is, of course, nothing new; it has often been reinforced not only by 'chain migration' within the immigrant community but also by discrimination in society at

---

1. In 1966 over 40 per cent of all New Commonwealth immigrants settled in Britain were between twenty-five and forty-four years old – not only prime working age but also prime child-bearing age – as compared with 25 per cent of the total population in this age bracket.

large, militating against dispersal. In 1966, eight of the 100 wards of the Greater London Council had a concentration of New Commonwealth immigrants higher than 20 per cent, though in Greater London as a whole they comprised only 3.2 per cent of the total population. Two-thirds of them were of West Indian origin, whereas in the West Midlands, the only other conurbation to show a proportion as high as this, a majority of the immigrants were from the Indian subcontinent. Here the highest concentration (4.8 per cent) was in Wolverhampton, Powell's birthplace and parliamentary constituency. Both London and the West Midlands were booming regions during this period; that is obviously why the immigrants went there. But, within those regions, it was the towns with falling populations which immigrants usually chose – again for the rational reason that the cost of housing would likewise be lower. So job vacancies plus cheap rents took Pakistanis to rundown houses in mean streets in declining towns like Wolverhampton – which had indeed seen better days before they arrived, just as unfriendly natives like Powell pointedly observed.

One question which Powell ducked was whether it was possible to *become* a Briton; whether nationality was irreducibly a matter of blood and race; whether national loyalty could be acquired, along with citizenship; whether cultural integration offered opportunities for fulfilment to a rising generation of ethnic minorities. Integration was certainly a frustratingly slow and discontinuous process for second-generation West Indians, even though they were brought up in English, participating in quintessentially English sports, notably cricket.

Arguably the finest writer of the century on cricket, quite apart from his work as a Marxist cultural historian, C. L. R. James became a distinguished resident of Brixton, where he died in 1989. Superb West Indian cricketers had long been familiar in England, not only in touring Test teams but as players for English clubs, like those in the Lancashire League which saw Learie Constantine in his prime in the 1930s. Truly an all-rounder, he was already a legendary figure long before he ended a distinguished career in London as High Commissioner for Trinidad and Tobago, 1962–4, and as the first black life peer in 1969. His work for better race relations came because Constantine, as his friend James put it, 'revolted against the revolting contrast between his first-class status as a cricketer and his third-class status as a man'.

Obviously many blacks, talented or untalented, faced setbacks from a pattern of discrimination that was 'not cricket'. But it could be said that, within twenty years or so, the presence of black soccer players, black rugby forwards and black fast bowlers, representing England in the national teams, was one conspicuous symbol of advance. The black sprinter Linford Christie was to become Britain's first world champion at his distance in more than half a century. Black pop stars made ethnic music like reggae and rap part of the British youth culture; a black comedian like Lenny Henry obviously had the power to make television audiences laugh with him, not at him; black newscasters gave a new face to the BBC (ITN too), both nationally and internationally. By 1992 there were to be several MPs from ethnic minorities – all Labour (though south Asian Conservative local councillors, often shopkeepers, had also emerged). In the Transport Workers' union Ernie Bevin's old chair was occupied by a black leader, Bill Morris; and the relative paucity of black students in higher education in 1990 was at least an improvement on their virtual absence fifteen years previously.

Integration was thus an uphill struggle but not an impossible one. Powell, however, had more of a point than his liberal critics allowed when he singled out the intractable difficulties in coming to terms with Islam. Pakistani communities, in particular, were notably determined to maintain their own culture intact, especially with the rise of Islamic fundamentalism during the 1980s. They presented an almost impermeable cliff-face to the conventions of their host country. This seemed reasonable enough when it took the form of claims for the recognition of the right of Muslim women and girls to wear the veil; but assertions of the primacy of a rival morality put it on a collision course with secular liberalism. Ironically, relativistic liberals who had purported to look benignly on the growth of a multicultural society were to find themselves pitched in confrontation with Islamic attempts to suppress Salman Rushdie's novel *The Satanic Verses* (1988), which, in the manner of a post-modernist Voltaire, cast a satirical eye over their revered prophet.

## TWEEDLEDEE

Edward Heath became prime minister in 1970 against most people's expectations (though not his own). Written off in advance as an ineffective party leader, with his lack of a personal touch and his absence of public charisma equally apparent, Heath was in a correspondingly strong position after he snatched victory, with a Conservative majority of 30. He was a lonely prime minister: not only because he was a bachelor but through long habit. Music served him for emotional fulfilment. He had learned to be circumspect while making his way as a scholarship boy in the gentlemen's party. The brusque camaraderie of the officers' mess, the whips' office and the yacht club – he had latterly become a successful competitive sailor – encompassed the masculine conventions with which he was comfortable. He did not find it easy to get on with the opposite sex. He appointed one woman to his cabinet – Margaret Thatcher at Education; this was not to prove a happy relationship, though she buckled down to her own job without dissent, furthering the comprehensive revolution. Heath's only close cabinet colleague was William Whitelaw, a bluff former Guards officer from a landowning family in the Borders, replete with innate political skills which the prime minister badly needed. Whitelaw put up with a great deal – even with being handed the Northern Ireland portfolio at one point.

Heath gave the Foreign Office to his predecessor, Douglas-Home, which was an equable arrangement; and the Home Office to his former rival Maudling, whose political fire was manifestly dying to its embers. In due course Maudling was caught in a messy financial scandal, which cast him as gullible rather than sinister but nonetheless spelled resignation in 1972; and his fire flickered out. This loss Heath could have weathered more easily had not Macleod suddenly died in July 1970, after only a month as Chancellor of the Exchequer. Macleod was the real political heavyweight in the new Government, with cabinet experience which outranked that of the prime minister himself, and plans for tax reform which he never had chance to implement. Faced with this yawning gap at the Treasury, Heath made a fateful choice in Anthony Barber, a relatively unknown politician, who never successfully proved that he was his own man rather than a client of the strong-minded prime minister. In fact Heath increasingly turned for political counsel as well as executive expertise to Sir William Armstrong. Another self-made man, brought up with both parents in the Salvation Army, Armstrong entered the higher civil service, of which he became a notably influential head.

The Conservatives talked of 'a quiet revolution'. This was in tune with the right-wing rhetoric which had emerged from their pre-election strategic planning conference at the Selsdon Park Hotel in January

1970. At the time this sort of talk had seemed a propaganda gift to Wilson, who uttered graphic warnings about the reactionary proclivities of 'Selsdon Man'. In fact there is little evidence that floating voters were alarmed – attracted rather – by the general notion of clamping down on big government and big unions alike. The Conservative manifesto was more specific on one point: 'We utterly reject the philosophy of compulsory wage control.' Sure enough, the Prices and Incomes Board was wound up by the new Government. Moreover its free-market image was enhanced by a striking appointment from outside Westminster. John Davies was parachuted into the Government, fresh from his post as director-general of the Confederation of British Industries – a bosses' counterpart to Bevin or Cousins. Sharing Heath's commitment to Europe and modernization, Davies was given charge of a big Department of Trade and Industry and, with a new boy's lack of dissimulation, came out with the opinion that taxpayers' money was not well spent in helping 'lame ducks'. He learnt soon enough how to eat his words, but not before they had acquired indiscriminate currency as a supposed insight into the Government's social as well as industrial policy.

For better or worse, therefore, the Heath Government represented itself, and was represented by its opponents, as promising a break with those interventionist policies – incomes policy above all – which had been pursued by successive governments throughout the 1960s. Instead market solutions would be sought, especially once the restrictive hold of the trade unions had been loosened by legal reform of their status. Pride of place therefore went to a long-prepared Industrial Relations Bill, which was the responsibility of Robert Carr, a personally emollient Minister of Labour, with whom, under other conditions, trade-union leaders might well have established cordial relations. But Carr was bound, against his better judgement, to abjure a piecemeal approach in favour of one big bill. The TUC, conversely, was in no mood to parley and opposed Carr's bill root and branch. It met bitter opposition from the Labour Party too – an unabashed Barbara Castle vehement in her denunciations. A new Industrial Relations Court was established, with wide-ranging powers to enforce ballots and cooling-off periods on registered unions. There was, however, a legal loophole which the TUC adroitly exploited: that if unions refused to register they would remain beyond the reach of the new court.

By the time the Act passed in 1971, the public standing of trade unions in the opinion polls stood at its highest level for three years; and after a year of its operation, it was apparent that the Heath Government, like the Wilson Government before it, had the worst of all worlds. It had inscribed a massive Act upon the statute book, at immense political, economic and industrial cost, but with no pay-off. The TUC had won the institutional struggle to prevent its constituent unions from registering. The Industrial Relations Court, so elaborately set up, had virtually no business; employers shied away from using it, fearful of the consequences to labour relations; when it did intervene, it made matters worse, turning cooling-off periods into hotting-up periods. Above all, when it procured the arrest of five shop stewards in the London docks in 1972, their case threatened to provoke a paralysing strike. Deadlock had been reached – broken in this instance by the opportune intervention of the Official Solicitor, as deus ex machina, securing the release of the 'Pentonville Five' for essentially political reasons. This pantomime was plainly not what the Conservatives had intended.

Nor was the Government in a happier position over the industrial strategy which Davies pursued. Early in 1971 he faced a moment of truth over an outsize lame duck, when Rolls-Royce faced bankruptcy. This was no obscure, marginal, dispensable firm but the country's major manufacturer of aircraft engines – and, of course, luxury motor-cars – which were a byword for the international status of British precision engineering. The Government took the painful decision to nationalize the company – a cause of much ideological glee to the Opposition. After this, when the collapse of Upper Clyde Shipbuilders threatened Glasgow with heavy unemployment (in a political context inflamed by the Nationalist surge) it was less of a surprise that a chastened Government should again come to the rescue. Moreover, its biggest humiliation was still to come.

The root of the trouble was inflation and how to cure it. This was the black spot in the economic legacy of 1970, with wages and prices leapfrogging at an accelerating pace, which had already pushed up the year-on-year inflation rate to over 6 per cent. The Conservatives made great play of the way the purchasing power of the pound was being snipped away; yet during three full years under Heath, 1971–3, price rises averaged nearly 9 per cent, while male industrial earnings increased by an average of nearly 14 per cent a year. Without annual productivity gains of 5 per cent a year to bridge this gap, the result was bound to be a further twist in the inflationary spiral.

Even with a devalued pound, British prices were again becoming uncompetitive, as a massive deterioration in the balance of payments showed. There was a slide from a record surplus of over £1 billion in 1971 to a record deficit of over £1 billion in 1973. To be sure, instability in the world currency markets did not help. This was the juncture at which the Bretton Woods system of fixed exchange rates broke down and sterling was left to find its own level in the market. Because of the weakness of the US dollar, under the strain of the Vietnam war, the pound continued to trade at around $2.40 during 1972–3; but the parity of sterling against the German mark told the real story. From 9.5 DM after the sterling devaluation of November 1967, the pound slipped to an average under 8 DM by 1972 and to 6 DM by 1974 – effectively, this was a further devaluation by more than 30 per cent.

The Government had abandoned a formal incomes policy, but obviously had a responsibility for pay settlements in the public sector, where grievances about inequitable treatment were building up. In 1972 the crunch came in the coal mines. Only fifteen years previously the National Coal Board (NCB) still had over 700,000 employees in the United Kingdom, but this total was thereafter run down fairly steadily to under 300,000. Notably under the direction of the Labour ex-minister Lord Robens, the NCB achieved this through natural wastage rather than sudden redundancies, in a process whereby the National Union of Mineworkers (NUM) implicitly traded job security against pay moderation. In the meantime, therefore, miners' earnings had increased less rapidly than those of industrial workers as a whole, exactly as one would expect in a declining industry. The NUM's president, Joe Gormley, came from the traditionally moderate Lancashire Miners; a pragmatic leader, he was now responsive to mounting pressure from his deputy, the Scottish Communist Mick McGahey, not to mention younger militants like Arthur Scargill of the Yorkshire Miners. A 14 per cent increase in miners' earnings in 1971 kept well ahead of the cost of living, but a big claim for 1972 was lodged by the increasingly restive union, intent on making up for ground lost in the Robens era.

It was natural that the Government should stiffen the resistance of the NCB, since pay settlements were already increasing at an alarming rate. The initially small gap which Gormley perceived between the two sides gaped wider as the dispute went on. In January 1972 the first national coal strike since 1926 began, and soon revealed the NUM much better prepared than the NCB. The use of 'flying pickets', marauding from Yorkshire under the flamboyant command of Scargill, was effective in closing a major supply depot, Saltley, as far away as the West Midlands – effective too in boosting Scargill's union career. This new concept of concentrated mass picketing made coal stocks inaccessible, and it was this rather than a shortage of coal itself which closed many power stations. The Government declared a state of emergency, with powers to put industry on a three-day week as part of a campaign to conserve energy. But this was an improvisation which failed to halt the slide into darkness. The Government capitulated. Not only did it concede big pay rises, as expeditiously recommended by a speedily convened committee of inquiry: when the NUM demanded more than this, Heath agreed to give them more – for overtime, for holidays, for pensions. Miners' earnings in 1972 jumped up by 16 per cent, more than double the rate of inflation.

This was an outright victory for the NUM, won by its industrial muscle. But it came also on a wave of public sympathy for the miners. Partly through an untutored gift for public relations, the union's simple pleas – forgotten men, blood on the coal, recompense for 1926 – evoked an unexpectedly warm public response. For Heath it was a moral defeat as well as an economic one. He now talked of finding a better way to resolve industrial problems, seeking active cooperation from both sides of industry, on a model generally associated with practice in Europe. This interventionist, neo-corporatist approach was also, of course, associated with Wilson's way of doing things: a bitter pill to swallow, but swallowed it was. Talk of U-turns in Government policy became common. Heath was less troubled by this than by the economic predicament he faced. When unemployment touched the emotive figure of a million, he resolved on a change of priorities. If the trade unions would not do business with him – this was the legacy of the Industrial Relations Act – the Government would have to do its duty single-handed.

Heath's own technocratic bent pulled him towards tidy administrative solutions, regardless of non-rational responses for which more astute politicians allowed. This was one reason why his loyal lieutenant Peter Walker was given carte blanche in the most fundamental reform of local government since the introduction of county councils in 1888. The Local Government Act of 1972 swept away historic counties – like Rutland and the Isle of Ely – the focus of local loyalties down the centuries, and imposed new boundaries, including off-the-shelf, ready-to-assemble counties like Avon, Humberside and Cleveland. Edmund Burke would have turned in his grave at the lack of conservative instincts betrayed in this blueprint for uprooting England's ancient oak trees; Conservative Party officials saw a more immediate threat to their traditional county elites under this radically rationalized new structure. Walker even refused to allow the customary partisan gerrymandering over the new boundaries, brushing aside pleas from Conservative Central Office. This object lesson in Heathite rationalization was thought magnificent by some (not very many) but it was not politics.

Heath found that modernization required political resources which he was ill-equipped to mobilize; and that, if anachronistic tribal loyalties stood in the way, they could not simply be ignored. In despising Wilson's purely tactical tergiversations, Heath underestimated the political subtlety necessary to achieve the sort of reorientation which he now believed necessary. Many Conservatives subsequently derided the Government's U-turns as a sign of weakness; Heath, conversely, saw himself as bravely facing up to the complex realities of a situation which had been inadequately grasped by Selsdon Man. In particular, by 1972 he was ready to adopt an incomes policy as the only means of reconciling higher growth and lower unemployment with lower inflation.

In his first budget Barber had reduced income tax and was to make a further change, not in its real incidence but in the way it was calculated. Standard rate had conventionally applied to all income, from whatever source; but earned income, since Asquith's time, had attracted a remission in the rate actually charged. So wage-earners under PAYE never actually paid the full standard rate at all. This confusing convention was superseded with effect from 1973 by a new arrangement, which allowed for this remission at source, and thus produced a (decimalized) 'basic rate' of income tax of 30 per cent – apparently lower, actually the same (at least for earned incomes). Albeit exaggerated in this way, the tax burden fell.

In 1970 Jenkins had passed on a big budget surplus. Government income was greater than expenditure by over 5 per cent of GDP. Yet within seven years, first under Barber and then under Healey, this big surplus was replaced by a government deficit of 6 per cent of GDP, a level totally unprecedented in peacetime. Deficits had built up steadily over four years (and were to take much longer to eliminate). Under the Conservatives, the deficit was not caused by any real increase in the share of central government spending. The explanation is that, over four years, Government tax revenue fell as a proportion of GDP by at least 7 per cent.[1]

Some of this relative fall in revenue was inadvertent and unpredictable, especially after the 'oil shock', when prices of crude oil soared, following the formation of a producers' cartel (OPEC). Yet this simply accelerated a trend which had already established an amazing momentum. The fiscal stimulus to the economy from this one-sided reduction in the burden of taxation was without precedent, in economic history or theory alike. Such a policy shift lay beyond the wildest imaginings of the fecund brain of the historical Keynes. This was Keynesianism in caricature.

Such was the 'Barber boom', which duly pushed up the annual growth rate, which had fluctuated around 2 per cent throughout 1969–72, to no less than 7.4 per cent in 1973. The stimulus was not only fiscal but monetary. The most widely used measure of the money supply (called M3 to distinguish it from other definitions), which had increased by around 25 per cent in the whole three-year period up to 1970, now showed increases of this order in *each* of the years 1972 and 1973. It is plain that credit was running wild. The 7 per cent bank-rate of 1970 was slightly more than the inflation rate, producing a real rate of interest of less than 1 per cent. (In practice, of course, actual high-street interest rates to private customers were set at higher levels than these.) In 1971 bank-rate was reduced, in two steps, to 5 per cent – at a time when the retail price index (RPI) was nudging 10 per cent. Real interest rates had thus become negative. Anyone able to borrow at prevailing rates would make money if they purchased an asset that would hold its value.

Little wonder, then, that 1971 saw the beginning of an explosion in house prices which left them, within a couple of years, at sometimes double their former levels, depending on the part of town and the part of the country. In London, in particular, the flood of money into the market created a wholly different scale of property values. This had its beneficial side, for example in the redemption of inner suburbs like

1. As shown in the traditional budget accounts (Consolidated Fund); meanwhile expenditure in 1973–4 was over 1 per cent lower than in 1970–71 (though local-government expenditure rose). Inflation introduces some distortion: the raw figures show revenue rising by 15 per cent, expenditure by 42 per cent and nominal GDP by 50 per cent.

Islington or Wandsworth, where 'gentrification' of decaying town houses led to real improvements in the housing stock. Nor did most of the owner-occupiers suffer, since the burden of breathtakingly large mortgages, necessary to finance purchases at fancy prices, was subsequently lightened in real terms by the same inflationary process. To ignore the fact that inflation suited many individuals is to ignore some of the reasons why it became socially entrenched, if only as a defensive strategy. The trick was to stay ahead of the game, by sitting on assets discounted for future inflation, while meanwhile securing pre-emptively large pay increases – to offset prospective as well as actual price rises. This revolution in expectations had its own self-reinforcing logic. In 1972 prices rose by 7 per cent, industrial earnings by 16 per cent.

Incomes policy was a logical way to break out of this collectively self-defeating spiral – without simply letting unemployment do the job. Interventionist policies were pressed further; the Industry Act of 1972 was welcomed by the born-again socialist Benn as a sign that the Tories too might be on the point of conversion – much to Tory embarrassment. When Heath failed to secure trade-union cooperation on wage restraint in the summer of 1972, the Government introduced its own statutory incomes policy. This might be ritually denounced as a Tory attack on working-class living standards, but in fact its provisions were markedly egalitarian. Its first phase, a wage freeze, allowed the Government to maintain the boom, hoping that this would feed into better industrial performance all round. A fall in unemployment was welcome to both Government and unions. The second phase of the incomes policy in practice allowed the unions more scope for negotiating better deals under these favourable bargaining conditions. It was, however, the third phase which came to grief, in the autumn of 1973.

Heath would have liked to strike an official deal with the TUC. Its general secretary, Victor Feather, was amenable but, facing retirement, realized that he could not deliver the support of his members. Heath and the indispensable Armstrong ('the deputy prime minister', according to Feather) nonetheless sought an unofficial deal with the NUM, the union of which they were most fearful. Again, Gormley himself was appreciative of Heath's goodwill, and he tipped the wink that a payment for 'unsocial hours' might be enough to appease the miners. What made a second coal strike inevitable was the fact that Heath guilelessly wrote this provision into the general guidelines for phase three, instead of keeping it up his sleeve as a special treat for the miners alone. The NCB therefore made its full and final offer at once, only to find it summarily rejected by the NUM, which began an overtime ban in November. Thus the Government became locked into a further conflict with the miners, this time with the complication that stage three had statutory backing. This meant that the miners could be represented as taking a political stand, intent on challenging the Government itself.

But this strict constitutional reading also meant that there was no scope for increasing the offer to the miners, whatever political or economic reasons should emerge – as emerge they did. For the oil shock suddenly altered the premises of all arguments about relative energy costs, in effect putting the bargaining strength of the oil sheikhs behind the miners' case. Far from being overpriced, coal was transformed overnight into a relatively cheap form of energy, and one with which Britain could hardly dispense until the North Sea wells came on stream. The increased costs of imported oil meanwhile caused the terms of trade to move sharply against the UK, putting an immense strain on the already weak balance of payments. The deficit of £1 billion in 1973 established a record which was to stand for only twelve months, whereupon the deficit soared to over £3 billion.

Here was a situation which patently required a quick political fix; Whitelaw, straight from his ordeal as Secretary of State for Northern Ireland, was drafted in to apply it. But he was unable to break the impasse and a second coal strike now loomed. This time the Government was well prepared, or thought it was. In December 1973 it pre-emptively instituted a three-day week for British industry. In a way this was a great success, given the national cult of reliving the hardships of 1940 in a safely miniaturized form; out came the candles, and the wartime lore, showing that Britain could take it – and make it too. For, despite predictions of a drastic fall in output, it turned out that manufacturing production in the first quarter of 1974 was 95 per cent of normal, which was itself a thought-provoking comment on the scope for productivity improvements.

None of this, however, helped the Government at the time. At the eleventh hour, the TUC offered an undertaking that other unions would not exploit a special settlement with the miners. This may have been an industrial nonsense, quite implausible in practice; but it was a political lifeline if the Government simply wanted to get off the hook.

Heath rebuffed the TUC; Armstrong collapsed and withdrew, like Montagu Norman in 1931; the prime minister seemed baffled, uncertain, isolated. Conservative partisans had long relished a confrontation in which unpopular unions would be subjected to the just wrath of the electorate. Heath did not want a general election on those terms; but in the end he concluded that there was nothing else for it and polling day was eventually set for the end of February 1974. As Whitelaw could well see, the Government needed an electoral victory not to chastise the miners but to settle with them.

'Who Governs?' demanded the Conservatives – a good question. But this election was not settled by constitutional issues, any more than in 1910, but by politics. The Government found its immediate case on coal falling apart, day by day, with more than one embarrassing revelation about errors in the official calculations of miners' pay and entitlements. It was not, however, the small print which sealed Heath's fate but the big picture: a hapless Government, hamstrung in the darkness of another three-day week, presiding over double-figure inflation. Conservative support slipped away during the campaign, with the Liberals rather than Labour making the running in the opinion polls.

The Liberals had scored some striking by-election gains in the previous sixteen months. As Liberal leader, Jeremy Thorpe seized his chances with panache and, although the general election did not yield quite as big a Liberal vote as predicted, it was, at 19 per cent, half as big as the Conservative vote. Needless to say, the Liberals did not get half as many MPs – only 14 to the Conservatives' 297. But together they clearly outnumbered Labour's 301 MPs. Such calculations seized Heath's imagination as the final results came in; moreover the Liberals supported an incomes policy. Heath did not resign, therefore, but saw Thorpe and dangled the prospect of a coalition. Whatever Thorpe's own temptation, the reaction in his party, as in 1951, ruled out such an option. Only at this point, with little sense that Labour had won the election, but only that Heath had lost it, was Wilson summoned back to office.

## QUESTIONS OF IDENTITY

When Powell invoked the verities of race and nationality, loyalty and identity, he was in deadly earnest, as was shown by his readiness to challenge the liberal consensus, not only over immigration, but over the old quarrel about Ulster and the new one about Europe. As a result, it was logical for him to end up as MP for one of the twelve Northern Irish constituencies, championing the Unionist cause, which the Protestant community had come to believe was in imminent peril.

After half a century, the Irish question came back on to the agenda of British politics. What is surprising, perhaps, is that it had for so long been forgotten. Yet for years neither of the major British parties had sufficient incentive to disturb the apparently quiescent devolved regime which had made Stormont, since its establishment in 1921, 'a Protestant parliament for a Protestant people'. The Conservatives were content to let sleeping dogs lie since, decade by decade, they enjoyed the virtually automatic support of up to a dozen Ulster Unionist MPs at Westminster, most of them returned with mountainous majorities from the Protestant parts of the province; indeed in 1951 four Ulster Unionists were returned unopposed – the last uncontested returns in a United Kingdom general election. So the Conservatives left their historic allies to rule the roost in their own backyard, with no awkward questions asked about the Stormont regime.

More surprisingly, neither did the Labour Party look for trouble; indeed the Attlee Government strengthened the position of Stormont, mindful of the wartime contrast between loyalist Ulster and neutralist Ireland. As a secular, working-class party, Labour had difficulty in establishing itself in Northern Ireland, where politics ran in grooves still deeply incised by sectarian loyalties which divided its natural supporters. It was not until the late 1960s, with the formation of the Social Democratic and Labour Party (SDLP) under the leadership of Gerry Fitt and later John Hume, that an effective constitutionalist challenge on behalf of the Catholic minority was mounted, in a field otherwise dominated by the uncompromising Nationalism of Sinn Fein, with its links to the gunmen of the (provisional) IRA.

What caused the brewing crisis in Northern Ireland to boil over was not an intensification of the manifold forms of discrimination against Catholics, which had long been endemic in the province, but a faltering attempt at reform. Captain Terence O'Neill, on becoming prime minister in 1963, started to inch Northern Ireland down the road of modernization, and was to be prodded by the Wilson Government to keep moving. Whether there was a consistent logic to 'O'Neillism', still less one driven by the economic imperatives of multinational businesses, may be doubted. If O'Neill claimed to be moved by his own sense of the sheer backwardness of a province locked into economic decline and social deprivation, he also had a partisan interest in neutralizing the threat which unemployment posed to the Unionists' working-class support. Whatever its origins, the effect of O'Neillism was to let the genie out of a bottle that had been corked up for half a century. Himself a landowner in the 'Big House' tradition of Ulster Unionism, O'Neill's perceived liberalism was anathema to the paranoid Orangemen, always alert to popish plots. Their populist Protestantism found its voice (a loud one) in the charismatic figure of the Reverend Ian Paisley. Here was the first sign of fracture lines within Unionism which, by 1974, was to divide the representation of the province at Westminster between Official Unionists, (Paisleyite) Democratic Unionists, and the Vanguard Unionist Progressive Party, with the SDLP marginally benefiting from the fragmentation.

When civil-rights marches, inspired by those in the USA, led to bloodshed, O'Neill fell, to be replaced from the same top drawer of Unionism by James Chichester-Clark: one final, desperate chance for the Big House. In a fast disintegrating situation he was in turn succeeded by a self-made Belfast businessman, Brian Faulkner, who hardly had time to savour his triumph as the first meritocratic Northern Irish prime minister, since he proved also to be the last. The fact was that the discredited Stormont regime was not robust enough to withstand the strains of implementing the reforms which the Westminster Government now required. The Royal Ulster Constabulary was deeply suspect as an agency of law enforcement; its paramilitary B-Specials were simply seen as Protestants in uniform. Having disbanded them in 1970, Callaghan as Home Secretary had little option but to replace them with British troops – a crucial stage in undermining Stormont, but little improvement in keeping the peace. The incoming Conservative Government exacerbated a bad situation by imposing internment without trial in a doomed attempt to isolate the IRA, which instead gained a new credibility in the Nationalist community. Protestant paramilitaries too were now in the field, linked to the Vanguard movement. Worse still, a (banned) civil-rights demonstration in Derry in January 1972 resulted in the deaths of thirteen unarmed Catholics in clashes with British troops. This was 'Bloody Sunday'. The Catholic community no longer believed that the Army could or would protect them. 'Bloody

Sunday' opened a new phase in 'the troubles', with the IRA escalating its campaign of violence, and a death toll for 1972 running into hundreds, with two civilians killed for each soldier. Meanwhile Heath decided to suspend Stormont altogether.

Thus, after a failed experiment of fifty years of devolved government, Britain became committed to direct rule in Northern Ireland. It was not intended as a permanent solution. With William Whitelaw as his lieutenant, Heath went to great lengths to devise a form of power-sharing between the different communities which would offer a constitutional way forward. But the Sunningdale Agreement of December 1973, involving not only Faulkner and Fitt but also the Irish Government, proved to be only a paper constitution. Holding a general election in February 1974 served to inflame all the old tribal allegiances at a highly sensitive juncture in the establishment of a power-sharing executive. Faulkner himself might now have seen the desirability of bridge-building; but the supporting piles were washing away beneath him. In May 1974 the unacceptability of Sunningdale to grassroots Unionists, who felt excluded and betrayed, was brought home by massive backing for a strike organized by Protestants. Faulkner resigned; Sunningdale became a dead letter; the impasse continued; the bridge-builders admitted defeat. Yet the Protestants' victory was hollow and their loudly proclaimed loyalism, though potent in thwarting a settlement, disclosed their own tragic dilemma. Blazoned with Union Jacks, they still defiantly proclaimed their loyalty to British culture and institutions – from which they actually felt a mounting sense of alienation. It was their plight, and their pleas, which seized the imagination of Powell, himself already alienated from the Heath Government because of its policy towards Europe.

The United Kingdom had finally become a full member of the EEC on 1 January 1973. This was Heath's dearest aspiration and his finest achievement. He understood, from bitter experience in the ante-rooms of Brussels, that the road into Europe went through Paris. Once de Gaulle had been replaced by Pompidou as French President in 1969, the application from the United Kingdom could be revived. In the tail-end of the Wilson Government, nothing was done; but Heath's election pushed Europe to the top of the agenda. In May 1971 he met face to face with Pompidou, the sort of pragmatic Gaullist who could be persuaded that Britons might make good Europeans. That Heath himself was one stood in little doubt; and his own coolness towards the USA – a not-so-special relationship in his eyes – was a positive advantage in winning over Pompidou.

With French support, the renewed negotiations in Brussels succeeded in resolving knotty problems which had seemed baffling in 1963 or 1967. Partly this was because Britain's main European trading partners, Denmark and Ireland, also proposed to join; and because Britain's Commonwealth suppliers had had ten years to get used to the idea that imperial preference was obsolescent. In 1960 4 per cent of UK imports still came from New Zealand; by 1970 little more than 2 per cent. Other world customers – like the Saudi Arabians, with their taste for fine lamb, and adequate means to gratify it – were to prove a profitable substitute for the cheapskate British consumer. The settlement still hurt, of course, as change of this magnitude was bound to; transitional arrangements for New Zealand, in particular, were a necessary part of the package. Such additional costs of entry could be regarded as a debt of honour – a post-dated cheque from 1940 which was met in the depreciated currency of 1971.

The real problem was that the EEC, as shaped from Messina onwards, obviously served the special interests of its six participating members better than those of a latecomer, historically orientated towards the open seas. For the United Kingdom, there was the grievous burden of the Common Agricultural Policy (CAP), imposed on consumers through higher food costs so as to subsidize uncompetitive small farmers – France's own price for opening its markets to the German industrial behemoth. Conversely, Britain was the supplicant in 1971, unable to exact conditions for joining the EEC: instead belatedly making the best of a bad job for itself while seeking to temper the wind to the antipodean lamb. The effect of the CAP was that British consumers were progressively denied access to cheap imports and supplied instead with the subsidized (but still dearer) produce of the EEC.

Much of the benefit went into the pockets of European farmers – including some British farmers. Within three years the market price of British wheat went up by 250 per cent – practically ten times the inflation rate. British farmers thus found in the CAP the answer to a century of prayers for protection in the domestic market. They had been forced by the rigours of competition in open markets to become the most efficient farmers in Europe; now they reaped their reward, both through price and through quantity, supplying a buoyant and guaranteed market. Wheat imports were cut by half and British wheat-growing increased by half during the 1970s. At 3.6 million acres in 1980, the acreage under wheat exceeded the wartime peak of 1943 and was the highest figure since 1874, at the onset of the so-called Great Depression. Moreover, with modern methods, yields were even higher – 8 million tons of wheat in 1980, twice as much as ten years previously and ten times as much as fifty years previously. The political economy of Free Trade imperialism had been turned upside down.

The consequent costs for the British consumer were exaggerated by the coincident acceleration of domestic inflation. By January 1974, the RPI stood at 25 per cent above its 1971 level; meanwhile food prices, which had previously kept pace with the overall cost of living, increased by no less than 40 per cent. Little wonder that many people were bemused – the more so since scales of money values which had long seemed second nature were now unsettled by a change in the money itself. After centuries of shillings and pence, sterling was decimalized in 1971; the pound was divided into 100 'new pence', each worth 2.4 old pennies. Shillings meanwhile continued in currency until they were eventually replaced by a virtually identical 5p coin; but though the demise of the half-crown (12.5p) was mourned, for it, as for the 'tanner' (2.5p), there was to be no such afterlife. Generations of British schoolchildren, who had sharpened their arithmetic skills by calculating sterling prices for quantities of stones, pounds and ounces, found that their lore was made redundant by a creeping process of metrication, signalling the long-resisted triumph of this Napoleonic scheme over a system of imperial measures which had once prevailed wherever the map was coloured red.

'The world as I had known it was coming apart,' so Powell recollected his feelings when Britain decided to quit India. A quarter of a century later, his feelings about joining Europe were no less anachronistic and no less passionate. He voiced the opposition of the Tory right-wingers, combining traditional conservative nationalism with a neo-liberal antipathy to economic interventionism from Brussels. This high-octane mixture was later to fuel Thatcherism. On the Labour benches, too, Europe was bitterly divisive, exposing a fissure which was, within ten years, to split the party. The current unpopularity of the EEC was seized upon by the left wing after Labour's electoral defeat in 1970, and used to rally opposition to the consensual approach adopted by Wilson in government. While in power, he had, of course, supported British entry – 'if the terms are right', as he liked to say. The available terms in fact changed little over the years; yet Wilson now found his excuse to trim to the prevailing wind in his party, whose unity was his own paramount consideration. It was left, therefore, to Brown's replacement as deputy leader, Roy Jenkins, to uphold some consistency in Labour's commitment. He led sixty-nine Labour MPs through the lobby in support of the principle of entry in October 1971. It was the most significant example of a transcending national issue overriding the party whip since the backbench Tory revolt against Chamberlain in 1940; and, as on that occasion, few of those who took this grave step subsequently repented.

Still, 1971 was not 1940, nor 1931, nor 1886, nor 1846 – occasions when the party system fractured and reset along new lines. Jenkins's position as Labour's deputy leader soon became intolerable and he resigned from it; but he and his supporters were ready to mend their fences with their party by voting with it, rather than finding a cross-party majority for a Conservative Government, on the necessary EEC legislation. Moreover, Wilson was soon beginning to trim to the right again. He had facilitated a move, originally inspired by Tony Benn, who was turning by inches into an anti-marketeer, to submit the issue to a referendum under a future Labour Government. Here was the opportunity to restore party unity while going no further than promising a 'renegotiation' with the EEC. And with Wilson unexpectedly back in power by 1975, this stratagem was put into effect. The other members of the EEC patiently engaged in new negotiations in Brussels which, in all essentials, left the terms much as they had been under Heath. But this was enough for Wilson to slide into renewed support for the EEC, thus (in the eyes of the left) betraying their cause just as (in the eyes of the right) he had betrayed that of Europe less than four years previously.

During the referendum on membership of the EEC in the summer of 1975, neither the prime minister nor the new leader of the Opposition, Margaret Thatcher, took a very visible part. The pro-European campaign was instead spearheaded by politicians who were fully committed to it: Jenkins for Labour, supported by the rising cabinet minister, Shirley Williams; and Heath for the Conservatives, supported by his ex-cabinet colleagues. They brought together an ad hoc centrist coalition which included the Liberals, the earliest and most consistent supporters of the EEC. The anti-Europeans meanwhile spanned a wider ideological gulf. Powell on the right, with his nationalist convictions, had nonetheless urged his supporters to vote Labour in 1974 because of Heath's alleged surrender of parliamentary authority to Brussels. Powell's unlikely allies on the left, like Michael Foot, Barbara Castle and Tony Benn, spurned the EEC as 'a rich man's club' (though, in that case, some might have thought it reassuring that Britain was still eligible). The results showed a clear vote in favour of British membership. The yes vote was highest in economically prosperous parts of England, north or south, with support topping 76 per cent not only in Surrey and West Sussex but also North Yorkshire; even in Tyne and Wear 63 per cent voted yes. In Scotland, admittedly, several counties saw a no vote above 40 per cent, and in the Western Isles over 70 per cent voted no. Ulster too was not readily persuaded, with only a bare majority voting yes.

It was, however, difficult for opponents to argue with the two-to-one majority in the United Kingdom as a whole. No doubt the propaganda on either side was less important in producing this than gut feelings about national allegiance and where Britain's destiny now lay. As usual in Britain, class distinctions made a difference. Those who voted yes – by and large the wealthier and better-educated classes – were much more likely to have travelled abroad recently than manual workers.[1] But the steeply increasing numbers of new passports issued, as of international flights, testified that foreign travel, mainly to the Continent, was fast becoming commonplace for Britons – fostering their sense of identity as, at least, insular Europeans. Politically, the outcome that was achieved was a triumph for the tortuous strategy pursued by Wilson: some compensation for the extent to which his own stature had been diminished in the process. For Britons, the referendum was a unique constitutional departure, albeit one improvised for tactical considerations, but one with a lot to commend it. With hindsight Jenkins had surely been mistaken to choose Labour's adoption of this device as the occasion (hardly the cause) of his resignation as deputy leader. On a clear national choice which cut across conventional party divisions, the referendum settled the issue in an impressively decisive way.

---

1. The influence of continental cuisine, similarly class-based, may also have signified a relaxation of insular prejudices. Standards of British cooking, both in restaurants and in the home, in pubs and in pizza houses, underwent marked – and much-needed – improvement in the course of a generation. The seminal influence of Elizabeth David's *French Provincial Cooking* (1960), with its enormous sales as a Penguin paperback, deserves historical recognition.

## TWEEDLEDUM

There were to be two general elections in 1974; the narrow result of the first at once made the second inevitable. Labour was in a minority of thirty in the House of Commons. Its position was actually rather stronger than this would suggest because none of the minor parties which held the balance – Liberals, SNP, Plaid Cymru, SDLP, variegated Ulster Unionists – wanted Heath back. Wilson was therefore relied upon by Labour to manage the electoral situation as nicely as in 1964–6, so as achieve a solid majority at the opportune moment. This came, much as expected, in October; and Heath was again expected to lose. His call for a government of national unity was consistent with his post-1972 policies. Having underestimated Labour's showing in February, the opinion polls now overestimated it, quite considerably. Wilson secured his majority – but only by three seats overall: a replay of 1964 not 1966. Labour still only had 39 per cent of the national vote, though it was now clearly ahead of the Conservatives, unlike in February; and the Liberal poll fell slightly to 18 per cent.

This was a bad result for the Conservatives. If not quite as bad as they had feared, it still left Heath vulnerable as a leader who had lost three elections out of four; within months he found himself ousted. But it was hardly a good result for Labour. True, Labour returned more MPs from England than the Conservatives, unlike 1964. But the low turnout, combined with Labour's failure to match its opinion-poll ratings, suggests that its supporters felt a lack of commitment, in sharp contrast to the Attlee era. As a share of the whole electorate, the Labour vote had topped 40 per cent in 1951, even in defeat; it had been over 36 per cent as recently as 1966; it slumped well under 30 per cent in both elections in 1974. This was hardly a firm footing on which to found a Government, still less one which was faced with the question of whether the country remained governable.

The unions seemed to be in the saddle. Wilson proclaimed that Labour had a 'social contract' with the TUC that would replace conflict with cooperation. This concept was vacuous; it hardly enhanced Rousseau's posthumous reputation. The Government determined to do nothing to aggravate the already appalling state of industrial relations; the Conservative labour legislation was repealed. Seventy million days had been lost through industrial disputes in 1970–74; this was comparable with the famous 'labour unrest' of 1910–14 (80 million), though still only half as bad as 1920–24 (150 million). Compared with 1950–54, however, over seven times as many days had been lost. Taking a hint from Churchill, Wilson found the socialist equivalent of Walter Monckton in Michael Foot, who was made Secretary of State for Employment.

The authorized biographer of Bevan, an ex-editor of *Tribune*, Foot was the acknowledged standard-bearer of the 'soft left' in the Labour Party. He was well suited to his role as oilcan, taking appeasement of the trade unions to lengths which made Monckton seem like an industrial warrior. First the coal strike was ended by buying off the miners, to widespread relief. Their 'special case' promptly pushed up the 'going rate' which other unions now felt entitled to demand. Honouring the social contract, the Government abolished Heath's Pay Board. The trail was laid for an enormous wage explosion; union leaders simply lit the matches. Industrial earnings, which had gone up by 15 per cent in 1973, went up by 19 per cent in 1974, and 23 per cent in 1975. The number of days lost in strikes, by contrast, declined to a fraction of its previous level – a temporary respite, as it turned out.

Foot, at sixty, was a novice in the cabinet. Otherwise it was a reshuffle of the same old faces at the top: Callaghan at the Foreign Office, Healey at the Treasury, Crosland at the Department of the Environment. These formed the inner core; by comparison, the two stalwarts of the last Wilson cabinet, Jenkins and Castle, were losing ground. When Jenkins was sent back to the Home Office, because his European views ruled out the Foreign Office, he was patently unenthusiastic, displaying little of the creative flair which he had brought to the job in the previous decade. Europhiles were balanced against Euro-sceptics, and left against right, showing Wilson's old tactical adroitness.

Despite Wilson's personal distaste, he realized that he had to find a prominent post for Benn, the champion of the 'hard left' in the Labour Party. Indeed Benn now linked the anti-EEC cause with the left-wing agenda, proposing an 'alternative economic strategy'. At its centre was a massive extension of public ownership – he had talked of nationalizing the twenty-five largest companies in the UK – and tariffs to shelter Britain's manufacturing industries. Though there was some alarm in business circles when Benn was given the Department of Trade and Industry, armed with the powers of Heath's Industry Act, in fact his influence in the cabinet was curbed and checked, not least by a watchful prime minister.

Benn's real constituency was in the Labour movement itself. He was not alone in being disturbed by the gap between the heady rhetoric, which went down well at party conferences, and the generally sober performance of Labour in office. On Europe, on incomes policy, on trade-union reform, conference decisions amounted to a virtual repudiation of the record of the first Wilson Government. On the right, Jenkins sought to maintain consistency with Labour's governing ethic; on the left, Benn sought to remove the inconsistency by bringing the Government into line with conference and the National Executive, where an alliance between the left and the unions now generally prevailed. In the middle, Wilson, Callaghan, Healey, and now Crosland too, affected unconcern with all this ideology, intent on preserving Labourism and party unity through tactical compromises. The leaders of the two biggest unions, Jack Jones of the Transport Workers and Hugh Scanlon of the Engineers, were pivotal figures. They had called the shots over 'In Place of Strife' – 'Get your tanks off my lawn,' Wilson had protested – and this lesson in power politics had gone home. So long as they remained adamant that wage restraint formed no part of the social contract, the Government continued to drift for more than a year, unable or unwilling to choose between the very different options urged upon it.

What brought matters to a head was Europe, the submerged issue in many crises during the next twenty years. The referendum in June 1975 settled Britain's continued membership of the EEC; thus it ruled out the isolationist 'siege economy' which was essential to an alternative economic strategy. Benn, the architect of the referendum, was hoist with his own petard; he was immediately demoted by Wilson, already poised to pounce. Sent to the Department of Energy, Benn was marginalized, though he clung to his seat in the cabinet while signalling his frequent dissent to his supporters. The hard left henceforth felt cheated of influence over a Labour Government that had again betrayed socialism; but the soft left, eloquently cajoled by Foot, generally identified with the leadership. So, crucially, did most of the unions. Responding to an earlier initiative from Jones, in June the TUC came forward with a proposal for wage restraint.

The whole idea was anathema to the hard left, which argued that incomes policy meant simply doing the capitalists' work for them, whereas organized labour was axiomatically right in every pay dispute. What Jones was now saying, however, sounded like common sense to most ordinary trade unionists. The term incomes policy was avoided, but the Government grasped eagerly at a deal with the TUC for moderate flat-rate rises across the board, to break an inflationary spiral which had driven up the cost of living by 24 per cent in 1975. For the next three years, after a U-turn almost as striking as Heath's, the Government was to pursue a prices and incomes policy – avowed and statutory on prices, euphemistic and voluntary on wages.

Year by year, the Government painfully scaled one false summit after another, believing each time that the worst must surely be over. Wilson took advantage of one such deceptive interlude to resign as prime minister in April 1976, thinking he would get out at the top: an innocent enough ambition for a man of sixty, especially one whose health was not to prove robust. Like Talleyrand, Wilson had built up such a reputation for duplicity that a deep-laid plot was suspected even in his demise. In fact he had confided his intention to several people, including Callaghan, who had long been regarded as the likely successor. Other candidates in the first ballot of the election for the Labour leadership had either less appeal than Callaghan to essentially the same constituency (Healey and Crosland) or a narrower appeal: Jenkins to Europhile social democrats, Benn to the hard and Foot to the soft left. On a second ballot Callaghan therefore convincingly defeated Foot.

The new prime minister showed malice towards none – except his old antagonist Castle, who was ejected from the cabinet. Jenkins also soon departed, in his case with the much more congenial option of a four-year term as President of the European Commission. This left the prime minister unchallenged in a united cabinet (apart from Benn, of course). The main flaw in Callaghan's cabinet-making was to concern his former post as Foreign Secretary. Crosland was gratified to land the job, but within months he died from a sudden stroke. Anxious not to have another reshuffle, Callaghan promoted Crosland's deputy, David Owen, who was unrivalled as Foreign Secretary since Eden in 1935 for youth, good looks and (some muttered) overweening vanity.

Callaghan was in many ways an impressive figure as prime minister, no less wily than Wilson in the arts of party management, but less transparently wily. Perhaps as a result, Callaghan aroused less bitterness on the left. The hard left at least knew where they stood with him;

and the soft left were kept in line by the partnership he formed with Foot, as well as Healey, on economic and industrial strategy. Callaghan felt that his tenure of all four great cabinet offices had given him unrivalled lessons in the hard school of experience. Statesmanlike, certainly, he nonetheless did not come across as aloof, like Jenkins, or arrogant, like Healey; instead the avuncular good sense of 'Jim' – the title of a popular television programme, *Jim'll Fix It*, was sometimes appropriated – was widely thought reassuring. In the opinion polls his own approval rating consistently ran ahead of the Government's. Fidelity to socialist dogma, genuine or purported, was simply not his priority. In his persona as candid friend to the whole country, the new prime minister went to the Labour Party conference in September 1976 with the sober message: 'You cannot now, if you ever could, spend your way out of a recession.'

Whether this statement marks the end of the Keynesian era is a moot point. Certainly many arguments which purported to be Keynesian had lost their relevance in the context of the mid-1970s. The simple idea that wage increases boosted demand and thereby reduced unemployment, though seized upon by some trade-union leaders as a desperate alibi in justifying wage claims, now sounded like a recipe for intensifying inflation, not to mention unemployment. While it is right, however, to recognize 1976 as a turning point, it did not necessarily mean a turn down a road signposted 'monetarism'. As Chancellor, Healey was too case-hardened to become a naive convert to the doctrine that tight control of the money supply was the only way to beat inflation. The annual growth of M3, which had been around 10 per cent in the two years 1975–6, averaged 12 per cent in the next three years; thus, if anything, monetary policy became less restrictive after 1976. Neither Keynesian nor monetarist, Healey prided himself on steering a pragmatic course, in so far as he was allowed by the constant buffeting to which the British economy was subject.

The fact is that, from the end of 1973, the economy had nose-dived into recession for two full years: the first time that output had shown a significant year-on-year decline since the early 1930s. This was a worldwide phenomenon, triggered by the oil shock, which produced immense economic dislocations. It took time for the implications to become clear. In the short term, since the oil sheikhdoms were simply unable to absorb a sudden increase in their revenues, a lot of the money came back to London anyway, looking for borrowers. But though external borrowing was obviously necessary to tide over the huge deficits in both the balance of payments and the Budget, this could not go on for long. Ineluctably, the claims of both public and private spending in the United Kingdom would somehow have to be brought into line with the current output of its economy. Though there were signs of recovery in 1976, the whole trend of economic growth was shifted to a lower level. From 1960 to 1973 economic growth had averaged over 3 per cent a year. But in 1974–9 growth averaged only 1.4 per cent a year. Over five years, therefore, national output (or income) turned out to be, say, 10 per cent smaller than expected.

If oil was largely to blame for the Conservative Government's immediate problems in 1973–4, and for the intractable difficulties which confronted the Labour Government from 1974 to 1979, it was, of course, a cloud with a silver lining. With the North Sea deposits about to come on stream, it was a matter of waiting for the sun to come out. In 1974 the UK imported over 100 million tons of oil and exported less than 1 million; by 1980 imports and exports almost balanced, in quantity and price alike. At the Department of Energy, Benn found unwontedly wide support for his interventionist instincts, seeking to maintain a direct stake for the British Government through the British National Oil Corporation (BNOC) as well as through tax revenues from the international oil companies. Compared with industrial competitors like Japan and West Germany, which lacked their own oil, the UK seemed on the verge of its silver age as a manufacturing country. The short-term problem was to hold tight till the oil account, which had plunged the balance of payments into a deficit of 4.4 per cent of GDP in 1974, in due course produced a surplus – which happened in 1977–8.

Not only economically, but politically too, the prospect of a crock of gold at the end of the rainbow made all the interim expedients seem worthwhile. In five years, Healey introduced more budgets than Gladstone did in a lifetime, often two or three a year, as he grappled with one unfolding emergency after another. The greatest of these was the sterling crisis of September 1976. What was demoralizing was the simultaneous persistence of so many alarming indicators: over 1¼ million unemployed, a balance-of-payments deficit approaching 1 billion, annual inflation at 16 per cent, sterling down to $1.57, interest rate up to 15 per cent, and government spending apparently out of control, producing a record budget deficit. Confidence was now badly shaken, and the need to secure a loan from the International Monetary Fund

(IMF) brought the second great moment of reckoning for the Government.

The IMF crisis was full of drama. At one moment Healey was leaving Heathrow for an international meeting, at the next he had turned tail to speed to the Labour Party conference instead. Then there was a knockdown, drag-out fight in the cabinet, which went into virtually continuous session at one stage in its deliberations on the terms demanded for assistance by the IMF. It was more like 1945 than 1931. The fact was that, unless Labour opted for a siege economy, a loan was necessary, and the terms available were naturally dictated by the lenders. These centred on cuts in overall government spending; and the political logic of acceding to these terms was conceded even by those ministers who still disputed their economic logic. Of course, the Treasury could be relied upon to make its own case for cuts, as it always had; but it could now appeal to a widespread conviction that radical surgery had become necessary.

The creation of the budget deficit, under Barber, may have come through a relative decline on the revenue side; but its growth, under Healey, was basically due to increased government expenditure, up by 6 per cent of GDP in two years (almost exactly the extent of the deficit itself). This was not Healey's own doing; but he was the person sitting in the Chancellor's chair when the music stopped. Expansive government commitments had been undertaken, especially in the 1960s, in expectation of full employment, high growth and low inflation – conditions which no longer obtained. Economic growth could no longer be relied upon to foot the tax bill. Instead the burden of personal taxation, which had once been a middle-class grievance, was now felt by nearly everyone in employment. In 1949 a married man with two children on average earnings escaped income tax altogether; but by 1975 such a man crossed the tax threshold before his earnings reached even half the national average.

When unemployment had briefly touched 1 million under the Conservatives, it had provoked Heath's great U-turn; yet under Labour a level of 1 million became commonplace. In every year from 1976 to 1979 unemployment averaged over 5 per cent – double the level in any year in the 1950s and 1960s. This represented not only lost output and lost taxes but also, for the state, an unforeseen expenditure to support the unemployed and their families. In April 1976 Healey had already imposed substantial spending cuts; the effect of the IMF crisis was to produce a further round of cuts that December. By 1979 a major fall in expenditure, especially on housing and education, and a (smaller) fall in the overall deficit had been achieved.

None of these measures made the Government popular. Indeed after the IMF crisis Labour's standing plummeted to levels not seen since the post-devaluation slough of 1968–9. By-elections were lost at Walsall, Workington, Birmingham Stechford (Jenkins's old seat) and – most shocking of all – the previously rock-solid mining constituency of Ashfield in April 1977. These were not just psychological rebuffs; they robbed the Government of its parliamentary majority.

It survived thanks to the minority parties. With the eruption of a scandal implicating Thorpe, the Liberals had had to replace him with an untested leader: David Steel, still under forty (like David Owen, the new Foreign Secretary). Callaghan affected a fatherly cordiality towards Steel and, more to the point, saw that the Liberals did not want to fight a general election in the shadow of the Thorpe case. Conversely, in Liberal eyes, the Callaghan Government was now pursuing policies which they could support; and coalition politics appealed to them in principle. Here was the basis for the 'Lib-Lab pact', which lasted from the spring of 1977 until the autumn of 1978. Like Baldwin after 1931, Callaghan could use Liberal susceptibilities as an excuse for following a course he wanted to follow anyway; but he would not concede electoral reform. Devolution was another matter, since proposals for elected assemblies in both Scotland and Wales were already part of the Government's strategy for countering the Nationalist challenge. These two bills took vast amounts of parliamentary time, partly because of lukewarm support from Labour MPs; but until they were passed in the summer of 1978 they ensured that not only Liberal but also Nationalist MPs would keep Labour in office.

It was the twin problems of inflation and the trade unions which dominated the life of the Government. Ideally the one could be solved through the agency of the other: by trade-union cooperation in making a prices-and-incomes policy work. Foot certainly did what he could to produce a friendly climate, not only repealing the Industrial Relations Act, but also passing his own labour legislation which, for the first time, gave trade unions significantly greater powers than they had enjoyed since the 1906 Trades Disputes Act, especially over the closed shop. A conciliation service was also set up. Yet the number of days lost in industrial disputes shot up in 1977, and stayed up in 1978, while 1979 was to be one of the worst years of the century – even worse than 1972.

The initial success of Labour's incomes policy, in winning consent for restraint, thus gave way to renewed industrial friction, threatening the policy itself. In 1976–7 rises in industrial earnings were held well below those in the cost of living, which was slower to decelerate. Thus the left was right when it claimed that living standards were being cut. Avoiding an overall cut, however, was not an option; the choice was really between managing the effects of economic decline through a prices-and-incomes policy or letting unemployment do the job via the free market. Hence the tacit alliance that emerged between the trade-union left and the monetarist right in defence of market forces in wage negotiations, unfettered by Government intervention. Moreover, incomes policy was a wasting asset; under Callaghan as under Heath, the crunch came after a couple of years of reasonable success. The retirement of Jack Jones, on whose industrial statesmanship the Government had come to rely, was another blow; his successor as leader of the TGWU, Moss Evans, championed free collective bargaining. In 1978 the rise in the RPI was only half that of the previous year; at 8 per cent it was the lowest for six years; but the problem of consolidating lower expectations of inflation on a long-term basis depended on union reactions in the 1978–9 wage round.

Trade-union membership had long fluctuated around 10 million; but in the mid-1970s it surged up, reaching a peak of over 13 million in 1979. Half the total workforce was now unionized. The TGWU, with 2 million members, remained the giant, followed by the Engineers with 1.5 million and the General and Municipal Workers with nearly a million. These remained the big three, as they had been since 1945; but whereas the Miners and the Railwaymen used to be next in size, there had been a shift from the traditional industrial unions to the sectors of fast expansion in white-collar jobs, especially in the public sector. In 1979 the National Association of Local Government Officers (Nalgo) and the National Union of Public Employees (NUPE) together had a total of 1.4 million members, more than three times as many as the combined membership of the NUM and NUR. Moreover, public employees were in the front line of industrial action (as it was still quaintly termed). One reason was that incomes policy had been tightly monitored for them, whereas 'wage drift' in practice pushed earnings in private-sector manufacturing firms above the norms calculated on basic rates of pay. Another reason why public-sector employees were often surprisingly militant was because they were immediately vulnerable to cuts in public spending. Like many proverbially ferocious animals, they bit back when they were attacked.

This was the making of the 'winter of discontent' in 1978–9. The Government had come up with a pay norm set at 5 per cent, from the first an unrealistically ambitious target. Moreover Callaghan, at the last moment, backed off from a general election in October 1978, as most people had come to expect. Buoyed up by the better economic news, Labour had been neck and neck with the Conservatives in the opinion polls for nearly a year. By March 1979, however, the Conservatives had an unassailable lead. What had occurred in the meantime was a collapse of the Government's policy in face of a series of damaging strikes. Not only had the TUC decided to flout the 5 per cent norm: the Labour Party conference also rejected it, leaving the Government in pitched battle with its own nominal supporters. First some key industrial unions, led – or not led, as cabinet ministers bitterly claimed – by Moss Evans at the TGWU, smashed the norm with big settlements; then the public-sector unions tried to catch up, with well-publicized strikes by NHS workers and, in particular, dustmen. The image of uncollected rubbish, piled high in the streets, was one which the public was not to forget, if only because the Conservative Party obligingly kept reminding them. In February 1979 the Gallup poll, which had put the Conservatives 5 per cent behind Labour only three months previously, now put them 20 points ahead.

The Government was on its last legs. Yet though the winter of discontent provided the fundamental cause of its downfall, the immediate cause was a nationalist backlash. At the end of March 1979 the Government lost a vote of confidence in the Commons (by one vote) because at the beginning of March the SNP had lost its reason for keeping Labour in office. With the end of the Lib-Lab pact, the Government had in practice been relying upon the SNP not to turn against it: at least not until the long-awaited referendum on Scottish devolution took place on 1 March. Wales voted on the same day and, as was no surprise, rejected devolution by four to one. The Scottish vote narrowly favoured the devolution proposal. The majority, however, was concentrated in industrial Clydeside, and areas currently enjoying prosperity from the North Sea voted no – as though telling Glasgow, 'It's *our* oil'. Worse still for the SNP, whereas 33 per cent of the whole Scottish electorate voted yes, an amendment had been inserted into the devolution legislation requiring support from 40 per cent. This served to abort the referendum. Within the month the SNP had joined Conservative and Liberal MPs in bringing down a Government itself elected by only 28 per cent of the electorate.

Under the most unpromising conditions, at a time not of his choosing, Callaghan nonetheless fought a plucky electoral campaign, clawing back some lost ground. For several months the Conservatives had been using a poster, produced by their new advertising agency, Saatchi & Saatchi; it showed a snaking dole queue under the caption 'Labour Isn't Working'. True, unemployment had stood at 1.6 million as recently as August 1978 and was still 1.3 million at the time of the general election. Whether the Conservatives could bring it down, however, was no longer what mattered most. Jobs had yielded to prices as the salient issue; and inflation was again back in double figures. Above all, the winter of discontent had changed voters' views as to which party was better able to deal with the unions. In six months this question had ceased to be a liability for the Conservatives and become a major asset. Even so, had 13 million trade unionists loyally voted Labour, none of this would have mattered; but in fact one in three of trade-union members now voted Conservative. Callaghan was right to sense that the election was slipping away from him, less because of particular campaign issues than a sea-change in the public mood. It was time for a fresh start.

# I I

# Rejoice?
## 1979–90

## GENDER

In 1975 the Conservative Party elected a woman as its leader. Women had, of course, been eligible as parliamentary candidates since 1918; there had been equal suffrage since 1928; and women had long played an active part in local government. Before the Second World War, however, a woman as a parliamentary candidate remained an oddity: less than one in twenty of all candidates, and with an even smaller chance of being elected. Most women stood as Liberal or Labour. Yet the Conservative triumph in 1931 produced the record number of 15 women MPs, because 13 out of 16 Conservative women candidates were elected. Since women candidates were less likely than men to be selected by their party in safe seats, the landslide helped them here; conversely in 1945, 21 out of the 24 women MPs were Labour. From 1950 to 1979 the number of women standing for the two major parties fluctuated around forty for Labour and thirty for the Conservatives – in a good year. But in a poor year like 1966 the number of women the two parties put up between them (51) was even smaller than in the 1930s, though the fact that in 1966 just over half (26) were elected was some compensation.

Still, Margaret Thatcher was one of only 7 women, as against 246 men, sitting on the Conservative benches in the 1966 parliament. She had got there through remarkable determination. The daughter of a grocer in the Lincolnshire town of Grantham, Margaret Roberts had gone from grammar school to Somerville College, Oxford, to read chemistry at the end of the Second World War. Resisting the egalitarian political tide of that era, she was more impressed by the polemic against planning and the welfare state in F. A. Hayek's *The Road to Serfdom* (1944). The truly formative political influence upon her remained that of her father, with his homely adages about thrift and hard work which had bridged his own evolution from Methodism and Liberalism to a locally influential role as a Conservative alderman. Marrying Denis Thatcher, a businessman who prospered through a family paint company which took him into oil at a propitious moment, was literally the making of Mrs Thatcher. It gave her not only the name under which she achieved fame, and a supportive spouse who enabled her to combine having children (twins) with pursuing her career, but also enough money to make all of this possible. Nonetheless, she was justly perceived as the grocer's daughter rather than the millionaire's wife.

That Margaret Thatcher proved to be an unusual woman should have come as no surprise. She had to make her way in a man's world. She did so conscious of the fact that clubbable Tory grandees dismissed her as 'that woman', as much through social as sexist condescension. Eventually she was able to turn this situation in her own favour, by projecting a populist appeal to the thwarted subaltern class of Conservative loyalists who recognized her as one of their own. In this respect gender drew the sting from some of the status disabilities which faced an outsider; whereas Heath had found trouble in being accepted into the club, Thatcher at least knew that she never could be and was thus spared the trouble. The remaking of the Conservative Party was to be part of her political achievement, finally undermining the long ascendancy of a traditional elite, part of whose traditionalism rested on assumptions about appropriate gender roles.

Under the prevailing circumstances, it took extraordinary luck to bring Thatcher to power. Admittedly, she was bound to be given a front-bench role after 1966: not only because of her incisive mind, or her capacity for hard work, but because her party had so few alternative options in finding at least one presentable woman. The Conservatives had never had a woman politician of the stature of Barbara Castle, self-evidently one of the inner core of the Wilson Government; and Shirley Williams, five years Thatcher's junior, was currently more often mentioned as a potential prime minister. If Thatcher entered Heath's cabinet as the 'token woman', however, within a year or two she emerged as a formidable minister, capable of fighting for her own department both in the cabinet and outside. What transformed her career was a combination of Heath's bad luck, or bad management, and her own facility in escaping from the wreckage.

That Heath himself would have to go was apparent after October 1974, except to himself. That the former Health minister Sir Keith

Joseph might make a challenge for the leadership briefly seemed possible; in opposition he had stepped into Powell's shoes as the right-wing standard-bearer but, like Powell, found his newly voiced views repudiated as extremist. Temperamentally unfitted to lead, Joseph found his métier as, if not quite the first, the foremost Thatcherite. That Whitelaw, the loyal Heathite, ultimately would prevail in a leadership election – the system allowed for several ballots – was generally assumed. But what happened in February 1975 was that Thatcher boldly stood against Heath and polled more votes; by which time the momentum behind her candidacy was enough to give her a convincing victory over Whitelaw when he was eventually free to come forward in the second ballot.

Rather to their surprise, therefore, Conservative MPs chose a woman, and one of whom they generally knew rather little. There was soon talk of the party having been 'hijacked', once unmistakable signs emerged that the new leader had embarked on the course charted by Joseph, whose damascene revelation of the real meaning of Conservatism had been prominently proclaimed in a series of speeches. Thatcher differed from him, however, in being a fully fledged political animal: never risking an exposition of doctrinaire economic liberalism when she could instead, like Adam Smith before her, appeal to the sort of prudent, domestic, bill-paying, debt-avoiding, book-balancing maxims which it was folly to ignore in a great kingdom. Thatcher's own twist was to invoke the supreme common sense of the housewife, a role in which this highly professional career woman could cast herself without any apparent sense of incongruity.

Thatcher was a political opportunist in the best sense: always quick to seize the opportunities which came her way and exploit them. When the Russians pejoratively dubbed her the Iron Lady, she took it as a compliment. She turned her lonely eminence as a woman into a unique asset. She exploited her femininity, teasing and coaxing favourite colleagues, teasing and upbraiding others, larded with a forthrightness which many of them had never before encountered. She carried a capacious handbag, from which pertinent documents could instantly be retrieved; the fact that it became a personal trademark was not only a boon to cartoonists but an indication of her own nose for public relations. She made no secret of her strong convictions, which she contrasted with the weakness implied by consensus. She had no time for socialism but could respect the old-fashioned socialist convictions of a

parliamentary opponent like Michael Foot; her real contempt was reserved for those Conservatives whom she called 'wet'.

Yet Thatcher also prided herself on proceeding with womanly caution, ruminating that, while her predecessor might have lost three elections, she would only be given the chance to lose one. She learnt from
her failings as leader of the Opposition: if her voice gave an opening for
sexist categorization as shrill, she took lessons to lower its pitch; if her
fussy clothes stereotyped her as a suburban matron, she took advice on
'power dressing' to create a strong, simple image. As prime minister she
came to radiate authority; but before 1979 Conservative Party managers were worried whether Britain was ready for a woman at the top.
For a couple of years she ran well behind Callaghan and her own party
in the opinion polls, and, luckily for her, it took the winter of discontent to put her ahead.

There is more than one paradox in the fact that the first woman
prime minister did so little for other women, and that, under a woman,
the Conservative Party relinquished a sixty-year electoral advantage
among women. While this 'gender gap' cannot be precisely quantified
in the era before opinion sampling, its long-standing nature is consistent with the demonstrable fact that in every general election from 1945
to 1979 women were more likely than men to vote Conservative. So
were older people; but the fact that there were more women among the
old does not explain this advantage, just exaggerates it. In 1955, while
only 47 per cent of men voted Conservative, 55 per cent of women did
so. The gender gap can thus plausibly be considered the reason for the
Conservative electoral ascendancy in the 1950s; but not for that in the
1980s. For the gap fairly steadily narrowed from 8 per cent to only 2 or
3 per cent in the 1970s. Furthermore, in Thatcher's great electoral triumphs of 1983 and 1987, women were, for the first time, no more likely
to vote Conservative than men. This can be read in more ways than one,
of course: as demonstrating the disappearance of male prejudice
against a woman leader, or as showing that women now voted 'just like
men'.

The political gender gap was surely closing because the social and
economic gender gaps had been closing too, giving men and women a
much more closely comparable experience of life and work. During the
first half of the twentieth century women's employment had shown
little proportionate increase, despite two world wars; indeed, the slump
in the 1930s had produced a substantial fall. In 1951 women comprised

31 per cent of the workforce, barely more than in 1911. This proportion had passed 35 per cent by 1970; but the sharp increase was to come over the next twenty years. Since women workers generally provided services of one kind or another, the economic explanation lies in the long-term growth in the service sector as a whole. From the time of the Second World War, a range of secretarial, clerical and sales positions replaced domestic service as the major source of employment for women. So a structural change in the economy saw traditionally male jobs displaced by conventionally female jobs.

The net result was a significant change in the composition of the British labour force. In 1975 total employment in metals and mechanical engineering – the largest industrial classification – was 4.2 million, compared to 1.5 million in banking, insurance and finance. By 1990 both figures were around 2.7 million, and were dwarfed by the 4.8 million employees classified under wholesale, retail, hotels and catering. Moreover the dramatic shift which took place in this period was further accentuated by the onset of high unemployment, which naturally hit the declining manufacturing sector much harder than the buoyant service sector. In 1990 the statistics for the total labour force, counting everyone available for work, showed that 43 per cent were women; but women workers were now more likely than men actually to have jobs – especially part-time jobs. Two women worked part-time for every three full-time; and whereas there were now a million fewer full-time jobs than in 1979, there were a million more part-time jobs. The net effect was that, by 1990, 11 million women were actually in employment, as against 11.7 million men – fast approaching statistical parity.

Parity of status and earnings, of course, was another matter. The statutory requirement for equal pay, passed in 1970 and implemented in 1975, was hardly a final victory; but this battle was made easier to fight, case by case, once the Sex Discrimination Act (1975) had established the Equal Opportunities Commission to monitor fair treatment. In 1970 women's average weekly earnings were, as they had long been, almost exactly half those of men in both manual and non-manual occupations; within ten years they rose to about 60 per cent. The rise in pay was associated with a rise in the number of women trade unionists to nearly 4 million in 1979, a rate of increase over the previous ten years twice as fast as for men. But further improvement was small after 1980; allowing for the fact that men worked longer hours, female pay rates seemed to be stuck at about two-thirds of the male average. Since an overt gender-based differential was now illegal, the reason lay in covert discrimination between gender-related skills and qualifications.

Professional qualifications for women usually depended on access to higher education, where a gender gap long remained entrenched. The proportion of full-time university students who were women had reached 28 per cent in the 1920s and actually declined by 3 or 4 per cent during the next thirty years. Until the Robbins era, a boy remained twice as likely as a girl to gain a university place within any social class. Conversely, in the subsequent expansion, while the number of men admitted by universities more than doubled in twenty years, the number of women quadrupled, with over 40 per cent of admissions by 1980, and rising. It was only in the 1980s that Oxford and Cambridge became fully coeducational, when the last male colleges agreed to admit women too – overwhelmingly from the same social and educational background as the male students, as it turned out.

The erosion of the gender bias in higher education showed that girls from professional families were at last getting the same treatment as their brothers. It is hardly surprising that women graduates should have gone on to demand the same treatment in society, and become prominent in feminist pressure-group activity, which notably revived in the 1960s. It did so, moreover, within a cultural context prominently shaped by articulate women.

The role of unacknowledged legislators, claimed for poets by Shelley, was exemplified by a striking cohort of women novelists, many of them graduates. Iris Murdoch was already a fine role model, successfully pursuing an academic career at Oxford as a philosopher during the years which saw the publication of thought-provoking novels like *The Bell* (1958) and *A Severed Head* (1961). By the time of her prize-winning books *The Black Prince* (1973) and *The Sacred and Profane Love Machine* (1974), she was perhaps the most respected English novelist of her generation.[1] Twenty years younger, Margaret Drabble made her mark very young, initially with *A Summer Birdcage* (1962), *The Garrick Year* (1964) and *The Millstone* (1966), showing confident

---

1. Her fame now eclipsed that of Angus Wilson, six years her senior: a latter-day E. M. Forster both in his sexual orientation and in the civilized liberal ironies of novels like *Anglo-Saxon Attitudes* (1956) and *The Old Men at the Zoo* (1961). When Wilson died in 1991 all his novels were out of print.

Oxbridge scholarship girls from the north making their own terms as young women who expected doors to open for them (rather than be opened by men). In their own right they now entered a sophisticated metropolitan world, of which people like the Denhams, in *Jerusalem the Golden* (1967), had long been been privileged denizens. Her sister, A. S. Byatt, like Murdoch, laid the foundations of a career as both an academic and a creative writer: an experience later to be distilled in her major novel *Possession* (1990). Angela Carter established her name with the publication of *The Magic Toyshop* (1967), with a girl's sensibility memorably informing its mysteriously unfolding themes. Fay Weldon was to disclose a hard-hitting feminist agenda in a string of novels like *Down Among the Women* (1971), *Remember Me* (1976) and *The Life and Loves of a She-Devil* (1984), which inimitably spiced realism with surrealism.

Women's liberation became the cry in the 1960s. Inspired partly by developments in the USA, and with a fearless champion in Germaine Greer, whose book *The Female Eunuch* (1970) became a best-seller, 'women's lib' meant claiming privileges which had long been enjoyed by men. Sexual liberty was certainly one of these, and since heterosexual activity required male partners, this was an area where male resistance was least likely to be encountered. Symbolic bra-burning had its innocent ripple-effect in a freedom of dress, especially among young women, which became part of the image of the 'swinging sixties'. Yet some of the protagonists of women's lib soon came to question the easy assumption that sexual inequalities could simply be willed away, least of all by such existential gestures.

Over the next twenty years, feminism was sometimes appropriated by militantly prescriptive campaigns, in which sexual warfare was the continuation of gender politics by other means. In a less sectarian spirit, recognition of the deep-seated nature of gender differences, requiring mutual understanding between men and women, became part of a feminist agenda. This spoke to fundamental problems, which were not susceptible to simple solutions like equal pay legislation. Women earned less in employment partly because roles traditionally associated with men – whether displaying physical prowess or exerting authority over others – remained generally more highly esteemed, whereas tasks requiring traditional female skills – from manual dexterity to sympathetic personal relations – were often less well rewarded. Moreover, at all levels of education, women seeking employment in better-paid jobs, with better prospects, found themselves not only competing against men but doing so under conventions which, having been instituted by men, implicitly favoured them. Highly qualified women still encountered barriers, both visible and invisible, leading some to speak of a 'glass ceiling' which effectively kept women out of the top jobs, or of a 'golden pathway' to promotion, informally signposted for and by men. In politics pressure-group methods had some effect in rectifying this situation. By 1992, the number of women standing for parliament easily set new records, not only overall and in the aggregate number elected (60 MPs), but also for each of the parties individually, with 144 Liberal Democrat, 138 Labour and 59 Conservative female candidates, over twice as many as in 1979, and clearly set to increase further.

Not only in the House but in the home, historic assumptions about gender roles increasingly came into question. Changes in patterns of employment were challenging the stereotyped distinction between the breadwinner and the housewife, living as a married couple, with a well-understood division of labour within the household. One official adaptation to new norms came with Nigel Lawson's reform of personal taxation, heralded in 1988, so that a man was no longer required to be responsible for his wife's tax return. More important, if more difficult to chart, were informal changes in everyday behaviour, like responsibility for household chores and child-rearing when both partners were holding down jobs. The 'new man' could certainly be seen (and sometimes made sure he was seen) taking his share of traditionally female tasks. This happened not only in trendy professional enclaves – Mark Boxer had long since caricatured Camden Town in his strip cartoon *Life and Times in NW1* – but increasingly throughout the country, not least in areas of high male unemployment. It became perfectly normal for men to push prams or change babies, shop in supermarkets or even cook the dinner – especially, perhaps, for guests. Indications are that the brunt of everyday chores continued to fall on women. In 1984 nine out of ten married women still coped alone with the washing and ironing; seven out of ten with household cleaning; five out of ten with shopping (though only one out of sixteen with domestic repairs). Such patterns increased the stress on women in responding to the dual pressures of their homes and careers.

The institution of marriage was in the process of redefinition. The average age of first marriage, after falling steadily for sixty years, started to rise again after 1970; by 1990 most brides in first marriages were over twenty-five and grooms over twenty-seven, levels not seen since the inter-war years. In those days, of course, it had been scandalous to 'live in sin', whereas fifty years later it was not unusual for couples to cohabit, often as a prelude to subsequent marriage. An increasing number of unmarried couples made a deliberate choice to have children. This was the main reason for a rise in the illegitimacy rate, which had crept up from a historic low of around 3 per cent of all births before the First World War to around 5 per cent after the Second. It was after 1960 that it began rising sharply, to about 10 per cent in the 1970s, and soaring to 25 per cent of all births by 1988. By then, admittedly, 70 per cent of births outside marriage were registered in the joint names of the father and mother, suggesting stable two-parent relationships. Undeniably, however, the trend towards illegitimacy also signalled an increase in the number of women bringing up children on their own, as did the increasing prevalence of divorce, since the ex-wife was usually the custodian of young children.

Before the Second World War, there had been roughly one divorce decree for every hundred marriages annually; after it, more like one for every ten, fewer in the 1950s but rising in the 1960s. The Divorce Law Reform Act of 1969, which replaced the concept of a matrimonial offence (usually adultery) with that of the breakdown of a marriage, was a response to rising pressure for easier divorce. Within a couple of years the number of divorces doubled, and during the 1980s there were over 160,000 decrees a year, not far short of half the number of marriages taking place. Divorce usually meant a drop in the standard of living of all concerned, for the obvious reason that two households needed support instead of one: a problem accentuated if either partner established a second family. Ex-wives caring for dependent children generally found their income worst hit. For them divorce remained literally a poor option. But at least it was now conceivable for them to escape from the trap of a failed marriage, especially since legislative changes in the early 1970s established a spouse's equal right to the property of a marriage and effectively gave wives tenure of the matrimonial home. Thus, especially in an era of fast-appreciating house prices, divorced men were more likely to lose their prime capital asset: a neat reversal of Victorian presumptions about real property. To say that divorce simply became easier is a misnomer; and whether it produced happier marriages, by dissolving more of the unhappy ones, is hard to know. Still, with increasing longevity, it took the higher divorce rates of the 1980s to get the average duration of marriage back to what it had been in the 1820s.


## THATCHERISM

There is something in the view that Thatcherism, like Bevanism, had to be invented by others to legitimate an essentially personal leadership style. The term came into use in the early 1980s, pejoratively introduced by the journal *Marxism Today*, but given favourable connotations by Nigel Lawson, formerly a high-powered financial journalist and now an increasingly influential minister in formulating economic strategy. His definition was a mixture of free markets, monetary control, privatization and cuts in both spending and taxes – combined with a populist revival of the 'Victorian values' of self-help and nationalism. The part played by Powell in preparing the ground for Thatcherism is apparent. So is the proselytizing activity on behalf of Hayekian economic liberalism, undertaken over many years by the Institute of Economic Affairs; and Keith Joseph played an important role in founding the Centre for Policy Studies in 1974, bringing a monetarist approach into the mainstream of Conservative policy-making. Thatcher's own indispensable achievement was to mobilize sufficient support to make Thatcherism the agenda of government.

Certainly Thatcher was an inconsistent ideologue. She was to disappoint the principled exponents of Thatcherism in her own cabinet when general doctrines about government non-interference clashed with her restless incapacity to refrain from interfering – because she felt she knew best. Though some of her ministers understandably saw her as upholding the tenets of nineteenth-century liberalism, its cosmopolitan outlook was literally foreign to her; when it came to nationalism, she was an old-fashioned Tory. She freely invoked the name of Churchill, while turning her back on many of the guiding principles in domestic policy adopted by his two Governments. Her convictions were temperamental rather than ideological. She made up policy as she went along and used off-the-cuff public utterances to bounce her colleagues into accepting initiatives that had not been previously agreed.

The Thatcher Government had a comfortable majority of over 40 in the 1979 parliament. The Conservatives had polled 44 per cent of the national vote to Labour's 37 per cent; the Liberals, on 14 per cent, had declined since 1974 but still saved 11 seats. The Conservatives had only half as many seats as Labour in either Wales or Scotland (despite picking up a few seats in the wake of the Nationalist subsidence). Moreover, much the same was true of the north of England, where there were 107 Labour MPs to 53 Conservatives. Here was a Government representing the prosperous south of England rather than the regions prone to high unemployment in manufacturing industry. This gave it some degree of electoral insulation in pursuing policies which, it was generally accepted, were likely to increase unemployment, at least in the short term.

Thatcher did not feel strong enough to exclude the leading 'wets', like Sir Ian Gilmour, Peter Walker and Francis Pym, from her cabinet. Whitelaw was in another category. First as Home Secretary and later as Lord President, he served Thatcher as he had served Heath before her, with impeccable loyalty and honest advice which was all the more important in sustaining her since it came from someone who was, at the very least, suspected of being damp. Heath himself was half-heartedly offered the Washington embassy, which he promptly refused, preferring to skulk (some said sulk) on the backbenches. But another of his former confidantes, Lord Carrington (sixth baron), was made Foreign Secretary. Such appointments helped defuse trouble in the party; by the time Heath spoke up against Thatcher, she was firmly in the saddle. The heavyweight support for Thatcherism in the cabinet initially came from Sir Geoffrey Howe, a dour but able lawyer who became Chancellor of the Exchequer; and, of course, from Joseph, who became Secretary of State for Industry. Committed Thatcherites like Nigel Lawson, Norman Tebbit, Cecil Parkinson and Nicholas Ridley had to bide their time in junior ministerial posts, before being shuffled into the cabinet, generally in place of ejected 'wets'.

In making appointments, administrative as well as ministerial, Thatcher became notorious for demanding whether the candidate was 'one of us'. She wanted to be served by people who believed in the mission of her Government, and she was initially suspicious of civil servants who had spent the best years of their lives in patching up the post-war consensus. She was to turn 10 Downing Street into a fortress, staffed by loyalists on whom she could implicitly rely. Professor Alan Walters, an unwavering monetarist, became a trusted economic adviser; Charles Powell became an indispensable private secretary from 1984. Bernard Ingham – an ex-socialist, like a number of born-again

Thatcherites – was throughout her premiership a uniquely influential press secretary, with a carefully maintained, blunt-speaking Yorkshire mien which translated policy issues and personal conflicts into a populist idiom. Ministers learned to dread a personally hostile, or insufficiently supportive, press briefing from Downing Street, as an early warning of the withdrawal of prime-ministerial favour. Through carefully culti- vated links with the popular press, Thatcherite propaganda reached a down-market constituency, traditionally Labour. The fact that Rupert Murdoch's *Sun*, Ingham's favoured tabloid, was a latter-day reincarna- tion of the TUC's own *Daily Herald*, combined with the fact that by 1979 its circulation of 4 million put it ahead of its Labour rival, the *Daily Mirror*, heralded a new epoch. In that Thatcherite dawn, it was bliss when the *Sun* came out for the Tories.

Despite Thatcher's suspicion of the Heathite Jim Prior as a 'wet', intent on industrial appeasement, he was given the Department of Employment, charged with implementing trade-union reform. The winter of discontent had served to harden public attitudes but had come too late in the day to upset Prior's plan of walking softly. This was a boon for the Government since the Prior Employment Act found widespread public support in 1980 for its minimal programme of out- lawing 'secondary' picketing (not at the place of work), and requiring a high level of workers' approval for a closed shop. Once this had been passed successfully, there was scope for further legislation to tighten its provisions, especially after Prior, increasingly isolated in the cabinet, was replaced by the uncompromising Tebbit, impatient to wield the big stick against the unions. The Tebbit Act in 1982 was a frontal attack on the closed shop and further restricted the scope of industrial action, while making unions legally liable for infringements. Incremental legis- lation over the next few years went on to require membership ballots, not only in the regular election of union officials and in sanctioning the existence of political funds, but also before any strike action. This highly effective fabian process avoided Heath's error of trying to do everything at once, while ultimately tying down the trade unions with a thousand silken cords.

A steady rise in unemployment also weakened the unions. During the 1980s their membership was to fall by 3 million, with half of this loss concentrated in the two years 1981–3. But at the outset the Thatcher Government was wary about which battles it would fight. The Conservatives had given a campaign pledge to honour whatever pay increases were recommended by the commission on public-sector pay, set up under Labour. This fuelled a pay explosion in 1979–80. The most significant confrontation the Thatcher Government faced – or refused to face, until it was ready – was with the the NUM, which bulked large in Tory demonology for supposedly bringing down Heath. Conscious of the political stakes here, Thatcher backed away from a conflict in the coal industry in 1981, preferring to buy off trouble for the moment. One way or another, until 1984 there was continuous improvement in the strike record. Again, the basic reason was unemployment.

The foundation of the Government's economic policy was the Medium-Term Financial Strategy (MTFS), adopted by Howe as Chancellor but drafted by Lawson as Financial Secretary to the Treasury. It sought to apply a monetarist approach to the problem of managing the economy, making the control of inflation the prime target. Once inflation was under control, it was argued, employment would look after itself, aided by reforms on the supply side of the economy that would liberate private enterprise from a dead weight of state intervention and onerous taxation. This was, as Conservative policy statements had proclaimed, the 'right approach' to the problem and, in adopting it, the Government needed determination. The secret of success lay in teaching the markets, not least the labour market, that financial discipline would be maintained, come what may. If only a set amount of money was available, inflation would thereby be contained, and inflationary wage settlements would simply lead to particular groups of workers pricing themselves out of jobs, or particular employers pricing themselves out of business. Some fall in output, or rise in unemployment, had to be envisaged as part of a learning process; but a couple of years after the money supply had been cut back, inflation would duly fall.

This simple theory was less easy to apply in practice. Immediate cuts in income tax were pushed through in the 1979 Budget as an earnest of the Government's commitment to fostering supply-side incentives. Basic rate came down from 33 to 30 per cent; the top rate from 83 to 60 per cent. To pay for this, Value Added Tax (VAT) was raised from 8 per cent to a full rate of 15 per cent. Here was the promised shift from direct to indirect taxes; here was a regressive redistribution of the tax burden, skewed in favour of the better-off; here too was an immediate stimulus to inflation, helping push the RPI up towards 20 per cent. But this was a Government unafraid to make things worse in order to make them better. The strategy remained that of squeezing inflation out of the economy by monetary means. Targets were announced for restricting the growth of the money supply (£M3) to progressively lower levels. Yet the Government had simultaneously robbed itself of the traditional battery of techniques for influencing the domestic money supply because, in pursuit of free markets, it had abolished exchange controls. It was left with the blunt instrument of interest rates.

Base rate went up as high as 17 per cent in the first year but £M3 still wildly overshot its range; much the same happened in the next year. If the targets were to be reached, interest rates would presumably have to go higher still. Yet they had already cut a swathe through British industry and, on the back of the oil boom, had at one point pushed up the parity of sterling to US$2.50 and 5 DM – further reinforcing the difficulties of exporters. Even dogmatic monetarists, like Lawson and Walters, sensed that enough was enough, and turned on £M3 as being the wrong target (though it continued to be published in different guises). What the Government opted for instead was a fiscal squeeze, which was consistent with its own emphasis on rolling back the public sector and cutting the Budget deficit.

Conservative policy was to control and reduce public spending by imposing cash limits, rather than planning the volume of services; thus if inflation proved higher than expected this would reduce services (admittedly in a rather arbitrary way) rather than increase expenditure. Public spending as a whole was in deficit by 5 per cent of GDP in 1979–80, rising to 6 per cent the next year. This rise may have upset the plan for real cuts but it was consistent with the structure of public spending in a slump, since the main reason was the increase in social-security payments due to high unemployment. While other types of social expenditure had peaked in the mid-1970s, the social-security bill continued to rise as a proportion of GDP. In the mid-1980s it absorbed 12 per cent of GDP, compared with 8 per cent a decade earlier. Hence the paradox that, for seven years under Thatcher, public expenditure continued to take a bigger share of national income than it had in 1979.

Howe responded in his 1981 budget, not only by cutting deeper on the spending side but also by putting up a whole range of taxes (except income tax, of course), in a determined effort to reduce the deficit by 2 per cent of GDP, which he succeeded in doing. The remarkable thing is that he set out to do this in the middle of the deepest slump for fifty years. It was an unmistakable rebuff to Keynesianism – except in one respect: its reliance on fiscal rather than monetary policy. Monetarism had thus become a mask for deflationary policies which abandoned the priority given to employment in post-war economic management. But as a means of tackling inflation, Howe's methods were vindicated. The fact that the £M3 targets were nominally met by 1983 was beside the point; this relied as much on continually revising the targets upward, regardless of the hypothetical effect upon inflation, as on bringing £M3 itself down to the levels originally projected. Yet inflation did fall steadily from 18 per cent in 1980 to 4.5 per cent in 1983.

The real reason was the impact of the slump itself. By the autumn of 1981 unemployment was 2.8 million, double the level in May 1979; and in the winter of 1982–3 it reached 3.3 million. There was an actual decline in the numbers in employment in each of these years; by 1983 over 2 million jobs had been lost. Most of the jobs lost were in manufacturing industry; most of them were full-time; most of them were held by men; most of them were in unionized plants; most of them were in the traditional industrial areas. Together these probabilities reinforced long-standing geographical and social differences, of which the most striking was between north and south. North, in this sense, stood for Scotland and Wales as well as the industrial north of England; and south mainly for the south-east of the country, a sort of greater Greater London which was spared the worst of the recession.

Measured from peak to peak of the economic cycle, growth was only 0.6 per cent in 1980–83, barely a quarter of what had been normal since the Second World War. In 1980 the economy shrank by a full 2 per cent, an even bigger contraction than in 1974; and 1981 was hardly better. This was the moment when the Thatcher Government showed its mettle. Predictions of a U-turn had been frequent. 'You turn if you want to,' Thatcher had told the Conservative Party conference in October 1980. 'The lady's not for turning.' After the Howe budget in March 1981, they knew that she meant it. Riots in deprived inner-city areas like Brixton in London and Toxteth in Liverpool likewise did not shake her. In September 1981 her cabinet reshuffle brought Thatcherites like Lawson, Parkinson and Tebbit into key positions, exiled Prior to Northern Ireland, and sacked two grandees among the wets. Gilmour went in a public huff, whereas Soames, Churchill's son-in-law, struck Thatcher as taking the news like 'being dismissed by his housemaid'.

The Government was at a crisis point; but so was the Opposition. Since losing office, the Labour Party had swung sharply to the left. This was shown not so much in the election of Foot as leader – he narrowly defeated Healey in November 1980 – but in Benn's renewed prominence as the champion of an ascendant left-wing coalition. This enlisted sufficient union support to carry the conference for a programme including a unilateralist defence policy, withdrawal from the European Community, and changes in the party's own constitution, making deselection of Labour MPs much easier. Conversely, with the emergence of a 'Gang of Three' – joint action by Shirley Williams, David Owen and William Rodgers to rally the social democratic wing – an actual split in the party became conceivable. Jenkins had floated the idea of a centre party in his televised Dimbleby Lecture in 1979, to a cool reception; but by the time he finished his stint with the European Community in January 1981, the left had inadvertently recruited him an army of potential followers. At a special conference of the Labour Party at Wembley, the left carried the day for its measures to entrench the influence of the unions. Conversely, the cry of 'one member, one vote' became the breaking point for the Gang of Three – or Four as it now became, as cooperation with Jenkins in establishing a new party became the strategy.

The formation of the Social Democratic Party (SDP) in 1981 was an attempt, as Jenkins put it, to 'break the mould' of British politics. It therefore needed electoral reform; but to get this it needed to make a breakthrough under the existing system – one reason for the pact which it made with the Liberal Party. Altogether, this was a tall order; only the ideological polarization of the major parties made it conceivable. The Thatcher Government seemed hell-bent on its monetarist experiment, despite record unemployment; the Labour Party seemed to be in thrall to the unions and, with the new electoral college in place, Benn came within a whisker of displacing Healey as deputy leader. During 1981, then, the SDP swept all before it. Fifteen Labour MPs had defected to it by the summer, and more were to come; in July Jenkins fought a by-election in Warrington and gave Labour a nasty jolt; in November Shirley Williams took the previously safe seat of Crosby from the Conservatives; and in its aftermath Gallup put the SDP–Liberal Alliance on 50 per cent nationally, with both other parties on 23 per cent. Clearly such a level of support was a bubble inflated by media hype, as opponents were not slow to allege; but in April 1982 the Alliance still had a lead of 6 points over the Conservatives and 8 points over Labour.

What decisively transformed the Government's position was not an economic upturn but a turn-up which nobody had thought was on the cards: a war in the South Atlantic. It caused Thatcher to lose her equanimity and her Foreign Secretary, but it enabled her to win the next general election at a time of her own choosing. Carrington's was a sad loss. He had presided over the Foreign Office with aplomb, persuading the prime minister to accept unpalatable decisions, not only over Europe, where the level of UK payments was a constant source of friction, but notably over Rhodesia. As leader of the opposition Thatcher had seemed sympathetic to the Rhodesia lobby in her own party, which supported Smith's new ploy – really a response to South African pressure – of seeking accommodation. He clearly hoped to divide the black nationalist forces and thereby marginalize their most forceful leader, Robert Mugabe. In power, however, Carrington prevailed upon Thatcher to accept a settlement which isolated Smith and paved the way for Mugabe to win power under black majority rule, as the leader of a legally independent Zimbabwe in 1980.

The Foreign Office found more difficulty in getting its own way, however, when it tried to engineer another piece of adroit appeasement, this time over the Falkland Islands. Long claimed by Argentina, these were an expensive ex-imperial commitment, harbouring a small, stubborn population of sheep-farmers. If their way of life was no longer economically viable, it was difficult to see why the British taxpayer should underwrite them indefinitely – or so a thoroughgoing economic liberal might argue. Nicholas Ridley, as Minister of State at the Foreign Office, had thus argued the case for a concession on sovereignty, combined with a leaseback agreement; but this was a solution which the small but vocal Falklands lobby in the House of Commons made impracticable. *Faute de mieux*, a continuing British commitment remained – though this was hardly signalled to Argentina by the Thatcher Government's withdrawal of the regular protection vessel as part of its defence cuts. Carrington had warned that this was unwise; Thatcher had sided against him. Nonetheless, when General Galtieri's military junta invaded the Falklands at the beginning of April 1982, paradoxically, the crisis was the making of Thatcher as a national leader, almost in the same way that Narvik had made Churchill or Suez Macmillan.

The Government was on the spot. Carrington accepted responsibility and resigned; and Pym was drafted as a stop-gap Foreign Secretary. Thatcher seized on the mood of shock and dismay which swept an emergency sitting of the House of Commons – Foot was unexpectedly hot for resistance – and announced a full-scale military expedition to retake the islands. Pym's efforts to find a peaceful settlement, brokered by the USA, were to prove as unavailing as Selwyn Lloyd's in 1956, and for the same reason: that the prime minister had a different agenda. One difference from Suez was that neither opposition party opposed the venture; indeed Owen, capitalizing on the fact that the islands had been effectively defended during his tenure as Foreign Secretary, now assumed a high profile, goading the Government to retrieve the situation. Of course, Galtieri and his regime had few apologists; in that sense he was the ideal enemy. An armada was massed to send British troops halfway round the world – as though Britain's defences were not already fully stretched – in a response which amazed most foreigners as quite disproportionate to the original injury.

Assuming that the expedition was worthwhile, Thatcher proved a courageous leader. In particular, she was ready to face the risk that Argentine missiles might score devastating hits on crucial vessels, like the troopship *Canberra*, which were vulnerably exposed. In fact it was the sinking of the Argentine cruiser *Belgrano* at the beginning of May, well clear of the Falklands, that caused the major loss of life. It was at this point that the *Sun* blazoned its front page with the headline: 'GOTCHA'. Within days, the loss of HMS *Sheffield* brought home the perilous nature of the whole enterprise; but once British troops had landed, the military operation was brought to an efficient conclusion with relatively light casualties. Thatcher drew her war cabinet, including Pym, Whitelaw and Parkinson, around her in pursuing her objectives with unflinching single-mindedness. She did not dwell on the financial costs of the war at a time of government cuts – the contingency fund proved elastic here – nor on how Britain would defend the Falklands in the future. For her the recapture of British territory was its own justification, even territory as bleak as glacial South Georgia, which, prior to the main assault, had been first to be retaken by the British forces. When the news was announced before the cameras in Downing Street, the prime minister swept aside questions with the simple injunction: 'Rejoice!'

Thatcherite triumphalism was born in the Falklands war: a style of politics which, for good or ill, depended on taking the Iron Lady at her own valuation. With victory achieved by the end of June 1982, Thatcher declared: 'We have ceased to be a nation in retreat. We have instead a newfound confidence – born in the economic battles at home and tested and found true 8,000 miles away.' It was this link which was crucial in vindicating her own leadership, with the war as a metaphor for eventual victory on the economic front, confounding the faint hearts. After the Falklands the prime minister's faith in her ability to triumph against the odds was shared by a wider section of the public. During eight weeks of crisis, her own approval rating in the opinion polls shot up, as did approval of the Government's record; by July 1982 the Conservatives stood nearly 20 points clear of either Labour or the Alliance. From this point onward, Thatcher had the ability to win a second term.

The improving economic news was thus assured of a more favourable electoral reception. The recession had bottomed out in 1981; growth was resumed in 1982 and approached 4 per cent by 1983. True, unemployment stood at 3.2 million in January 1983 but there was a seasonal fall below the psychologically important level of 3 million by June. Figures of such magnitude would surely have been sufficient to condemn any other post-war government; the political achievement of Thatcherism was to refocus the economic argument. The Government's record in reducing inflation was thus crucial. This was what it had promised, this was what it had delivered – how, or at what cost, or how permanently, became academic questions. Moreover this story looked better because mortgage payments were included in the RPI. This had exaggerated its rise somewhat at the peak of interest rates in 1980–81, but by 1983 mortgage rates had fallen by 4 per cent, mainly in the months before the election, which in turn brought the RPI under 5 per cent. For owner-occupiers who had kept their jobs, there was some comfort by 1983. Since unemployment had stabilized at 12–13 per cent, this implied that 87 per cent were in work. It was the *rise* in unemployment, now apparently contained, which seems to have inspired widespread fears among the majority. But the unemployed themselves were, as in the 1930s, a minority interest, concentrated in parts of the country which voted Labour anyway.

What finally secured Thatcher's position in the 1983 general election was the stance of the Labour Party. Foot, for all his literary gifts and parliamentary experience, did not look like an effective prime minister. Labour's copious manifesto – 'the longest suicide note in history', according to one shadow minister – not only called for the restoration of the trade unions to their former position: it proposed Britain's withdrawal from the EEC and from the Nato defence policy. Healey's social-democratic wing of the party were cowed into an embarrassed acquiescence. This was the opportunity for the Alliance, which went into the campaign in May at only 17 per cent in the polls. Jenkins, labouring under the title of 'prime-minister designate', fought a lack-lustre campaign, but Steel's refusal to break ranks was vindicated when the polls, day by day, showed the Alliance closing the gap with Labour. In fact, in the national vote it ended up 2 per cent behind Labour, which, at under 28 per cent, had its worst showing since 1918. The gap between the two forces in seats, of course, was much wider: 209 Labour MPs as against 23 for the Alliance. The breakthrough which the SDP needed had not occurred, leaving it with Jenkins, Owen and four other MPs; instead the effect was to augment the number of Liberal MPs to 17. The logic of fusion between the two wings of the Alliance was, however, resisted by Owen, who now succeeded Jenkins as leader of the SDP.

The disarray of the Opposition was a bonus for the Conservatives. With only 42 per cent of the vote, they managed to return nearly 400 MPs and increase their working majority to around 150. In Greater London they now had twice as many seats as Labour; in the rest of the south of England, 168 MPs to only 5 Liberals and 3 Labour. Here the advance of the Alliance had succeeded brilliantly in displacing the Labour Party as challenger, but almost completely failed to unsettle the Conservative Party as incumbent. Thatcher's mastery of the field was shown in her ministerial changes. At last free to rid herself of Pym, she found herself unable to replace him at the Foreign Office with the victorious chairman of the Conservative Party, Parkinson, because of a looming sex scandal, which was to blight but not end his career. Instead, Howe became Foreign Secretary, and Lawson had the gratification of moving into his inheritance as Chancellor of the Exchequer. Ridley too was promoted, entering the cabinet as Transport Secretary.

This looked a thoroughly Thatcherite cabinet. Its only prominent 'wet' member was now Peter Walker, but in his new role as Energy Secretary he was at one with the prime minister. While it would be unfair to accuse the Government of courting a collision with the miners, it had taken purposeful steps to be ready for one, along lines sketched by Ridley as early as 1978. The lessons of Saltley had sunk home in ensuring, not only that coal stocks should be at a high level during a miners' strike, but that they should be accessible, and alternative energy sources secured. The new laws on secondary picketing also reduced the efficacy of the tactics which the NUM had used during the last two coal strikes. The hero of Saltley, Arthur Scargill, was now president of the NUM; his uncompromising class-war rhetoric made him a worthy successor to Galtieri as a Tory hate-figure. From 1983 he confronted a new chairman of the NCB, Ian McGregor, a tough-minded Scottish-American industrialist who had just spent three years cutting back excess capacity in the British Steel Corporation; his brief was to do the same for the coal industry.

These were the ingredients for a major confrontation. In April 1984 Scargill called for industrial action over pit closures and miners went on strike throughout the country. Technically, however, this was not a national strike, since Scargill refused to call the national ballot which would then have been necessary; instead he relied on each area of the NUM to make it effective. This flawed approach, betraying some lack of confidence in his members, proved damaging since the Nottingham-shire miners, least at risk and least militant, went on working. More-over Scargill discovered that mass picketing, notably by his own Yorkshire miners, had limited effects in stopping the coal moving, though it provoked violent clashes with the police that made for vivid televised images. There remained much public sympathy for the miners, despite Scargill; and the NCB under McGregor showed little finesse in public relations. But McGregor was not really in charge; despite denials, Walker was in fact determining strategy, reinforced by the resolve of the prime minister to 'see off' this further challenge.

The coal strike lasted a year; more days were lost than in any dispute since 1926. There was little prospect of a negotiated settlement between Scargill and Thatcher, both intent on complete victory, cost what it might. The costs on the Government side were seen in a setback to economic recovery; on the miners' side, the families of men on strike bore the main suffering, and with impressive fortitude and resilience. But privation drove increasing numbers of miners back to work at the beginning of 1985 and the strike petered out. Scargill remained unrepentant, citing an acceleration of pit closures as testimony to his own foresight. The NUM lost half its membership.

The humbling of the miners, with their reputation as the shock troops of the labour movement, was shortly to be complemented by the equally forthright defeat of the newspaper printers, whose tight hold over Fleet Street had made them a byword for restrictive practices. When Murdoch, intent on asserting his 'right to manage', installed new computerized technology for Times Newspapers at a vast, fortified, new plant at Wapping, in the old docklands, he was able to invoke the cover of the law in a final confrontation with the old print unions. Neither of these bitter industrial disputes was over pay. The coal strike had the greater political resonance but the Wapping dispute had the wider economic significance, by overcoming union resistance to changes in working practices. At Wapping the print unions were brutally stripped of the power to resist; many other unions lost the will to resist. Their readiness to negotiate productivity deals, at the expense of job losses, was one reason why those who kept their jobs were fewer but more efficient, and still relatively well paid. Here too Thatcher could rejoice in her battle honours.

## VALUES

'Economics are the method,' said Thatcher in 1981; 'the object is to change the heart and soul.' Thatcherism was both more and less than a programme of economic liberalism, intent on maximizing the freedom of choice of the individual. Thatcher was never tempted by the thoroughgoing libertarian position which enjoined laissez-faire in matters of moral, personal and sexual conduct. The 'permissive society' was reviled, along with a liberal elite whom it was the mission of Thatcherite populism to dispossess. Tebbit caught this nicely in 1990 in a diatribe against 'the insufferable, smug, sanctimonious, naive, guilt-ridden, wet, pink orthodoxy of that sunset home of that third-rate decade, the 1960s'. Even at the height of her power as prime minister, Thatcher's public posture was still that of an outsider, appealing to public opinion over the heads of her own cabinet. She would voice popular discontent as though an unspecified 'they' ought to do something about it; she would openly applaud pro-hanging speeches at Conservative Party conferences, to the embarrassment of her own Home Secretary. Thatcher's politics of moral populism, practised with a success unmatched since Gladstone, helped give her Government its authentic streak of radicalism – yet its project of economic liberalism was to be tempered, perhaps hampered, by her conservative instincts.

Thatcher saw no inconsistency in preaching a crusade for economic modernization which relied upon a return to 'Victorian values'. These were selectively interpreted, with particular attention to restoring a distinction between the deserving and undeserving poor. Thatcher was often branded as a class warrior, for obvious reasons. She was viscerally against the unions; yet she was confident that she spoke *for* an influential section of the working class and she challenged the stereotypes of the old class system. Her undying quarrel with the Tory 'wets' is focused in her memoirs by a revealing image of 'the false squire', with all his outward show of John Bull, but in fact pursuing the politics of calculation and accommodation. 'Noblesse oblige' and 'One Nation' were other code words for this supposedly Disraelian tradition, which had been much invoked under Churchill, Eden and Macmillan. Indeed the aged Macmillan, ennobled as the first Earl of Stockton in 1984, hobbled into the House of Lords to deliver a characteristically memorable and oblique rebuke to Thatcherism, evoking the fine qualities which the miners had revealed on the Somme. Yet the unspoken premise of this kind of Tory paternalism was that the Establishment, not only in Church and state but society too, was naturally Tory – something that could no longer be taken for granted.

When Anglican bishops persisted in drawing attention to the plight of the poor in deprived cities like Liverpool, it certainly showed that the Church of England had ceased to be the Tory Party at prayer. Archbishop Runcie, a mild enough man, displeased Thatcher with the insufficiently martial tone of the Falklands commemoration service. The Church became linked with the BBC and the universities as part of a deeply suspect liberal establishment. The epithet 'chattering classes' nicely described the articulate impotence of middle-class liberalism. In the 1987 election the Conservatives were supported by only one in three voters with a university education.

The disaffection between the Government and the traditional professions, long the backbone of Conservatism, was mutual and self-reinforcing. Highly paid lawyers found their own restrictive practices challenged by the Government's radical agenda. Doctors were upset by sweeping, market-driven reforms in the NHS. Higher civil servants, schooled in a mandarin tradition, had to master a new managerial jargon and sometimes found that, under the 'Next Steps' programme, their jobs were hived off to semi-autonomous agencies. Professors groaned under the double affliction of a reduction in university funding and an increase in paperwork, much of it replicating business-style schemes of appraisal – of colleagues, of research output and of teaching quality. The 'caring professions' were the butt of Thatcherite scorn for institutionalizing 'compassion' as a welfare bureaucracy, to their own career benefit. To some extent this was the widening of an existing fissure between the self-interest of those employed in the public sector, vulnerable to spending cuts, and those making a living in the market sector who were increasingly resentful of high taxes. It sharpened a clash of cultures in ways well caught by David Lodge's *Nice Work* (1988), as much a novel about the dichotomy between 'two nations' as Disraeli's *Sybil*.

Thatcher spoke up for small businesses. Her own loyalty to the ethic of the corner shop made her sympathetic to the parallel growth of the service sector and of self-employment. Between 1979 and 1990 there was no net increase in employment in the UK, but the number who were self-employed went up by 1.5 million, from 8 per cent to 15 per cent of all employed persons. There had already been signs of a consumer rebellion against standardized marketing; the Campaign for Real Ale (CamRA) had focused the sentiment that small is beautiful on the pub, forging a highly effective alliance with small independent brewers to promote traditional (or 'live') English bitter ale, threatened by the mass production of pasteurized beer. This campaign had been so successful that the big brewers responded by reviving their own traditional ales (though lager was more profitable for them). Corner-shop bakeries showed the same trajectory. A taste for real ale hardly betokened Thatcherite politics – in fact the increased consumption of lager was associated with the rise of self-employed skilled workers – but both were working with the grain of economic change. The growing number of estate agents who were Conservative activists was often remarked.

The proper scope of public and private provision became a key issue. Whereas previous Conservative governments had tolerated the public sector, this one dismembered it. Privatization had not been a major theme in 1979 but it became the most dynamic policy of Thatcher's period in office, and the one with which her name was linked worldwide. Part of the state holding in BP (British Petroleum) shares had been sold off by Healey after the IMF crisis, straightforwardly to raise revenue and plug the budget deficit. This remained one motive for privatization but it was subsumed in an ideological drive towards 'popular capitalism'. Truly public ownership, it was suggested, meant putting shares in the hands of the public. The new Government accordingly sold more BP shares, as well as two nationalized companies, British

Aerospace and Cable & Wireless. What raised the stakes was Lawson's period as Secretary of State for Energy, 1981–3, during which he launched the privatization of Britoil (the former BNOC) for a billion pounds. Success bred success, and well-publicized flotations of cut-price shares on an increasingly buoyant market became a common pattern. By 1990, BP had gone for a total of £6 billion, British Gas for nearly £7 billion, British Telecom for nearly £5 billion. These were the giants, but Rolls-Royce, British Steel, British Airways, the airports and the water companies were also among the concerns privatized. The result was to cut the share of the public corporations in the economy by more than half: reducing employment in them from 8 million to 3 million, and cutting their contribution to GDP from over 10 per cent to under 5.

In so far as privatization replaced public with private monopolies, it simply mirrored the original nationalization process, and stored up a similar likelihood of disappointing hopes for transformative change. Radical Thatcherites, like Lawson and Ridley, were conscious of this problem. Yet the introduction of real competition was difficult to achieve, partly because some services were natural monopolies, partly because fragmented ownership would reduce profitability, and partly because it might leave some operations vulnerable to bigger foreign competitors. Such arguments were deployed by the powerful chairmen of British Gas and British Airways to keep their empires intact under privatization, knowing that the Government did not want to spoil the market price of the assets. The Government in the end cared more about instituting private ownership than breaking up monopoly. It did, however, impose new mechanisms for public regulation, arguing that these would be more effective if the Government were at arm's length, with its defence of the customer facilitated by the fact that it was no longer the proprietor. Targets were thus specified for reducing prices, year by year, below the rate of inflation, policed by regulatory authorities with Newspeak names like Ofgas and Oftel.

Privatization undoubtedly made share ownership more accessible than before. During the 1980s the number of shareholders in the UK showed a threefold increase, to a total of 9 million. Yet the proportion of all shares in the hands of individuals (rather than institutional investors) fell by a third in the same period, to around 20 per cent. The fact is that these new shareholdings were puny in economic terms. Their importance to the individuals holding them was another matter; and this may not have been financial so much as psychological, helping to inculcate more favourable attitudes towards business. If not popular capitalism in a full sense, privatization temporarily made capitalism more popular. But the greatest coup for privatization was in sustaining the older Conservative conception of a 'property-owning democracy'. The policy of giving council tenants the right to buy their own homes, at prices discounted according to their length of tenure, was implemented in 1980 by Michael Heseltine, as Secretary of State for the Environment. It caught on fast, with the political bonus that it embarrassed Labour councils which initially resisted. By 1987 1 million dwellings had been transferred from the public sector to owner occupation.

Owner-occupiers had long been recognized as a uniquely favourable constituency for the Conservatives. When their number became a majority of all households after 1970 it spelt danger for Labour. What privatization did was to help push owner-occupation up from 55 per cent of the market in 1980 to 67 per cent by 1990, by bringing it within reach of upwardly mobile skilled workers (C2s). At the outset finance was guaranteed by local councils; but the building societies soon saw their opportunity in advancing the vast majority of mortgage loans – thus returning to their artisan origins in an authentic triumph of Victorian values. Among skilled workers, traditionally a key element in the labour movement with their craft-union tradition, the Conservatives were to have a 7 per cent lead over Labour in the 1987 general election. On council estates, a freshly painted front door and a copy of the *Sun* in the letter-box was a signal of Thatcher's achievement in remaking the Conservative Party. It became a coalition of strong bargainers in all classes.

Owner-occupiers were championed by the prime minister, albeit at the expense of free-market principles. As Chancellor, Lawson considered himself the true Thatcherite with his radical agenda of tax reform. It rested on the doctrine of tax neutrality, meaning that the state should raise revenue in ways that did not distort the free play of market forces between equally legitimate economic activities. His aim was to devise a rational structure of incentives for wealth creators by removing historic anomalies which had crept into the tax system. But he soon discovered that his plans fell foul of Thatcher's solicitude for the owner-occupier and that she vetoed any attempt to reform the system of tax relief on mortgage-interest payments which, to the tax-reforming Chancellor, stood out as an expensive state subsidy, costing £7 billion by 1987, almost twice the UK public housing budget.

Moreover, the political salience of mortgage-interest rates was to become increasingly apparent in a nation of owner-occupiers. A demonstrable relationship between voting intentions and interest rates emerged in the 1980s. It meant that any rise in interest rates sent Government popularity plummeting – in much the same way that any rise in unemployment had done in an earlier period. This was a major change in electoral behaviour.

Public-service broadcasting was obviously unaccustomed to the market climate in which the BBC found itself operating in the 1980s. It was open to Government pressure, not only through appointments to its board, but also because of its continual need to renegotiate the level of the licence fee. Economic liberals, of course, argued ideally for a free market in broadcasting, commercially financed. The Peacock Report in 1986, however, produced a sophisticated 'second-best' defence of public regulation as serving the consumer interest, and recommended against introducing advertising on the BBC. The main new commercial opportunity came through the development of satellite television, which required heavy initial investment before it became viable. The result here was that the first company to be licensed, BSB, was cavalierly pre-empted by Murdoch's SkyTelevision, which managed to get on the air first. Truly dished, BSB settled for a merger as BSkyB in 1990.

Rather than a major extension of cable facilities, Britain was distinguished by a faster spread of video than in either the USA or Europe; by 1990 one family in three had video. Moreover, three times out of four it was used to record programmes from the BBC or ITV networks. Since Channel 4, as a second commercial-television channel, had been on the air since 1982, terrestrial television output was evenly balanced between alternative popular and minority channels, one of each run by the BBC. In fact Channel 4, acting like a publisher rather than as a production company, was often closer to the BBC in general ethos and output, and was notably successful in commissioning British films made for television.

It was, above all, through television that Britain projected its image in the world. Not only did the quality of British television win widespread international recognition, which could be considered a tribute to its public-service tradition: the export of a relatively large proportion of programmes displayed an entrepreneurial ability to sell these cultural products, thus passing the test of the competitive market too.

The surrealistic extension of the conventions of television comedy in *Monty Python's Flying Circus* achieved a worldwide impact, reinforced by subsequent films from this team. Their *Life of Brian* (1979) showed a naive and misunderstood hero who ended up being crucified two thousand years ago; its concluding song, sung from the cross, 'Always Look on the Bright Side of Life', was calculated to affront its audiences and make them laugh. They did so, in varying proportions. John Cleese subsequently recaptured and domesticated the animal spirits which had run wild in *Monty Python*, in the widely exported television series *Fawlty Towers*. Here the comedy lay in the tension between the tight, polite, English conventions observed in a small hotel and the suppressed hysteria welling up in its choleric proprietor. Cleese took similar themes into the cinema, first with *Clockwise* (1986), scripted by the novelist and playwright Michael Frayn, chronicling the disintegrating dignity of an obsessive headmaster, and in the portrayal of an inhibited English barrister falling in love in *A Fish Called Wanda* (1988). There were some compromises here to reach an international audience but also welcome signs of life in the hard-pressed British film industry.

The distinctive British forte lay not in blockbuster movies, where Hollywood was unrivalled, but in a sector where the line between the big and the small screen was often transgressed, on the production side by films made for television and on the consumption side by the spread of video. The adaptations for television of Evelyn Waugh's *Brideshead Revisited* (1981) and Paul Scott's Raj Quartet of novels, set in the last days of British India, as *The Jewel in the Crown* (1982), acquired a cachet as much-discussed series. Such prestige productions, with an afterlife on video, could creditably stand alongside the filmed adaptations that were successively made from E. M. Forster's oeuvre. David Lean's *A Passage to India* (1984), his last film, showed the possibilities for a big-production treatment, memorable for Peggy Ashcroft's performance as Mrs Moore. Subsequent adaptations by Ismail Merchant and James Ivory worked meticulously to a smaller scale – though, following *A Room with a View* (1986) and *Maurice* (1987), their more ambitious *Howards End* (1992), with Anthony Hopkins and Emma Thompson nicely matched, was to become a major box-office success. These were fine productions by any standards, delicately translating many of the nuances of the original books on to the screen with a control of pace and sureness of touch which evocatively reconstituted the period settings.

Yet the very success of the Merchant–Ivory films, like that of the English-cottage-garden fabrics of the Laura Ashley label, could readily be bracketed by critics of a 'heritage industry', fostering backward-looking (and often factitious) perceptions of Britain. It is true that the tide of architectural conservation had turned since the 1960s, when fine old buildings were still being demolished in favour of urban motorways and tower blocks. By the time of his death in 1984, John Betjeman's lifelong defence of Victoriana no longer seemed merely quaint; as Poet Laureate from 1972 he not only found wide appreciation for his un-pretentiously accessible and often witty verse, but used his position to campaign for the preservation of threatened buildings, such as the Vic-torian gothic St Pancras Station. Not only were ancient monuments more zealously protected: schemes for the conservation and renovation of whole neighbourhoods, rather than comprehensive redevelopment, were now the fashionable idiom, even during the property boom of the late 1980s.

Now that tourism had become big business, was the country reduced to trading in nostalgia? The National Trust, founded in 1895 primarily to conserve the countryside, became the custodian of an increasing number of historic houses, with record-breaking numbers of visitors from home and abroad. But though foreign tourists often came to see historical sites, many also appreciated the vitality of the performing arts. In Scotland, the Edinburgh Festival had become a major draw every summer, attracting international recognition for the high calibre of the programme of music and drama which it mounted over a period of several weeks. It had famously generated a 'fringe' for aspiring visit-ing productions, commemorated in the title of the irreverent revue *Beyond the Fringe* (1960), which first made the names of Jonathan Miller, Alan Bennett, Dudley Moore and Peter Cook. In England, the six-week season of promenade concerts at the Albert Hall, sponsored by the BBC, was simply the most conspicuous part of a wide annual repertoire of classical music, available not only in London with its four major orchestras, but in cities like Birmingham where there was greater readiness to introduce modern composers.

The role of the Arts Council in disbursing public money had been important in generating a more vital climate for the arts in post-war Britain. The reopening of the Covent Garden Opera House was given a high priority and its running costs remained a major burden on the Arts Council budget. Criticized as elitist both from the egalitarian left and from the populist right, this policy nonetheless succeeded in helping British opera and ballet achieve a level of international status unprecedented in earlier generations. Building on established tradition, the Royal Shakespeare Theatre, based at Stratford-on-Avon, was eventually complemented by the opening of the National Theatre in London, initially using the Old Vic, which had long been home to Shakespearian productions. As the first director of the National, and the first actor to gain a peerage, Laurence Olivier crowned a long and uniquely distinguished career, with Kenneth Tynan as literary director giving an innovative twist to the selection of plays. Productions from both the RSC and the National subsequently had long runs in the West End, or on Broadway – for example, Peter Shaffer's *Amadeus* (1979; filmed, 1984) – thus helping sustain a reputation for the London stage unrivalled in the English-speaking world.

Not until 1976 did the National Theatre acquire its own new building, on the South Bank, now a fine central site for the arts, looking across the Thames, upstream to Big Ben and downstream to St Paul's. The external severity of Denys Lasdun's chunky design, softened only by the wood-grain mouldings on the concrete façades, enclosed an airy functional interior, creating spacious amenities on several levels for audiences in either large auditorium, one with a traditional proscenium, the other with an open stage. Very much a building of its own time, it contrasted nicely with another period piece on the South Bank site: the Royal Festival Hall, with its sweeping lines and bold use of glass, designed by the London County Council's architects' department under Robert Matthew and Leslie Martin for the Festival of Britain in 1951. Held one hundred years after the Great Exhibition, the Festival of Britain symbolized an aspiration, not least on the part of the young team who planned it, for Britain's creative and aesthetic regeneration – high hopes of which the present cluster of public buildings on the South Bank stands as a gloriously post-Victorian affirmation.

The one symbol of Britain which commanded instant international recognition and media attention remained the monarchy. It had, of course, acquired its late-twentieth-century glamour partly through astute media promotion, with a relaxation of television coverage over the years so that tantalizing glimpses of domesticity conveyed more personal and informal impressions of the whole royal family, now replete with four children of marriageable age. Charles, Prince of Wales, broke new ground for royalty in gaining a good honours degree at Cambridge and was not deterred from expressing his concern on a range of environmental issues, from architecture to the social plight of the inner cities. In 1981, at the age of thirty-three, he married Lady Diana Spencer; she was just twenty, virtually uneducated, in a casual upper-class way, and apparently a virgin (an important consideration in the making of this match, or mismatch). Their wedding went round the world as a television spectacular, to be repeated when Prince Andrew married in 1986. The birth of their respective children helped to domesticate fairy-tale romance as ongoing soap opera, enhancing a happy, if increasingly cloying, impression. Once the media had got so close, however, the successive onset of marital breakdown, culminating in separation or divorce for all of the Queen's three married children by 1992, was equally over-exposed. This hardly represented values which their great-great-great-grandmother would have acknowledged.

Victorian values, indeed, proved as elusive as a salvation for Britain as they were elastic in definition. If British culture, as some argued, had proved resistant to the entrepreneurial spirit for generations, a change of heart and soul might well need more than a few years to accomplish. Perhaps that is what Thatcher meant by saying in 1990: 'Thatcherism is not for a decade. It is for centuries.' Thatcher's electoral successes did not create a Thatcherite electorate, with 58 per cent voting against her in 1983 and 1987 alike. Moreover, survey evidence in the late 1980s suggests that only one in five respondents – considerably fewer than a decade before – agreed with the proposition that if people were poor, their own lack of effort was to blame. The National Health Service remained popular, and people told pollsters that they preferred increased welfare spending to tax cuts – though tax cuts seem to have proved a stronger motive in the solitude of the polling booth.

All told, it is easier to show that Thatcherism had notable successes in modifying the immediate behaviour of the British people at a particular stage in the economic cycle, than to point to a fundamental transformation of attitudes. The years of recession had left plenty of room for a strong recovery in the 1980s, if only a recovery of an essentially cyclical kind. Talk of ending a century of decline often meant reversing a decade of decline – a worthwhile but less heroic undertaking, and one that need not be mistaken for either an economic miracle or a historical watershed.

## BOOM AND BUST

Nowhere was Thatcher more warmly received than in the USA. Just as Heath's had been the least pro-American, and most pro-European, Government since the Second World War, Thatcher's was quite the reverse. An idealized USA was held up by Thatcherites as a model of a society based on the free market, minimal government, anti-Communism, the mighty dollar and Almighty God. After Ronald Reagan was elected President in 1980, Thatcher found a real ally, with her trenchant expositions of their common outlook complemented by his benignly bemused concurrence. This was indeed a special relationship, which helped to inflate Thatcher's international standing. As her Foreign Secretary, Sir Geoffrey Howe was put, and kept, very much in the shade. Thatcher knew that covert US support had been vital during the Falklands war. For all of this she was thankful and she showed it in her unwavering public support for the USA. This tallied with her convictions in facilitating the deployment of the mobile Cruise missiles at two bases in England – despite long-running protests organized by CND – in exchange for a promise of Trident missiles to update the British nuclear force. The real test came when the President's thinking and Thatcher's diverged.

The Strategic Defence Initiative (SDI) purported to give the USA a high-technology defence system against Soviet nuclear attack, thus cancelling the premise of mutually assured destruction (MAD) which was assumed to have secured both sides from the threat of attack. To Reagan, 'star wars' opened the possibility of a world freed of all nuclear weapons, and he was accordingly set on going ahead. To Gorbachov, the new Soviet leader, the SDI was destabilizing to the nuclear balance, and its abandonment by the USA a prerequisite of peace. Thatcher agreed with neither. Nor did she accept that, because the SDI was appallingly expensive and technically unproven, it was therefore not worthwhile to pursue it. Instead she considered that even an inefficient SDI still tipped the nuclear odds against the Soviet Union – and that any effort it made to develop its own equally costly system would bring the Soviet economy to its knees. In the short term, therefore, Thatcher was horrified by the outcome of the Reykjavik summit in 1986, when Reagan had been on the point of accepting a phased reduction of all strategic missiles, the 'zero option', in return for not implementing the SDI. One implication was that the Trident missiles destined for the UK would also go. Much to Thatcher's relief, such an agreement proved abortive, and a hastily arranged visit to Washington gave her the reassurance she needed.

Not that Thatcher was personally hostile to Gorbachov. An invitation for him to visit Chequers, while the ailing Chernenko was still Soviet leader in 1984, had paid off handsomely; Gorbachov proved to be a man she could do business with, as Thatcher readily told the press. During the Gorbachov era, Thatcher welcomed reform but the Iron Lady did not belie her sobriquet. She braved Soviet disapproval to voice strong support for the struggle by the Solidarity movement in Poland, even if this made her into an unlikely champion of trade-union methods. A reciprocal enthusiasm for Thatcherism was displayed in eastern Europe, at least temporarily, as the Communist regimes crumbled. When the Berlin wall came down at the end of 1989, she could claim a part in bringing the cold war to an end – fit reason to rejoice.

The personal fortitude which the public had glimpsed in her during the Falklands campaign was put to a severe test during the Conservative Party conference in October 1984, when an IRA bomb exploded in Thatcher's Brighton hotel, severely injuring the Tebbits in an adjacent room and killing the wife of the chief whip. Thatcher's insistence that the conference debates continue as planned next day, with an undaunted speech from herself, showed that her image as the Iron Lady had stuck with her for good reason. It was an important part of her appeal, at home as well as abroad. Defence policy became one of the Conservatives' big electoral assets; correspondingly, the unilateralist stance of the Labour Party in two general elections was fundamental to its lack of credibility.

Since January 1983 Michael Heseltine, a forceful minister with a charismatic hold over the Conservative Party conference, had assumed a high profile as Secretary of State for Defence. In 1981, thirsting for cuts, the Government had accepted the findings of a major defence review; it proposed scrapping a number of naval surface vessels, which within months played a key role in retaking the Falklands. The review was then scrapped instead. But defence procurement continued to pose acute problems, as shown by Heseltine's difficulties over the Westland helicopter company, based at Yeovil. What made the Westland crisis so explosive by December 1985 was the way it triggered two other issues. One was the EC dimension, since Heseltine wanted to explore European alternatives to a projected US takeover of Westland; but the real dynamite lay in Thatcher's relations with her cabinet colleagues.

The new Secretary of State for Industry, Leon Brittan, was a rising star in the cabinet, clearly 'one of us'. It was hardly surprising that his free-market outlook made him ready to approve the US takeover; Thatcher supported him, regarding talk of a European option as a waste of time and as sheer anti-Americanism. Heseltine insisted that he was being denied proper discussion in cabinet. In an attempt to counter him, Brittan's department was drawn into leaking sensitive material to the press, seemingly with the connivance of Downing Street. Heseltine's resignation in January 1986 – striding out of 10 Downing Street in front of the television cameras – did nothing to quell damaging speculation. Moreover the trail led back towards the prime minister, whose apparent duplicity suddenly made her position very shaky. She was much assisted at this point by Brittan's resignation – pained but, above all, discreet. (Thatcher was later to appoint him one of the two British members of the European Commission: the least she could do for him.) In the event, then, Thatcher survived, aided in the House by the Opposition's failure to press the issue effectively. The whole episode, however, especially the sacrifice of Brittan, gave her colleagues uneasy thoughts about her concept of loyalty; and it set up Heseltine as a backbench critic, nursing his grievance while biding his time.

The curious uncertainty of the Government's standing was revealed by its vulnerability in by-elections. The Alliance showed that it had staying power by unexpectedly winning Portsmouth South in June 1984 and in the next summer all three parties were neck and neck in the polls, a position which Westland helped to prolong. Not until June 1986 did the economic boom float the Conservatives out of third place nationally, and not until the end of the year did Gallup put them ahead again. By May 1987, when an election was called, the Conservatives were ten points clear – but with the Alliance rather than Labour in second place.

When Foot stepped down in 1983, the Labour leadership passed from an old unilateralist to a young unilateralist. Neil Kinnock, just turned forty, won acceptance from the left partly because he was untainted by ministerial office under Wilson and Callaghan. It also meant, of course, that he lacked front-bench experience. He came out of the Welsh Bevanite tradition; all his emotions and rhetoric tugged him to the left, his current thinking on a viable electoral strategy for Labour drew him to the centre. His ringing denunciation of the hard-left Militant Tendency at the Labour Party conference in October 1985 was an open step; but privately he knew that Labour was still hobbled by its unilateralist stance. The Conservatives' credentials on defence were also enhanced by disputes within the Alliance, where Owen had used his position as leader of the SDP to make support of Trident into a matter of faith. Like the Conservatives, he insisted that the independence secured by a British deterrent (albeit one supplied by the USA) was the overriding issue, whereas the majority position in the Alliance had always been that British commitment to Nato was the crux.

It was in this context that the Opposition's disarray over defence became so damaging. The strong showing for the Alliance was actually less threatening to the Conservatives than it seemed; it simply meant that there would be fierce competition for second place throughout Tory-held southern England. The Labour Party certainly fought a much more effective campaign in 1987 than four years previously. A party political broadcast, entitled *Kinnock*, enlisted the talents of Hugh Hudson, whose film *Chariots of Fire* (1981) had given a thrilling depiction of Britons striving for medals at the 1924 Olympics – skills which were enlisted, sixty years on, to suggest Kinnock's golden potential. The campaign showed how much Labour Party managers had learned under Thatcherism: how to market their product in a way that appealed to customers who were ready to shop around, irrespective of brand loyalty.

Yet Labour policy had changed little, as Conservatives kept pointing out. As for the Alliance, the handicap of a dual leadership – Steel for the Liberals, Owen for the SDP – was brought home by the fact that they plainly spoke in different tones: Owen essentially as a candid friend of the Government, Steel as an opposition critic. Jenkins and Williams plainly sided with Steel rather than their increasingly isolated SDP colleague. A post-election split thus emerged between, on the one side, the bulk of the SDP, who wanted a merger with the Liberals, and, on the other, the rump of independent Owenites who clung to the title SDP; and the subsequent formation of the Liberal Democrats was to bear these disabling scars.

What is surprising in hindsight is that the Conservatives were ever worried about the election result. Yet a week before polling day, a rogue poll was enough to provoke 'a ding-dong row' (Thatcher's own description) between herself and the party chairman, Tebbit. Their relations never fully recovered from 'wobbly Thursday'; and it is significant that such a committed Thatcherite was arraigned, in effect, for not building the campaign more around the prime minister herself. Certainly she took the election verdict as a personal endorsement. Compared with 1983, the Conservative vote was steady on 42 per cent, Labour up three points to 31 per cent – just like 1931 – with the Alliance fading to 23 per cent. The Conservatives had 376 seats, still leaving them a parliamentary majority in three figures, while Labour gained 20 seats to give them 229 MPs, with 22 for the Alliance. This was again a victory achieved in the south of England, where Labour retained only three seats outside Greater London – and this time a new post-war low of 23 out of 84 London constituencies. In Scotland, by contrast, Labour now had 50 seats to the Conservatives' 10, and in Wales Labour had 24, the Conservatives only 8. Rather than One Nation, there were now at least three.

The state of the economy was, of course, fundamental. Conservatives boasted that British productivity now showed the best record in Europe. In the small print, this claim applied only to *gains* in productivity. Since the manufacturing base had contracted faster than in other countries during the 1980s, shedding a couple of million of the presumably less efficient workers, higher output per head was indeed achieved with the leaner and fitter workforce that remained. The real test was to consolidate these gains once unemployment began to subside.

The headline figures for the registered unemployed reached a peak of 3.4 million in January 1986 and thereafter showed a steady fall to 1.6 million in June 1990. The changes which the Government introduced in counting unemployment not only exercised the Opposition, who cried fraud, but obscured the true trend. Measured on a standard basis, OECD figures showed British unemployment at its peak as early as 1983, at over 12 per cent of the labour force, two points above the EEC average, with a fall to 6 per cent by 1990, a couple of points under the European average. Two conclusions are clear: that, however unemployment in the UK was measured, its best year in the 1980s was worse than its worst year in the 1970s, and that it went through a more volatile cycle, both up and down, than in comparable countries. The good news lay in the strength of the recovery. Measured from peak to peak, economic growth was 3.7 per cent in the five years 1984–8 – beating the previous records in 1961–4 and 1969–73.

The Lawson boom thus takes its place in history alongside Maudling's 'dash for growth' and the Barber boom. In each case a strong pattern of cyclical recovery was further fuelled by an injection of consumer demand which left the economy overheated. The difference, in the case of the Lawson boom, was that this could hardly be attributed to an excess of Keynesian zeal. Lawson thought of himself as a principled monetarist, though some were left puzzled as to what the Chancellor's principles actually were. Certainly the old target of £M3 was defunct, as Lawson's Mansion House speech in 1985 finally acknowledged. The problem was what to put in its place. By 1985 he saw the real alternative to £M3 in the discipline of a fixed parity for sterling, much like the old gold standard. This was his argument for joining the European Exchange Rate Mechanism (ERM); by locking sterling into this system, he hoped to lock the UK into a permanently lower rate of inflation, which remained the essential objective.

If the UK were ever to join the ERM, this was surely the moment. Labour had spurned it when it was established in 1979, but the experience of the early 1980s, when sterling exhibited the volatility of a petrocurrency, brought home the need of British export industries for stable exchange rates. But whenever Lawson broached his proposal to the prime minister he found it vetoed, or at least stalled. The logic of Thatcher's argument against the ERM – maintaining that it would impair the Government's freedom of action on economic policy – was that in the last analysis she preferred to retain the option of devaluation. In practice she often flinched from rises in interest rates even though they were indispensable in running a tight monetary policy – because of the effect on the politically sensitive mortgage rate. This was not the immediate problem since base rate moved generally downward, albeit in irregular steps, from 14 per cent at the beginning of 1985 to under 8 per cent in the spring of 1988. Mortgage rates followed, a step or two behind.

However, signs of a lack of trust between 10 and 11 Downing Street became increasingly apparent. The prime minister preferred to rely on the advice of Professor Walters, an unabashed opponent of the ERM. Lawson, who liked to play his cards close to his chest, resorted to his own informal exchange-rate mechanism. It became common knowledge that the pound was in fact shadowing the German mark at a parity of 3 DM, though Thatcher subsequently purported to have no knowledge of this. Government unity showed signs of cracking in March 1988, when Thatcher's statement in the Commons that there was 'no way in which one can buck the market' was taken as challenging Lawson's exchange-rate policy. The prime minister backed down, for the moment.

Yet an extraordinary public euphoria persisted for more than a year in the afterglow of Thatcher's third election victory. Combined with the private conflict in Downing Street, this helps to explain two steps which, in hindsight, were widely regarded as blunders: the 1988 Budget and the poll tax. Because the prime minister and her 'brilliant Chancellor', as she publicly called him, were jointly credited with achieving an economic miracle, they were inseparably yoked together, despite their deadlock on the twin issues of the ERM and monetary policy. There was, however, one major area of agreement between them: that tax cuts were a good thing. Lawson was therefore unconstrained in introducing his great tax-cutting Budget in March 1988. The basic rate of income tax, which had already been brought down to 29 per cent in 1986, and to 27 per cent in 1987, was now cut to 25 per cent. Further, the top rate of income tax was cut from 60 to 40 per cent.

The Conservatives had thus fulfilled their pledges to cut income taxes. The overall burden of taxation in the UK actually increased during the 1980s, as in most comparable countries, but its distribution certainly altered, with an increase in indirect taxes financing a cut in personal taxes. This in turn had powerful redistributive effects; while the poor got relatively poorer, the rich got absolutely richer, before as well as after tax.[1] Not only were the tax gains very considerable for high earners, many of these were simultaneously benefiting from big pay rises, notably in recently privatized companies. The conspicuous affluence of 'yuppies' in the City had solid fiscal arithmetic behind it. Lawson's guiding axiom was that, through creating such incentives, he was priming the engine that would in turn create future wealth. Indeed in 1988 he claimed success on all fronts simultaneously – prices and interest rates down, employment and growth up, and a Budget surplus despite his tax cuts.

The sincerity of Lawson's convictions need not be doubted, since a cynical Chancellor would have introduced a giveaway budget before rather than after an election. The inflationary effects of the boost in consumer demand, however, soon showed through; the rate of inflation

1. By 1990–91 individual taxpayers paid £27 billion less than at 1978–9 rates; more than half of this remission went to the 4 million taxpayers currently earning over £20,000 a year, with the remainder divided among the other 22 million taxpayers. More generally, by 1989 the managing director of any medium-sized firm could expect to earn over £50,000 a year, a rise of well over a third in ten years, after allowing for inflation; and taxpayers in this range benefited from reduced income tax to the tune of £9,000 a year.

rose from 4 per cent at the beginning of 1988 to over 10 per cent in the autumn of 1990. As in the Barber boom, there was an explosion of house prices. As in Maudling's dash for growth, the balance of payments rapidly deteriorated. One reason why consumer goods were sucked in is that the slump of the early 1980s had destroyed so much manufacturing capacity at home; a quick increase in production was now impossible. It was oil which had hitherto cushioned the balance of payments. In 1985 the oil surplus peaked at £8 billion; a sharp price fall then cut this in half. This did not matter in the short term since the balance of payments was still (just) in balance in 1986. But by 1989 the total deficit had opened up to a record of £20 billion, or 4.4 per cent of GDP – as bad as 1974.

Lawson affected unconcern, saying that it was for the private sector to cope with a deficit of its own making. If only because of its implications for the exchange rate, such a view was unsustainable, the more so since a parallel deficit in the Budget soon appeared. Again, this had been masked by windfall gains, since the proceeds of privatization were counted against expenditure. No less than £13 billion of the Budget surplus of £14.5 billion which Lawson realized in 1988–9 came from the sale of public assets, which was not to be repeated on this scale. As these problems mounted, confidence ebbed, and the Government uneasily woke up from its dream. Interest rates were steadily jacked up from 7.5 per cent in the springtime of 1988 to 15 per cent in the far from contented winter of 1989–90.

If the 1988 Budget was the product of Lawson's hubris, Thatcher's nemesis came with the poll tax. There had long been a Conservative commitment to reform local government finance, by replacing household rates; it took Thatcher to declare this the flagship of her legislative programme after 1987. Hence the scheme for a flat-rate 'community charge', to be paid personally by every adult inhabitant, not just property-owners. The aim was to restrain the free-spending policies that were associated with Labour councils, an area in which Conservatives felt impotent.[1] Thatcher's defiant response was to mobilize the

1. The reason the Conservatives were relatively weak in local elections was partly that they were over-represented in national elections. The electoral system gave Thatcher two landslide victories in the 1980s because anti-Conservative votes were inefficiently distributed. But in local elections support for Labour and the Alliance was much more efficiently distributed, and was maximized by the ability of these parties to run against an often unpopular Government.

power of central Government against her enemies. The (Labour-controlled) Greater London Council was thus abolished in 1985, while rate-capping measures, restricting the level of local expenditure, hobbled other councils.

The poll tax promised a more radical solution: that was its charm for Ridley as the minister responsible for implementing it. It would strip Labour of its ability to milk local property-owners by making each and every voter bear a full share of the costs incurred by prodigal spending. Thus democratic accountability would remove the need for rate-capping. Here was the biggest alteration in local government finance since the reforms of the late 1920s, implemented by Chamberlain only when he had secured Treasury support. By contrast, Thatcher and Ridley pressed on with their plan without squaring Lawson, who mocked the idea.

Had the transition to a poll tax been sweetened by the Chancellor from his overflowing coffers in 1988, it need not have been an electoral disaster. Instead, radical change came, in Scotland in 1989, elsewhere in 1990, when the boom had already gone sour, leaving more losers than gainers. The fact that the only conspicuous gainers were again the wealthy excited real anger, even among some Conservatives. Moreover, the great principle of local accountability was thrown over when Thatcher decided she needed rate-capping as well as the poll tax. Worst of all, not only did Labour councils exploit the confusion to increase spending regardless, the voters apparently held the Government accountable. By the spring of 1990 opinion polls put the Conservatives at under 30 per cent, more than twenty points behind Labour. A by-election in Mid-Staffordshire gave Labour its biggest victory in years.

It was not, however, the poll tax which triggered Thatcher's downfall. True, the anniversary of her ten years as prime minister, in May 1989, had produced a curiously cool response, and she had to face a token backbench opponent for the party leadership in December. But she could have soldiered on with a united cabinet at her back. This she did not have by 1990, and the reason was not the poll tax but Europe. Britain's relations with the European Community formed the submerged reef on which the Thatcher Government foundered in successive ministerial crises. It had played a part in the resignation of Heseltine, who was now widely seen as a real challenger for the leadership. It was the reason why Ridley, perhaps Thatcher's staunchest supporter, had to resign in June 1990, after making xenophobic remarks about the

Germans. Finally and fatally, European policy was behind the resignations of Lawson and Howe.

With Whitelaw's retirement, following a stroke in 1988, Howe was Thatcher's most senior colleague, yet she treated him with scant respect, for which she paid dearly in the end. As Foreign Secretary, he wanted to improve relations with the EC; he had prevailed on Thatcher to sign the Single European Act in 1985, which committed Britain to the principle of closer integration. When Thatcher still refused to consider joining the ERM in 1989, claiming in Wilsonian style that the time was not ripe, Howe was prepared to join forces with Lawson in putting pressure on her. Together they confronted her before the Madrid summit of EC leaders, threatening resignation. For the moment she held them off; indeed she was able to take her revenge on Howe by moving him out of the Foreign Office in July, in favour of the more compliant figure of John Major – a startling promotion. Howe consoled himself meanwhile with the rather empty title of deputy prime minister.

Lawson was generally disturbed by what he saw as the prime minister's increasingly truculent chauvinism, pandering to tabloid prejudices; but he was more immediately upset by the subversive role of Walters as her personal economic adviser, especially his declared scorn for the ERM. Since this had become public, and Thatcher refused to part with Walters, Lawson felt he had no alternative but to resign in November 1989. Thatcher professed to find this incomprehensible. Unabashed, she again filled the gap with Major, most of whose ministerial experience had been at the Treasury. Douglas Hurd, an old Heathite, became Foreign Secretary, leaving this a far-from-Thatcherite cabinet. It was Major who now secured the prime minister's consent for entry to the ERM. This was certainly no panacea; from the outset, the weakened state of the economy made it an uphill struggle to maintain the parity of sterling. Like Britain's entry to the EC in the first place, here was an object lesson in the importance of doing the right thing at the right moment.

Almost exactly a year after Lawson's resignation came Howe's, which Thatcher recognized as almost exactly a rerun, right down to her professed incomprehension about the reasons for the coincidence. Again it was commitment to European integration which was at issue. This time Thatcher's carefully coached acquiescence could not hold under questioning in the Commons on 30 October 1990 – 'No, no, no!'

Howe decided to go. The incident came within a couple of weeks of the Conservatives' loss of a by-election in the safe seat of Eastbourne – not to Labour, of course, but to the supposedly defunct Liberal Democrats, whom the poll tax had put back in business as a third party. Talk of a serious challenge for the leadership – Heseltine's was the obvious name – was rife among worried Conservative MPs. What made this certain was Howe's resignation speech, its subfusc delivery a perfect foil to its deadly impact, as he spoke of wrestling with a conflict of loyalties, 'for perhaps too long'. When Heseltine declared his candidature, he was supported by both Howe and Lawson.

That Thatcher's leadership was now caught in a spiral of disintegration was apparent – except to her campaign managers, who felt they need not actively canvass support. Yet in the first ballot she polled only 204 to Heseltine's 152. True, under the revised rules, she fell a scant handful of votes short of being declared outright winner; but for a sitting prime minister, who had led the party through three successive parliaments, such calculations were beside the point, if two out of five Tory MPs had withdrawn their confidence. Her decision to resign followed because only her withdrawal could ensure Heseltine's defeat.

But by whom? Again Major slipped into the vacant role. He had hardly been groomed for the succession, but a series of temporary favourites had stumbled – or been pushed – and Major, a mere Chief Secretary to the Treasury sixteen months previously, took the final step in a dizzy ascent. Facing not only Heseltine but the old Etonian Hurd in the second ballot, Major found his humble origins an asset in projecting himself as the candidate who would keep the Government safe for Thatcherism, which was enough to give him the votes he needed. Thus in November 1990, the Conservative Party, awed at the thought of what it had done, gave Thatcher a fine send-off, with some pangs of guilt that her eleven and a half years as prime minister had ended in this way.

It is not true that Margaret Thatcher did untold harm, if only because the chattering classes constantly told each other about the harm she was doing. Yet the fruits of her reforms were accepted by many long-standing opponents. Though their hearts might have bled for the miners, they did not propose to put the unions back in the saddle; though they might have been scornful of privatization, they did not propose to go back to a regime of nationalized industries and council houses. The post-Thatcher Labour Party bore a closer resemblance to the SDP of ten years previously than partisans of either cared to acknowledge.

Thatcher achieved her victories at a terrible cost, usually borne by others. By any test, from statistical surveys of relative incomes to the striking reappearance of beggars on the street, Britain became a more unequal society. Moreover, in carrying out her grand design, Thatcher relied on rough-and-ready improvisation far more often than she liked to think. The main plank of her 1979 programme, monetarism, was soon splintered; yet the fact that its chief object was realized provided Thatcherites with sufficient justification for such departures from plan. As Lawson put it in his Mansion House speech of 1985: 'The inflation rate is judge and jury.' When Thatcher left office, the rise in the RPI had again hit double figures. Unemployment, on the other hand, was below 2 million. Just as, with the onset of a cyclical recession, inflation was subsequently to fall again, so unemployment was to rise. Some trade-off between the the two was plainly not unique to the Keynesian policies which Thatcherism claimed to have superseded. Asked what she had changed, Maragaret Thatcher once assured an interviewer that she had 'changed everything'. In her memoirs she was to strike a different note: 'In politics there are no final victories.'

# Epilogue

During the twentieth century, the perspectives adopted by historians of the United Kingdom naturally changed. In 1900 the existence of the British Empire had dominated, or at least framed, the picture; and the mood of the picture itself was that of triumphalism, albeit tinged with apprehension. Imperial history was to modify its stance as liberal historians, from Ramsay Muir in the 1920s to Nicholas Mansergh in the 1960s, presented a vision of the evolution of the Empire into the Commonwealth; though this version was itself renounced as Whiggish by a new generation of revisionist historians. The history of England long continued to be written in ways that silently subsumed Scotland and Wales, as shown in the original series for the Oxford History of England and the Pelican History of England, both completed in the 1960s. G. M. Trevelyan, often called the last of the Whig historians, was Regius Professor of Modern History at Cambridge from 1927 to 1940. He owed his pre-eminence, however, not to exact scholarship but to a fine literary sense and an imaginative broadening of the scope of history for the general reader. His *English Social History* (1944), which notched up staggering sales, captured a sense that 1940 had vindicated the robustness of British society as well as a tradition of enlightened liberal leadership. 'Tout va très bien, Madame l'Angleterre,' commented one French review, in a prickly admonition to Trevelyan's anglocentric complacency.

If this was still a Whig interpretation, presenting the story of the past as a benign progress towards an increasingly enlightened present, it was deeply rooted among British historians. Accounts of social policy, for example, often orchestrated a variation on the same theme, with poverty submitting to a painfully achieved but finally successful conquest by beneficent state intervention. It was as though the rise of the welfare state simply compensated for the decline of the British Empire. When

A. J. P. Taylor, a diplomatic historian by training and a political radical by conviction, turned his hand to the volume *English History, 1914–45* (1965), he did not mourn his country's downfall as a great power but celebrated the fact that 'England had risen all the same'.

If Taylor meant that life expectancy at birth had increased by some seventeen years since the beginning of the century, or that GDP per head in 1948 was 35 per cent higher in real terms than in 1900, he was quite right. But these snapshots were of a dynamic, continuing process. By 1990 life expectancy was to lengthen by a further ten years, and per capita GDP, allowing for inflation, was to be 150 per cent higher than in 1948. On this showing, Britons had never had it so good as after their finest hour. Yet, writing towards the end of the twentieth century, it is difficult to escape the issue of decline, as the titles of numerous books immediately confirm.

Relative decline in Britain's position during the century was, of course, inevitable; and since relative power is what matters in a military or political sense, that issue is clear. But economic decline is relative in more complex ways, and can indeed be absolute. Two world wars radically depleted Britain's assets, thus extorting a high price for victory in both blood and treasure. It should be noted, however, that the war economy, by requiring full use of resources, also brought some benefits. The Second World War thus mopped up the unemployment left by the years of recession which preceded it. Moreover, in the period from 1945 to 1990 there were only four years of significant absolute decline – all of them between 1974 and 1981. It is indisputable that in this period the British economy enjoyed secular growth unprecedented in its history, albeit less than that of some major competitors.

The question is, therefore, whether the British people could in some way have done better, had they seized their historical opportunities by making different collective choices. Economically, the relevant comparison is surely with other major European countries, like France and Germany. In 1950 the British economy was still larger than either; only later did both overtake Britain. It is difficult to resist the conclusion that both of them bounced back from the setback of the Second World War more effectively than the only combatant European country to remain unconquered throughout. Yet it would be bizarre to suppose that Britain would have benefited from defeat, and naive to think that accommodation with Nazi Germany offered a means of preserving British power and prosperity – still less national self-respect. In the end these remain choices with a moral dimension, not simply alternative strategies in maximizing immediate material self-interest.

Given that Britain did the right thing in 1939–40, did the country take the wrong course after 1945? At home, the post-war settlement involved a commitment to implementing a welfare state and to maintaining high levels of employment. Again, the relevant comparison is with similar European countries, most of which were soon spending at least as much as the United Kingdom on social services, albeit organized in different ways. It is odd to suppose that in Britain alone such provision inhibited economic growth: more reasonable to think that the welfare state and virtually full employment were interdependent. The long era of economic expansion which followed the Second World War provided ample resources for social security – so long as unemployment remained low. Britain's experience here, as in much else, was not so different from that of other European countries.

It is easy now to see that Britain's pretensions as a great power in the post-war world were unsustainable; that defence spending was a crippling burden; that imperial geopolitical thinking was outmoded. Yet it should not be forgotten that a potential power vacuum existed for some years after 1945, before the USA adopted a clear role in the sort of Atlantic alliance apparently necessary to guarantee the security of western Europe. Nor should it be overlooked that British decolonization was to prove relatively successful, leaving few of the scars suffered by other ex-colonial powers in their own extrication from empire. Whatever its other deficiencies, the continued existence of the Commonwealth showed that British governments had not wholly lost their talent for appeasement, when this was the appropriate strategy for accommodation to the reality of declining power. Only after Suez did France more purposefully turn from post-imperial illusions to the constructive pursuit of its national objectives within a framework of European integration.

Here is the most obvious missed opportunity. For by the time Britain joined the European Community, the once-for-all boom was already exhausted and the British people were to be denied an economic object lesson in the benefits of the Common Market. More crucially, the developing European institutions had already been moulded in many ways that ill-suited British traditions and interests. This was the penalty for British failure to participate in laying the foundations, arguably from the time of the Schuman Plan in 1950, certainly after the Messina conference in 1955. Little wonder that European issues were to play such a divisive role in British politics. Until the mid-1980s it was the Labour Party that was most sceptical and most divided; since then, in a curious reversal, it has been the Conservative Party. Within the span of a generation, the fracture lines in politics have increasingly stemmed from issues concerning Britain's relationship with the European Union – issues which can hardly remain unresolved into the twenty-first century.

*Appendix*
# Governments and Elections
## 1895–1990

## UNIONIST GOVERNMENT, 1895–1905
Prime minister: 3rd Marquess of Salisbury, 25 June 1895

*General election, 28 September/24 October 1900*
Electorate 6.7 million; turnout 75 per cent; 243 unopposed returns

|                  | Liberal | Unionist | Labour | Irish Nationalist |
| ---------------- | ------- | -------- | ------ | ----------------- |
| Total votes (%)  | 45.0    | 50.3     | 1.3    | 2.6               |
| MPs              | 184     | 402      | 2      | 82                |
| (Unopposed MPs)  | (22)    | (163)    | —      | (58)              |

Prime minister: Arthur James Balfour, 12 July 1902

## LIBERAL GOVERNMENT, 1905–15
Prime minister: Sir Henry Campbell-Bannerman, 5 December 1905

*General election, 12 January/7 February 1906*
Electorate 7.3 million; turnout 83 per cent; 114 unopposed returns

|                  | Liberal | Unionist | Labour | Irish Nationalist |
| ---------------- | ------- | -------- | ------ | ----------------- |
| Total votes (%)  | 49.4    | 43.4     | 4.8    | 0.6               |
| MPs              | 400     | 157      | 30     | 83                |
| (Unopposed MPs)  | (27)    | (13)     |        | (74)              |

Prime minister: Herbert Henry Asquith (Liberal), 7 April 1908

*General election, 14 January/9 February 1910*
Electorate 7.7 million; turnout 87 per cent; 75 unopposed returns

|                  | Liberal | Unionist | Labour | Irish Nationalist |
| ---------------- | ------- | -------- | ------ | ----------------- |
| Total votes (%)  | 43.5    | 46.8     | 7.0    | 1.9               |
| MPs              | 275     | 273      | 40     | 82                |
| (Unopposed MPs)  | (1)     | (19)     |        | (55)              |

*General election, 2–19 December 1910*

Electorate 7.7 million; turnout 82 per cent; 163 unopposed returns

|  | Liberal | Unionist | Labour | Irish Nationalist |
|---|---|---|---|---|
| Total votes (%) | 44.2 | 43.6 | 6.4 | 2.5 |
| MPs | 272 | 272 | 42 | 84 |
| (Unopposed MPs) | (35) | (72) | (3) | (53) |

## FIRST COALITION, 1915–16

Formed 25 May 1915 with Asquith remaining prime minister

## LLOYD GEORGE COALITION, 1916–22

Prime minister: David Lloyd George, 7 December 1916

*General election, 14 December 1918*

UK electorate 21.4 million; turnout 57 per cent; 107 unopposed returns

|  | Liberal | Coalition | Labour | Sinn Fein | Others |
|---|---|---|---|---|---|
| Total votes (%) | 13.0 | 53.2 | 20.8 | 4.6 | 8.4 |
| MPs | 36 | 523 | 57 | 73 | 18* |
| (Unopposed MPs) | (4) | (65) | (11) | (25) | (2) |

\* Including 7 Irish Nationalist MPs; Sinn Fein did not take their seats at Westminster.

## CONSERVATIVE GOVERNMENT, 1922–3

Prime minister: Andrew Bonar Law, 23 October 1922

*General election, 15 November 1922*

Electorate 20.9 million;* turnout 73 per cent; 57 unopposed returns

|  | Liberal | Conservative | Labour | Others |
|---|---|---|---|---|
| Total votes (%) | 28.3 | 38.5 | 29.7 | 3.5 |
| MPs | 115 | 344 | 142 | 14 |
| (Unopposed MPs) | (10) | (42) | (4) | (1) |

\* Great Britain and Northern Ireland only.

Prime minister: Stanley Baldwin, 22 May 1923

*General election, 6 December 1923*

Electorate 21.3 million; turnout 71 per cent; 50 unopposed returns

|  | Liberal | Conservative | Labour | Others |
|---|---|---|---|---|
| Total votes (%) | 29.7 | 38.0 | 30.7 | 1.6 |
| MPs | 158 | 258 | 191 | 8 |
| (Unopposed MPs) | (11) | (35) | (3) | (1) |

## LABOUR GOVERNMENT, 1924
Prime minister: J. Ramsay MacDonald, 22 January 1924

*General election, 29 October 1924*

Electorate 21.7 million; turnout 77 per cent; 32 unopposed returns

|  | Liberal | Conservative | Labour | Others |
|---|---|---|---|---|
| Total votes (%) | 17.6 | 48.3 | 33.0 | 1.1 |
| MPs | 40 | 419 | 151 | 5 |
| (Unopposed MPs) | (6) | (16) | (9) | (1) |


## CONSERVATIVE GOVERNMENT, 1924–9
Prime minister: Stanley Baldwin, 4 November 1924

*General election, 30 May 1929*

Electorate 28.9 million; turnout 76 per cent; 7 unopposed returns

|  | Liberal | Conservative | Labour | Others |
|---|---|---|---|---|
| Total votes (%) | 23.6 | 38.1 | 37.1 | 1.2 |
| MPs | 59 | 260 | 287 | 8 |
| (Unopposed MPs) | — | (4) | — | (3) |


## LABOUR GOVERNMENT, 1929–31
Prime minister: J. Ramsay MacDonald, 5 June 1929


## NATIONAL GOVERNMENT, 1931–40
Formed 24 August 1931 with MacDonald remaining prime minister

*General election, 27 October 1931*

Electorate 30.0 million; turnout 76 per cent; 67 unopposed returns

|  | Liberal | National | Labour | Others |
|---|---|---|---|---|
| Total votes (%) | 7.2 | 60.5 | 30.8 | 1.5 |
| MPs | 37* | 521 | 52 | 5 |
| (Unopposed MPs) | (5) | (56) | (6) | — |

* Thirty-three of these Liberals, as well as 35 Liberal National MPs included in the National column, were elected as supporters of the National Government; until 1932 only 4 (Lloyd George) Liberals were independent of it.

Prime minister: Stanley Baldwin, 7 June 1935

*General election, 14 November 1935*

Electorate 31.4 million; turnout 71 per cent; 40 unopposed returns

|  | *Liberal* | *National* | *Labour* | *Others* |
|---|---|---|---|---|
| Total votes (%) | 6.8 | 53.3 | 38.1 | 1.8 |
| MPs | 21 | 429 | 154 | 10 |
| (Unopposed MPs) | — | (26) | (13) | (1) |

Prime minister: Neville Chamberlain, 28 May 1937

## COALITION GOVERNMENT, 1940–45
Prime minister: Winston S. Churchill, 10 May 1940

## CONSERVATIVE GOVERNMENT, 1945
Formed as a 'caretaker' administration, Churchill remaining prime minister, 23 May 1945

*General election, 5 July 1945*

Electorate 33.2 million; turnout 73 per cent; 3 unopposed returns

|  | *Liberal* | *Conservative* | *Labour* | *Others* |
|---|---|---|---|---|
| Total votes (%) | 9.0 | 39.6 | 48.0 | 2.4 |
| MPs | 12 | 210 | 393 | 25 |

## LABOUR GOVERNMENT, 1945–51
Prime minister: Clement Attlee, 26 July 1945

*General election, 23 February 1950*

Electorate 34.4 million; turnout 84 per cent; 2 unopposed returns

|  | *Liberal* | *Conservative* | *Labour* | *Others* |
|---|---|---|---|---|
| Total votes (%) | 9.1 | 43.5 | 46.1 | 1.3 |
| MPs | 9 | 298 | 315 | 3 |

*General election, 25 October 1951*

Electorate 34.9 million; turnout 83 per cent; 4 unopposed returns

|  | *Liberal* | *Conservative* | *Labour* | *Others* |
|---|---|---|---|---|
| Total votes (%) | 2.6 | 48.0 | 48.8 | 0.6 |
| MPs | 6 | 321 | 295 | 3 |

## CONSERVATIVE GOVERNMENT, 1951–64
Prime minister: (Sir) Winston Churchill, 26 October 1951
Prime minister: Sir Anthony Eden, 6 April 1955

*General election, 26 May 1955*
Electorate 34.9 million; turnout 77 per cent

|  | Liberal | Conservative | Labour | Others |
|---|---|---|---|---|
| Total votes (%) | 2.7 | 49.7 | 46.4 | 1.2 |
| MPs | 6 | 345 | 277 | 2 |

Prime minister: Harold Macmillan, 10 January 1957

*General election, 8 October 1959*
Electorate 35.4 million; turnout 79 per cent

|  | Liberal | Conservative | Labour | Others |
|---|---|---|---|---|
| Total votes (%) | 5.9 | 49.3 | 43.9 | 0.9 |
| MPs | 6 | 365 | 258 | 1 |

Prime minister: 14th Earl of Home/Sir Alec Douglas-Home, 19 October 1963

*General election, 15 October 1964*
Electorate 35.9 million; turnout 77 per cent

|  | Liberal | Conservative | Labour | Others |
|---|---|---|---|---|
| Total votes (%) | 11.2 | 43.4 | 44.1 | 1.3 |
| MPs | 9 | 304 | 317 | — |

## LABOUR GOVERNMENT, 1964–70
Prime minister: Harold Wilson, 16 October 1964

*General election, 31 March 1966*
Electorate 36.0 million; turnout 76 per cent

|  | Liberal | Conservative | Labour | Others |
|---|---|---|---|---|
| Total votes (%) | 8.5 | 41.9 | 48.0 | 1.5 |
| MPs | 12 | 253 | 364 | 1 |

*General election, 18 June 1970*
Electorate 39.3 million; turnout 72 per cent

|  | Liberal | Conservative | Labour | Others |
|---|---|---|---|---|
| Total votes (%) | 7.5 | 46.0 | 43.0 | 3.2 |
| MPs | 6 | 330 | 287 | 6* |

(Unopposed MPs)

* Four of these (one Protestant Unionist and 3 Republicans) from Northern Ireland, which is given separately below; also one MP for the Scottish National Party (SNP), given below with Plaid Cymru (PC).

## CONSERVATIVE GOVERNMENT, 1970–74
Prime minister: Edward Heath, 19 June 1970

*General election, 28 February 1974*
Electorate 39.8 million; turnout 79 per cent

|               | Liberal | Conservative | Labour | SNP/PC | N. Ireland | Othe |
| ------------- | ------- | ------------ | ------ | ------ | ---------- | ---- |
| Total votes (%) | 19.3 | 37.9 | 37.1 | 2.6 | 2.3 | 0.8 |
| MPs | 14 | 297 | 301 | 9 | 12 | 2 |

## LABOUR GOVERNMENT, 1974–9
Prime minister: Harold Wilson, 4 March 1974

*General election, 10 October 1974*
Electorate 40.1 million; turnout 73 per cent

|               | Liberal | Conservative | Labour | SNP/PC | N. Ireland |
| ------------- | ------- | ------------ | ------ | ------ | ---------- |
| Total votes (%) | 18.3 | 35.8 | 39.2 | 3.5 | 2.4 |
| MPs | 13 | 277 | 319 | 14 | 12 |

Prime minister: James Callaghan, 5 April 1976

*General election, 3 May 1979*
Electorate 41.1 million; turnout 76 per cent

|               | Liberal | Conservative | Labour | SNP/PC | N. Ireland |
| ------------- | ------- | ------------ | ------ | ------ | ---------- |
| Total votes (%) | 13.8 | 43.9 | 36.9 | 2.0 | 2.2 |
| MPs | 11 | 339 | 269 | 4 | 12 |

## CONSERVATIVE GOVERNMENT, 1979–
Prime minister: Margaret Thatcher, 4 May 1979

*General election, 9 June 1983*
Electorate 42.2 million; turnout 73 per cent

|               | Alliance | Conservative | Labour | SNP/PC | N. Ireland |
| ------------- | -------- | ------------ | ------ | ------ | ---------- |
| Total votes (%) | 25.4 | 42.4 | 27.6 | 1.5 | 3.1 |
| MPs | 23 | 397 | 209 | 4 | 17 |

*General election, 11 June 1987*
Electorate 43.2 million; turnout 75 per cent

|               | Alliance | Conservative | Labour | SNP/PC | N. Ireland |
| ------------- | -------- | ------------ | ------ | ------ | ---------- |
| Total votes (%) | 22.5 | 42.3 | 30.8 | 1.6 | 2.2 |
| MPs | 22 | 376 | 229 | 6 | 17 |

Prime minister: John Major, 28 November 1990

# Bibliographical Essay

In one sense, my sources have been everything I have read in thirty years as a professional historian of twentieth-century Britain; and reconstructing a bibliography is thus impossible. In another sense, the books continually at my elbow while I was writing are fairly easy to list. My debt to B. R. Mitchell, *British Historical Statistics* (Cambridge, 1988), is outstanding for a whole range of statistics on the period up to 1980. Post-Mitchell, most of the economic statistics in Chapter 11 come from the fifty pages of tables in the useful appendix to Christopher Johnson, *The Economy under Mrs Thatcher* (Penguin, 1991). For social statistics I leaned heavily on A. H. Halsey (ed.), *Trends in British Society since 1900. A Guide to the Changing Social Structure of Britain*\* (1972) and, less heavily, on his completely new edition, *British Social Trends since 1900*\* (1988). David Butler and Gareth Butler, *British Political Facts, 1900–1994* (7th edn, 1994) was published in time for me to update some of my figures. My chief source for electoral statistics, however, remained F. W. S. Craig, *British Electoral Facts 1885–1975* (3rd edn, 1976). These indispensable works must have supplied 90 per cent of the statistics cited in my volume.

I have, of course, frequently turned to other reference books, notably the *Annual Register*. For office-holders, the authoritative guide is E. B. Fryde, D. E. Greenway, S. Porter and I. Roy, *Handbook of British Chronology* (3rd edn, 1986). *The Dictionary of National Biography*, specifically *The Twentieth Century DNB*, was a great standby, especially the volumes (by dates of death) for 1951–60 (ed.) E. T. Williams and Helen M. Palmer (Oxford, 1971); for 1961–70, (ed.) E. T. Williams and C. S. Nicholls (Oxford, 1981); for 1971–80 and 1981–5 (ed.) Lord Blake and C. S. Nicholls (Oxford, 1986 and 1990); and the volume of afterthoughts, *Missing Persons* (ed.) C. S. Nicholls (Oxford, 1993), which repaired some notable omissions, notably of women. For those persons who still fell through the cracks – or had, up to the time of writing, still happily escaped the necessary condition for being memorialized by the *DNB* – I turned to *Who's Who*, especially the volumes for 1908, 1932, 1946, 1972 and 1990 which happen

---

\*An asterisk indicates a work containing a fuller bibliography.

to sit on my own shelves. The many volumes of the *Dictionary of Labour Biography*, (ed.) Joyce M. Bellamy and John Saville (1972–, in progress), supplied further specialist guidance, as did John Eatwell, Murray Milgate and Peter Newman (eds.), *The New Palgrave: A Dictionary of Economics* (4 vols., 1987).

Previous historians of twentieth-century Britain, of course, have had a shorter period to cover than mine. Thus when David Thomson concluded the old Pelican History of England with *England in the Twentieth Century, 1914–63* (1965), this covered less than fifty years, barely half my stint here. I reread Thomson's chapters, with enhanced respect, after I had written my own, and thus discovered some unexpected echoes of his own earlier treatment – an experience repeated when I returned to Kenneth O. Morgan's path-breaking account, *The People's Peace, 1945–89\** (Oxford, 1990). In both cases I suppressed my first instinct to change my own text. I have a different sort of debt to two other general histories, each covering a couple of decades. Volumes 5 and 6 of Élie Halévy's classic and irreplaceable *History of the English People in the Nineteenth Century* made a foray into our own century with *Imperialism and the Rise of Labour, 1895–1905* (1926; English edn, 1929) and *The Rule of Democracy, 1905–14* (1932; English edn, 1934). To publish a work of such insight within twenty years of the close of the period which it explored is a heartening demonstration of the possibilities of recent history. Exactly the same can be said of of Charles Loch Mowat, *Britain between the Wars, 1918–1940* (1955), to which A. J. P. Taylor paid a well-deserved tribute – 'I have found myself constantly relying on it despite a struggle for independence' – when he published his own vastly influential volume in the Oxford History of England, *English History, 1914–1945\** (Oxford, 1965). In turn, part of my own struggle for independence lay in keeping my distance from Taylor.

An unusually rich recent crop of synoptic works covers broad fields of British history in this period. P. J. Cain and A. G. Hopkins, *British Imperialism* (2 vols., 1993), use the concept of 'gentlemanly capitalism' to mount a challenging interpretation, with which I am broadly in sympathy, of the political economy of empire and its aftermath. David Reynolds's *Britannia Overruled: British Policy and World Power in the Twentieth Century* (1991) is an authoritative and incisive account of the making of British foreign policy. The second edition of Roderick Floud and Donald McCloskey (eds.), *The Economic History of Britain since 1700\** (Cambridge, 1994), appeared too late to influence the main lines of my treatment. Still, I was able to derive appreciable benefit from Volume 3, covering 1939–92, picking up points from essays by Peter Howlett on the war economy, Charles Feinstein on growth, Leslie Hannah on state ownership, Susan Howson on monetary policy, Jim Tomlinson on economic policy and Barry Supple on the question of decline.

The study of English cultural history owes an inescapable debt to a succession of (diminishingly) Marxist studies by Raymond Williams, among which *The Country and the City* (1975) is my own favourite. In a wholly different style, John Gross sensitively retrieved a lost literary and political context in *The Decline and Fall of the English Man of Letters* (1969). F. M. L. Thompson (ed.), *The Cambridge Social History of Britain, 1750–1950\** (3 vols., 1990), contains a fine survey on Scotland by T. C. Smout. On Welsh history, I have frequently turned to Kenneth O. Morgan, *Rebirth of a Nation: Wales, 1880–1980* (Oxford, 1982). K. T. Hoppen, *Ireland since 1800: Conflict and Conformity* (1989), is an excellent concise treatment; F. S. L. Lyons, *Ireland since the Famine* (rev. edn, 1973), is fuller and almost over-scrupulously balanced in its judgements. More engaged in its revisionist interpretation, and equally engaging in its elegant exposition, is Roy Foster, *Modern Ireland, 1600–1972* (1988).

John Benson's admirable overview, *The Rise of Consumer Society in Britain, 1880–1980* (1994), indicates many new directions in social history. Persistent links between social trends and a 'centrist' political tendency are eclectically illustrated in Brian Harrison, *Peaceable Kingdom: Stability and Change in Modern Britain* (1985). Keith Middlemas, *Politics in Industrial Society: The Experience of the British System since 1911* (1979), elaborated a model of 'corporate bias' in interpreting the accommodation of interest groups by the state during the twentieth century. Robert Blake, *The Conservative Party from Peel to Thatcher* (2nd edn, 1985) and Henry Pelling, *A Short History of the Labour Party* (9th edn, 1991), equally concise and fair-minded, are the standard works on the two major political parties. The classic statement of the thesis that their adversarial form in fact concealed substantial convergence is Robert McKenzie, *British Political Parties: The Distribution of Power within the Conservative and Labour Parties* (1955); and J. P. Mackintosh, *The British Cabinet* (1962), is likewise the classic exposition of the case for regarding prime-ministerial power as distinctive of twentieth-century government. Mackintosh edited a useful collection of essays, *British Prime Ministers of the Twentieth Century* (2 vols., 1977–8), while – single-handed, alas – Peter Clarke, *A Question of Leadership: Gladstone to Thatcher* (1991), used a dozen biographical essays to examine a surprisingly neglected theme.

The following works are grouped under the chapters where I found them most pertinent. It is necessarily a selective list, and thus subjective too. It includes what I regard as the landmark books which have shaped the historiography; also a number of recent articles, especially in *20th Century British History* (abbreviated to *20thCBH*); references to theses by younger scholars whose work has influenced me; and a scattering of sources – memoirs or other contemporary publications which I think worth reading.

## CHAPTER I

On the political system at the turn of the century Martin Pugh, *The Making of Modern British Politics, 1867–1939* (1982), is attentive to developments at the grass roots, while Robert Rhodes James, *The British Revolution, 1880–1939* (1978) develops a more traditional narrative of high politics. There is a brilliant study of the fortunes (in all senses) of the traditional elite in David Cannadine, *The Decline and Fall of the British Aristocracy* (1990). The pioneering work from probate records by W. D. Rubinstein forms the core of his major book, *Men of Property: The Very Wealthy in Britain since the Industrial Revolution* (1981), though the implications of this research have been queried, notably in M. J. Daunton, '"Gentlemanly capitalism" and British industry, 1820–1914', *Past & Present*, 122 (1989). The classic development of ideas of 'informal empire' was in J. Gallagher and R. E. Robinson, 'The imperialism of free trade', *Economic History Review*, vi (1953).

The significance of Chamberlain's background as a businessman is well brought out in Peter Marsh, *Joseph Chamberlain: Entrepreneur in Politics* (1994), while Richard Jay, *Joseph Chamberlain: A Political Biography* (Oxford, 1981), gives the most coherent account of his later career. Andrew Porter, *Britain and the Origins of the South African War* (1980), shows Chamberlain at work as the impresario of imperialism, and Richard Price, *An Imperial War and the British Working Class* (1972), casts a (perhaps unduly) sceptical eye over the popular appeal of jingoism. Bernard Semmel's innovatory study, *Imperialism and Social Reform, 1895–1914* (1960), may have overstated its thesis about a social-imperialist conjunction but was notable in anticipating many themes of later scholarship. Alan Sykes, *Tariff Reform and British Politics, 1903–13* (1979), is a good account of Chamberlain's last crusade. A commanding study of both the intellectual roots and the electoral impact of radical Conservatism is now provided in E. H. H. Green, *The Crisis of Conservatism, 1880–1914* (1994).

Despite its title, the interesting revisionist book by L. G. Sandberg, *Lancashire in Decline* (Columbus, Ohio, 1974), takes a more benign view than I do of the cotton industry's performance and prospects. The authoritative history of trade-union organization and activity has long been H. A. Clegg, Alan Fox and A. F. Thompson, *British Trade Unions,*\* vol. I, *1889–1910* (Oxford, 1965). This is particularly lucid on legal issues, on which Norman McCord, 'Taff Vale revisited', *History*, lxxviii (1993), is also pertinent. On the politics of organized labour, the classic study is Henry Pelling, *The Origins of the Labour Party, 1880–1900* (1954), with its sequel, Frank Bealey and Henry Pelling, *Labour and Politics, 1900–1906* (1958). These now need to be supplemented by David Howell, *British Workers and the Independent Labour Party, 1888–1906* (1983). The nature of working-class political culture is nicely conveyed in Ross McKibbin, 'Why was there no Marxism in Great Britain?', *English Historical Review*, xcix (1984), reprinted in McKibbin, *Ideologies of Class* (1990), which also reprints seminal essays on working-class gambling and hobbies.

On electoral politics, the fine study by Paul Thompson, *Socialists, Liberals and Labour: Struggle for London, 1885–1914* (1967), took a 'pessimistic' view of the revival and prospects of the Liberal Party, while P. F. Clarke, *Lancashire and the New Liberalism* (1971), stated the 'optimistic' thesis. This still seems to me to have a lot in it and not to be vitiated by demonstrations of the continued strength of 'old Liberalism', like that in Kenneth D. Wald, in *Crosses on the Ballot: Patterns of British Voter Alignment since 1885* (1983). Judicious historiographical surveys are offered by Michael Bentley, *The Climax of Liberal Politics, 1868–1918* (1987), and G. R. Searle, *The Liberal Party: Triumph and Disintegration, 1886–1929*\* (1992).

## CHAPTER 2

The thoughtful reinterpretation by Jose Harris, *Private Lives, Public Spirit: A Social History of Britain 1870–1914*\* (Oxford, 1993), has a wealth of suggestive detail and advances an overarching thesis about the strong continuities in social norms into the third quarter of the century. This was adumbrated in her earlier contribution to F. M. L. Thompson (ed.), *The Cambridge Social History of Britain, 1750–1950*\* (3 vols., 1990), which also contains fine essays by the editor on town and city, by Michael Anderson on demographic change, by Leonore Davidoff on the family, by Patrick Joyce on work, by Pat Thane on government and society, and by F. K. Prochaska on philanthropy. I had the advantage of reading Pat Jalland's persuasive, if harrowing, study, *Death in the Victorian Family* (Oxford, 1996), before its publication. Roderick Floud, Kenneth Wachter and Annabel Gregory, *Height, Health and History: Nutritional Status in the United Kingdom, 1750–1980* (Cambridge, 1990), further the debate on living standards by using new sorts of evidence.

Michael Freeden's *The New Liberalism* (1978) is a coherent account of Liberal ideology, though a better sense of the impact of events like the Boer War is given in H. C. G. Matthew, *The Liberal Imperialists* (1973), which brings out this group's preoccupation with social issues at home, and in G. R. Searle, *The Quest for National Efficiency, 1902–11* (1971), which explores the Fabians' attempts to accommodate imperialism and work with it. Peter Clarke's *Liberals and Social Democrats* (1978) is a study of how New Liberals like Hobson, Hobhouse and Wallas established a distinctively liberal kind of social-democratic thinking; and the intellectual ramifications of such a position are elegantly traced in Stefan Collini, *Liberalism and Sociology: L. T. Hobhouse and Political Argument in England, 1880–1914* (1979).

Norman and Jeanne Mackenzie, *The First Fabians* (1977), is an accessible group biography which can be supplemented by the exhaustive treatment in Michael Holroyd, *Bernard Shaw*, vol. 1, 1856–98: *The Search for Love* (1988; Penguin 1990), and vol. 2, 1898–1918: *The Pursuit of Power* (1989; Penguin 1991). Much shorter – not of insight, only pages – is Margaret Drabble, *Arnold Bennett* (1974); and another informative biography is Janet Adam Smith, *John Buchan* (1965). H. G. Wells, *Experiment in Autobiography*

(2 vols., 1934) shows his preoccupations; and the state of scientific education is the theme of D. S. L. Cardwell, *The Organization of Science in England* (1957; rev. edn, 1972).

Gareth Stedman Jones, 'Working-class politics and working-class culture 1850–1914', reprinted in his *Languages of Class* (Cambridge, 1983), is especially good on music hall, on which much has recently appeared in print. Peter Bailey examines the complicity between performers and audience in 'Conspiracies of meaning: music hall and the knowingness of popular culture', *Past & Present*, 144 (August 1994). Michael Rosenthal, *The Character Factory: Baden-Powell and the Boy Scout Movement* (1986), is a somewhat uncharitable view, open to revision from Martin Dedman, 'Baden-Powell, militarism, and the "invisible contributors" to the Boy Scout scheme, 1904–20', *20thCBH*, iv (1993). There is now an interesting literature on the informal imperialism of sport, with two particularly apt essays by James Bradley and Harold Perkin in J. A. Mangan (ed.), *The Cultural Bond: Sport, Empire, Society* (1992). Tony Mason, *Association Football and English Society, 1863–1915* (Sussex, 1980), was a pioneering study of leisure.

Asquith has attracted two good modern biographies: Roy Jenkins, *Asquith* (1964), inclined towards an indulgent judgement, whereas Stephen Koss, *Asquith* (1976), adopted a more astringent view. At the time of writing, John Grigg's three well-wrought volumes, *The Young Lloyd George* (1973), *Lloyd George, the People's Champion, 1902–11* (1978) and *Lloyd George, from Peace to War, 1912–16* (1985), stopped short of the premiership. The most durable single-volume study has long been Thomas Jones, *Lloyd George* (Oxford, 1951), though Martin Pugh, *Lloyd George* (1988), is an admirable modern account of his career.

On the politics of welfare, Bentley B. Gilbert, *The Evolution of National Insurance in Great Britain* (1966), is especially good on the friendly-society background; Jose Harris, *Unemployment and Politics, 1886–1914* (1972), is exemplary on policy developments. The tensions within the Royal Commission on the Poor Law are sensitively recaptured in A. M. McBriar, *An Edwardian Mixed Doubles: The Bosanquets versus the Webbs* (1988). Avner Offer, *Property and Politics: Landownership, Law, Ideology and Urban Development in England 1870–1914* (1981), is a multifaceted study of the Edwardian fiscal crisis, and Lloyd George's response to it is well surveyed in Bruce K. Murray, *The People's Budget, 1909–10* (1980). The authoritative study of the 1910 elections is Neal Blewett, *The Peers, the Parties and the People* (1972).

A stimulating perspective on Irish history in this period is J. J. Lee, *The Modernization of Irish Society 1848–1918* (1973), while the Home Rule crisis receives a lucid treatment in Pat Jalland, *The Liberals and Ireland: The Ulster Problem in British Politics to 1914* (1980). The classic account of this period has long been George Dangerfield, *The Strange Death of Liberal England, 1910–14* (1936), now historiographically superseded but still compelling reading. Newer approaches to trade-union history are well exemplified by Alastair Reid's essay in Wolfgang J. Mommsen and Hans-Gerhard Husung (eds.), *The Development of Trade Unionism in Great Britain and Germany, 1880–1914* (1985).

Michael Howard, *The Continental Commitment* (1972), is a trenchant analysis of the thinking behind British strategy and Paul Kennedy likewise accessibly encapsulates much learning in *The Realities behind Diplomacy: Background Influences on British External Policy, 1865–1980* (1981). Zara Steiner, *Britain and the Origins of the First World War* (1977), picks its way sure-footedly through a minefield of contention. Keith Robbins has written with dispassionate insight both about Grey's foreign policy in *Sir Edward Grey* (1971) and about its radical critics in *The Abolition of War: The Peace Movement in Britain, 1914–19* (1976).

## CHAPTER 3

A. J. P. Taylor, *The First World War* (1963), showed the author's incomparable gift for making lucid narrative look easy, though it is still profitable to go back to B. H. Liddell Hart, *History of the First World War* (1970), originally published in 1930 in a slightly different format. John Keegan, *The Face of Battle* (Penguin, 1976), brings out some historically distinctive features of the soldiers' experience of the western front, compared with earlier eras. For British propaganda, I have drawn on Cate Haste, *Keep the Home Fires Burning* (1977); and Jon Silkin (ed.), *The Penguin Book of First World War Poetry* (Penguin, 1979) contains most of the poems quoted. Like many other readers, I have been much influenced by Paul Fussell's evocative book, *The Great War and Modern Memory* (1975), and also by Samuel Hynes, *A War Imagined* (1988). Jay Winter, *Sites of Memory, Sites of Mourning* (1995) has many insights on the cultural impact of war; and on commemoration, David Cannadine's vignette on Curzon's role in *Aspects of Aristocracy* (1994) can be supplemented by Adrian Gregory's fine survey, *The Silence of Memory: Armistice Day, 1919–46* (1994). For the war artists the indispensable study is Maria Tippett, *Art at the Service of War* (1984).

Trevor Wilson's *The Myriad Faces of War* (1988) is a vast and comprehensive work of scholarship. Strategic issues are among the many themes cogently argued in John Turner, *British Politics and the Great War** (1992); and on the imperial and naval logistics of food supplies I found Avner Offer, *The First World War: An Agrarian Interpretation* (1989), stimulating and (almost) wholly persuasive.

Arthur Marwick, *The Deluge* (1965; 2nd edn 1991), remains the most accessible account of the domestic impact of the war, and can be supplemented by his *Women at War* (1978). Jane Lewis, *Women in England, 1870–1950* (1984), deftly illustrates the significance of many long-term trends in both work and welfare. Susan Pedersen, *Family, Dependence, and the Origins of the Welfare State: Britain and France, 1914–45* (1993), uses comparative history to bring out significant aspects in the British treatment of the family, while Joanna Bourke gives a sympathetic account of married women's domestic role in 'Housewifery in working-class England, 1860–1914', *Past & Present*, 143 (May 1994). Margaret Llewelyn Davies (ed.) *Life As We Have Known It* (1931; republished 1977) was a pioneer edition of autobiographical writings by working women.

Jay Winter, *The Great War and the British People* (1985), brings out the relative demographic impact of both military participation and changing living standards. There has now been much useful research on political repercussions, culminating in the 1918 Reform Act, well explained in Martin Pugh, *Electoral Reform in Peace and War 1906–18* (1978). The allegedly strong class bias of household suffrage was the theme of a much-cited article by H. C. G. Matthew, R. McKibbin and J. Kay, 'The franchise factor in the rise of the Labour party', *English Historical Review*, xci (1976), reprinted in Ross McKibbin, *The Ideologies of Class: Social Relations in Britain, 1880–1950* (1990). But Duncan Tanner's authoritative study, *Political Change and the Labour Party, 1900–18* (1990), makes a convincing revision here, and his book should be read alongside the distinguished earlier study by Ross McKibbin, *The Evolution of the Labour Party, 1910–24* (1975).

Trevor Wilson, *The Downfall of the Liberal Party, 1914–35* (1966), remains the best study of the party itself, though the disintegration of a Liberal mind-set is nicely observed in Michael Bentley, *The Liberal Mind, 1914–29* (Cambridge, 1977). An unpublished thesis with a penetrating treatment of the making of the peace is David Dubinski, 'British Liberals and Radicals and the the Treatment of Germany, 1914–20' (Cambridge PhD, 1992). The *War Memoirs* which David Lloyd George wrote at such length in the 1930s are now under-read and underrated, though the two-volume edition (1938) is easily available. A. J. P. Taylor (ed.), *Lloyd George: A Diary by Frances Stevenson* (1971), contains unique glimpses of the prime minister through the eyes of his mistress and political secretary, while Harold Nicolson, *Peacemaking 1919* (1933 and subsequent editions), is interesting in juxtaposing a young diplomat's diary with his later reflections.

For the post-war period, Kenneth O. Morgan, *Consensus and Disunity: The Lloyd George Coalition Government, 1918–22* (Oxford, 1979), is the definitive work. It can be supplemented on high-political manoeuvres by Maurice Cowling, *The Impact of Labour, 1920–24* (Cambridge, 1971), which suggests that a return to a two-party system was not preordained. Robert Blake seized the benefit of early access to the Beaverbrook archive in writing *The Unknown Prime Minister: Bonar Law* (1955), which still holds the field. There are challenging new perspectives on the evolution of an independent Ireland in J. J. Lee's weighty tract, *Ireland 1912–85: Politics and Society* (Cambridge, 1989).

CHAPTER 4

The inaugural lecture by F. M. L. Thompson, *Victorian England: The Horse-Drawn Society* (Bedford College, London, 1970), wore its learning lightly but broached many provoking ideas. Two major landmarks in the history of newspapers are Alan J. Lee, *The Origins of the Popular Press in England, 1855–1914* (1976), and Stephen Koss, *The Rise and Fall of the Political Press* (Volume 2 on the twentieth century) (1984) – each of them, sadly, the last book before the premature death of its author. David Ayerst, *Guardian: Biography of a Newspaper* (1971), is particularly good on the golden age of C. P. Scott. The most fascinating press lord of the era has attracted two biographies of high calibre: A. J. P. Taylor's candidly hagiographical *Beaverbrook* (1972) and the altogether more candid appraisal by Anne Chisholm and Michael Davie, *Beaverbrook* (1992). My account of broadcasting and film, as well as the press, is much indebted to Dan LeMahieu, *A Culture for Democracy: Mass Communication and the Cultivated Mind in Britain between the Wars* (Oxford, 1988). Such cultural dilemmas are picked up in several of the essays in Peter Mandler and Susan Pedersen (eds.), *After the Victorians: Private Conscience and Public Duty in Modern Britain* (1994), notably LeMahieu on Reith and Chris Waters on Priestley.

The confused electoral politics of the early 1920s are analysed in Chris Cook, *The Age of Alignment: Electoral Politics in Britain, 1922–9* (1975), and the maps in Michael Kinnear, *The British Voter: An Atlas and Survey since 1885* (1968), are particularly useful for this period. At the time of writing there was no wholly satisfactory life of Baldwin: Roy Jenkins's urbane extended essay, *Baldwin* (1987), is too slight, though often acute, whereas the doorstop by Keith Middlemas and John Barnes, *Baldwin* (1969), errs in the other direction. Meanwhile the essay by Philip Williamson, 'The doctrinal politics of Stanley Baldwin', in *Public and Private Doctrine*, (ed.) M. Bentley (Cambridge, 1993), is persuasive in retrieving a religious ambience, and this era in the history of the Conservative Party is well treated in John Ramsden, *The Age of Balfour and Baldwin* (1978). MacDonald was lucky, at least posthumously, in attracting a biographer of the calibre of David Marquand, whose *Ramsay MacDonald* (1977) achieved a proper rehabilitation of a formidable figure, scorned since his death. Bernard Wasserstein's fair-minded biography, *Herbert Samuel* (1992), spoke with particular authority on Palestine and John E. Kendle, *The Round Table Movement and Imperial Union* (Toronto, 1975), is useful on the origins of the concept of the Commonwealth.

Paul Addison is so refreshing, in *Churchill on the Home Front 1900–55* (1992), by dint of taking the future war leader seriously in the role he was actually playing at the time. Norman Rose, in *Churchill: an Unruly Life* (1994), has written the best single-volume biography, and writes well on the Zionist theme in Robert Blake and Roger Louis (eds.), *Churchill* (Oxford, 1993), in which Addison contributes a shrewd essay on Churchill and social reform and

Peter Clarke also writes on Churchill's economic ideas. On Treasury policy scholars have the benefit of the excellent unpublished thesis by Mary Short, 'The Politics of Personal Taxation: Budget-making in Britain, 1917–31' (Cambridge, 1985). The authoritative study of the return to gold is D. E. Moggridge, *British Monetary Policy, 1924–1931* (Cambridge, 1972). There is a useful wide-ranging survey of all aspects of the unemployment problem in W. R. Garside, *British Unemployment, 1919–39*\* (Cambridge, 1990). H. A. Clegg, *A History of British Trade Unions*, vol. 2, *1911–33*\* (Oxford, 1985), sets the strikes of the 1920s in context, and for an exemplary account of the intractable problems of the coal industry see Barry Supple's coverage of the period 1913–46 in volume 4 of *The History of the British Coal Industry* (Oxford, 1987).

Neville Chamberlain is diligently chronicled by David Dilks, *Neville Chamberlain*, vol. 1, *Pioneering and Reform, 1869–1929* (Cambridge, 1984), and his work at the Ministry of Health copiously explained in Bentley B. Gilbert, *British Social Policy 1914–39* (1970). Paul Johnson is illuminating on 'The employment and retirement of older men in England and Wales, 1881–1961', *Economic History Review*, xlvii (1994). The impact of women within the political system is the theme of Martin Pugh, *Women and the Women's Movement in Britain, 1914–59* (1992). The Liberal revival, intellectual as much as electoral, is well covered in John Campbell, *Lloyd George: The Goat in the Wilderness* (1977).

## CHAPTER 5

A good starting point for the social history of the inter-war period is John Stevenson, *British Society, 1914–45* (1984); and see the essays by M. J. Daunton on housing and James Obelkevich on religion in F. M. L. Thompson (ed.), *The Cambridge Social History of Britain, 1750–1950* (1990). Simon Pepper writes well on architecture in Boris Ford (ed.), *The Cambridge Cultural History of Britain*, vol. 8, *Early Twentieth Century Britain* (Cambridge, 1992), which also has good essays on literature by Jacques Berthaud and John Beer. A. D. Gilbert, *Religion and Society in Industrial England: Church, Chapel and Social Change 1740–1914* (1976), establishes a sound methodology for estimating change in religious observance over time; this is followed up in the chapter by Gilbert and Robert Currie in A. H. Halsey (ed.), *Trends in British Society since 1900*\* (1972).

A recent spate of publications has transformed the literature on the political economy of this era. On Keynes himself two major biographies were published almost simultaneously: Donald Moggridge, *John Maynard Keynes: an Economist's Biography*\* (1992), and Robert Skidelsky, *John Maynard Keynes*, vol. 2, *The Economist as Saviour 1920–37* (1992). There are essays on Treasury thinking by George Peden and Peter Clarke in Mary Furner and Barry Supple (eds.), *The State and Economic Knowledge* (1990). Peter Clarke, *The Keynesian*

*Revolution in the Making, 1924–36* (Oxford, 1988), tells the story of an argument over economic policy with both theoretical and practical implications, especially as it developed in the Macmillan Committee. The earlier account of the parallel arguments within the EAC by Susan Howson and Donald Winch, *The Economic Advisory Council* (Cambridge, 1977), remains indispensable.

The obstacles to implementing a Keynesian programme are brought out in J. Tomlinson, *Problems in British Economic Policy, 1870–1945*, (London, 1981), and in several of the essays in A. Booth and M. Pack, *Employment, Capital and Economic Policy* (Oxford, 1985). G. C. Peden, 'Sir Richard Hopkins and the "Keynesian revolution" in employment policy', *Economic History Review*, xxxvi (1983), gives a sympathetic account of the career of this notable civil servant. Roger Middleton, *Towards the Managed Economy* (London, 1985), usefully subjects contemporary policy models to modern economic analysis.

On the economic policy of the Labour Government, Robert Skidelsky, *Politicians and the Slump* (1967), remains well worth reading, though his biography, *Oswald Mosley* (1975), intended as an exercise in retrieval of a fallen reputation, has not worn well. Skidelsky's perspective received an early challenge from Ross McKibbin's article, first published in *Past & Present* in 1975, 'The economic policy of the second Labour Government', reprinted in his *Ideologies of Class* (1990). On the politics of this period, students can now turn with confidence to Stuart Ball, *Baldwin and the Conservative Party* (1988), Andrew Thorpe, *The British General Election of 1931* (1991), and Philip Williamson, *National Crisis and National Government, 1926–32* (1992). Some of these revisionist readings, it should be acknowledged, were adumbrated in Reginald Bassett's pioneering scholarly study, *1931: Political Crisis* (1958). John Stevenson and Chris Cook, *The Slump* (1977), is particularly strong on electoral analysis, and can be supplemented by D. H. Close, 'The realignment of the British electorate in 1931', *History*, xvii (1982), and Tom Stannage, *Baldwin Thwarts the Opposition: The General Election of 1935* (1980).

One theme explored in Stefan Collini's distinguished book *Public Moralists* (1992) is the role of literary influences in defining a shift away from a Victorian sensibility. Noel Annan, *Our Age* (1990), is an idiosyncratic and subjective view of British political culture since the First World War. Samuel Hynes, *The Auden Generation: Literature and Politics in the 1930s* (1976), is a good account of the response of younger writers, while Gary Werskey, *The Visible College* (1978), usefully focuses on a number of scientists of the same generation. Among numerous biographies, Quentin Bell, *Virginia Woolf* (2 vols., 1972) and Peter Ackroyd, *T. S. Eliot* (1984), are particularly illuminating; and I also drew on Nigel Nicolson (ed.), *The Letters of Virginia Woolf*, vol. v, *1932–5* (1979).

## CHAPTER 6

On Churchill and India, Robert Rhodes James, *Churchill: A Study in Failure, 1900–39* (1970), makes many good points; though I have also benefited from the useful unpublished thesis by Graham Stewart, 'Churchill and the Conservative Party, 1929–37' (Cambridge PhD, 1995). Max Beloff makes the best case for Churchill's prescience on India in Robert Blake and Wm Roger Louis (eds.), *Churchill* (1993), while Clive Ponting, *Churchill* (1993), is alert to Churchill's atavistic mind-set.

The literature on appeasement has always been notable for both copiousness and tendentiousness. Churchill's own apologia was influentially set out in Winston S. Churchill, *The Second World War*, vol. 1, *The Gathering Storm* (1948), and later buttressed by his official biographer, Martin Gilbert, *Winston S. Churchill*, especially volume 5, 1922–39 (1976) with its useful documentary Companion Volumes. A. J. P. Taylor's *The Origins of the Second World War* (1961) was a cause of affront when it was published and of a historiographical revolution in subsequent decades. Gordon Martel (ed.), *The Origins of the Second World War Reconsidered* (1986), provides a sober retrospect. Curiously, one of the best early revisionist works, extenuating the position of Churchill's opponents, came from the later official biographer, Martin Gilbert, in *The Roots of Appeasement* (1966). Keith Robbins, *Munich 1938* (1968), was a notably successful attempt to transcend partisanship and remains well worth reading, while John Charmley, *Chamberlain and the Lost Peace* (1989), gives the most sympathetic portrayal of Chamberlain's policy. Many of his points were anticipated in Maurice Cowling's trenchant study, *The Impact of Hitler: British Politics and British Policy, 1933–40* (1975). There is now a balanced appraisal, based on deep scholarship, in R. A. C. Parker, *Chamberlain and Appeasement* (1993). The management of public opinion provides a good subject for Richard Cockett in *Twilight of Truth: Chamberlain, Appeasement and the Manipulation of the Press* (1989).

The constraints on British policy exercised by economic perceptions are lucidly explicated in G. C. Peden, *British Rearmament and the Treasury* (1980), while the tensions in relations with the USA are effectively brought out in David Reynolds, *The Creation of the Anglo-American Alliance, 1937–41* (1981). The unfolding crisis is expertly described, step by step, in Donald Cameron Watt, *How War Came* (1989). Henry Pelling, *Britain and the Second World War* (1970), is a concise survey, nicely anti-heroic in tone, whereas some of the debunking in Clive Ponting, *1940: Myth and Reality* (1990), mars an otherwise salutary study. John Charmley, *Churchill: The End of Glory* (1993), suggests that a negotiated peace might have better served British interests, though the contrary case, as summarized in David Reynolds, 'Churchill and the decision to fight on in 1940: right policy, wrong reasons', in Richard Langhorne (ed.), *Diplomacy and Intelligence during the Second World War* (1985), remains more persuasive. The inescapable tragic dimension in Churchill's stance is well caught in Keith Robbins, *Churchill* (1992), and his private secretary, John Colville, happily preserved many contemporary insights in *The Fringes of Power: Downing Street Diaries, 1939–51* (1985).

Michael Balfour, *Propaganda in War, 1939–45* (1979) – more wide-ranging in scope than its title might suggest – provides an admirably sustained view of the course of the war. F. H. Hinsley offers an insider's account of the significance of Ultra in the volume he edited with Alan Stripp, *Codebreakers* (1993). David Reynolds's fine study, *Rich Relations: The American Occupation of Britain, 1942–5* (1995), has much to offer both on grand strategy and on social history. The war's domestic impact and thwarted revolutionary potential is the theme of Angus Calder's rich chronicle, *The People's War* (1969); and three pertinent articles on cultural issues are: F. M. Leventhal, ' "The best for the most": CEMA and state sponsorship of the arts in wartime, 1939–45', *20thCBH*, i (1990); Nicholas Joicey, 'A paperback guide to progress: Penguin books, 1935–51', *20thCBH*, iv (1993); and Sian Nicholas, ' "Sly demagogues" and wartime radio: J. B. Priestley and the BBC', *20thCBH*, vi (1996).

The long-term role of war in driving up government spending commitments is the theme of Alan T. Peacock and Jack Wiseman, *The Growth of Public Expenditure in the United Kingdom* (Oxford and Princeton, 1961); this process is analysed in a more explicit political context in James Cronin, *The Politics of State Expansion* (1991). Two good studies which use public records to chart the development of a Keynesian approach to economic management are Jim Tomlinson, *Employment Policy: The Crucial Years, 1939–51* (Oxford, 1987) and Alan Booth, *British Economic Policy, 1931–49: Was There a Keynesian Revolution?* (1989). Correlli Barnett, *The Audit of War* (1986) presents an acerbic indictment of Britain's failings, targeting a misguided aspiration for a 'New Jerusalem'. There is a sharp critique of this view in 'Enterprise and welfare states: a comparative perspective', *Transactions of the Royal Historical Society*, xl (1990) by Jose Harris, whose biography, *William Beveridge* (1977), is authoritative on the architect of social-security plans. Paul Addison, *The Road to 1945* (1975), remains the most persuasive account of the making of a new consensus, though it can now usefully be supplemented by Stephen Brooke, *Labour's War* (1992), which stresses the persistence of partisan commitments. Rodney Lowe, 'The Second World War, consensus, and the foundation of the welfare state', *20thCBH*, i (1990), makes a critical appraisal of the extent of consensus here. Steven Fielding, Peter Thompson and Nick Tiratsoo, *'England Arise!' The Labour Party and Popular Politics in 1940s Britain* (1995), by examining social and cultural attitudes, suggests a sceptical view of the possibilities for radical change.

## CHAPTER 7

The essays collected in Peter Hennessy and Anthony Seldon (eds.), *Ruling Performance: British Governments from Attlee to Thatcher* (Oxford, 1987), provide a good introduction to the party politics of the post-war period. The biography by Kenneth Harris, *Attlee* (1982), had the advantage of drawing on personal contact with its subject; Trevor Burridge, *Clement Attlee* (1985), is more distant, perhaps more objective. Alan Bullock's *Ernest Bevin, Foreign Secretary, 1945–51* (1983) completes a fine trilogy on the life and times of a major figure, convincingly portrayed throughout, despite the fact that he left such a thin personal archive – a problem also faced by Bernard Donoughue and G. W. Jones in their sympathetic but scholarly study, *Herbert Morrison* (1973). Ben Pimlott is not only the editor of the two illuminating volumes, *The Political Diary of Hugh Dalton, 1918–40, 1945–60* (1987) and *The Second World War Diary of Hugh Dalton, 1940–5* (1986), but also author of a masterly biography, *Hugh Dalton* (1985). Cripps now needs similar attention.

A pre-publication inkling of Simon Szreter's *Fertility, Class and Gender in Britain, 1860–1940* (Cambridge, 1996) informed my text on demographic issues. Correlli Barnett, *The Lost Victory: British Dreams, British Realities, 1945–50* (1995), casts a jaundiced eye over the allegedly misguided commitment to a welfare state; a useful corrective is the trenchant analysis in Jim Tomlinson, 'Welfare and the economy: the economic impact of the welfare state', *20thCBH*, vi (1995). On the making of the National Health Service, its official historian, Charles Webster, writes pertinently in 'Conflict and consensus: explaining the British Health Service,' *20thCBH*, i (1990), and 'Doctors, public service and profit: GPs and the NHS', *Transactions of the Royal Historical Society*, xl (1990). Michael Foot, *Aneurin Bevan, 1945–60* (1973), deals with this phase of his hero's career, invariably in heroic terms; a necessary corrective is supplied by John Campbell, *Nye Bevan and the Mirage of British Socialism* (1987).

On economic policy two formidable studies complement each other: Alec Cairncross, *Years of Recovery: British Economic Policy, 1945–51* (1985), and Susan Howson, *British Monetary Policy, 1945–51* (1993). On nuclear policy I relied on Margaret Gowing's massively documented volumes, *Britain and Atomic Energy, 1939–45* (1964) and *Independence and Deterrence: Britain and Atomic Energy, 1945–52* (2 vols., 1974). Kenneth O. Morgan, *Labour in Power, 1945–51* (1984), was a path-breaking account of the Attlee Government in context, and Henry Pelling, *The Labour Governments, 1945–51* (1984), was admirably concise and precise in explaining its official policy stance, while its critics received more sympathetic treatment in Jonathan Schneer, *Labour's Conscience: The Labour Left, 1945–51* (1988). The achievement of Peter Hennessy in *Never Again: Britain 1945–51* (1992) was to realize how much more than a simple political history was still needed to reconstitute the texture of post-war life. Two useful articles by Ina Zweiniger-Bargielowska, 'Bread rationing in Britain, 1946–8', *20thCBH*, iv (1993) and 'Rationing, austerity and the Conservative party recovery after 1945,' *Historical Journal*, xxxvii (1994), now substantiate the political as well as economic impact of austerity.

The compendious volume edited by Anthony Seldon and Stuart Ball (eds.), *Conservative Century*\* (1994), contains a wealth of important essays: those by Stuart Ball on party organization, by Richard Kelly on party conferences, and by John Barnes and Richard Cockett on ideology and policy are particularly relevant to this period. On its own ground, J. D. Hoffman's study, *The Conservative Party in Opposition, 1945–51* (1964), still holds the field. As authorized biographer, Anthony Howard proved no hagiographer in *RAB: A Life of R. A. Butler* (1987), though Butler's crucial role in post-war Conservative politics is not diminished. The last Churchill Government is the subject of Anthony Seldon's scholarly account, *Churchill's Indian Summer, 1951–5* (1981), and a similar autumnal glow infuses Paul Addison's *Churchill on the Home Front 1900–55* (1992), with its engaging portrait of the old warrior as peacemonger.

## CHAPTER 8

Arthur Marwick, *Culture in Britain since 1945* (1991), is a bold, broad-brush introduction, bubbling with bright ideas. While Robert Hewison's stimulating synthesis, *Culture and Consensus: England, Art and Politics since 1940* (1995), does not replace his earlier books, it usefully draws together some of their themes. Boris Ford (ed.), *The Cambridge Cultural History of Britain*, vol. 9, *Modern Britain* (Cambridge, 1992), has useful essays by Roy and Gwen Shaw on the cultural context, by Neil Sinyard on film, and by the editor on the Third Programme. The role of the media is well covered in James Curran and Jean Seaton, *Power without Responsibility: The Press and Broadcasting in Britain*\* (4th edn, 1991). Vernon Bogdanor and Robert Skidelsky's (eds.) *The Age of Affluence 1951–64* (1970) was a pioneering attempt to make sense of this period and contains several pertinent and wide-ranging essays.

Robert Rhodes James's *Anthony Eden* (1986) extends sympathy to its subject, sometimes justifiably. On Suez, though Hugh Thomas, *The Suez Affair* (rev. edn, 1970), succeeded in getting near the truth on many contentious points, Keith Kyle's *Suez* (1991) must now be regarded as definitive, testing the contemporary hunches of a working journalist against subsequent archival research. Harold Macmillan's voluminous *Memoirs*, especially the disingenuous account of Suez in Volume 4, *Riding the Storm* (1971), did nothing to unravel the enigma of its author. Alistair Horne's *Macmillan* (2 vols., 1987–8), though often candid on personal aspects, bears too many of the marks of an official biography. It left plenty of room for John Turner's acute (though far from hostile) *Macmillan* (1994); and Anthony Sampson, *Macmillan: A Study in Ambiguity* (1967), is still full of insight. D. R. Thorpe's scholarly biography,

*Selwyn Lloyd* (1989), successfully rescued its subject from condescension. On what the archives reveal, and do not reveal, about the Sandys defence review, see Simon J. Ball, 'Harold Macmillan and the politics of defence', *20thCBH*, vi (1995). The salience of electoral motivation in influencing policy is well brought out in Ritchie Ovendale, 'Macmillan and the wind of change in Africa, 1957–60', *Historical Journal*, xxxviii (1995), and in the unpublished thesis by Richard Aldous, 'Harold Macmillan and the Search for a Summit with the USSR, 1958–60' (Cambridge PhD, 1992).

For the creation of Supermac, along with many other sharply observed images from this period, Russell Davies and Liz Ottaway's *Vicky* (1987) serves as a handsome guide. On voting behaviour, the survey which the Gaitskellite magazine *Socialist Commentary* commissioned from Richard Rose and Mark Abrams, *Must Labour Lose?* (1960) was a seminal inquiry, helping to stimulate subsequent academic as well as political debate. Thus a more sophisticated examination of the *embourgeoisement* thesis was mounted in David Lockwood and John Goldthorpe, *The Affluent Worker: Political Attitudes and Behaviour* (1968); while Robert McKenzie and Allan Silver, *Angels in Marble* (1968), was a reminder of traditional sources of working-class Toryism. The two editions of the major work by David Butler and Donald Stokes, *Political Change in Britain* (1969 and 1974), constituted a conceptual as well as an empirical advance in understanding generational change. Frank Parkin, 'Working-class Conservatives: a theory of political deviance', *British Journal of Sociology*, xvii (1967), brilliantly redefined the whole problem as turning on the hegemonic pervasiveness of Conservative values: a line of analysis profitably deepened in Andrew Gamble, *The Conservative Nation* (1974).

On Labour politics, the book on Arthur Deakin by V. L. Allen, *Trade Union Leadership* (1957), still has a lot to offer, though superseded as an institutional study by Lewis Minkin, *The Labour Party Conference* (Manchester, 1978). Philip Williams was a committed Gaitskellite whose *Hugh Gaitskell* (1979) was nonetheless fair as well as full in its scholarship. These virtues made Williams a good editor for *The Diary of Hugh Gaitskell, 1945–56* (1983), while Janet Morgan's edition of *The Backbench Diaries of Richard Crossman* (1981), despite its great length, is riveting as a chronicle from the Bevanite camp (really from a Wilsonian viewpoint).

## CHAPTER 9

F. M. L. Thompson (ed.), *The Cambridge Social History of Britain, 1750–1950*\* (1990), vol. 3, contains a good section on education by Gillian Sutherland, whose monograph, *Ability, Merit and Measurement: Mental Testing and English Education 1880–1940* (1984) is indispensable in understanding issues about selectivity. Deborah Thom on 'The 1944 Education Act', in H. L. Smith (ed.), *War and Social Change: British Society in the Second World War* (1986), is also very useful. John Carswell, *Government and the Universities in Britain: Programme and Performance 1960–1980* (1985), is the best guide to the expansion of the Robbins era. Since A. H. Halsey has unrivalled expertise in this area it is not surprising that both *Trends in British Society since 1900** (1972) and *British Social Trends since 1900** (1988) contain valuable material from him on education, especially on participation at university level. Ralf Dahrendorf's *LSE* (1995) is, more than an institutional history, a fine contribution to the intellectual history of the period. Maurice Kogan (ed.), *The Politics of Education: Conversations with Edward Boyle and Anthony Crosland* (1971), recaptures the tone of contemporary debate between two essentially liberal political opponents; see also Susan Crosland's vivid portrait of her husband, *Tony Crosland* (1987). The accessible discussion of the discovery of DNA by Edward Yoxen in Roy Porter (ed.), *Man Masters Nature* (BBC, 1987), can be prefaced to J. D. Watson's highly subjective but enthralling account in *The Double Helix* (1970). Arthur Marwick, *British Society since 1945* (1982), has an engaging spontaneity, particularly good on the sixties.

The scorn with which the left viewed Wilson while he was alive and well is faithfully conveyed in Paul Foot, *The Politics of Harold Wilson* (1968), with its telling use of quotation. The emergence of a more indulgent posthumous view was already signalled with Ben Pimlott's scrupulous exercise in reconstitution of the historical context, *Harold Wilson* (1992), followed by Philip Ziegler's sympathetic biography *Harold Wilson* (1993). David Howell, *British Social Democracy: A Study in Development and Decay* (1976), is a knowledgeable overview. Clive Ponting, *Breach of Promise: Labour in Power, 1964–70* (1989), though severe in judgement, is scholarly in method, making excellent use of US documents. There are a number of dispassionate and searching essays by younger historians in R. Coopey, S. Fielding and N. Tiratsoo (eds.), *The Wilson Governments, 1964–70* (1993).

Most of the essays in Wilfred Beckerman (ed.), *The Economic Record of the Labour Government, 1964–70* (1972), took a critical view of the Government's strategy, especially on exchange-rate policy; and Michael Stewart framed this analysis in the context of adversarial politics in *The Jekyll and Hyde Years* (1977), republished as *Politics and Economic Policy in the UK since 1964* (1978). The suggestive essay by Paul Johnson on the welfare state in Roderick Floud and Donald McCloskey (eds.), *The Economic History of Britain since 1700* (Cambridge, 1994), vol. 3, can be buttressed by the fuller treatment in Rodney Lowe, *The Welfare State in Britain since 1945** (1993), which contains a useful appendix, clarifying statistical measures of public spending. Geoffrey Finlayson, *Citizen, State, and Social Welfare in Britain, 1830–1990** (Oxford, 1994), offers a complementary 'non-statist' frame for understanding welfare issues over a long period.

The internal politics of the Wilson cabinet have been documented by a unique trinity of diarists. The publication of Richard Crossman's *The Diaries of a Cabinet Minister, 1961–70* (3 vols., 1975–7) created a precedent, for which historians have been more thankful than serving politicians, in its unbridled bean-spilling. His colleague Barbara Castle duly and copiously followed with *The Castle Diaries, 1964–70* (1984) and the first two volumes of Tony Benn, *Diaries* (5 vols., 1987–93), cover the period 1963–72. Still, Peter Jenkins showed how much a well-informed contemporary journalist could fathom, even without such access to privileged archives, in *The Battle of Downing Street* (1970), which stands up well as an account of Labour's troubled trade-union proposals.

## CHAPTER 10

On immigration Juliet Cheetham's chapter in A. H. Halsey (ed.), *Trends in British Society since 1900\** (1972), drew together much useful evidence at an interesting moment. Tom Nairn's arresting book, *The Break-up of Britain* (1977, new edn 1981), was timely in speaking to the theme of nationalism. For developments in Wales Kenneth O. Morgan, *Rebirth of a Nation: Wales, 1880– 1980* (Oxford, 1982), is authoritative, and I have likewise turned to the new edition of Paul Bew, Peter Gibbon and Henry Patterson, *Northern Ireland, 1921–94* (1995). Patrick Cosgrave, *The Lives of Enoch Powell* (1989), helps make sense of its subject's preoccupation with issues of race and nationality.

John Campbell has produced a well-rounded biography, *Edward Heath* (1993), which offers a convincing interpretation of the divagations of the latter's Government. Much less charitable, as might be expected, is the view conveyed in the volume of Margaret Thatcher's memoirs dealing with this period, *The Path to Power* (1995); while William Whitelaw, *The Whitelaw Memoirs* (1989), blandly sees the best in both the old leader and the new, and includes a revealing chapter on the Irish question. Michael Crick's Penguin Special, *Scargill and the Miners* (1985), traces the shifts occurring within the NUM. Michael Charlton, *The Price of Victory* (1983), originally undertaken for the BBC, used archive footage and interviews to flesh out a persuasive study of perceptions of Britain's post-war international role. The detailed account by Uwe Kitzinger, *Diplomacy and Persuasion: How Britain Joined the Common Market* (1973), gains more than it loses by its closeness to the developments it describes; conversely, John W. Young, *Britain and European Unity, 1945–1992* (1993), benefits from its longer perspective on the trajectory of British relations with Europe. Roy Jenkins's *European Diary, 1977–81* (1989) contains some first-hand impressions of the difficulties in resolving Britain's relations with the EEC.

There is a coherent, corrosive Marxist analysis in David Coates, *Labour in Power? A Study of the Labour Governments, 1974–9* (1980), while a more sympathetic understanding of the Government's difficulties is conveyed in M. Artis, D. Cobham and M. Wickham-Jones, 'Social democracy in hard times: the economic record of the Labour Government, 1974–9', *20thCBH*, iii (1992). Two important studies of the actual workings of the machinery of government are Hugh Heclo and Aaron Wildavsky, *The Private Government of Public Money* (2nd edn, 1981); and Peter Hennessy, *Whitehall* (1989), which draws on interviews given to a well-connected journalist with his own academic agenda. Likewise, Bernard Donoughue, *Prime Minister: The Conduct of Policy under Wilson and Callaghan* (1987), nicely combines an academic's concern with the nature of policy-making with the I-was-there verisimilitude of an insider in Downing Street; and a similar immediacy infuses the intelligent account by the cabinet minister, Edmund Dell, *A Hard Pounding: Politics and Economic Crisis, 1974–6* (1991). This should be read alongside Kathleen Burk and Alec Cairncross, *Goodbye, Great Britain: The 1976 IMF Crisis* (1991), which is a triumph for contemporary history, and Keith Middlemas, *Power, Competition and the State*, vol. 3, *1974–91* (1991).

Following the publication of Peter Kellner and Christopher Hitchens's *Callaghan: The Road to Number Ten* (1976), their highly critical view seemed to be confounded by the ease with which Callaghan stepped into the premiership, but the book showed some prescience about the barren prospects for old-fashioned Labourism. The apologia in James Callaghan, *Time and Chance* (1987), does not really come to grips with the nature of the dilemmas which he faced. On the Lib-Lab pact, see David Steel, *Against Goliath* (1989) – the title is not a reference to Callaghan – and the chronicle produced at the time by Alastair Michie and Simon Hoggart, *The Pact* (1978). The best volume of memoirs from this period is Denis Healey, *The Time of My Life* (1989), which abjures petty self-justification while offering a literate and robust defence of the Labour right.

## CHAPTER II

Jane Lewis, *Women in Britain since 1945* (1992), is an admirable introduction to a number of gender-sensitive issues, well supported with relevant statistics. There is an excellent chapter on women by Joni Lovenduski, Pippa Norris and Catriona Burgess in Anthony Seldon and Stuart Ball (eds.), *Conservative Century** (1994), which also contains pertinent chapters by Vernon Bogdanor on the selection of Tory leaders, Keith Middlemas on industry and the City, Andrew Taylor on trade unions and Robert Waller on electoral support. On Thatcher herself, Peter Jenkins's *Mrs Thatcher's Revolution* (1987) showed a good deal of biographical insight in a (surprisingly sympathetic) appraisal of her record at its zenith; and Kenneth Harris likewise brought a journalist's skills to bear in his biography, *Thatcher* (1988). The best and fullest biography, however, is now Hugo Young, *One of Us: A Biography of Margaret Thatcher* (1989, final edn. 1991), which will be difficult to replace.

Dennis Kavanagh, *Thatcherism and British Politics* (Oxford, 1987) adroitly set the politics of this period in context, and Denis Kavanagh and Anthony Seldon (eds.), *The Thatcher Effect* (Oxford, 1989), followed up with a useful range of essays. Stuart Hall, *The Hard Road to Renewal* (1988), reprinted some seminal articles, notably from *Marxism Today*, giving its author's reading of the nature of Thatcherism. Andrew Gamble, *The Free Economy and the Strong State* (1988), nicely distinguished the liberal economic agenda from the centralizing political tendency of Thatcherism. Richard Cockett, *Thinking the Unthinkable: Think Tanks and the Economic Counter-revolution* (1994), has some useful material on the genesis of the IEA. The two books by William Keegan, *Mrs Thatcher's Economic Experiment* (1984) and *Mr Lawson's Gamble* (1989), were both percipient and prescient; and for another cogent analysis from an economic journalist see David Smith, *From Boom to Bust: Trial and Error in British Economic Policy* (1993). There are valuable essays, generally effective in their criticism, in Jonathan Michie (ed.), *The Economic Legacy, 1979–92* (1992). My own heaviest debt, not least for invaluable statistical support, is to Christopher Johnson, *The Economy under Mrs Thatcher, 1979–90* (1991).

Jad Adams's *Tony Benn* (1992) is a workmanlike biography, much helped by the Benn diaries, with insights on the rise of the hard left in the Labour Party which can be supplemented by Michael Crick's account of the Militant tendency, *The March of Militant* (1986). The authoritative institutional study of Labour's union links is Lewis Minkin, *The Contentious Alliance: Trade Unions and the Labour Party* (1991). Two serviceable contemporary accounts of the career of the SDP were Ian Bradley, *Breaking the Mould? The Birth and Prospects of the SDP* (Oxford, 1981), and Hugh Stephenson, *Claret and Chips: The Rise of the SDP* (1982), while the authoritative study is now Ivor Crewe and Anthony King, *SDP: The Birth, Life and Death of the Social Democratic Party* (1995). Kenneth Harris's *David Owen* (1987) helps explain the rise and fall of an abrasive figure. The elegantly executed memoirs of Roy Jenkins, *A Life at the Centre* (1991), are as shrewdly dispassionate on this phase of his career as on his earlier period of cabinet office under Wilson. For the 'Falklands factor', see *Contemporary Record* (autumn 1987 and winter 1988) for contributions by Lawrence Freedman and Helmut Norpoth. The 'Nuffield' series of electoral studies, which has long been invaluable to historians, is well sustained in recent volumes by David Butler and Denis Kavanagh, *The British General Elections of 1979/ 1983/ 1987/ 1992* (1980/ 1984/ 1988/ 1992). David Butler, Andrew Adonis and Tony Travers, *Failure in British Government: The Politics of the Poll Tax* (1994), is a multidimensional account of a key episode in the fall of Thatcher. A notable examination of survey evidence by Ivor Crewe, suggesting scepticism about a mass conversion to 'Thatcherite' attitudes, appeared in Robert Skidelsky (ed.), *Thatcherism* (1988), a wide-ranging collection of essays which also included Patrick Minford's appraisal of Thatcher's economic record – a notably stout defence.

Not so stout, however, as that in Margaret Thatcher, *The Downing Street Years* (1993). This is, of course, a unique source, compiled with privileged access to official papers, marshalled relentlessly in vindication of her own position. It thus engages in a set-piece battle of the books, notably contesting the account presented with such cogency in the thousand pages of Nigel Lawson, *The View from No. 11** (1992). Thatcher is in turn the butt of some effective fusillades in Geoffrey Howe's engagingly literate memoirs, *Conflict of Loyalty* (1994). A critical stance towards the whole project of Thatcherism is trenchantly conveyed in Ian Gilmour, *Dancing with Dogma* (1992). For a more visceral, spontaneous – and often self-deprecatingly witty – record of the hazards and temptations of ministerial life, Alan Clark's *Diaries* (1993) are not to be missed.

Harold Perkin, *The Rise of Professional Society: England since 1880* (1989), sets the backlash against collectivism and its associated professional bearers in a convincing historical context, and Brian Harrison, 'Mrs Thatcher and the intellectuals', *20thCBH*, v (1994), illuminates the culture-clash enacted in these years. Jeremy Paxman, *Friends in High Places: Who Runs Britain?* (1990), provides a good deal of fresh journalistic evidence on the entrenchment of a new Thatcherite elite. On perceptions of the past, Martin Wiener's stimulating study, *English Culture and the Decline of the Industrial Spirit* (1982), has been widely cited, though also often misconstrued in the process, innocently or otherwise. The outlook of two vastly influential historians is well captured respectively in David Cannadine's sensitive essay in retrieval, *G. M. Trevelyan* (1992), and in Adam Sisman's revealing biography, *A. J. P. Taylor* (1994).

# Index